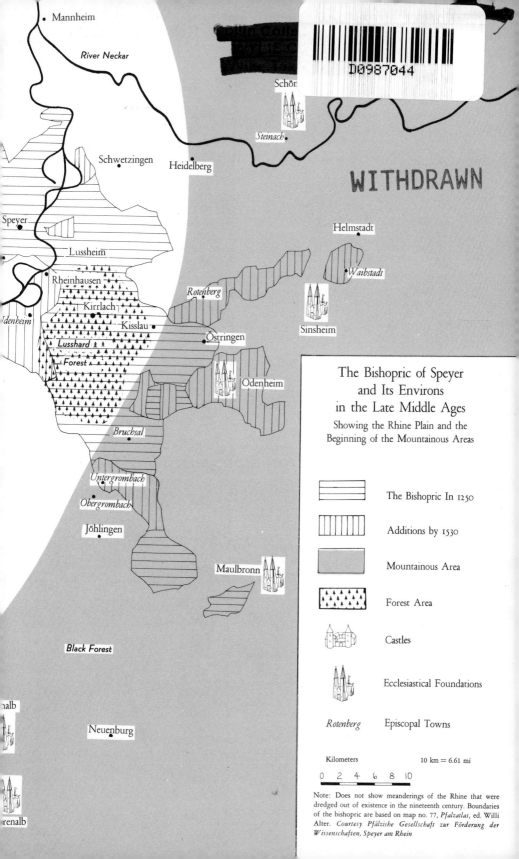

Mannheim

River Neckar

Schön...

Steinach

D0987044

WITHDRAWN

Schwetzingen

Heidelberg

Helmstadt

Speyer

Waibstadt

Lussheim

Rheinhausen

Rotenberg

Idenheim

Kirrlach

Kisslau

Sinsheim

Östringen

Lusshard
Forest

Odenheim

Bruchsal

Untergrombach

Obergrombach

Jöhlingen

Maulbronn

Black Forest

nalb

Neuenburg

renalb

The Bishopric of Speyer
and Its Environs
in the Late Middle Ages

Showing the Rhine Plain and the
Beginning of the Mountainous Areas

	The Bishopric In 1250
	Additions by 1530
	Mountainous Area
	Forest Area
	Castles
	Ecclesiastical Foundations
Rotenberg	Episcopal Towns

Kilometers   10 km = 6.61 mi

0   2   4   6   8   10

Note: Does not show meanderings of the Rhine that were
dredged out of existence in the nineteenth century. Boundaries
of the bishopric are based on map no. 77, *Pfalzatlas*, ed. Willi
Alter. *Courtesy Pfälzische Gesellschaft zur Förderung der
Wissenschaften, Speyer am Rhein*

Bishop and Chapter

STUDIES PRESENTED TO THE
INTERNATIONAL COMMISSION FOR
THE HISTORY OF REPRESENTATIVE
AND PARLIAMENTARY INSTITUTIONS
LXII

Bishop and Chapter

The Governance of the Bishopric of Speyer to 1552

Lawrence G. Duggan

RUTGERS UNIVERSITY PRESS
NEW BRUNSWICK, NEW JERSEY

Publication of this book was supported in part by the University of Delaware and the bishop and cathedral chapter of Speyer.

LIBRARY OF CONGRESS CATALOGING IN PUBLICATION DATA

Duggan, Lawrence G   1944–
    Bishop and chapter.

    (Studies presented to the International Com-
mission for the History of Representative and
Parliamentary Institutions; 62)
    Bibliography: p.
    Includes index.
    1. Catholic Church.   Diocese of Speyer—History.
I. Title. II. Series: Études présentées à la
Commission internationale pour l'histoire des
assemblées d'états;   62.
BX1538.S6D83   282'.43'43   78-18868
ISBN 0-8135-0857-6

Copyright © 1978 by Rutgers, The State University of New Jersey
Manufactured in the United States of America

To
DELIA COYNE DUGGAN
AND
LAWRENCE GERALD DUGGAN, SR.

Contents

Glossary

Amt (pl. *Ämter*)	administrative district
Amtmann (pl. *Amtleute*)	chief official of an *Amt*
Bede	property tax on land and houses
decimatio	extraordinary tax of ten percent on ecclesiastical revenues or benefices
fl.	gulden
Landfrieden	a general peace declared by a prince or a union of princes
Landvogt	imperial protector or bailiff
Landvogtei	imperial protectorate or bailiwick
Oberamtmann	one of the bishop's two chief administrative officials, resident at Bruchsal and Lauterburg
Schultheiss	bailiff of the bishop in a town or a village
subsidium caritativum	voluntary subsidy granted by the clergy
Schatzung	extraordinary capital levy rendered by the bishop's subjects
Ungeld	excise
Vogt	advocate; in the later Middle Ages, equivalent to an *Amtmann*
Vogtei	advocacy; in the later Middle Ages, protectorate with the right to exercise high justice

List of the Bishops of Speyer, 1090–1552

John I (1090–1104)

Gebhard II von Urach (1105–1107)

Bruno von Saarbrücken (1107?–1123)

Arnold II (1123–1126)

Philip I (1126)

Siegfried II von Wolfsölden (1127–1146)

Gunther von Henneberg (1146–1161)

Ulrich I von Dürrmenz (1162–1163)

Gottfried II (1164–1167)

Rapodo von Lobedenburg (1167–1176)

Conrad II (1176–1178)

Ulrich II (1178–1189)

Otto von Henneberg (1190–1200)

Conrad III of Scharfenberg (1200–1224)

Beringer von Entringen (1224–1232)

Conrad IV of Tann (1233–1236)

Conrad V von Eberstein (1237–1245)

Henry II von Leiningen (1245–1272)

Frederick of Bolanden (1272–1302)

Sigibodo of Lichtenberg (1302–1314)

Emicho von Leiningen (1314–1328)

Bertold von Buchek (1328–1329)

Walram von Veldenz (1329–1336)

Gerhard von Ehrenberg (1336–1363)

Lambert von Born (1364–1371)

Adolf von Nassau (1371–1381)

Nicholas of Wiesbaden (1381–1396)

Raban von Helmstadt (1396–1438)

Reinhard von Helmstadt (1438–1456)

Siegfried von Venningen (1456–1459)

John Nix von Hoheneck zu Entzberg (1459–1464)

Mathias Ramung (1464–1478)

Louis von Helmstadt (1478–1504)

Philip von Rosenberg (1504–1513)

George, count palatine of the Rhine (1513–1529)

Philip von Flersheim (1529–1552)

Preface

Choosing a title for this book has been one of the most difficult tasks involved in writing it. The title of the original doctoral dissertation on which it is based was at once more precise and more cumbersome: "The Parliamentary Activity of the Cathedral Chapter in the Ecclesiastical Principality of Speyer to 1552" (Harvard, 1970). It is not a straightforward political history intended to replace the two-volume history of the bishops of Speyer by Franz Xaver Remling. Remling's work, while admirably grounded on extensive archival research, is, nonetheless, more a chronicle than a history and nowhere systematically treats, if it raises at all, questions of interest to modern historians. Nor is this a study in administrative history; the word *governance* I have chosen deliberately. My concern, more fully described in the introduction, is to discuss certain aspects of the government of the bishopric in the late Middle Ages, and in particular the activity of the cathedral chapter as the functional diet of the principality during a crucial period when the bishopric experienced a variety of challenges. This has required both extensive narrative and detailed analyses of inextricably related problems in ecclesiastical, legal, economic, political, and social history, which—it is hoped—should interest historians of these areas without having obscured the central thesis.

Narrative history—as distinct from the analytical variety—is currently unfashionable. Less questionable is a focus on local or regional history rather than on topics or "problems"; but it still seems to call for some justification, particularly in the case of one of the less conspicuous bishoprics of the empire. Although some historians have hinted at the main argument of this book and others have explored isolated aspects of it, the nature, novelty, and complexity of the thesis compel one to examine a specific see that can be studied both in depth and over a long period of time. It will be explained shortly why the half millennium from the eleventh to the sixteenth centuries constitutes such a logical unit. The mountains of sources, however, discourage one from investigating the entire range of activities of the cathedral chapter at Mainz or Cologne, Salzburg or Münster over such an extended length of time. Speyer can be so investigated. Many readers will doubtless be impatient, if for totally opposite reasons, with the amount of detail in my account. Germans reading it as local history will seek more details; non-Germans, with their more general interests, fewer. This is perhaps unavoidable. In any event, the methods and findings of this study can be applied to bishoprics throughout Europe, not merely the empire. It therefore serves as a framework and a model for future research.

Several remarks on orthography and other usage are necessary. First, the German spelling of place-names has been followed except in the case of well-known Anglicized variations. At the risk of alienating some scholars, I have used "Speyer" instead of "Speier."[1] I have also Anglicized proper given names. Second, for reasons that will become evident in chapter one, "of" instead of "von" has been employed for the proper names of members of the emerging lower nobility until the second quarter of the fourteenth century. Third, *Electors* always refers to the Electors Palatine of the Rhine, *electors* to the electors of the Holy Roman Empire. Finally, I have used the terms *loans* and *interest* purely for convenience's sake, for in order to circumvent the prohibition on usury, such transactions almost invariably took complicated forms which cannot be explained here.

This study could never have come to light had it not been for generous assistance given by many institutions and people over a period of seven years. For grants that made possible the research, I owe great thanks to the Danforth Foundation, the German Academic Exchange Service, Harvard University, and the University of Delaware. For handsome subsidies that facilitated publication, I am most grateful to the bishop and the cathedral chapter of Speyer as well as to the University of Delaware. For acceptance of this book as volume sixty-two in the series of "Studies Presented to the International Commission for the History of Representative and Parliamentary Institutions," I extend my thanks to Professors Emile Lousse and Antonio Marongiu.

More intangible but no less great is my debt to many colleagues and friends for their patience and sage counsel. First, thanks for their many criticisms and constant encouragement go to Giles Constable, who directed the dissertation, and Ronald Witt, who served as its second reader. For their comments and advice, I am deeply obliged to Professors Peter Blickle, D. F. Callahan, F. L. Carsten, Franklin L. Ford, R. H. Rogers, S. W. Rowan, Lewis Spitz, Gerald Strauss, and J. A. Vann III; Drs. Henry Cohn and Hans-Joachim Köhler; Karl Lutz, former episcopal archivist in Speyer; and Messrs. J. G. Hiester and J. C. Hobbins, Jr.

My archival work was made most pleasant by the unfailing courtesy and helpfulness of the staffs of the archives in which I did research, especially that of the Generallandesarchiv in Karlsruhe and above all Herr Helmut Weber. I also wish to thank the Pilger–Verlag, Speyer, for permission to draw upon Ludwig Stamer's *Kirchengeschichte der Pfalz* in compiling the charts that appear on pages 22 and 120. Finally, to the staff of the Rutgers University Press I shall be forever grateful for making the final stages in the birth of this opus as painless as possible. My wife Devon has helped me in more ways than she can ever know.

NEWARK, DELAWARE
MARCH 1977

Introduction

Representative institutions rank among the greatest achievements of Western civilization and finest legacies of the Middle Ages to the modern world. The continuity of their development in many places on the Continent was broken by the age of absolutism, but in the last hundred-and-fifty years, they have been everywhere revived and reinstituted, although they now reflect the presuppositions of a democratic, rather than of an estatist, society.[1] Even the parliaments of the British Isles have not remained immune to the consequences of the "rise of the masses" and the decline of aristocratic society. Modern democratic institutions are now no longer confined to the West. The rest of the world imitates not merely its science and technology, but its methods of government as well, in name if not in substance. What country now lacks the temerity to call itself a republic? East Germany, Uganda, the USSR, China, Haiti? No, curiously—the constitutional monarchies of Western Europe!

These developments have not been without effect on the writing of history. It is a commonplace that historians often formulate the questions they address to the past after having taken thought from contemporary phenomena or attitudes. Examples that come to mind are the wide allegiance commanded by Marxist analyses of society and economy and the partly related democratic (and romantic) concern with peasants, both of which have spawned entirely new areas of historical investigation.

Similarly, the passing of the monarchical into the democratic order may have subtly influenced the study of representative institutions. In the nine-

1

teenth and early twentieth centuries, historians, particularly of the French school, tended to stress princely initiative in the formation of assemblies.[2] In the past forty years, on the other hand, fresh insights and a new impetus toward reexamination of old issues have been provided by proponents of the *corporatist* viewpoint, who emphasize the role played by the various estates in that process and specifically the necessity of princely consultation with and reliance on them for legal and economic reasons. Much of the credit for this revival, as Helen Cam pointed out, must go to Émile Lousse, both for his vigorous advocacy of the importance of corporatism in the rise of parliaments and for his able leadership in the founding of the International Commission for the History of Assemblies of Estates in 1935.[3] Under its auspices have appeared many distinguished contributions in the series of *Études presentées à la Commission internationale pour l'histoire des assemblées d'états*,[4] and in the journal *Anciens pays et assemblées d'état* (also called *Standen en Landen*).[5] Perhaps not all writers will concur with Otto Hintze's opinion that in the emergence of estates and of the corporatist state lies the touchstone of late medieval history and the root of modern democratic government,[6] but the work of the corporatists has underscored the significance of estates for a proper understanding of European history and society from the High Middle Ages down through the cataclysmic ending of the ancien régime.[7]

Nevertheless, there remain three areas of neglect in the study of representative institutions where the possibilities of fruitful research are great. First, although German historians have long recognized the importance of the appearance and triumph of the corporatist state (*dualistischer Ständestaat* or *ständischer Dualismus*) in the fourteenth and fifteenth centuries, they have until recently devoted surprisingly little attention to particular studies of parliaments in Germany. This is understandable for several reasons. There were hundreds of principalities in the empire, for many of which exist vast numbers of unpublished documents. Moreover, the extraordinarily complicated structure and levels of government within the empire[8] also discouraged even the most fervent scholar and vindicate Pufendorf's assessment of the imperial constitution in the seventeenth century as something of a monstrosity.[9] There is perhaps another explanation, however, more profound and more disturbing. Until recently, German historians have, in the main, regarded their parliaments and estates under the First Empire as an aberration in German history, as interest groups far more concerned to maintain and extend their own privileges and powers than to champion the genuine and common interests of their territories; one sometimes wonders whether the estates are censured because they failed to check the rise of the absolutist state or rather because they proved to be noisome hindrances to the necessary victory of the princes.[10]

Second, if the parliaments in the secular principalities have elicited little interest, those in the ecclesiastical principalities have received even less. Indeed, the ecclesiastical principalities of the empire have not been well regarded historically. In the Middle Ages they were viewed with frequently covetous eyes by kings;[11] in modern times, with often perfunctory disdain by historians.[12] One cannot deny that they occupied a less conspicuous place in the empire from the thirteenth century onward and that at least some of the prominence they retained derived largely from their functioning as appanages of the great princely families.[13] Still, they deserve careful consideration and fuller treatment, if only because they covered roughly fifteen percent of the surface area of Germany,[14] because they served the empire faithfully and well on the whole, and because—although this has barely been investigated, much to our loss—they may well have devised various institutions and administrative methods imitated later by the lay principalities.

The third and last aspect of parliamentary studies meriting comment is that historians have placed an inordinately heavy and legalistic emphasis on formally constituted parliaments. To be sure, one ought to focus primarily on these national or territorial assemblies. Here the various estates gathered to give counsel and aid to their princes and to safeguard their own liberties. It was at this level above all that the constant give-and-take between the lord and his subjects took place. Yet excessive concentration on assemblies of estates can lead one to neglect salient facets of governance that simply cannot be treated within that perspective. For instance, ordinarily only the privileged orders were invited to attend.[15] What, then, of the peasants, who formed an estate principally in alpine and some maritime regions and were otherwise represented, if at all, indirectly by their lords or as members of an administrative district?[16] Had they no part in government, no way to protect their rights? On occasion some privileged groups had no right to attend parliaments. Imperial collegiate churches[17] and imperial knights,[18] who achieved immediacy (*Reichsunmittelbarkeit*, "direct subjection only to the emperor") in the sixteenth century, held no seats in the Reichstag, even though the knights and the imperial towns bore a disproportionate share of the imperial tax burden.[19] Again, too legalistic an approach and too much attention to formal parliaments preclude consideration of the relationships between princes and the individual orders and classes, the relations between estates themselves as they bore on the larger questions of government, and the many and complex levels of administration and rule. In a word, as Bryce Lyon has recently proposed, medieval constitutionalism must be viewed as a functioning balance of power whose specific contours and outcome depended on a host of factors and fortuities.[20] Before instinctively reacting by charging Professor Lyon with imposing a modern concept on the past, one ought to note Helen Cam's reminder that even so magnificently successful an achievement as the English Parliament rested on layer upon layer of representative institutions and practices, down to the level of the vill, all participating in the total process of government.[21]

There is another reason why I insist on the inadequacy of the point of view induced by narrow preoccupation with formal assemblies: It cannot explain why parliaments did not appear in some states of medieval Europe. Whereas formally convened parliaments arose in most of Europe in the late Middle Ages, they by no means developed in all the ecclesiastical principalities of the empire (of which there were nearly one hundred in the fourteenth century),[22] although they appeared in many more than I had once thought.[23] When they did arise in some principalities, they often appeared late, met infrequently, and achieved little stature. In Würzburg, for example, where the bishop held the title duke of Franconia and governed a very extensive territory, a diet composed of the upper clergy, the knights, and representatives from about twenty-nine towns and twenty-five *Ämter* first convened only in the sixteenth century. Later meetings did not always include all the estates. Although they won briefly the right to collect and administer taxes (1566–83), they lost ground rapidly during the Thirty Years War and disappeared after 1701.[24] A similar pattern can be discerned in the bishopric of Basel; where a formal diet existed only between 1566 and 1730 and never acquired any significant power.[25]

Why this late and stunted development of full-fledged estates? F. L. Carsten in his fine study of *Princes and Parliaments in Germany from the Fifteenth to the Eighteenth Century* has already hinted at the answer, though he excluded the ecclesiastical principalities from his consideration. He noted that, even in those bishoprics where parliaments did develop, the cathedral chapters generally dominated the estates.[26] How did they come to do so? The principal argument, advanced in the present study of one principality, but applicable to others, is that cathedral chapters achieved a singularly powerful position in the structure of German bishoprics in the course of the twelfth and thirteenth centuries in virtue of (1) the constitutional significance accorded them in the revived and rapidly changing canon law, (2) their substantial ecclesiastical jurisdiction and control gained largely at episcopal expense, (3) the great financial resources at their disposal, and (4) their increasingly aristocratic composition and, hence, outlook. So fitted and so placed, they gradually came, in responding to challenges and difficulties similar to those found in most European states in the late Middle Ages, to perform more and more parliamentary functions and to acquire many of the rights and prerogatives traditionally associated with the diets of the German principalities.

One enormous advantage they enjoyed in contrast to regularly constituted diets, and which goes far in addition to the reasons given above in explaining their predominance (and also makes them very difficult to study as parliaments), was that they were permanently established and largely autonomous corporate bodies that met regularly and therefore did not depend on the will of the prince for their convocation. On the other hand, their stability and prosperity, their very existence, were inextricably bound up with that of the bishopric. Hence, eminently practical reasons, as well as their ecclesiastical responsibilities, compelled them willy-nilly to come to the aid of their prince-bishops and to seek solutions to the critical problems faced by all governments in late medieval Europe. As a rule, only when they proved unequal to the task, for any number of reasons, did the other estates begin to participate noticeably in the general territorial government. In some cases the bishops turned to and negotiated with the estates, either individually or collectively; in others, the estates united against their lords to curb their dissipate ways;[27] in virtually no case did cathedral chapters enjoy the right to assent unilaterally to taxation of their bishops' nonclerical subjects.

The ambiguous character of the imperial ecclesiastical principalities ought by now be clear. The bishops and abbots of immediate bishoprics and monasteries were simultaneously prelates of the church and princes of the empire, governing dioceses (if they were bishops) and territories whose boundaries were by no means coterminous.[28] Similarly, the cathedral chapters and monastic communities acted both as churchly bodies dedicated to the worship and service of God and as councils to their lords spiritual in the administration of the land. To them, there was no necessary contradiction between the two realms, although they were frequently not well distinguished by our standards.[29] Although the modern mind might find cause for embarrassment or scandal in these notions, it should also check itself against imposing its own conceptions of the church on the past, a not very distant one at that. Most of the imperial prince-bishoprics were abolished in 1802–3, the Papal States in 1870–71. In the High Middle Ages, in fact, the church was quite literally a state that issued laws, exercised jurisdiction, and collected taxes to which all were subject.[30] In addition, the church in pre-Napoleonic times fulfilled numerous functions, particularly in relation to the aristocracy, that are alien to our experience,[31] yet deserve impartial and thorough examination if the church is to be understood in all its richness as an historical institution.

To return to the point: the character and structure of the ecclesiastical principalities owed as much to their being integral parts of the church as it did to their membership in the Holy Roman Empire. Canon law played a significant part in the shaping of the constitutions of the prince-bishoprics. Its influence was not confined to the church. Whereas some historians have perhaps exaggerated the role of the church in the spread of representative institutions,[32] others have found that its importance in general, and on specific points of political and legal thought and practice, is by no means to be underestimated.[33] The following chapters illustrate how much the fortunes of cathedral chapters as parliaments depended frequently on changes in the law of the church.

This study is restricted to one southwest German bishopric, Speyer, the favorite see of the Salian emperors. In Speyer they built a red-and-cream sandstone cathedral where they all came to rest, together with four of their successors, Philip of Swabia, Rudolf of Habsburg, Adolf of Nassau, and Albert of Austria. The church has not been favored with tranquility or good fortune. Fire gutted it several times during the Middle Ages. French troops burned it again in 1689, and so the cathedral stood till the middle of the eighteenth century, when reconstruction with inadequate funds resulted in a whole church shored up by ugly half measures, especially obelisks cornering the stubby western facade; yet even then it evoked the wonder and admiration of so fine a sensibility as Goethe's.[34]

Napoleon's troops plundered it and tethered their horses in the nave, and only luck brought about the revocation of the demolition orders that arrived from Paris in 1806. "Restoration" recommenced in the nineteenth century under Habsburg and Wittelsbach auspices, the era unabashedly leaving its stamp everywhere on the work. Aversion to Wilhelmine tastes and a desire to recreate the majesty of the original swept all that away between 1957 and 1963.[35] The reaction, like the effort that kindled it, was too extreme. The church today, the largest Romanesque building in the world, elicits awe and a sense of the monumental and is much lighter than the other Upper Rhenish cathedrals, all of which are constructed entirely of red sandstone. Yet it is too huge, too formidable, and a bit cold and empty; its austerity by no means corresponds to the colorful processions and other liturgical functions that filled it in the Middle Ages, when eventually some seventy vicars in addition to the thirty canons were required to staff its altars.[36]

Between the thirteenth and nineteenth centuries, the bishops of Speyer were compelled to reside elsewhere than in their cathedral city[37]—at first at various castles in circuit, later at Udenheim (the Phillipsburg of the Treaty of Westphalia), and finally in Bruchsal. From these places they governed their lands and their subjects. By 1366, they held in whole or in part eighteen castles, six towns, and sixty-six villages,[38] to which they added, by 1541, another six castles, thirty-eight villages, and three tolls.[39] Despite losses suffered during the Reformation and to France in the seventeenth century, the bishops still ruled, in the later eighteenth century, about 608 square miles (1,575 km^2) and about fifty thousand subjects settled in 119 places.[40] With these modest resources, Bishop Damian Hugo, cardinal and count of Schönborn (1719–1743), was able not only to discharge many of the debts of the bishopric reaching back to the fifteenth century, but also to build at Bruchsal a baroque palace with several dozen outbuildings and still leave a surplus of a third of a million gulden.[41] For some of this work he commissioned the distinguished architect Balthasar Neumann (1687–1753), who was, however, primarily engaged in creating a far more magnificent residence for Damian's brothers who held the see of Würzburg.

To my knowledge or that of the learned and generous archivists in Speyer and Karlsruhe, no diet ever assembled in the prince-bishopric of Speyer.[42] The primary reason, I have already suggested, lies in the position and work of the cathedral chapter, which in time became the ordinary, functioning "parliament" of the principality. Chapter one is of necessity a long chapter. In it I have sought to describe the cathedral chapter's rise to prominence and power and to account for it. The reasons historians usually give for the sudden blossoming of cathedral chapters in the twelfth centuries are at best partial or cursorily sketched, at worst completely wrongheaded. All of a sudden, we are often told, the lust for power, materialistic concerns, or just plain *Egoismus* prompted the chapters of the empire, even of all Europe, to unfold and to appropriate to themselves large shares in the administration of their bishoprics.[43] Such reasoning is most implausible, for it implies that a tidal wave of greed and selfishness swept across the cathedral chapters of the Continent. It ascribes to incredible changes in the hearts of men at the local level what can only be explained by more general tendencies at work throughout Europe. It ignores the growth of corporatism and the revival of law with its passion for rationalization. It ignores the evolution of the college of cardinals into the senate of the Roman pontiff and the parallel development of cathedral chapters in fact and in law. It ignores the whole spirit of the Gregorian reform movement, which, in its concern to free the church from lay control, inevitably and ironically "secularized" the clergy, and in its later concern with pastoral care, partly inspired chapters to assume some episcopal responsibilities that bishops simply could not discharge.

All of this is the stuff of chapter one, in particular the slow delineation in canon law of a cathedral chapter's rights to elect bishops, to rule during vacancies, and above all to govern the corporation of the bishopric jointly with the bishop. This legal approach does not suffice, however; chapters soon claimed many rights merely implicit in canon law or sometimes explicitly forbidden by it. They needed practical power, as well as the law, to gain their leading position. This power they wielded not only through their control of ecclesiastical jurisdiction and offices, but also through their great financial resources. A final source and manifestation of their power was their ever-growing domination by the aristocracy, who considered themselves the natural and exclusive ruling class. Chapter one treats these interrelated legal, ecclesiastical, economic, and social aspects involved in the ascendance of the cathedral chapter of Speyer in the High Middle Ages.

The following three chapters, more narrative than analytical in nature, chronicle in detail the cathedral chapter's activities in the bishopric and its growth to "parliamentary maturity" between the thirteenth and the mid-sixteenth centuries. These chapters, too, differ from most conventional treatments in that they do not focus solely on electoral capitulations or solely on the constitution of the chapter or solely on its social composition or solely on its finances. These and other matters all properly bear on a comprehensive study of the role of the cathedral chapter in the governance of the bishopric.

The character and limitations of the cathedral chapter, however, produced fascinating nuances and unique twists to its operation and success as a parliament. Although it "represented" the estates of the land in many vital senses of the term, it oftentimes acted selfishly and irresponsibly. On such occasions it often faced, ironically, the bishop as the advocate of the best interests of his subjects! Furthermore, the cathedral chapter was not always competent to speak for the other estates, above all when the issue was extraordinary taxation. They too negotiated with the bishops individually, enjoyed protection of their rights and privileges, and participated in large measure in the governance and administration of the territory. All this is the subject of chapter five. Finally, in chapter six, by way of conclusion, the whole political, social, and economic history of the bishopric in the late Middle Ages is scrutinized again, from a different perspective, in search of answers to another question: Why did a formally established diet fail to appear in the ecclesiastical principality of Speyer?

This study begins with the full emergence of the ecclesiastical principality in the High Middle Ages and its sharp break away from a tradition of centuries of service and support rendered to the empire. A major reason why the study ends with the middle of the sixteenth century is simple respect for the masses of documents that mushroom in the early modern period (e.g., 622 volumes, alone, of privy council minutes); yet three substantive reasons also justify this decision. First, the bishopric by then had reverted to a close imperial connection after three centuries first of independence, then of drift, and finally of mounting subordination to the Electors Palatine in Heidelberg. Only the threat of total incorporation into the Palatinate or of complete secularization drove the bishops back to that distant, ineffectual, but willing protector, the emperor. Second, the Reformation clarified a fundamental ambiguity about the extent of the bishops' rule. The loss of nearly two-thirds of the churches and of most of the monasteries in the diocese[44] meant that the bishops' spiritual dominion was thereafter effectively limited to those lands they governed temporally. The diocese and the principality became, for all practical purposes, coterminous. Third, by this time the essential modes of governance and administration that characterized the bishopric down to its dissolution by Napoleon had taken shape. The rule of Damian Hugo von Schönborn rested at root on principles and practices worked out by his fifteenth-century predecessors.[45]

This is not to pass judgment on the question of whether the chapter's position declined in the later period. It was doubtless relatively displaced, inasmuch as the bishops gradually created both sufficient regular sources of income and a bureaucracy capable of enforcing their will. Some of the useful functions performed by the chapter in the parlous late Middle Ages were simply overtaken by other institutions and procedures. How effectively it checked, or should or could have checked, the growth of "absolutism" after 1648 cannot be answered here.

In any case, we cannot speak of a "decline" in the chapter's position by the mid-sixteenth century. On the contrary, the minutes of its meetings, extant from 1500 onwards, demonstrate in detail at every turn how much it shared in the administration of the principality by then. Happily, the minutes between 1500 and 1531 have been published in digest form in two volumes by Manfred Krebs, former director of the Generallandesarchiv in Karlsruhe.[46] The desire to use these materials to penetrate into the day-to-day realities of governance and thereby to assess the role of the chapter was one of the principal reasons for carrying this inquiry down to the Reformation. To add some flesh to this otherwise impersonal study, I have added an appendix recounting in detail some meetings of the chapter. This book could never have come to light, however, had it not been for the patient research and editing done by Krebs, Remling, F. X. Glasschröder, Emil Friedberg, and many others. The frequency of their citation in the notes will be, if not adequate thanks, at least proof sufficient of my debt to them.

Chapter 1

The Ascendance of the
Chapter, 1101-1272

I

On 3 March 1272 the twenty-four prelates and canons residentiary of the cathedral of Speyer drew up in solemn convention an oath. They were met to choose a new bishop. Henry, count of Leiningen, bishop of Speyer (1245–1272), and chancellor to William of Holland, had died scarcely a week before. Before proceeding to the election of his successor, however, they were moved by consideration of persistent violations of the rights and liberties of the church of Speyer by "certain recent bishops" to list their grievances and somehow to try to prevent their recurrence in future. The points were stated as articles of an oath to be taken by every voting canon prior to the election and by the new bishop immediately upon election. Each swore under pain of sin to uphold its provisions as best he could.[1]

The oath, issued in charter form, contained some forty-three clauses that may be roughly divided into three different groups according to their bearing. Least important, judged by both their number and their positioning, were the six articles dealing with certain general interests of the bishopric. The bishop pledged himself to administer justice fairly and impartially and not to grant fiefs or mint money without the consent (*consensus*) of the cathedral chapter. In another eleven articles he promised to maintain peace within the clergy of Speyer, to make no uncustomary demands upon them (including the confiscation of the goods of an intestate cleric), and to defend them against all lay and ecclesiastical aggressors, in particular the townspeople of Speyer and the archbishop of Mainz. By far the greatest number of articles, twenty-five in all, significantly, and to some extent uncanonically, limited the power and jurisdiction of the new bishop. Not only was he to defend and maintain the already extensive privileges, properties, rights, and customs of the cathedral chapter, but he was also obliged to exercise no jurisdiction over the clergy subject to the four collegiate churches of Speyer, to secure the consent of the chapter to major ecclesiastical transactions (including all incorporations and alienations of any church property in the diocese), and to appoint cathedral canons to certain major offices in the episcopal administration (chamberlain, chaplain, and judges-delegate). A final clause forbade the bishop to seek nullification of any of these statutes by appeal to higher authority.

This document is the first extant electoral capitulation of the bishops of Speyer[2] and may also be regarded as the first formal manifestation of the parliamentary activity of the cathedral chapter. It reflects the mixed motives inspiring the unions (*Einungen*) of the privileged orders in the empire against their princes in the thirteenth century and after. It also reflects characteristics of the treaties or agreements that the estates forced their princes to concede: a desire to protect the genuine interests of the principalities, but an even greater concern to safeguard the estates' rights and privileges against princely excesses and incursions and often to extend them at the expense of their lords.[3] Although in the course of the next two centuries the parliamentary consciousness of the Speyer cathedral chapter developed gradually but steadily, it never forgot its own interests and was always quick to insist on its prerogatives and to forestall the creation of precedents potentially prejudicial to its own rights.

Before looking forward from 1272 to trace that story, we ought perhaps look backward to understand why the chapter acted so strongly to control the bishop and how it had achieved a position of such strength as to be able to lay down these demands. The capitulation of 1272 represents the culmination and the fusion of two distinct yet very much connected strands of development that reach back to the twelfth century and beyond. The first was the rapid emergence of the cathedral chapter as a powerful and, in some important ways, closed corporation with more and more rights and responsibilities in the coadministration of the bishopric. The second, discussed in chapter two, concerns the background of the various political, ecclesiastical, and economic problems and threats faced by the bishopric, the clergy, and the chapter as reflected in the clauses of the electoral oath.

II

Little is known about the constitution of the Speyer cathedral chapter before 1100. The sources provide some scanty illumination on but one aspect of its history: its economic basis. The first reference to the cathedral clergy occurs in 859,[1] and in 865 Louis the German confirmed the first attested donation made explicitly to the canons.[2] This charter provides clear proof of a division of the property of the bishopric into lands assigned to the bishop's keep (the *mensa episcopalis*) and lands reserved for the use of the cathedral clergy for ecclesiastical purposes (the *mensa capitularis*), a separation effected throughout the disintegrating Carolingian empire in the ninth and tenth centuries.[3] This division, however, in Speyer as elsewhere,[4] proved short-lived, and time and time again the charters of the tenth and eleventh centuries fail to specify to whom a pious gift was being made, the bishop or the canons.[5] More revealing are indications furnished by eight imperial charters of 1046 and others of 1074 and 1101–2 of episcopal violations and usurpations of lands belonging to the cathedral clergy.[6] In one of the 1046 charters, in fact, Henry III transferred to sole ownership of the canons, probably by way of compensation, some property originally granted jointly to the bishop and canons in 1024.[7]

From the turn of the twelfth century onward, by contrast, the impression one receives from the sources of an amorphous body of clerics serving at the cathedral dissolves quickly upon the sudden appearance of a strong, sensitive, and increasingly well-defined corporate body enjoying legal personality and marked autonomy from the bishop. Although as late as 1091 an imperial charter leaves unclear the question whether the bishop or the chapter was the recipient of a donation,[8] Bishop John I (1090–1104), in his foundation charter for the monastery of Sinsheim in 1100, declared that "I have freed all parochial churches pertaining to that abbey from all episcopal service, so that just as the churches of the canons of Speyer are free from the exaction of customary payments, no tribute from the abbey's churches may be requested by the bishop."[9] Curiously, this clause has not elicited commentary from scholars, but what savors of recently acquired strength is confirmed by an imperial charter of the following year which has been called "the Magna Carta of the Speyer cathedral chapter."[10] This may be something of an exaggeration, for this long privilege, running to well over four printed pages, is considerably more complex than has been thought and deserves full study in its own right. For example, it is not altogether clear, in many instances, whether Henry IV was actually introducing novelties or merely confirming established practices. The charter is nevertheless extremely important. Whereas individual prebends and living quarters appear to have been the rule for some time, the chapter now received the power of exercising disciplinary control over its members, including ultimate deprivation of prebend; the clear right to administer its own property (which was divided into prebendal and common lands); and certain claims to the effects of bishops and canons who died intestate. The emperor also conceded, to the chapter, territorial immunity from all authorities, and to the canons and certain of their servants, personal immunity from secular laws. Those accused of violations of the laws of Speyer (*ius civium*) were to be tried before the dean within the chapter precincts by the bishop's magistrate (*tribunus*). Henry furthermore transferred jurisdiction over the domestic servants of the canons from the civil courts to the chapter and granted that no canon could be compelled to provide hospitality for any emperor, king, or imperial bishop or abbot.[11]

There are no clues as to the background of this remarkable document. The last two clauses cited smack of concessions wrung from Henry as the price of continued support during the investiture struggle and foreshadow the bitter conflict between the clergy and townspeople that dominated the next centuries.[12] Whether the chapter was merely reacting to the heightened political awareness and hostility of the burghers, or taking its cue from the new corporatist spirit that was beginning to pervade Europe,[13] or imitating changes in the college of cardinals within the last half century,[14] is open to conjecture. What is worth noting is that by this very early date the chapter had acquired some essential facets of a corporate body: the possession and administration of common property, certain powers of self-governance and discipline, the legal immunity of its grounds and its members, and the enjoyment of a distinct autonomy from the bishop.[15]

Other features of a full corporatist constitution appeared during the next two centuries. The use of a capitular seal is referred to possibly in 1137 and 1152.[16] New prelacies and offices were added to the existing list (i.e., provost, dean, custodian, and chancellor of the school) as the responsibilities of the chapter increased: cellarer and porter by 1137,[17] and chanter in

1213.[18] The term *universitas* was first applied to the chapter in 1178.[19] As such, enjoying legal personality, it could sue, be sued, and be represented by proctors. The first attested legal action independently undertaken by the chapter occurred before Frederick Barbarossa in 1184,[20] and canons deputed by the chapter to act as proctors in its behalf are mentioned in a charter of 1220.[21] When the chapter obtained the right to convene its members without the permission of the bishop is not clear, but it is implied in a document of 1220, which tells of a temporary union of the clergy of Speyer against the bishop.[22] Given the frequent absence of the bishops on imperial business in the second half of the twelfth century, it is probable that the chapter exercised the right even then. The electoral capitulation of 1272 finally and formally excluded the bishop from all its deliberations except by special invitation of the chapter.[23]

Certain limitations on the chapter's independence naturally arose in virtue of its position in the hierarchical structure of the church. The bishops retained their right of consent to all statutes and changes in statutes drawn up by the chapter. Although the canons seem to have gained a measure of freedom in this respect during the later twelfth century,[24] they never achieved independence of the bishop's right of approval.[25] In the fifteenth and sixteenth centuries, in fact, the bishops at times made use of their prerogative to pit the cathedral vicars against the canons.[26]

Nor did the chapter have absolute control over its membership despite the assertion in the 1272 capitulation of its right of free choice of new canons.[27] Frederick Barbarossa revived the strong imperial sway over Speyer that had obtained under the Salians. He and his successors had much to say about the choice of bishops, and probably of canons too, well into the thirteenth century.[28] They were well served by the clerics of what came to be known in the late twelfth century as the "Speyer school of imperial diplomats" (*die Speyerer Diplomatenschule*), which flourished most brilliantly under Bishop Conrad III of Scharfenberg (1200–1224), chancellor to Philip of Swabia, Otto IV, and Frederick II.[29] Papal interference replaced imperial control once the decline of the Staufens began. Although, in one of nine privileges granted to the chapter between 1244 and 1246, Innocent IV conceded that the chapter could refuse to accept anyone provided to a canonry or prebend unless he held a special papal mandate,[30] Innocent III had some time before established the priority of papal appointees over canons elected from within.[31] Papal provisions to the chapter became increasingly common from the later thirteenth century. They went mainly to members of the German high nobility (e.g., Eberhard von Zweibrücken in 1264[32]) or of the papal or imperial courts.[33] In addition, the emperor retained the right to name canons under certain circumstances.[34] In the fourteenth century, ecclesiastical offices and benefices were swept up into the battle between the empire and the papacy. Bitter struggles, particularly over bishoprics and other high church offices, often broke out, and the principality of Speyer was among those that suffered the most as a result. This is taken up in a later chapter.

III

The transformation of the cathedral chapter into a somewhat autonomous corporate body endowed with legal personality, property, and a generous measure of self-governance did not of necessity give it much leverage against the bishop, nor does it account for the exclusive and paramount position it occupied in the bishopric by the mid-thirteenth century. To understand this, we must turn first to the law of the church as expressed in papal bulls, conciliar decrees, and the canonistic collections compiled by Gratian and supplemented and revised by the popes through the mid-fifteenth century. As Geoffrey Barraclough has reminded us, "it must be borne in mind that the law never developed so rapidly as during the period" of the twelfth and thirteenth centuries.[1] The profound changes effected in the structure of the church and its relationship to secular society between 1050 and 1250 by successive reform movements, aided by the revived Roman and canon law, resulted in shattering conflicts between church and state and upset and polarized even men of good will throughout Europe.[2]

It is not our purpose here to describe those efforts at reform, but rather to see how they altered the constitutional position of cathedral chapters. In brief, the results were two: first, in canon law, the circle of episcopal electors was, between the Concordat of Worms of 1122 and the Fourth Lateran Council of 1215, gradually restricted to cathedral chapters to the exclusion of the laity and of the other clergy; and second, and much more important, chapters in canon law came to share with their bishops ever greater responsibilities in the coadministration of the bishopric. Not that practice provided a perfect mirror image of what the law prescribed; then as now, it frequently lagged or deviated considerably according to place and circumstance, and sometimes, in fact, long-standing and widespread custom assumed the lead, or at least proved so resistant to change that the law eventually was bent to fit the inflexible reality. Still, the essential leadership came from the popes and the canon lawyers,[3] and of new developments in that law the clerics at Speyer were well aware. Many elements of canon law appear in charters issued between 1237 and 1239 by the ecclesiastical court of Speyer, over which trained masters presided as judges-delegate of the bishop.[4] By 1260 the court had drawn up a textbook of procedural canon law, of which there now exist five manuscript copies.[5] In the electoral capitulation of 1272, the canons, on grounds of canonical prohibition, explicitly forbade anyone to use bribes or other illicit means to secure election as bishop.[6]

Canon law also made its influence felt indirectly through imperial law, by way of certain decrees of Frederick Barbarossa[7] and the concessions wrung from Philip of Swabia, Otto IV, and Frederick II by the papacy.[8] It should be noted, however, that the laws of the church and the empire, according to Gaines Post,[9] drew much from a common source, the Roman law. From the second half of the twelfth century, for example, imperial edicts did much to revive the principle of Roman law regarding the inalienability of church property.[10]

The steady narrowing of the episcopal electoral circle from the clergy and people to the chapter followed, with a lag of some seventy-five to one-hundred years, the limitation of the papal electors to the college of cardinals, even though, in the end, some significant differences remained between the two.[11] In 1059 Nicholas II had issued a decree establishing the cardinal-bishops, in consultation with the other cardinals, as the sole electors of the popes, although the clergy and other people of Rome retained the right to approve the choice by acclamation.[12] In 1179 Alexander III in *Licet de vitanda* abolished the right of approbation and, to prevent future conflicts among the cardinals, declared a two-thirds majority sufficient for valid election.[13]

Similarly, in the Concordat of Worms of 1122, Calixtus II allowed "free and canonical elections" to take place in Germany in the presence of the emperor.[14] The meaning of this has provoked some scholarly dispute,[15] but it probably referred to the centuries-old formula of election by "the clergy and the people" as the term was then understood: neighboring bishops, the chief abbots and prelates of the diocese, the nobility and other lay potentates, and possibly the bishop's ministerials and the people of the epis-

copal town.[16] Here Rome was concerned primarily to curb excessive imperial control over the church, to restore regular elections, and to establish the proper order of investiture and consecration, not to alter the composition of the electorate.

The papal election of 1130, on the other hand, signaled the triumph of a new generation of ecclesiastical reformers who put positive content into the Gregorian program of *libertas ecclesiae*, defined the competent ecclesiastical electors, and studied the many technical problems that arose from reshaping the church's constitution.[17] The new attitude was reflected in canon 28 of the Second Lateran Council of 1139, although scholars disagree on what exactly the council had in mind. The decree forbade cathedral canons to exclude from episcopal elections "religious men" (*religiosos viros*) and declared null and void any election taken without their advice and consent.[18] This has ordinarily been taken to mean the monks, or at least the abbots, of the cathedral city and of the diocese;[19] but André Desprairies argued that the term included bishops, archdeacons, and the urban and rural clergy as well.[20] In any event, two points remain clear. First, by 1139 the canons constituted the principal electors. Second, the laity was implicitly excluded from the body of electors.[21] In a famous letter of 1169 to the chapter at Bremen, Alexander III, in repeating substantially the conciliar decree, explicitly denied the laity any right to participate, although he did concede that the chapter ought to seek the assent of the prince.[22]

In time the rest of the clergy lost most of their rights as well, though they often struggled as bitterly as the laity to preserve their rights and, in some instances, achieved partial success.[23] In numerous election cases between 1164 and 1182, the popes addressed themselves only to the cathedral canons.[24] Clement III formally granted the sole right of election to the chapter at Clermont in 1190, as did Innocent III to Sutri in 1200 and to Canterbury in 1205.[25]

During the pontificate of Innocent III (1198–1216), elections by canons capitular alone became the general rule.[26] There were of course exceptions in law and even more so in practice. Innocent allowed deviations in the case of well-established local customs, as he admitted in the privilege to Sutri mentioned above.[27] Even in his famous bull *Venerabilem* (1202) (in which, according to one interpretation, he proposed reform of the imperial electoral system by adoption of the capitular model),[28] he spoke vaguely of the electoral right as belonging to the chapter or the diocesan clergy. He may have left the way open, partly because he was a practical and flexible man;

partly because the Romano-canonical principle of consent expressed in the phrase *quod omnes tangit, ab omnibus approbetur* (which he did so much to spread and institutionalize in the church)[29] perhaps prohibited him from drawing circumscribed lines; and partly as well because he recognized both the abuses that could occur within capitular elections (as some of his letters reveal)[30] and the local pressures to which the chapter might be subjected.[31]

Nevertheless, in most of the letters and bulls of Innocent that found their way into the *Decretales* of Gregory IX (1234), he referred to election by canons alone.[32] He extracted from Otto IV in 1209 and from Frederick II in 1213, in the so-called Constitution of Eger, the promise to recognize as bishop or abbot that man chosen by the chapter or by the *maior et sanior pars* thereof.[33] He devoted, in fact, much attention to trying to establish reasonable election procedures and the principle of valid election by the *maior et sanior pars* to prevent internecine conflicts between rival candidates and factions and yet protect the rights of the minority.[34] What both presuppose is the chapter's right to act as the sole body of electors. This applies as well to the famous canons 23 and 24 of the Fourth Lateran Council of 1215: even though the references to the electors are vague and indirect, and even though others appear to be allowed to attend the proceedings, the cathedral canons were to be the final arbiters.[35] The phraseology is capable of misconstruction because here, too, Innocent's canon lawyers were trying primarily to define more precise yet more flexible election procedures; hence the obliqueness of the references to the canons.[36] Again, the electoral right of the chapter was assumed. Bishop Henry II of Speyer acknowledged it in a charter of 1265,[37] and the canons convened to choose his successor in 1272 presumed it as well.[38]

The chapter at Speyer had not won that right very easily, for others did not renounce their participatory rights so quickly, especially in the transalpine empire, where the emperor could require elections to be held in his presence and where, after the sharp decline of imperial power in the thirteenth century, the political significance of the ecclesiastical principalities enticed prince, pope, and local dynast alike to seek to control and eventually even to secularize them. Speyer was particularly exposed to these dangers, originally because of its close association with the Salians and the Staufens, later because of its smallness and vulnerability to neighboring, predatory lay princes. As an integral component of the imperial church system (*Reichskirchensystem*)[39] and as the Salian family church,[40] Speyer served the empire well with troops, administrators, counsellors, and loyalty. Some of its bishops were relatives of the emperors.[41] Many went on the expeditions to Italy, and some died there.[42] Imperial influence over the see of Speyer remained strong down to the 1230s, despite the facts that, according to Remling, capitular elections took place there from 1124 on[43] and that Bishop Ulrich II in 1190 mentioned in a general way the election of his successors and their reception of the regalia from the emperor.[44]

Still, it was not difficult for the crown to reconcile canonical procedures with its desires. There is unfortunately in this period little direct evidence for Speyer by comparison with other imperial bishoprics,[45] where turmoil often reigned at elections, generated largely by the claims of ministerials to participate.[46] On the other hand, this may denote strong imperial control, and for that argument there exists some convincing circumstantial evidence, at least for the second half of the twelfth century and onward.

In 1162 Frederick Barbarossa's chancellor, Ulrich von Dürrmenz, was chosen bishop.[47] Little is known of his three successors,[48] but Bishop Ulrich II von Rechberg (1178–1189) came of a family closely related to the Staufens and appeared often in Barbarossa's entourage.[49] Bishop Otto von Henneberg (1190–1200), probably chancellor of the cathedral school since 1164 and possibly brother of Bishop Gunther von Henneberg (1146–1161), was much in the company of Henry VI.[50] The Staufen sway reached its acme under Bishop Conrad III of Scharfenberg or Scharfeneck.[51] Born of a family of Palatine imperial ministerials, he was probably the first bishop of Speyer of unfree origin and became chancellor of the empire in 1208, having worked in the imperial administration since 1187. Provost of Saint Germain's in Speyer since ca. 1186, once thought to have been cathedral dean since 1196, bishop of Speyer from 1200 and simultaneously of Metz from 1212 to his death in 1224, he led the so-called Speyer imperial *Diplomatenschule* to its height and served his king, if not his dioceses, with great devotion, although perhaps at a price.[52] His successor, Beringer von Entringen (1224–1232), scion of a Swabian noble family and dean of Speyer since 1220, remained unobtrusively loyal to the Staufens,[53] as did Conrad IV of Tann (1233–1236), whose election was attended by King Henry (VII).[54] He was counsellor to the young king and had been provost of the chapter.[55]

A distinct shift of allegiance commenced after 1236 that mirrored the increasing bitterness of the struggle between empire and papacy and the decline of imperial fortunes. Although the German church had by and large remained steadfastly loyal to the emperors since the investiture struggle (and Speyer conspicuously so), the growth of princely particularism, loss of faith in imperial promises to desist from spoliation of the church, and the enormous pressure brought to bear by Rome by the 1230s led to the defection of most of the German hierarchy to the papal cause.[56] Bishop Conrad V von Eberstein of Speyer (1237–1245) was one of the prelates who in 1240 assured the pope that they would remain faithful to the church should peace negotiations with Frederick II fail.[57] Between 1244 and 1252, Bishops Conrad and Henry,[58] members of their immediate families,[59] the cathedral chapter,[60] and some canons of the collegiate churches of Speyer[61] received numerous privileges from Innocent IV to win their allegiance and reward them for adherence to the papal cause. Although Bishop Conrad may not have been anti-imperial at the outset of his episcopate, Henry II (1245–1272) had little compunction about throwing in his lot on the papal side; he participated in the elections of Henry Raspe (1246–1247) and William of Holland (1247–1256), acted as William's chancellor, and unsuccessfully attempted to gain the see of Würzburg in 1254–1255.[62] Not all the bishops who followed him took an anti-imperial stance, or certainly not as extreme a one, nor did the see of Speyer escape its obligations, military and financial, to the empire. On the contrary, they became more burdensome in time. The centuries-old association of the bishopric with the empire had, however, passed, never to return; Henry II, count of Leiningen, was the harbinger of the future.

If the chapter had entertained hopes of winning a greater measure of freedom by breaking loose from the imperial connection, they were soon dispelled. Bishop Conrad V was uncle to Henry II, and Henry uncle to Bishop Frederick of Bolanden; and so with all the bishops save two for a century (1237–1336), as the chart on page 22 makes clear.[63]

Domination of German sees by princely and comital families became a common phenomenon in the thirteenth century.[64] However impossible it may be to pinpoint the exact reasons for this subordination or the methods by which it was attained in any particular case, the general factors accounting for it are easily enough discernible. With the enervation of imperial power and the concomitant increase of lay depredation of the church,[65] many churches felt the need to seek protection from local rulers. Philip Schneider has suggested that many chapters, in particular those of the ecclesiastical principalities, appointed to canonries members of the surrounding aristocracy in order to form tacit or explicit alliances with them to secure protection of the rights and property of the bishopric and chapter.[66]

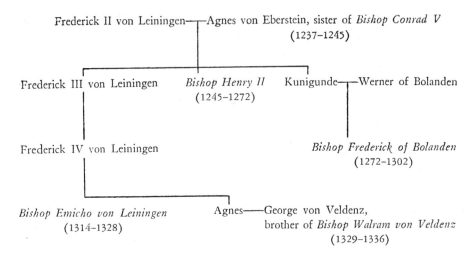

On the other hand, one would be naive to think in terms of such unilateral initiative. For centuries before and to come, the nobles of the empire had relied on the church for fiefs to expand their territories, for prebends for their numerous sons and daughters, and for prayers for their salvation. The great weakening of imperial power in the thirteenth century multiplied these opportunities and exposed many imperial monasteries and bishoprics to the threat of subjugation, direct or covert, to local powers;[67] hence the efforts of the imperial abbeys to secure the privilege of inalienability from the empire (*privilegium de non alienando de imperio*) at the imperial court in 1198, 1209, and 1216.[68]

Both factors were undoubtedly at work at Speyer. The counts of Leiningen were related to the Staufens and had put together a sizable territory (by southwest German standards, at any rate) in and about the Hardt Mountains.[69] More important, between 1205 and 1331, they very often held the office of imperial *Landvogt* in Speyergau, making them the chief vicegerents of the emperor in the area bounded to east and west by the Rhine and the far side of the Hardt, to north and south by Mannheim and Weissenburg i. E.[70] The counts of Eberstein were settled in the Black Forest near Gernsbach. Their principal holdings were fiefs from the sees of Speyer and Strasbourg.[71] Bishop Frederick of Bolanden came of one of the most eminently successful ministerial families in the service of the Staufens.[72] The Leiningens and the Ebersteins were among the most power-

ful families in the diocese of Speyer, and the chapter no doubt realized the
need to come to terms with them. The counts appear frequently in the witness lists of episcopal and capitular charters from the 1220s onward,[73] and
during the middle decades of the thirteenth century, they cooperated with
the bishop on numerous occasions to keep the peace and arbitrated disputes
between the bishop and his cathedral city.[74]

Nevertheless, the evidence, most of it circumstantial, suggests that the
century-long rule of Leiningen-related bishops owed more to the pressure
from these families than to any positive feelings toward them on the part
of the chapter. These bishops were consistently neither good princes nor
good pastors, and the chapter's relations with them were, on the whole,
wretched, as will become clear; yet there were never canons from these
families, or even from the high nobility, sufficient in number to constitute
a majority that could railroad its candidates through an election.[75] If the
papal provisions and other favors showered on the Leiningens and the
Ebersteins in the 1240s and on the other members of the high nobility then
and later may be taken as representative,[76] papal concessions cannot be excluded from consideration, although nothing can be conclusively demonstrated. The peasants in 1525 and soldiers, later, burned most of the records
of the Leiningen and other families, thereby destroying any evidence for
this hypothesis that might have existed.[77] More probable and more susceptible of proof, however, was simple pressure brought to bear on the
chapter by puissant local powers. Their sons became canons and irresponsible bishops who granted their families innumerable fiefs, often without
the consent of the chapter, and neglected their episcopal duties;[78] yet they
continued to succeed each other, one bad bishop giving way to a worse one.
What other conclusion is possible than that the Speyer chapter acquiesced
in a situation over which it had little control?

To recapitulate: by the early thirteenth century, the Speyer cathedral
chapter had won the exclusive right in canon law to choose the bishop, but
other agreements and prevailing political circumstances could result in considerable abridgment of that right or in limitation of the chapter's theoreti-
cal freedom of choice. When close imperial control passed away in the
1230s, substantial influence by the local aristocracy was immediately sub-
stituted. Exclusion of noncapitular participants in episcopal elections hardly
implied exclusion of their influence. The bishopric was simply too small
and too weak to permit the chapter to enjoy anything but a restricted freedom of choice within procedurally free elections.

Even at that very moment, that right was being infringed from another
direction: the papacy. For reasons good and ill, the popes of the second half
of the thirteenth century, beginning with Innocent IV (1243–1254), introduced and gradually extended a general right of reservation of all cathedral and metropolitan churches, that is, they could prohibit an election
from taking place and nominate the prelate directly. Particular precedents
for intervention, such as the right to decide in disputed elections, had
existed from the late twelfth century. Finally in 1249, Innocent IV flatly
interdicted all elections in the empire conducted without special papal permission. Though, on his assumption of office in 1254, Alexander IV rescinded the order, the first great breach had been made, and thereafter
cathedral chapters fought bitterly but vainly against what they considered
usurpations of their rights.[79] "The electoral system of the *Corpus juris
canonici*," Barraclough has noted, "lasted in full vigor for hardly more than
half a century."[80] We return to this conflict and its consequences in chapter
three.

IV

If the chapter at Speyer was only rarely allowed to make full use of its
electoral prerogatives, it normally experienced, from the High Middle Ages
on, little interference in exercising its responsibilities in helping to govern
the bishopric. Even in the antique and early medieval church, of course, the
clergy attached to a cathedral had played an important role, both in the
episcopal administration and as the bishop's council to advise him on many
questions. The diocese was regarded as one body of which the bishop was
the head and his *familia* the members. The cathedral clergy's rights of
counsel and consent were, however, ill-defined; they were but the inner
core of a much larger group of clergy and laity who also could demand to
be consulted. During vacancies, however much of the practical work they
performed, the administration of the see ordinarily devolved to another
power, be it the metropolitan, the *oeconomus*, or the crown.[1]

It was the aim and the achievement of the reforming movements in the
church in the twelfth and thirteenth centuries, first, to limit to the cathedral
chapter the right and the duty to help the bishop govern his see, and
second, to precisely define and to extend the tasks and privileges of the
chapter, especially its rights to advise and consent to all important acts of

the bishop and to act in his stead under certain conditions. In establishing the power of the chapter, these rights proved far more important than its rather restricted electoral responsibility.[2]

This could conceivably have taken place without the aid of the reformers and canonists for several practical reasons. The chapter's development into a fully corporate, largely autonomous body with its own property set it conspicuously apart from the bishop, the rest of the clergy, and the laity and probably led to attempts to clarify the relationships with the bishop and to exclude all others from its deliberations.[3] Furthermore, although the chapter now enjoyed a separate and distinct status, its property and its interests remained very much tied up with those of the bishopric and always depended on the fortunes of the see. Again, the emperors' loss of control over the church, and especially their renunciation of the right to administer vacant sees (the *ius regalium*) between 1209 and 1216[4] and to confiscate the movable estate of a deceased imperial prelate (the *ius spolii*) between 1198 and 1220,[5] suddenly left a vacuum: to whom did the administration of a vacant bishopric fall? The problem of governance during vacancies was not the only question raised by the recession of imperial power, for in its place there emerged an ecclesiastical principality, independent to be sure, but also subjected to enormous stresses from within and without: loss of lands in the form of fiefs to the surrounding nobility, rising expenditures and inadequate incomes, and a series of incorrigible bishops.

No doubt all these factors contributed somehow or other to the ascendancy of the cathedral chapter, but they might equally well have led to entirely different results, with the chapter, in the end, not occupying as eminent or as exclusive a position as it in fact came to hold. What conferred that unique place and those substantial rights in the bishopric on the cathedral chapter was canon law, which in turn was partly the child of Roman law as applied to the church.[6] Capitular initiative, practice, and even abuse also helped shape the law, but in the end, the direction and the sanction given by the laws of the church proved essential.

The rights and responsibilities of the chapter varied considerably in the thirteenth century, depending on whether a bishop ruled at the time. It is therefore necessary to consider the chapter's canonical position both during vacancies and at the time of occupation of the see. Diocesan administration during vacancies does not appear to have received detailed study by scholars. In any event, it was marked by flux and by a lack of fixed rules. The letters of the third and fourth centuries cited by Schneider bear this out, even though the priests and the deacons of the episcopal city normally took over the day-to-day supervision of affairs.[7] This later gave way, according to Schneider, to the vesting of practical authority in the most important clerics, the archpriest, the archdeacon, and often the so-called *oeconomus*, "the administrator of diocesan property." Their authority was eventually superseded by that of the metropolitan, who customarily delegated supervision of the see and the responsibility for conducting the election of a new bishop to a *visitator* (variantly called *intercessor, interventor,* or *commendator*), who tended to be a neighboring bishop.[8] The Carolingians, in turn, came to win substantial influence over the disposition of sees at the expense of the archbishops; this system of royal control reached its peak under their German successors in the empire.[9] During the twelfth century, it came to be technically limited to the *temporalia,* the exercise of the rights and the collection of the incomes appurtenant to the *mensa episcopalis,* but abuses continued.[10] H. A. L. Fisher considered this and the spoliation of the estates of imperial prelates the principal points of contention between Frederick Barbarossa and the church, which nearly cost him its support and helped finally to alienate the German church from Frederick II.[11] Barbarossa was forced on several occasions to restrict his use of the *ius regalium* to one year,[12] and Otto IV and Frederick II finally renounced it entirely between 1209 and 1216.[13] The general weakening of imperial power insured against frequent violations of these pledges thereafter.

This created an acute problem, if not at that very moment,[14] at least by the time of the Interregnum. Who was to administer a bishopric during a vacancy? The whole weight of recent developments at Speyer pointed to the cathedral chapter. It had probably been administering the *spiritualia* for some time, given the extensive ecclesiastical jurisdiction it had acquired since the mid-twelfth century[15] and given the absence of any suitable official at the time to act for the bishop. The first and last allusions to the *chorepiscopus* at Speyer occur in 1100 and 1103,[16] those to the first vicars-general and suffragan bishops in 1296 and 1311, respectively.[17] The early decretist Master Rufinus at one point in his *Summa* (1157–59) assigned the administration of the temporalities of a see to the archdeacon but otherwise held that the chapter could exercise a bishop's powers during a vacancy.[18] A letter of Honorius III, written sometime between 1216 and 1227 and later incorporated into the *Decretales* (also called the *Liber extra*) of Gregory IX (1234), implies that chapters by then normally took over upon the death or removal of the bishop.[19]

Still, before the *Liber sextus* of Boniface VIII (1298), there was little formal theory in conciliar decrees or in the canonistic collections to ratify the situation.[20] Canons 28 of the Second Lateran Council of 1139 and 23 of the Fourth Lateran of 1215 reflected only a concern to have elections held within three months of a bishop's demise.[21] The few relevant passages in Gratian's *Decretum* treat the inventories to be made of the bishop's effects.[22] The *Decretales* also said little, and although one can infer from the few germane passages that chapters in normal practice assumed the responsibility,[23] the old principle was strongly reasserted that no innovation might take place during an episcopal vacancy.[24]

Certain practical exigencies, however, buttressed by the spread of the Roman legal tenet that the rights of a corporation lived on in its surviving members, and coupled with the canonists' desire to codify and standardize ecclesiastical custom, soon led to modification of that position on some issues. In one of his decretals, Lucius III (1181–1185) had empowered chapters to judge heretics during vacancies,[25] and in the course of an often hot and always complicated debate during the thirteenth century, it was more and more acknowledged that a chapter could administer certain episcopal rights and could otherwise generally govern in the absence of the bishop.[26] All this was consecrated in the canonistic collection of Boniface VIII, the *Liber sextus*.[27] By the time it was compiled in 1298, however, the popes (just as they had done with respect to the chapter's rights of electing the bishop and of choosing its own members) had made great inroads on the chapter's equally short-lived right to govern the bishopric, *sede vacante,* and these ideas, too, found their place in the Bonifatian collection. The appointment of an administrator of a cathedral church in things spiritual and temporal was reserved to the pope alone, as was the delegation of a visitator to a vacant see.[28] Inasmuch as the consequences of these doctrines appear in our documents only after 1272, and inasmuch as the chapter first devoted its attention to the administrative problems raised by vacancies in the fourteenth century, I have deferred a specific discussion of these developments at Speyer to chapter three.

Besides, the far more easily won, more extensive, and more perduring rights of the chapter concerned its position vis-à-vis the bishop in the ordinary governance of the bishopric. Nevertheless, the various interrelationships of theory, law, and practice became extremely complex in the twelfth and thirteenth centuries, while those prerogatives and duties were hammered, not to say fought, out within the church and between the church and the empire.

In the early church, the bishop was regarded as the pastor of his people and the administrator of his church. He was the head of a body ecclesiastical, the members of which had a right to be consulted on all major changes and transactions affecting the bishopric. These conceptions were reasserted with vigor by the councils and popes of the High Middle Ages. The Lateran Councils of 1123, 1179, and 1215 all spoke of the bishop as the pastor and administrator of all church affairs and property.[29] Alexander III, writing to the patriarch of Jerusalem in 1168, said that "whereas you and your canons (*fratres*) are one body," of which he was the head and they the members, "it is not fitting that you take counsel with others while ignoring the members."[30] To that extent, the canonists of the High Middle Ages merely made explicit, and more precise, views and customs that bore the approbation of the centuries.

The canonists also went beyond tradition in several respects. For the sake of legal precision, they applied the Roman law on corporations to bishoprics and came to regard the bishop as the proctor of that corporation, representing it, acting for it, and accountable to it.[31] The equally important principle in Roman law of *quod omnes tangit*, which actually had been one of the fundamental principles of church government for centuries,[32] led them to require the bishop to consult with or obtain the consent of the other members of the corporation on all matters affecting the bishopric.[33] They also formulated these matters more carefully, although lack of rigorous distinction between such basic words as "counsel" and "consent" prevailed until the later thirteenth century.[34]

At the same time, they greatly narrowed the group of people who had a right to be consulted ordinarily. The clergy and notable laymen who, down into the thirteenth century, on solemn occasions or in synods, witnessed and assented to the bishop's acts and gave counsel on ecclesiastical governance gradually disappeared from episcopal charters and were replaced by the cathedral chapter.[35] The rights and responsibilities of the corporation that was the bishopric came to be vested in the chapter alone. Practical necessities, given the increasing legal paperwork of the bishops, helped force the issue, as did the newly emergent corporate sense of the cathedral canons, the reformers' desire to minimize lay interference in the church and achieve *libertas ecclesiae,* and the impulse toward the rationalization of law in the High Middle Ages.[36]

The college of cardinals, furthermore—which took on decisive form in the second half of the eleventh century, becoming the advisory body of the popes at the expense of synods and losing most of its originally purely liturgical character—served as a prototype of collegial organization at the episcopal level.[37] Although cathedral chapters eventually differed from the college in major respects, they did follow the model it provided as the exclusively electoral and consultative body in the bishopric. They were to help the bishop to discharge his duties and to cooperate with him, and if need be to oppose him, to maintain the best interests of the bishopric. In a very real sense, then, chapters were held accountable in canon law to represent the commonweal of their churches. Given the nature of bishoprics in the early Middle Ages and of the immediate ones in Germany until the Napoleonic era, that responsibility subsumed the property, castles, lands, and subjects of bishoprics, not merely ecclesiastical discipline and administration.

The chapter's position in canon law developed rapidly in the century between the appearance of Gratian's *Decretum* (ca. 1140) and Gregory IX's *Decretales* (1234), just as its electoral rights had. At the time of Gratian, the constitutions of chapters were still embryonic, and the canons were not yet always distinct, particularly with respect to their authority or powers, from the other clergy in the episcopal town. The terms for the bishop's consultative body used at the First Lateran Council (1123) and in Gratian are *presbyterium* or *clerici,* not *fratres* or *canonici.*[38] Their consultative rights moreover were not always well indicated, exclusive, or comprehensive. Canon 22 of the council's decrees forbade ordinations or alienations of church property of any sort made by bishops or abbots "without the common consent of the clergy of the church,"[39] but canons 7 and 18 emphasized only the importance of the bishop by prohibiting the conferral of prebends or of cures of souls and also the reception of tithes or churches by priests from laymen, without the consent of the bishop.[40] Gratian cited prohibitions on bishops' ordaining clerics without the advice of their clergy or hearing cases in their absence.[41] A comparison of his texts indicates more complexity on the question of alienation of church property. Depending on the nature of the property, a bishop might not need the counsel, much less the consent, of his *fratres* (in the case of unproductive lands or of unreturnable fugitive serfs)[42] or else might simply have to consult with two or three neighboring bishops (as in the case of cottages),[43] but as a rule, the consent of the clergy was necessary.

The *Liber extra* of 1234 epitomized a century of law making by popes who had for the most part been trained in canon law. It reflected both the growth in subtlety and profundity and the shortcomings of legal thought. The greatest single problem, so far as we are concerned, was the careless use of the terms *consensus, consilium, collaudatio, approbatio, subscriptio,* and the like with regard to the exact collegial rights of chapters.[44] Hostiensis complained in vain about this uncritical approach.[45] Within this still inadequately charted framework, however, the rights and duties of the chapter as the bishop's collegial council had come to be established. Some of the passages occur in book III, title 10, chapters 1–8 of the *Decretales*.[46] They are set out here in roughly chronological order and in themselves map the historical progress of the cathedral chapter.

The Council of Valence of ca. 529 had forbidden bishops to alienate any church property (including donations and exchanges) "absque collaudatione et subscriptione clericorum" (chap. 1). In the next two chapters were recorded decretals of Alexander III (1159–1181) permitting temporary alienations made with at least the tacit consent of the chapter (note well: the *chapter*). Chapters 4–5 contained excerpts of an earlier letter of Alexander to the patriarch of Jerusalem, which have been cited already (n. 30). There, he spoke of the patriarch as the *caput* and of his *fratres* as the *membra* of *unum corpus,* and the pope ordered the patriarch to consult with them regarding "concessions and confirmations and the other affairs of your church" and to conduct its business with their counsel or that of the *sanior pars* thereof.[47] In chapter 8 appeared an extract from Innocent III's letter of 1201 to the archdeacon of Metz in which he denied the right of the bishop to donate churches to other churches without the consent of the chapter, even if he held the patronage rights involved.[48]

Alienation of ecclesiastical property, one of the gravest threats faced by the church and always large in the legislation of the High Middle Ages,[49] was treated elsewhere in the *Decretales*. Although the sale, donation, exchange, or any other change in the status of ecclesiastical property tantamount to alienation was flatly forbidden,[50] it was granted that, with the advice and consent of the chapter, less profitable possessions might be severed.[51]

The *Liber sextus* (1298) of Boniface VIII revealed the achievements of the intervening sixty years. By then the collegial rights of chapters had become so well established that attention was now directed primarily to the resolution of technical difficulties such as the collation of benefices during vacancies.[52] All alienations of the immovable goods and the rights of a church, including the granting of them in any way to laymen, were declared de facto null and void unless done with the consent (*consensus*) of the chapter "and the special permission of the Holy See."[53] Again, the papacy was beginning to restrict the prerogatives of chapters just when they had been achieved.[54] The decree indicated great concern on the part of the popes and the decretalists about the loss of church property. Archbishops receiving the pallium in Rome from the twelfth century on, and bishops consecrated there from the thirteenth century on, promised in their oaths to the pope not to alienate without his assent. The clause was later incorporated into the general oath of bishops to the pope taken upon their entrance into office.[55] In similar fashion, the Council of Lyons of 1245 condemned the impoverishment of bishoprics by usury and required new bishops, within one month of their elevation, to prepare an inventory of the debts on the *mensa episcopalis*.[56]

It goes without saying that under normal conditions the popes were far less able to exercise this right of consenting to alienations in distant dioceses than of providing to canonries and sees. Cathedral chapters assumed the ordinary responsibility and insisted on the observance of their right of consent. Clauses to this effect figured prominently in electoral capitulations extracted from bishops, such as those at Verdun in 1231, Paderborn in 1247, Osnabrück in 1265, and Speyer in 1272.[57] Whereas chapters might ignore, for example, Paul II's order of 1468 that no sale, leasing, or enfeoffment of church land for more than three years was to take place without special papal dispensation,[58] they tended to try conscientiously to execute these canonical regulations within their limited means.

In so doing they did much to maintain the territorial integrity of their bishoprics in the turbulent late Middle Ages and took over an important function performed in the secular principalities by unions of estates or estates general. These states from the late thirteenth century on were ravaged by endless partitions and wasteful wars among the members of the ruling houses, whose subjects were sometimes driven to unite against them.[59] Although the nonheritability and indivisibility of bishoprics prevented at the outset the appearance of these difficulties, analogous threats arose in the form of wars between rival candidates in an election, family control of sees, and lay depredation to the point of mediatization or secularization. To be sure, cathedral chapters bore part of the blame for these situations, but frequently they had little choice in the matter. And they attempted to establish, with substantial success, what control they could in fulfillment of their mandate in canon law.

In the empire, that mandate to preserve inviolate the endowment of churches came from imperial legislation as well, although in a manner that temporarily compromised the rights of chapters. Gaines Post has emphasized the role of Frederick Barbarossa in bringing into imperial law the prohibition in Roman law on the alienation of church property.[60] In 1153 an imperial-court decision concerning alienations made by Archbishop Arnold II of Cologne, Frederick delivered the sentence of the judges forbidding alienation of church property.[61] The significant point is not so much that the emperor backed the principle, but rather why he backed it. Frederick and his legists, all familiar with Roman law, viewed it as an imperial right and duty, a concomitant of the *iura regni*, to conserve and defend the clergy and ecclesiastical rights and liberties. The *iura ecclesiastica* were conceived as falling within the structure of the state and subordinate to the *iura regni*. Hence Frederick's assumption of a kind of superior advocacy (*Obervogtei*) over the church as a whole and of the *Vogteien* over many bishoprics and monasteries, including Speyer; hence his free, nearly calamitous, use of his rights of spoliation and of disposition over vacancies; and hence too his and his successors' assertions of their right to consent to major transactions affecting church property and finances.[62]

Thus at Milan in 1184 the Archbishop of Mainz declared, on behalf of Frederick and all the attendant princes, that no ecclesiastical prince was bound to pay debts contracted by his predecessor without the consent of the emperor and the advice of his chapter, and that he could neither sell nor pawn ecclesiastical property without imperial consent.[63] Frederick II defined the rights of the chapters in similar fashion. In 1219 he delivered the sentence of the imperial curia at Hagenau that any alienations made by a bishop "without the advice of his church and the authorization of the empire" were devoid of legality.[64] His son Henry (VII) in 1222 forbade bishops to alienate in any way the income of the four court-offices (*Hofämter*) without the consent of their chapters (*chorum*) and of their ministerials.[65] In 1234 chapters were not even mentioned in a sentence given at Foggia declaring illegal enfeoffments made by bishops without imperial permission.[66] By 1240, however, the massive papal bid for support in

Germany forced Conrad IV to relent somewhat: in the *Sententia de juribus episcoporum*, he and the princes decreed that newly elevated bishops could rescind any pawns, infeudations, or other alienations of episcopal property done without the consent of both emperor and chapter.[67] The strength of these claims deteriorated so much with the imperial position during the next two decades that the Mainz provincial synod of 1261 could order bishops and abbots to administer their churches in accordance with the sense of the "maiori et saniori parte capituli."[68]

Local claims and customs as well as imperial prerogatives further retarded the attainment by the chapter at Speyer of the exclusive position it held in canon law. The Salians had exercised a strong personal sway over the bishopric of Speyer, both as an important see in the imperial church system and even more as their home diocese. They lavishly endowed it,[69] procured further donations for it,[70] cooperated closely with the bishops (holding at least one castle jointly with them),[71] and often consented to their acts.[72] The advocates of the bishopric, whoever they were in the first seventy-five years of the twelfth century, appear in documents giving their consent only twice, around 1164 and 1180.[73] On both occasions, the chapter also assented, but neither consent appears to have carried much weight, for the bishops issued many charters without their consent.[74]

Frederick Barbarossa restored substantial imperial control over the bishopric, though under different circumstances and with a slightly different rationale. For a time (of disputed duration)[75] he and his son acted as the advocates of the church of Speyer.[76] It has already been noted that the Staufens until the 1230s succeeded in having their candidates elected to the see. They were well served by these bishops and by the clerics under them. The sees of Speyer, Worms, and Mainz played a significant part in the political activities of the early Staufens, and Speyer, along with Bamberg, continued to occupy a special position under them until the early thirteenth century.[77] Barbarossa and his successors held many fiefs of the bishops,[78] and an unusual number of ministerials belonging to the church served the empire simultaneously.[79] One of them became bishop and chancellor, Conrad of Scharfenberg.

The emperors paid a price for this support. At the complaint of Bishop Otto von Henneberg, Henry VI, around 1193, forbade appeals by Speyer burghers from decisions of the episcopal court before pronouncement of the verdict, thereby temporarily checking the movement of the town toward ever greater independence from the bishop.[80] Three years later Henry VI settled a dispute between bishop and chapter over the coinage minted in Speyer by decreeing what the weights and values of the coins were to be and that no changes be effected "without the common consent and wish of our prelates and canons" at Speyer.[81] He clarified an unclear situation by establishing an important legal right of the chapter.[82] Whether these men who acted as the notaries and diplomats of the empire extracted this from Henry in return for their work can only remain a matter of conjecture, but one not easily dismissed.

On the other hand, it is clear that Bishop Conrad of Scharfenberg forced Philip of Swabia to halt construction of a castle on Speyer property at Kreuznach.[83] He also obtained a second see, Metz, in 1212. His role in the making of the *Privilegium in favorem principum ecclesiasticorum* is questionable,[84] but in any event, this agreement generalized, for the whole imperial church, concessions to individual archbishoprics and bishoprics spanning several decades and may be said to mark the beginning of the ecclesiastical principalities and of a new chapter in the relations between the empire and the imperial church. Despite Frederick's son Henry's receiving another *Vogtei* in 1231[85] and his presiding at the election of Bishop Conrad IV in 1233, the bishopric did not appear on the famous imperial tax list of 1241–42 (in contrast to the neighboring abbey of Weissenburg in Alsace),[86] and the subsequent collapse of the Staufens put an effective end to close imperial suzerainty over the principality.

The position of the chapter as the bishop's sole collegial body was nevertheless not yet assured. The amorphous "clergy and people" who on occasion ratified the acts of the bishops in the eleventh century[87] gave way in the twelfth to the sometimes more easily definable members of the *familia* of the church of Speyer. Sometimes they merely bore witness,[88] sometimes they gave counsel,[89] sometimes they assented;[90] there was no uniform development in this respect. In 1104 the bishop exempted the abbey of Schwarzach from all services to the see on the advice of the emperor and his *fideles*.[91] A donation by Bishop Gunther to the monastery of Schönau around 1150 received the assent of "the more notable clergy and ministerials of our church."[92] The canons, the vassals, and the ministerials all joined Frederick and Henry VI in 1188 in agreeing to an exchange of lands between Bishop Ulrich II and Rudolf, count palatine of Tübingen.[93] In an exchange of property with the cathedral chapter in 1223, Bishop Conrad III made sure that "this exchange pleased persons both clerical and lay pertaining to the church of Speyer."[94] As late as 1241,

Bishop Conrad V, because of financial distress, sold to the chapter some lands, tithes, and incomes upon the advice of "the clergy of all the churches of Speyer and of our ministerials."[95]

Several factors account for this persistence of extracapitular influence on the affairs of the bishopric. First, until the thirteenth century, diocesan synods were attended by the clergy and prominent laymen and treated matters of general administration as well as "purely ecclesiastical" matters, insofar as one can distinguish the two in the High Middle Ages.[96] For Speyer, such synods are clearly attested for the years 1023, 1149, 1180, 1211, and 1232.[97] Second, the principle *quod omnes tangit*, the importance of which in ecclesiastical affairs was understood by the cathedral chapter,[98] plus the sheer tenacity of local custom, kept the chapter from acting alone in all affairs. This becomes evident in later chapters, in extraordinary taxation, first of the clergy, and later of the peasantry. Third, the ministerials enjoyed great power in all German bishoprics, not solely Speyer. This is discussed shortly,[99] as is the special relationship between the cathedral chapter and the other three collegiate churches in Speyer.[100] It helps explain, for instance, why all four chapters assented to the foundation of the monastery of Heilsbruck in the diocese in 1232.[101] The cathedral chapter nevertheless guarded its privileges jealously, and by the time of the 1272 electoral oath, the bishop was required in virtually all matters to obtain the consent of the chapter alone.[102]

This tendency can be observed by the late twelfth century. The chapter had consented to donations by the bishops to the monastery of Maulbronn in 1152 and 1183,[103] but on most occasions in the latter half of the twelfth century, as has been already shown, witness or consent was usually given by any combination of other parties with the chapter, whether it was the emperor, the advocate, the ministerials, or the rest of the clergy. The breakthrough came with the concession to the chapter by Henry VI in 1196 of the right of assent to all changes in the weight and value of the coins struck by the bishop.[104] The privilege indicates that the chapter had by then taken on an aggressive stance and also possessed the means to achieve its aims. Its activity in the next decades confirms this suspicion. References in charters to its exclusive consent increased appreciably.[105] To the assent of the appropriate archdeacon, the cathedral chapter was careful to add its own to incorporations, donations of tithes to churches, and the like.[106] On at least one occasion, it wisely issued a separate charter of consent to a donation made by Bishop Conrad III.[107]

The chapter experienced considerable frustration at the hands of Bishop Conrad III. While many of his charters attest capitular consent to his transactions, some mention counsel given,[108] others only witnesses,[109] others no one at all.[110] At all these levels, Conrad did not always seek out the chapter;[111] even when he did, the canons were frequently but one of the witnessing or consenting groups.[112] Here Conrad relied particularly heavily on burghers of Speyer,[113] ministerials,[114] and the counts of Leiningen and Eberstein[115] to counterbalance the chapter.

Steady progress achieved during the twenty years after Conrad's death was again checked, this time even more markedly, by Bishop Henry II. Many of his charters bear no trace of consent whatsoever, and most of these concerned important matters. On one occasion, he pawned some incomes to his brother Emicho, count of Leiningen;[116] on another he granted the income of the church at Dertingen to Herrenalb Abbey;[117] on two others he, as ordinary, affirmed sales of land by the monastery of Hirsau.[118] When, to improve the financial condition of a religious confraternity attached to the cathedral (the *fratres sedis* or *Stuhlbrüder*), he decided to use, for the support of its income, that of the first vacated prebend for a year, he did so only with the advice of "prudent and good men."[119] Neither archdeacon nor chapter is mentioned. The tension that naturally came of this is disclosed by two charters of 1256. With the permission of King William of Holland as collator, and to whom Henry was chancellor, the bishop granted all patronage rights at Altrip (in the diocese of Speyer) to the monastery of Himmerod. Six months later Berthold von Eberstein, provost of the cathedral chapter and the archdeacon affected, issued a separate charter of confirmation.[120] The chapter's consent is of course recorded on a number of charters,[121] but at times Henry preferred to seek the assent of others[122] or at best the counsel of the chapter.[123]

Canon law by no means required the chapter's endorsement in all these cases. That did not bother the chapter in 1272. Neither did the lack of clarity then regnant among canonists over the distinctions between counsel, consent, and ratification. Very few charters from Speyer after 1200 record the chapter's counsel without mention of its consent, and inasmuch as the bishops in question were Conrad III and Henry II, the possibility of deliberately chosen phraseology must be considered.[124] In the oath of 1272, the canons demanded simply that the bishop do none of the following "without the consent of the chapter" (*sine consensu capituli*): mint coinage, convene the chapter outside the cathedral precincts, attend capitular meetings or elections (here unanimous assent to his presence was requisite), exempt any canon from the customs of the church of Speyer, enfeoff or otherwise alienate any possession in the bishop's keep or appurtenant to the bishopric, use reverted or recovered fiefs for the exchange or recuperation of other properties, permit alienations of possessions by any church or monastery in the diocese, or allow any monastery or church to enjoy the income of any parish. This list expanded considerably in the following centuries as new circumstances arose and the chapter's power increased.[125]

What was the nature of that power? What practical means did the chapter have in hand to force the bishop to acknowledge its canonical rights and much more? What of substance could it offer in return to relieve the distressing financial situation of the bishopric from the thirteenth century on, inasmuch as all its rights in law availed nothing to pay debts? Finally, what clues to the understanding of this new strength and assertiveness may be found in the changing duties and social background of the canons?

V

By the turn of the sixteenth century, the cathedral chapter had become very wealthy. Three great copybooks of that time, now in the Generallandesarchiv in Karlsruhe, record the many scattered possessions of the chapter. The last of them, an inventory drawn up around 1520, could encompass within its hundreds of folio pages only the lands and incomes in places whose names ran from A to L.[1] The extent of the chapter's resources in the period just before the Reformation has been recognized, if not studied in detail.[2] What has received at best cursory recognition, much less investigation, are the beginnings of that affluence in the thirteenth century and signs of the chapter's financial acumen in the twelfth.

Henry IV in his charter of 1101 to the chapter listed the donations he, his father, and his grandfather had made to the chapter. They comprised holdings in seventeen places and the church and tithes at Schifferstadt.[3] The capitulation of 1272, by contrast, spoke of the extensive manors, tithes, incomes, and services subject to the chapter, and this was by no means a complete list.[4] In the intervening generations, particularly since the turn of the century, it had accumulated substantial holdings in various ways. Donations, whether outright grants or lands or rights or else exemptions from tolls or property taxes, continued to be important. They came primarily from the emperors,[5] the popes,[6] neighboring princes,[7] the bishops,[8] monasteries,[9] and nobles or ministerials.[10] The prelates and canons as well gave land and money, most of it to support new benefices.[11] The chapter further supplemented its income by using for capitalization the revenues from vacant prebends. Pope Honorius III in 1220 confirmed the chapter's custom of sequestering the income of vacant prebends for three years,[12] and by the end of the fifteenth century, further extensions had increased to five years and thirty days the period a newly elected canon had to wait before taking possession of his prebend.[13] Lastly, the chapter also purchased, at great cost, other lands and rights, particularly from impoverished monasteries and noble families.[14]

Among the more valuable of these holdings were those in Speyer: the small tithe, lands farmed by *censuales,* and several mills. Bitter litigation with the burghers of Speyer occurred often over these matters as well as over the clergy's wine-selling privilege.[15] The chapter showed equal firmness in securing no fewer than six charters of confirmation of Frederick II's donation in 1213 of the royal church at Esslingen in Swabia,[16] which Stamer called "the richest possession of the cathedral chapter until the days of the Reformation."[17] Perhaps an exaggeration, but the three-page list of the revenues from the church in 1268 is most striking.[18] The chapter also owned a mint at Kreuznach, which it leased out.[19] It had leased property since the twelfth century, and by the 1230s it was not uncommon for the canons to lease land immediately to the person from whom they had just bought it.[20] On occasion, the chapter exchanged property[21] or simply alienated it, as it did the barren forest near Offenbach in 1219.[22] The organization of its lands into administrative units, called *officia,* under the supervision of a canon or of a lay *officiatus,* appears to have antedated by about half a century the bishops' division of their lands into *Ämter.*[23] The chapter issued detailed regulations for the management of its revenues, although it experienced considerable difficulty in their collection from both its clerical and lay officials.[24]

Even in the twelfth century, scattered pieces of evidence hint at the ability and tenacity of the chapter in the governance of its affairs. In 1157 Bishop Gunther issued a charter that recorded events several years past. King Conrad III had compelled the bishop against his will to enfeoff his son Henry with Ilsfeld, which Henry IV had donated to the church of Speyer in 1102.[25] Gunther had demanded compensation and was accordingly dispensed from the obligation of joining an imperial expedition, probably the journey to Rome planned for September 1152. Now, some years later, feeling himself bound to indemnify the chapter, Gunther redeemed two fiefs (each a curia) with, curiously, his own resources rather than those of the church, and donated them to the chapter. The long interval of time, Gunther's carping references to his duty to make good the chapter's loss, and the use of his own funds all suggest that the canons may have pressured him into it.[26] Other charters point, if not to this conclusion, at least to the chapter's strong-mindedness on matters of wealth and property. In 1184 it brought before Frederick Barbarossa a suit against a certain Conrad of Boyneburg and his nephew concerning a fief they held from the chapter.[27] About the year 1200 the canons demonstrated little compunction about forging a charter to support their claims in Kreuznach against those of the counts of Sponheim, since the eleventh-century original had been lost.[28]

The substantial assets of the chapter undoubtedly made it one of the wealthiest landowners of the principality. They by no means equalled those for which the bishop was responsible, but at the same time the chapter did not have to maintain castles or troops. Its lands, in fact, insofar as they fell within the bishop's territorial domains, were protected by the bishop; and where they did not, the continued independence of its possessions depended ultimately on that of the lord bishop's. Beyond its responsibilities to the bishopric in canon law, therefore, the chapter had a vital and concrete interest in the preservation of the territorial integrity and financial stability of the bishopric. Looked at from another point of view, its extensive resources, landed and monetary, also permitted it to fulfill a potentially major role in the finances of the principality. The chapter could lend the bishop money or negotiate loans for him should his credit be low. It could also receive, in fief or in pawn, castles, incomes, or *Ämter* of the bishopric without the bishop's having to fear permanent loss of these properties. It could recover holdings already lost and thereby restore them indirectly to the bishopric. Finally, in a pinch the chapter could be relied on to supply a large portion of any extraordinary levies exacted by the bishops.

The bishops realized some of these possibilities when they began to encounter financial difficulties in the 1230s. Bishop Conrad V in 1241 wanted to purchase all the lands in Zeutern and Stettfeld owned by the nobleman Rudolf of Kisslau. To raise the money, he sold to the chapter, on the counsel of the clergy of the Speyer churches and of his ministerials, a yearly income of 96 measures (*modii*) of wheat and 40d. (*unciae*) from two episcopal granges as well as an allod with all appurtenances (including tithes) at Deidesheim for 260 marks of silver. He made this arrangement, he announced, "thinking the sale of these holdings safer than the resale of the newly acquired ones, especially since the bishopric could be hard pressed by another powerful possessor of the lands we have bought."[29] His premonition was to prove well founded.

At the same time, the bishops appear to have embarked on a policy of recuperation of fiefs from the high nobility to quash the threat of lasting deprivation to the church of its lands.[30] Although Bishop Conrad III had perhaps already undertaken such a program,[31] toward the end of Bishop Beringer's episcopate it blossomed into a full-scale operation in which the chapter participated. In 1232, Count Gottfried of Vaihingen and his nephew Count Gottfried of Calw resigned to Beringer their fief at Öwisheim, which they had subinfeudated to Rudolf of Kisslau, with the request that he donate it to Maulbronn Abbey.[32] Aware that Maulbronn, in present-day Württemberg, lay more within their reach than his (the bishop was technically the advocate of the monastery), Beringer instead granted it jointly to Maulbronn and his chapter to foil pressure that might be brought to bear.[33] Four years later Frederick, count of Zollern, in resigning to the bishop a fief at Rödersheim, sold it to the chapter for 340 marks. The bishop then gave it to the chapter to support prebends.[34] A similar pattern was followed again in 1241: resignation, purchase, and donation of the tithes at Lachen.[35]

While Bishop Henry II pursued his own vigorous efforts to win back control over several major possessions of the bishopric,[36] the chapter continued to reclaim episcopal lands. It purchased in 1263 for £60 Heller a fief-rente of £6 Heller per year.[37] From the counts of Leiningen, the canons acquired a manor at Bühl for 140 marks (1256),[38] one third of the tithe at Walsheim held in fief from the bishop (1254),[39] and, twelve years later, more feudal lands in the same place.[40] The canons, moreover, remained alert to the possibilities inherent in Henry's policies. Financial distress drove him in 1249 to sell the forest at Ketsch (near Schwetzingen) to Maulbronn Abbey for 160 marks. On the same day, but in a separate charter, the chapter announced that it had joined the monastery in buying the forest. The canons evidently paid a price for their eagerness to buy in, for they ceded to Maulbronn half the income from their chapel at Öwisheim. Six years later, in 1255, the canons exchanged with the abbey their half of the revenues of the forest for 100 measures of wheat per year.[41]

To be sure, the chapter's policy was a two-edged sword. Although the alienated lands and incomes reverted to the bishopric in a way, in practice only the chapter could enjoy their use. The separation of the *mensa episcopalis* from the *mensa capitularis* proscribed the bishop's usufruct of chapter property. His advantage was at best indirectly served: the chapter's endowment increased through these additions, thereby potentially putting at his disposal more money in the form of loans and pawns. This purely legal point of view, however, is too narrow even to encompass all the constitutional nuances in the relationship. As the members of the corporation, the chapter bore, with the bishop, a primary responsibility for the health of the body corporate, although the other clergy might be taxed if necessary.[42] The inadequacy of the *mensa episcopalis* could not be ignored, furthermore, because from it the bishop provided defense, administration, and services for the good of all, including the chapter. The chapter could not idly stand by watching the decline of the bishop's revenues and lands and face possible bankruptcy, mediatization, or, later, secularization. Practical considerations and legal accountability compelled the chapter to act in such menacing situations, and its resources put it in a position to respond forcefully. Some historians have laid undue stress on chapters' rights and attempts to seize power and have barely mentioned their responsibilities.[43] (In certain ways, ironically, the more influence and power chapters gained in bishoprics, the more responsible they had to become, for their stake in stability had grown.) Admittedly chapters were altogether too often neglectful of their duties, too selfish and irresponsible. What is worth noting about the few examples cited above, however, is that the chapter at so early a date showed itself willing to cooperate with the bishops for the good of the principality and to recoup fiefs that otherwise would gradually have drifted beyond the pale of recoverability. This was but an adumbration; the chapter's efforts to maintain fiscal viability and territorial coherence first became full-blown only in the fourteenth century and attained real success only in the fifteenth.

The chapter wielded a final kind of power, less ambiguous in character, but equally complex in its implications. By the mid-twelfth century the exercise of much of the bishop's jurisdiction over the lower clergy, over church property and benefices, and over the cases to be tried by the courts ecclesiastical had passed into the hands of archdeacons. Although in the ancient church the archdeacon as one of the bishop's principal helpers discharged major administrative functions and came in time (particularly since the ninth century) to have his own *jurisdictio propria,* in the diocese of Speyer the archidiaconate is first attested only in 1152[44] and it probably developed from the office of the *chorepiscopus,* last mentioned in 1100 and 1103.[45] There is some scholarly dispute concerning the order in which the diocese was carved up into archidiaconates and the division of the city of Speyer among them, but this does not concern us here.[46] Suffice it to say that, by the middle of the thirteenth century, four archidiaconates had been formed.[47] To one fell that part of the diocese on the left bank of the Rhine, while the rest of the diocese on the right bank was subdivided among the other three.

The archdeacons themselves were the provosts of the four collegiate churches of Speyer: the cathedral, Saint Germain (founded ca. 600 probably by King Dagobert I),[48] Saint Guido (founded in 1030 by Emperor Conrad II),[49] and Holy Trinity or (as it was called more and more after 1200) All Saints (established by Bishop Sigibodo [1039–1051]).[50] The four provosts, furthermore, were, from the second quarter of the twelfth century, members of the cathedral chapter.[51] Until the mid-thirteenth century, the provostships of the other chapters were ordinarily held by the prelates or dignitaries of the cathedral chapter, thereafter in general by canons.[52] In the fifteenth and sixteenth centuries, the other collegiate churches on several occasions attempted to break this control by electing their own canons as provosts, usually, but not always, without success.[53]

The scanty sources available to us, taken at face value, suggest that the cathedral chapter had gained the four provostships before the provosts became the archdeacons. Witness lists in charters of 1137, 1147, ca. 1150, and 1152 indicate the personal union of the offices before the first attestation of archdeacons in 1152 and 1160.[54] These references, on the other hand, show archidiaconates that had already gone beyond an elementary level of organization and the further expansion of which Bishop Gunther may well have been trying to curb. In the first document bishop and chapter donated to Maulbronn Abbey a *curtis* belonging to the *mensa capitularis.* The provost of the chapter was flatly forbidden to invest the priest for the chapel on the *curtis* without being so requested by the abbot.[55] In the second (1160), the bishop, in incorporating the parish church of Saint Michael at Backnang into the collegiate church of Saint Pancratius there, noted that the provostship of Saint Guido's, and hence the archdeaconry, lay in his disposition.[56]

Whatever the hazy origins and early development of the archidiaconal system, during the thirteenth century the four archdeacons became firmly established with substantial rights and authority. They conducted much of the day-to-day business in matters strictly religious, sacerdotal, and paro-chial. Their consent was necessary for ecclesiastical transactions such as investiture, incorporation, and the like. They supervised the installation, organization, and discipline of the diocesan clergy, often working through the deans of rural chapters. They collected sizable revenues in fees for the dispensation of their *jura archidiaconalia* as well as the *cathedraticum* (paid by parishes upon visitation) and *synodalia* (paid, it seems, by the laymen in parishes) every leap year. They also possessed the competence to try most cases falling within the jurisdiction of the ecclesiastical courts, from which they derived further income.[57] In short, they were, in the words of Clement III, "the eye of the bishop" or his vicar and, according to In-nocent III, came second in rank only to the bishop.[58]

However much the rise of the archdeacons in Germany and their great increase in authority in the twelfth century may be attributable to the need to fill a vacuum left by bishops preoccupied with imperial or their own princely business,[59] the bishops of Speyer, like their colleagues elsewhere, came to regard the growing power of the archdeacons, and especially of their courts, as a threat to be dealt with.[60] The main battles arose only in the late thirteenth and again in the fifteenth centuries and hence are taken up again later.[61] There were, however, in the early thirteenth century, portents of the troubles to come. In 1210 a dispute between the villages of Herxheim and "Bruchwilre" was adjudicated before two archdeacons, the provosts of Saint Guido and All Saints, acting as the episcopal judges.[62] Bishop Conrad IV may have tried to displace the archdeacons by appointing canons of Saint Guido's as his *judices delegati*,[63] but without lasting success. Later judges were members of the cathedral chapter,[64] and the electoral capitulation of 1272 required that at least one of the bishop's judges be a cathedral canon.[65]

The archdeacons had so encroached on the bishop's sphere that by the 1270s they were appointing *officiales* to represent them in court and handle many of their duties.[66] When the bishop countered by creating an *officialis* of his own, the chapter demanded in the first article of the capitulation of 1302 that the episcopal *officialis* be a canon.[67] The struggle continued in this fashion until the dissolution of the bishopric by Napoleon, and to the end, the chapter managed to retain a great deal of power. It ceded rather little to the bishops in the fifteenth century, successfully circumvented efforts by the vicars-general to restrict their privileges, and largely ignored the decrees of the Council of Trent that affected archdeacons.[68]

The chapter's ecclesiastical prerogatives bore on its position in the principality in several ways. They furnished another point of friction between the bishop and the chapter. The chapter's prominence was all the more enhanced, its potential leverage against the bishop all the more augmented. At the same time that its control of the four provostships, and hence the archdeaconries, added to the chapter's substance, it also tied the cathedral chapter more closely to the other three collegiate churches in Speyer and modified somewhat its exclusive place in the bishopric, for the chapter had to act in conjunction with the other chapters more than it otherwise might have. This union, nonetheless, lent a broader base, and therefore greater stability, to the chapter's "representation" of the other orders of the principality, especially of the clergy, and that particularly in connection with extraordinary taxation. The immediate causes of the formation of this union had little to do, however, with these specific links between the canons and the other chapters; they are discussed in chapter two.

The great increase of the chapter's possessions, rights, and duties during the twelfth and thirteenth centuries brought with it corresponding alterations in the responsibilities and attitudes of the canons. They had originally been responsible for the celebration of the liturgy, the singing of the divine office, and the ministration of the sacraments. Henry IV's charter of 1101 to the chapter indicates that some of the canons held benefices or cures from the bishop in the countryside.[69] All these necessarily suffered, however, when the canons' nonsacerdotal duties began multiplying rapidly.

These new obligations partly promoted the growth of nonresidence and, to a lesser extent, pluralism from the later twelfth century,[70] and because canons did not ordinarily have to be priests to discharge many of their responsibilities, they were increasingly content to receive nothing more than the subdiaconate. Although it was set down in statute at Speyer only in 1343 that canons had to have received at least the subdiaconate,[71] this was merely the formulation of a custom that probably reached back to the twelfth century, for in 1207 Innocent III, in acceptance of the general practice, had admitted the subdiaconate to the major orders.[72] (Only the major orders belonged to the episcopal *presbyterium* and enjoyed the right of consultation.)[73] By the end of the twelfth century, according to the revised version of 1569 of the *Regula chori,* the need for priests had become so great that two canons were moved to found four vicarages specifically for priests.[74] Four more were established in 1229.[75] The chapter itself allocated at some time six of the original forty capitular prebends for noncapitular priests. It may have done so before the first sacerdotal vicarages were created, although the first evidence of their existence dates from a charter of 1273 in which the chapter spoke of the forty prebends and thirty canons in the cathedral.[76] The difference of ten is explicable by the fact that six prebends were reserved for nonvoting priests, two other prebends had been set aside in 1245 to be shared by four deacons and subdeacons,[77] and the last two were incorporated into the offices of dean and chancellor of the school.[78]

Vicarages continued to be founded for the performance of specific duties at particular altars throughout the course of the late Middle Ages. As early as 1220, the vicars appear to have acquired considerable influence in clerical affairs, as revealed by the fact that the clergy of the four collegiate churches of Speyer in that year decided, on the advice given by the cathedral canons and vicars, to suspend services because Bishop Conrad had not rendered them the customary *servitium*.[79] Not all the vicars were priests,[80] and dispensations were granted even for prebends stipulated for priests.[81] The vicars, like the canons, had many nonsacerdotal and administrative duties, and by the late fifteenth century they had won a certain voice in capitular deliberations in virtue of their numbers (ca. seventy)[82] and their responsibilities.[83]

This decline of the cathedral chapter as a purely religious body and its transformation into a well-endowed, privileged corporation has often been lamented by modern historians and variously ascribed to the decline of the common life, the deleterious effects of its wealth, or the aristocratic origins of the canons.[84] This is not the place to offer an apology for this phenomenon, were it necessary or possible. In fact, the common life fully observed seems rarely if ever to have been the norm in cathedral chapters.[85] Furthermore, we have seen that in the High Middle Ages canons acquired, not only substantial holdings to administer, but also great and new tasks to discharge in the government of their bishoprics and the empire.[86] Vicars came to perform duties that canons had once executed, just as canons, archdeacons, and, later, suffragan bishops and vicars-general came to assist overtaxed bishops.[87] These developments paralleled in many ways changes in the character of the college of cardinals in the second half of the eleventh century.[88] If this be "secularization," it might be noted that it was, ironically, a direct consequence of the Gregorian reform movement which, in seeking to free the church from lay control, necessarily forced clerics to assume "secular" responsibilities. What has usually been viewed as a sign of decline was, on the contrary, a consequence of reform; and the reformers, in turn, conscientiously provided for new officials to carry out the ongoing and proliferating duties of the church's primary mission, the pastoral care of souls.[89]

VI

Another facet of the structure of the cathedral chapter that is intriguing and perhaps incomprehensible to many modern minds and that, in a different way, illuminates and accounts for the chapter's predominant place in the principality and its relationship to the bishops and the other estates, has now to be discussed and to have its significance evaluated: the social background of the canons.

In 1910 Aloys Schulte published a major work on the nobility and the German church in the Middle Ages. There he set out the thesis that the aristocracy dominated most of the sees, abbeys, and chapters down to the end of the medieval period, particularly those belonging to the so-called imperial church system (*Reichskirchensystem*) established by the Saxon emperors on foundations laid by the Carolingians.[1] Leo Santifaller has more recently compressed much of the information collected by Schulte and later historians on the imperial church. He too thought that nobles were very much in control and that nonnobles had access to the newer orders and to the older foundations only through imperial or papal promotion.[2] Like Schulte, however, he tended to extrapolate from the well-known aristocratic exclusiveness of the German foundations in the late Middle Ages and to conflate it in a distorting fashion with the earlier Middle Ages. To cite but one example: of the 106 archbishops and bishops in the Mainz and Cologne church provinces in the ninth century, according to Schulte, 44 were noble, 18 "presumably" (*vermutlich*) noble, but of a full 42 nothing is known. The figures are scarcely better for the tenth century: We have no indications about the origins of 39 out of 107 bishops, and 17 of the remaining 68 were "presumably" noble. The sources are better for the eleventh and twelfth centuries, in which the backgrounds of only 31 and 22 prelates cannot be demonstrated out of 154 and 161 bishops, respectively.[3] But if the investigation of the episcopate presents such obstacles, one can only imagine how many thousands of monks, canons, and nuns failed to break into history for want of a single citation.

Although these findings may be valid for the German church as a whole, one must be careful about assuming in a facile manner that what is true of the whole is a fortiori true of any of its parts. Scholars have not always avoided this pitfall in their discussions of the composition of the cathedral chapter of Speyer.[4] The little evidence available supports the conclusion that only from the early fourteenth century at best did the Speyer chapter exclude nonnobles from its membership. In his famous 1101 charter to the chapter, Henry IV granted detailed testamentary rights to "each canon of the church of Speyer, born of either noble or humble kind."[5] The first positive indication of the chapter's exclusively noble composition appeared in 1362, when the emperor Charles IV conceded it the privilege of rejecting nonnoble postulations to prelacies or canonries and promised that none whatsoever would be made without the express and special permission of the papacy.[6] This clearly confirmed the chapter's already established practice of electing only nobles. When that had become customary is the decisive question, to which no precise answer can be given, but two different sorts of evidence preclude the possibility that it was so before 1310.

First, as late as 1302, burghers of Speyer could be admitted to the chapter. The cellarer of the chapter, who subscribed to the oath of 1272, was Master Diether, son of the Speyer *Schultheiss* Sigulo.[7] In 1264 the four collegiate churches of Speyer had barred all benefices and prebends in the diocese to all Speyer burghers and their relations to the fourth degree.[8] The ban was rescinded in 1272,[9] but reimposed in 1302.[10] Seven years later, the bishop and the chapter, on those grounds, explicitly forbade acceptance of Master Nicholas Bernhoh, a native of Speyer and canon of Saint Germain's, into any canonry or dignity of the chapter; he was not rejected for lack of aristocratic ancestry.[11]

Second, during the thirteenth century, and to some extent in the late twelfth, *ministeriales* and their descendants gained access to the canonries and prelacies of the chapter, and some ascended to the episcopate as well. Bishops Conrad of Scharfenberg, Conrad of Tann, and Frederick of Bolanden were all ministerials or of ministerial origin.[12] Conrad of Scharfenberg did not serve as dean of the chapter, as was once thought, but at least two later deans, Siegfried of Lachen (1228–1249) and his brother Adelvolk (1262), were ministerial offspring. Since 1241 Adelvolk had also been chancellor of the cathedral school, and, since 1248, provost of All

Saints.[13] From scattered and incomplete witness lists, one can garner the names of canons of similar birth: Ulrich of Staufen in 1248 and 1252,[14] and Helfric of Talheim, Egenolf of Landsberg, and Henry of Tann in 1270.[15] Of the twenty-four canons' names given at the close of the 1272 electoral oath, fully nine can be identified as having ministerial background. The dean, Albert of Musbach, came of ministerial ancestry.[16] The family of Berthold of Scharfenberg, canon since 1232 and chanter since 1235, had given the see Bishop Conrad III.[17] Chancellor of the school, Adelvolk of Lachen, was the uncle of Canon Master Albert of Lachen.[18] Their family had for some time held dual ministerial posts from bishop and emperor.[19] So, too, had the relatives of Frederick of Bolanden, Hugh of Spiegelberg, Albert of Remchingen, and the brothers Henry and Peter of Fleckenstein.[20] A tenth canon, Richwin of Schonenberg, might also have had ministerial ancestors. A Theodoric of Schoneberg, *miles*, appears in a charter of 1267.[21] Given the close connection between *ministeriales* and *milites* discussed shortly, it is not impossible that Richwin and Theodoric or their parents were sired by ministerials.

For many decades historians had thought quite simply that all ministerials were unfree. E. F. Otto caused that view to be modified somewhat by demonstrating the diversity of their origins and their status.[22] Karl Bosl, too, cautioned against drawing sharp "class" lines in medieval history, especially in those hazy areas of flux between "classes." He found that, by and large, ministerials were unfree, "a particularly qualified upper layer of the unfree," however, noted for their ambition and their rapid achievement of power and influence.[23]

Ministerials in the bishopric of Speyer were sharply distinguished from freemen in witness lists as late as 1238,[24] but at the same time they were often indiscriminately confused with, or listed elsewhere as, *milites*. This is not surprising, because ministerials in the principality of Speyer,[25] as in most of Germany,[26] discharged primarily military duties. One cannot be certain Bishop Conrad III in 1216 meant *ministeriales* when he alluded to "ministrorum nostrorum vel aliorum militum,"[27] but the lack of precision at the time is apparent in references of 1220 to Anselm, the bishop's advocate: In one place, he is counted among the ministerials, in another among the *milites*.[28] Adelvolk and Albert of Lachen are similarly labeled in various fashions in charters of 1232 and 1237.[29] A witness list appended to an episcopal charter of 1241 described three men in the following manner:

"Eberhardus pincerna de Mattenberg, Adelvolcus et Heilwicus de Landesheim milites, ministeriales ecclesie."[30] Similar terminology was applied to Conrad of Sulzfeld in 1220.[31]

The confusion was not restricted to this level: *miles* too was not very strictly used. The son of a *miles* was manumitted in 1256.[32] On the other hand, Johannes of Franckenstein appears in charters of 1235 as *miles*, of 1236 as one of *nobilium virorum*, and of 1237 as *dominus*.[33] Bertold of Remchingen is called *miles* in documents of 1257 and 1263, but in 1271 he and his brothers are *domini*.[34] Before one succumbs to the temptation of crediting these men with aggressive and successful social climbing, one ought to consider nine witnesses of a Bruchsal charter dated 13 January 1282, of which six were *milites* and three *servi nobiles*—a most unusual term.[35]

This apparent want of discrimination springs not from the celebrated medieval unreliability in matters where the modern scholar would have accuracy. Rather, it indicates enormous flux and mobility within the military and administrative orders in the thirteenth century. The contours and boundaries of these newly emerging social patterns were uncertain and ever changing. Still, though they elude attempts at exact description, rough plotting of the stages of transformation is possible. For all the confusion between ministerials and *milites*, ministerials were distinguished from freemen as late as 1238 and from episcopal vassals in the electoral capitulation of 1272.[36] They are mentioned infrequently after the middle of the century and not at all after 1280.[37] Thereafter the dominant distinction drawn was between *milites* and *castrenses*[38] or *nobiles* or *armigeri*.[39] *Milites*, furthermore, came to hold the principal offices of the bishopric, which had been filled by ministerials since the mid-twelfth century.[40] A complicating factor arose in the second quarter of the fourteenth century, when German began to supplant Latin as the ordinary language of the charters and other records of the bishopric. *Milites* and the like gave way to *Dienstmann*, *Herr*, *Jungherr*, *Ritter*, and *edler Knecht*, yet behind these initially disconcerting transpositions of terminology lay real changes in attitude and status. In 1238 ministerials who did castle duty for their bishop still bore the mark of being unfree. A century later their successors had gained, not merely freedom, but nobility as well. In 1339 Bishop Gerhard traveled to the castle at Kirrweiler (about fourteen miles west of Speyer at the foot of the Hardt range) to conduct a feudal inquest. The eighteen castellans deposed concerning their residence duty there and other obligations towards the bishop. Those unable to fulfill them, they said, should under pain of forfeiture of fief "send in their place a fully armored noble knight."[41]

It is not impossible that the chapter at Speyer had, about the same time, adopted a similar attitude regarding its membership, because its canons came increasingly from this same ambitious class of *Ritter,* the lower nobility formed essentially from the fusion of the *milites* and *ministeriales* and their achievement of noble status through their power and influence.[42] The first bishop of lower noble origins elected to the see of Speyer was Gerhard von Ehrenberg in 1336, and from 1396 to 1719, every bishop of Speyer save one was a baron (*Freiherr*). The high nobility had always been, and continued to be, represented in the chapter, but from the thirteenth century at the latest, they constituted a distinct minority. Many canons from the high nobility, furthermore, since the 1240s and above all in the fourteenth century, gained their seats in the chapter only by papal or imperial advancement, rather than by election from within;[43] so, too, many of the comital bishops of the fourteenth century. As we have already seen, it is not inconceivable in view of the almost constant bad blood between the chapter and the series of Leiningen-related bishops (1237–1336) that some of these bishops were forced upon the chapter.

By the early decades of the thirteenth century, a certain pattern of governance had begun to establish itself in the bishopric, which remained essentially the same down to the eighteenth century, however much the individual names or arrangements varied from generation to generation. In short, at any given time, certain ministerial or, later, knightly families who were settled in and around the bishopric occupied most of the high positions in the principality. Ordinarily highly interrelated by marriage, they provided the bishops, the canons, the retainers, the court and castle officials. The bishops commonly had several relatives in the chapter, frequently as its prelates, and, on their accession, granted their brothers and other kinsmen fiefs, *fief-rentes,* benefices, and administrative offices. The "system," if one may call it such at the risk of presenting a rigid picture where rigidity was not present, became more conspicuous in the fourteenth century, when the names "von Ehrenberg," "von Randeck," and "von Fleckenstein" recur constantly in the rosters. It became full blown in the fifteenth, when three von Helmstadt bishops ruled for 86 out of 108 years (1396–1504) and saw many of their von Venningen, von Gemmingen, and Goler von Ravensberg relatives in the chapter and appointed others to numerous positions in their service.

The outlines of this loosely interlocking maze of families were beginning to take shape in the thirteenth century. Some of the families that had risen in imperial or episcopal service, or both, as ministerials and that had obtained canonries for their sons have already been indicated: the Lachen, the Talheim, the Remchingen, the Bolanden, the Spiegelberg, the Landsberg, the Staufen, the Musbach. The Lachens had been particularly successful. Siegfried held the deanship from 1228 to 1249. His brother Adelvolk became chancellor of the school in 1241, provost of All Saints in 1248, canon of Worms and provost of Saint Andreas collegiate church in Worms in 1256, and dean of Speyer in 1262, which office he held concomitantly with the mastership of the school. Adelvolk's nephew, Master Albert, first appeared as canon in 1272 and as cellarer in 1292.[44] His nephew in turn was Eberhard *genannt* ("called") Sniteloch of Lachen, the high steward (*Truchsess*) of Bishop Frederick.[45] He was hardly the first of his line to distinguish himself in the bishops' employ; many others had done so since the early years of the thirteenth century, in many instances simultaneously ministerials of bishop and emperor.[46]

Less long-lived at Speyer but even more significant in their heyday were the Scharfenbergs and their collateral line, the Scharfenecks,[47] both in imperial ministerial service.[48] Bishop Conrad III, the later chanter Berthold of Scharfenberg, and Canon Johannes of Scharfeneck (who was mentioned only once in the sources, in 1286)[49] all had seats in the cathedral while their relations held positions and fiefs under the Staufens and the bishops.[50] Anselm, the advocate of the church of Speyer between 1204 and 1220, was probably a close relative of the bishop, as the following section of a witness list of 1212 indicates: "Albertus camerarius, Anselmus advocatus et filii eius duo, Henricus et Bertoldus de Scarphenburc."[51] His son Gerlach was referred to as a canon in 1218 and 1220[52] and is undoubtedly the same Gerlach named as chanter between 1230 and 1237.[53]

Not all the ministerial or formerly ministerial families represented in the chapter lived in the diocese or found their principal employ there. Some advanced quickly through the ranks of the imperial ministerials by ambitious accumulation of fiefs and advocacies and by carefully planned marriages into the upper nobility. The famous Bolandens used all possible resources to build up and consolidate their holdings on the middle Rhine. In

1212 they gained the office of imperial high steward (*Reichstruchses-senamt*), and by the middle of the century, they possessed twenty-one castles.[54] Bishop Frederick of Bolanden, nephew of his predecessor, Count Henry II of Leiningen, and the youngest canon at the time of his election, was but one member of this family who achieved great distinction.

Other families of lesser note failed to have any sons raised to the see of Speyer but did install many canons in the chapter. The Fleckensteins, whom Bosl called one of the most eminent imperial ministerial families in Lower Alsace, made their way primarily as imperial castellans at Hagenau, added to their stature by marriages with the Bolandens and Scharfenecks, and, in the church, placed sons in the Strasbourg chapter, in the collegiate churches of Selz and Surburg, and in the commandery of the Teutonic Knights at Tann i. E., as well as five in the Speyer chapter between 1270 and 1342.[55] The Randecks, another important group of imperial castellans, found canonries for six sons in the Speyer chapter in the decades between 1280 and 1340.[56] A final ministerial family from Alsace who made their mark in the twelfth and thirteenth centuries by serving the bishopric of Strasbourg and the Staufens was the Landsbergs. Two of the five Landsberg canons in the necrology of the Speyer chapter between 1270 and 1340 had matriculated at the University of Bologna. Both were elected provost of the collegiate church of Lautenbach, and one was later appointed vicar-general to the bishop of Constance. Of the remaining three, one held simultaneously the provostship of All Saints and a canonry at Saint Peter's church in Strasbourg, and another gained the deanship at Speyer.[57]

The wide geographical sweep represented in the composition of the episcopate and the chapter in the thirteenth and early fourteenth centuries and the speed with which the ministerials and their descendants gained ascendancy in the chapter underlines their ambition, the role of the Staufens in bringing about their success, and the ease with which they came to power. Although episcopal ministerials are attested as early as 946,[58] they obtained a major voice in the conduct of affairs only in the middle of the twelfth century. Bishop Gunther in 1149 subordinated Naumburg Priory to Limburg Abbey after taking the counsel of his abbots, provosts, nobles, and ministerials in synod.[59] A year later he donated land to the monastery of Schönau with the assent of "the more notable clergy and ministerials of the church of Speyer."[60] By 1160 ministerials filled all four court offices.[61] Their position improved much more rapidly once Frederick Barbarossa and his successors assumed the direct advocacy of the see and revived close imperial control over it. Many if not most of the bishop's ministerials doubled as imperial officials and soldiers, whereas the emperors advanced their own men in the bishopric[62] and promoted the consultative rights of ministerials in the imperial churches.[63] Imperial sway was maintained, although ever more tenuously, until the 1230s and undoubtedly accounts for the conspicuous silence of the sources on ministerial turbulence at Speyer. Franklin Geselbracht found that ministerials proved to be the main obstacle to the achievement of closed canonical elections in the last quarter of the twelfth century,[64] and as late as 1221 and 1223, they interfered with elections at Hildesheim, Eichstätt, and Paderborn.[65] Complaints about ministerial usurpations and excesses occurred frequently as well.[66] Nothing of this sort is recorded at Speyer in connection with elections or the chapter's authority.[67]

The collapse of the Staufens did not bring with it that of the ministerials in the principality. On the contrary, under imperial aegis they had arrived at the point where they could continue to evolve independently. As late as 1241, the ministerials joined the cathedral chapter and the clergy of the other churches of Speyer in assenting to a sale by the bishop.[68] The chapter won its exclusive right of consent within a few decades without any evident opposition from the ministerials. In the 1272 electoral capitulation, in fact, it stipulated that the bishop's chamberlain be either a canon or a ministerial, which suggests the absence of conflict between them.[69] The explanation for this is twofold. First, the ministerials were not denied admission to the chapter. The lineage of nine and possibly ten of the canons signatory to the electoral oath was, we have seen, ministerial. Formally barred from its deliberations by canon law, the powerful families in the bishopric obtained seats in the chapter and thus sustained their influence under a different guise. (Desprairies discerned a parallel phenomenon in twelfth-century France, where many abbots and archdeacons gained permanent places in cathedral chapters to compensate for their exclusion.)[70] Second, their participation in the governance of the principality was in any event by no means abolished, but, rather, circumscribed. They continued to be consulted on matters that affected them, specifically as castellans, administrative officials, and counsellors of the bishop. Indeed, the bishops of the following centuries often tried, sometimes with success, to play off their "friends and advisors" (*frunde und rete*) against the chapter.

What did all this imply for the chapter as the functioning "parliament" of the principality? Canon law guaranteed the chapter's exclusiveness and predominance in the bishopric. The canons' increasingly aristocratic outlook not only reinforced that tendency, but also led them to extend their claims to cogovernance far beyond those permitted in church law. Heinrich Dannenbauer, Karl Bosl, and Heinrich Mitteis, to select but a few historians, have all underlined the significance of the aristocracy in medieval society and culture. Bosl sketched some aspects of that picture in a fine, short essay, "The Aristocratic Structure of Medieval Society."[71] What Dannenbauer wrote is more pertinent to our considerations:

> The world of the Middle Ages is an aristocratic world. State and church and society are governed by the nobility. A number of great families, distinguished by noble birth and extensive possessions, and closely related to each other, rule the land and its people. The king himself is their equal, the first nobleman of the land. Together with him they rule the state—imperial princes in Germany, barons in France, lords in England, grandees in Spain. Their brothers, their sons and cousins occupy the bishoprics of the land. With them they elevate the king, surround him at his court, define his policies, support him in administration and law-finding, accompany him on his campaigns with their vassals, or engage him in feuds and indeed depose him just as they had raised him up.[72]

Mitteis went so far as to say that the conflict between the nobility and the prince constituted the central problem of medieval constitutional history.[73]

Certainly the struggle between bishop and chapter formed the crucial issue in the internal polity of the principality down through the dissolution in 1802–3. The personalities and the issues often changed, but always in the foreground stood the chapter's essential insistence on cogovernance (*Mitherrschaft, Mitregierung*) of the bishopric. In time, it came to demand the appointment of canons to the major offices ecclesiastical and secular: judges, *officiales,* chamberlains, regents, provostships, vicars-general. Canons were also to supervise the bishop's accounting officials and the collection of extraordinary taxation. The chapter required that the bishop undertake no important transaction or policy and alter no customs without its express consent. The bishop was to curb expenses, collect the chapter's incomes, provide adequate defense for his subjects, and devote himself to the amortization of the debts of the principality. The chapter was to rule during vacancies, and a new bishop could not take possession of the castles until he had sworn to an electoral capitulation, guaranteeing and sometimes extending the chapter's rights in the government of the bishopric.

It is conceivable that, given the unique character of an ecclesiastical principality of which canon law did not take account, things might have developed this way even if the chapter had not closed its doors to all but nobles. Certain exigencies had to be tended to, and the chapter was in the best position to do something about them, but at the same time its outlook was so stoutly and consistently aristocratic that one would do grave injustice to the facts simply to ignore it. The unmitigated hostility with which the chapter treated the only burgher to occupy the see of Speyer, Nicholas of Wiesbaden (1381–1396); the difficulties experienced by the occasional nonnoble, university-trained canons in the fifteenth century; the clause in the 1464 electoral oath that the bishop's courts consider the eminence of the personage appearing before them; the chapter's petulant carping about its rights and privileges; its occasional attempts to shift the burden of extraordinary taxation to the peasantry; and the savagery with which the peasants in 1525 pillaged those seats of the aristocracy, the castles and the ecclesiastical foundations—all bear witness to the chapter's attitudes and help explain its often bitter contests with the bishops. Most of these signs and claims appeared only later, in the fourteenth and fifteenth centuries. In other words, they developed *pari passu* with the restriction of the chapter to nobles and the rise in southwest Germany of social orders more and more antagonistic to each other.[74]

The fact that the bishops, canons, and their highly placed relatives came from the *lower* nobility deserves emphasis, for it significantly affected their attitudes toward the bishopric. It is, in the course of the next three chapters, made clear that the bishopric was not well served by the high nobility, who tended to exploit it for their own advantage, personal or familial. By contrast, it can in fairness be said that the knightly born bishops, canons, and officials of the principality, especially in the fifteenth and sixteenth centuries, showed remarkable concern for the well-being of the bishopric, despite the strongly aristocratic tone of that concern. To be sure, on the whole they were by no means dedicated primarily to the bishopric; their families sought employment and ecclesiastical benefices where they could obtain them, nor had they any qualms about achieving immediacy in the early sixteenth century to avoid subjugation to local princes, nor were they, with some exceptions, distinguished as reform-minded churchmen. Unlike the high aristocracy, however, they possessed no public rights or extensive lands or power to be increased by spoliation of churches in one form or another. Rather, they depended on neighboring lords or the empire to provide them with income, prestige, and positions for their sons and daughters. Just as they have been adjudged by some historians the most loyal servants of the Holy Roman Empire in the early modern period,[75] so too, for different reasons and in a different way, can they be considered the best servants of the bishopric of Speyer in the late Middle Ages.

Chapter 2

The Background of the Electoral Capitulation of 1272

I

Although canon law and the financial strength and changing social makeup of the chapter at Speyer go far to account for its conspicuous position in the structure of the bishopric at the death of Frederick II, they do not explain why the chapter acted so strongly in the electoral capitulation of 1272 or why it did so at that moment. To understand *that* requires direction of our attention to the intricate political, economic, and ecclesiastical history of the bishopric in the High Middle Ages, to both its internal evolution and its relations with external powers—the town of Speyer, local lords, the emperors, and the popes.

One of the most direct ways of isolating some of the salient features of that development lies in a close examination of the articles of electoral capitulations. They epitomized the current problems of the principality, or more precisely those dominant during the rule of the late bishop, as well as the tensions that had prevailed between him and his estates, particularly the chapter. It would be an error, however, to regard them as merely negative documents of reaction or as a résumé of the grievances of but one estate. Feine regarded them as genuinely analogous to the agreements (*Herrschaftsverträge*) concluded between many imperial princes and their estates in the late Middle Ages, the nature of which has been well described by Otto Brunner; and Feine went so far as to call them "the fundamental law of the elective ecclesiastical state."[1]

Like *Herrschaftsverträge*, capitulations represented attempts to define the respective spheres of competence, power, and responsibility of princes and their important subjects, and like them, they exhibited good and bad features. On the one hand, they required the prince, not only to respect and preserve inviolate the rights and privileges of the estates, but often to increase them at his own expense as well; on the other, they legitimately demanded that he act in accordance with the best interests of the principality and insisted on his accountability to his politically active subjects in all matters affecting the commonweal.

To be sure, the comparison fails in certain respects. In some ecclesiastical principalities, especially the larger ones, formal estatist constitutions were drawn up, by the estates meeting together, in addition to the electoral capitulations exacted by the chapters. This was the case at Liège in 1316, at Cologne in 1463, at Trier in 1501 (after an abortive effort in 1456), and also at Münster and Paderborn.[2] Only in the bishopric of Osnabrück did the other estates—in this case the knights and the sworn council (*geschworener Rat*)—assist in the formulation and promulgation of the electoral capitulation.[3] Elsewhere chapters jealously guarded this prerogative and successfully parried attempts by the other estates to secure the right of participating in the capitulation, as was the case at Bamberg in 1481, Würzburg in 1623, and Mainz in 1675 and 1710.[4] This narrowness was at the same time balanced by the early recognition, enjoined upon chapters by canon law and embodied in the capitulations, that all members of the ecclesiastical corporation shared in the responsibility for its continued well-being and specifically for its financial stability. In most lay principalities positive acceptance of this responsibility by the estates came about much more slowly.[5]

Electoral capitulations also generally antedated their secular counterparts. Although they may have been extracted as early as 1089 at Arles and 1167 at Augsburg, the first clear example in the empire dates from 1209 at Verdun, which was quickly followed by others at Hildesheim in 1216, Würzburg in 1225, Mainz in 1233, Worms in 1234, Paderborn in 1247, and Eichstätt in 1259.[6] Oaths taken by prelates had been common in the church for some time: by bishops to their archbishops since the eighth century (at least in England), by archbishops to the pope since the reign of

Paschal II (1099–1118), and by exempt bishops to the pope since the early thirteenth century.[7] These were rendered, however, to ecclesiastical superiors by their subordinates, whereas electoral capitulations involved a reverse relationship: the oath of a bishop (or abbot) to his chapter (or community). More accurate parallels of this sort may be found in the coronation oaths of English kings from the time of Ethelred the Unready (998–1016) and in the oaths of the Roman (German) kings to individual princes since 1257 and of the popes to the college of cardinals since 1352, although less formal promises of German kings and of popes went much farther back in time.[8]

The oath taken by Frederick of Bolanden, then, before and after his election in March 1272 was hardly unique, whether viewed from an ecclesiastical or secular standpoint, but it was lengthy, specific, and demanding, and no mere vague affirmation of the customs and liberties of his subjects. Its forty-three articles required of him concessions in addition to execution of the duties of his office. In terms of their content and the levels of analysis they suggest, we have seen that they fall into three different categories. Twenty-five attempted to set out general relationships between the bishop and his chapter and clergy. In a further eleven he abjured aggression against the clergy and promised to protect them against attacks by the archbishop of Mainz, the townspeople of Speyer, and any other lay powers. In another six he agreed to certain limitations on his powers as a prince.[9] If all these clauses combined to give the impression that the chapter dealt from a position of great strength, the effect was vitiated by the final article which forbade appeal to higher authority to obtain abrogation of the oath. The canons had reason to fear papal nullification, for the whole tenor of the oath, as well as of many of its provisions, ran counter to canon law. These apprehensions were realized on 5 September 1288, when Nicholas IV condemned the capitulation of 1272 for its violations of episcopal rights and of the prohibition at canon law on the introduction of innovations during vacancies.[10]

Taken at face value, the articles themselves of the oath belie the achievements and the abilities of the chapter. Although the canons claimed substantial rights and powers, they could frequently do little to impose their will on bishops determined to have their own way. For centuries this often intensely bitter struggle was carried on between bishop and chapter over the division of power and authority in the principality and the diocese. At the same time the chapter found itself seriously threatened by the burghers of Speyer, who by the latter half of the thirteenth century had effectively emancipated themselves from episcopal lordship and had focused their energies on the abolition of clerical privileges in the town. The stout resistance of the collegiate chapters resulted in frequent and bloody encounters between the adherents of the two factions, culminating in the murder of the cathedral dean, Albert of Musbach, in 1277.[11] Behind its assertiveness in the capitulation, therefore, stood a chapter distinctly on edge.

II

Although the twenty-five articles dealing with the bishop's relations with the chapter and clergy bulk largest in the oath, many are vague or redundant. A large number, furthermore, emphasized simple respect for the existing customs, privileges, possessions, and rights of the canons and the other clergy. Of these, five listed specific manors and holdings of the chapter, and another two forbade episcopal interference in the collection of capitular incomes. Three treated the exact status of the canon who was to serve as the bishop's court chaplain. Two stipulated that the bishop appoint a competent goldsmith and carpenter for the cathedral and the episcopal palace. Another barred him from appointing to benefices to which he did not possess the right of collation.

The chapter did, however, go considerably beyond these moderate and reasonable demands. At least one canon was to sit as a judge on the ecclesiastical court of Speyer. The bishop was also to appoint a canon or a ministerial as his chamberlain and, "if he should desire," a canon as court chaplain, whose sustenance and clothing the bishop had to provide and who "will be with him continually unless by times he have sent him off into the country for the conduct of his business."[1]

In another two articles the chapter forbade the bishop without its agreement to consent to the alienation of the property of any monastery or church anywhere in the diocese or to the enjoyment by any church or monastery of the income from a parish. If canon law did not clearly support either of these claims, it flatly contradicted the chapter's attempt to secure exemption of its members and dependent clergy from episcopal jurisdiction. Totally exempt chapters were common in France and Spain, where they were often sustained by papal or episcopal privilege. Exemption occurred far less frequently in the empire, and the degree of exemption attained varied considerably. By such standards, noted Hofmeister, Speyer enjoyed great independence.[2] The canons did not merely express a legitimate concern to guarantee their freedom of episcopal election, cooptation, and internal disciplinary control; they also forced the bishop to grant that "he shall have no jurisdiction, nor shall anyone in his name, over the prelates, canons, and other clerics of whatever order or condition bound to the chapters of Speyer, or their dependents (*familia*), unless the dean and chapter have been negligent, or unless the dean and chapter have denounced someone as disobedient."[3] This usurpation of the bishop's lawful power was explicitly condemned by Nicholas IV in 1288.[4]

The scope of the clause, "other clerics . . . bound to the chapters," is not readily apparent. It clearly encompassed the vicars and other clerics directly dependent on the four collegiate churches. At the other extreme, it did not subsume the entire diocesan clergy. One might try to argue that it did, given the extensive power of the archdeacons in the thirteenth century and the fact that the four archdeacons held canonries in the cathedral and ex officio the provostships of the four collegiate churches, but the clause refers only to the jurisdiction exercised by the dean and chapter alone and hence concerned only the internal affairs of the chapter. Although the constitutional position of the provost-archdeacons at Speyer vis-à-vis their respective chapters was finally settled only in the fourteenth century by their formal exclusion from all ordinary proceedings, the dean had by the mid-thirteenth century replaced the provost as the effective head of the chapter in all four cases, and their spheres of authority had already become distinct.[5] It is probable, however, that the canons meant to extend their control to clergy holding benefices at the collation of one of the four collegiate churches, the number of which was large, particularly in Speyer.[6] The canons' attempt to withdraw themselves, their vicars, and their dependents completely from episcopal control represented a major advance beyond the imperial concession of 1101 and a substantial infringement of the bishop's rightful authority.

The canons made the breach all the more noteworthy by asserting exemption for all four collegiate churches, not merely for the cathedral chapter. Why this departure from a normal policy of exclusiveness? To some extent it was a continuation of many common policies and practices of the eleventh and twelfth centuries, when less rigid distinctions between the cathedral chapter and the other churches had obtained. As late as 1159, certain regulations valid for all four foundations were passed and approved by the bishop.[7] Furthermore, down to the early sixteenth century, when parish organization was at length introduced (1513/16), the four churches remained the principal level of organization of the secular clergy in Speyer. The cathedral chapter styled itself "capitulum maioris ecclesiae Spirensis," the three collegiate chapters "capitula trium aliarum ecclesiarum Spirensium."[8] Common liturgical celebrations and processions remained important throughout the Middle Ages.

These bonds that might otherwise have fallen into desuetude were reinforced in the twelfth century by the cathedral chapter's gaining control of the four archidiaconates of the bishopric as they were created, which were united with the provostships of the four chapters and which had to be held by cathedral canons. In the later Middle Ages one or other of the collegiate churches from time to time contested this custom, but usually without success. The situation tied the chapters more closely to each other. The cathedral chapter found its independence to a degree hampered, but at the same time its power had been substantially increased.[9]

Its basis of power had also been considerably broadened. Common action by the four chapters gained what would have been more difficult if not impossible of achievement had they not worked in concert. In May 1226 they secured, from Bishop Beringer, freedom from payment of tolls on the Rhine at Speyer, and they may have worked together to win this privilege.[10] On the arrival of the mendicant orders in Speyer, the four chapters moved swiftly to guard their prerogatives. In 1266 the bishop of Regensburg effected a settlement between the Dominicans of Speyer on the one hand and the bishop and chapters of Speyer on the other. The Dominicans agreed to pay damages to the bishop and the secular clergy for encroachments on their prerogatives and to abide by restrictions on their own rights to minister the sacraments and bury the dead.[11] Such troubles persisted. The Magdalene convents without the walls of Speyer in 1281 reached an accord over similar issues with the bishop and secular clergy in which they promised not to alienate any of their property to the Dominicans or the Franciscans.[12]

All these threats to the chapters paled in comparison with others that threw them directly on the defensive and forced them to protect their collective interests by concluding a formal union in 1264, which they renewed periodically thereafter as the occasion demanded. The cathedral chapter went beyond this by including in the electoral capitulation of 1272 eleven articles designed to compel the bishop to aid his clergy—both to desist from his own abuses against them and to protect them against attacks of one sort or another on them by the archbishop of Mainz, lay aggressors, and above all, by the townspeople of Speyer.

III

The complaints the clergy raised against the bishop covered wide ground. Some that affected the cathedral chapter alone have already been discussed, such as Bishop Henry II's failure to procure its assent to many of his important acts. Others strictly concerned the bishop's activity as a prince and hence, although they touched the clergy in general, are treated in the next section.

The sources of the thirteenth century offer little specific information on the background of most of the grievances. Some retrospective light is cast on them by their frequent recurrence in future, which also reflects the ineffectiveness of the protests. The canons, for example, required the bishop to render to the chapters of Speyer their accustomed *servitia*. Bishop Conrad of Scharfenberg's refusal to do so in 1220 had led to a convocation of the chapters and their decision, sustained by the archiepiscopal court of Mainz, to suspend the celebration of services in Speyer until he relented.[1] The nature of those *servitia* is first, and then only partly, clarified by a charter of 1290 issued by Bishop Frederick in which he promised to pay the four chapters the usual £48 Heller in *servitia* annually.[2] In 1307 Bishop Sigibodo II refused to render the cathedral chapter its *servitia* and *pensiones,* but he too was eventually forced to give way.[3]

Bishop Frederick in 1272 foreswore the use of threats to gain services or other exactions from his clergy. Again, the documents fail to illuminate the realities behind the legal formulation. It might well refer to some bishop's attempts to collect an extraordinary levy (*subsidium caritativum,* as it was normally called) from the clergy; but, outside of the permission granted by Innocent IV to Bishop Conrad von Eberstein in 1244 to tax all the foundations and clergy of the diocese (the collection of which is not attested by local sources),[4] such levies at Speyer are first mentioned only fifty years later.

Bishop Sigibodo in 1302 swore not to apply pressure to obtain the temporary usage of the income from vacant benefices. This was probably implicit in Bishop Frederick's more vaguely phrased oath, but in any event it by no means covered all possible abuses.[5] Thus the chapter insisted in 1272, in one article, that the bishop not usurp the right of disposing of the property of deceased clergy of the four chapters, even if they died intestate, and in a second, that the dean or the other priests of the rural deaneries dispose of the estates of intestate diocesan clergy according to law.[6] Such legacies frequently offered the prospect of lucrative incomes to financially hard-pressed bishops, who were reluctant to relinquish their established rights, and hence it comes as no surprise that protestations against the practice reappeared again and again in the late Middle Ages.

The capitulation charged the bishop not to neglect his duty to protect the clergy against attacks and violations of their rights from several quarters. The vagueness of these implied accusations against Henry II concerned his failure to stand by the clergy in their opposition to visitations by the archbishop of Mainz, but nothing in the sources clarifies the situation, not even the registers of the archbishops.[7] One cannot infer from this that therefore nothing happened. The archbishop of Mainz intervened frequently in diocesan affairs, particularly to lend his consent to donations;[8] in 1296 just such a major incident occurred, when the cathedral and collegiate chapters of Speyer and Strasbourg united to resist the extortionate visitations by Archbishop Gerhard.[9]

The chapter showed more anxiety with regard to lay assaults against the clergy and its possessions, and Bishop Henry seems to have acted by times on their behalf. Margrave Rudolf of Baden took an oath by proxy in February 1255 to desist from further depredations on the clergy in and around Speyer and submitted himself to the decision of four prelates and canons of the cathedral chapter regarding compensation for the destruction he had wrought.[10] General violence against the clergy is very conspicuous in the sources of the 1260s. When a certain Conrad "miles de Megensheim" pillaged and set fire to the chapter's property at Horheim in 1262, the count of Vaihingen, apparently his lord, negotiated a settlement with the chapter in which he renounced all future infringements of the chapter's liberties there and on its tithes at "Güdratbach."[11] Far more serious was the general upheaval at Speyer three years later, when a band of marauders from the town subjected it for a time to a reign of terror. After taking its defenses, they plundered at will, forced the citizens to render them services, ran roughshod over the immunity of the clergy, and, in the words of Bishop Henry, committed other atrocities "which we cannot put down in writing."

Worst of all in the bishop's eyes was their attempt to set another lord over the town. Henry and his brother Emicho, count of Leiningen, allied with the town council, banished the revolutionaries, and promised not to rest until order had been restored.[12] Henry in 1268 also quashed the claims of some of his vassals to the advocacy of the chapter's lands at Weingarten.[13] On the other hand, he did little to help his clergy against the growing independence and belligerent policies of the magistrates and burghers of Speyer. This, the greatest threat of all, finally compelled the four collegiate churches to enter into a formal protective union in 1264, and it weighed heavily on the canons' minds when they convened to elect a new bishop in 1272.

The seeds of this conflict were planted in the tenth century, when the bishop was made lord of Speyer through concessions of rights and privileges by Conrad the Red, duke of Lotharingia (944–953) and son-in-law of Otto I, and by the emperors Otto I and Otto II.[14] In an imperial effort to stem the increasing autonomy of lay counts and to develop new bases of support, the bishop became one of many prelates fitted out with public rights that they exercised in the name of the emperor. Through his advocate, the bishop dispensed high and low justice; through his ministerials and other officials, he collected tolls, minted money, and provided for the defense and governance of the city.

Under the aegis of emperor and bishop, the town expanded greatly in size and importance during the eleventh century. Emperor Conrad II commissioned the construction of the enormous cathedral in 1029 on a site that linked the town more closely with the Rhine, an act of more than symbolic import. Speyer's favorable position on both the north-south and east-west land and water trade routes facilitated its development into a commercial center of the first rank on the upper Rhine. To accommodate the merchants who settled there in the late tenth and the eleventh centuries, an extension of the walls was undertaken, from 1061 on, which increased the space encompassed, by one estimate, from about 8 hectares to 70 hectares (or from 20 to 173 acres).[15] The boast of Bishop Rüdiger (1075–1090) that he had made an *urbs* out of a *villa* must be interpreted guardedly, for walls stood around the town by 969,[16] but he did promote economic growth by encouraging Jews to settle in a separate quarter he built for them and to take advantage of the financial, trading, and legal privileges he awarded them. These concessions appear to have attracted Jews from Mainz.[17] In the following centuries, Speyer achieved a central place in the Rhenish cloth industry and concluded trade agreements with Nuremberg and Regensburg as well as other cities on the Rhine. Its growth was reflected in the appearance of three more *suburbes* around the old center during the twelfth and thirteenth centuries.[18]

With the advent of prosperity, the townspeople came to desire political power commensurate with their economic strength. Friction with the clergy is suggested in the imperial charter of 1101 to the cathedral chapter, in which Henry IV removed the immediate household servants of the canons from the jurisdiction of the civil law and subjected them to the episcopal tribunal.[19] The clergy had reason to be apprehensive, for what the king had granted the king could take away. In August 1111 Henry V initiated that delicate teetering act between town and bishop that characterized imperial policy for centuries. At one stroke he abolished many features of the personal dependence of the inhabitants on the bishop and ceded significant liberties to them. They were freed from mortmain, all episcopal and imperial tolls, and various arbitrary exactions in money and kind; they could not be summoned to courts outside Speyer by the bishop's advocate; they had to be consulted on all changes affecting the coinage; and anyone possessing a house or a plot of ground for a year and a day without challenge could thereafter hold it in freedom.[20] Episcopal efforts to circumvent some of these provisions moved Frederick Barbarossa to renew these privileges in 1182.[21]

If these documents fail to reveal the motives behind this shift in imperial policy, the privilege granted to Speyer by Philip of Swabia in January 1198 stated them frankly. In return for the burghers' aid in victualing his army prior to its embarkation and for their participation in the defense of the bishopric, Philip agreed not to quarter troops in the town (although the burghers consented to receive him together with no more than thirty soldiers), exempted their property from all exactions by all lords outside of customary dues, agreed himself to make no demands and to take only what they gave freely, and allowed them to choose a town council of twelve members.[22] It was thought for a long time that the last of these rights had been ceded in 1111, but this interpretation is based on a faulty reading of the texts and there is no evidence to support it.[23]

Events at Speyer now developed their own momentum. Already in the 1160s Bishop Ulrich von Dürrmenz (1162–1163) was hotly embroiled in strife with the citizenry.[24] The early decades of the thirteenth century witnessed a marked increase in independence and influence of the burghers.

Around 1207 the town negotiated a reciprocal reduction of tolls with Worms in the presence of King Philip and with permission of Bishop Conrad, but an agreement concluded with Strasbourg twenty years later concerning the summoning of debtors bore no mention of emperor or bishop.[25] At the same time, Bishop Conrad and his successors felt compelled to seek the burghers' assent to some of their more important acts, possibly as a counterweight to the growing influence of the cathedral chapter, and in any event, in recognition of the town's power.[26] This is clear from a charter of 1207 in which Bishop Conrad granted to the monastery of Denkendorf the church near the Thieves' Bridge in Speyer, with the proviso that no buildings be erected on the spot that could threaten the town.[27] Within the next few decades, the town made such great strides that it was able to negotiate with Bishop Beringer in 1230 over the division of the profits of justice.[28]

The clergy ordinarily proved less flexible, however, and conflict resulted over its extensive privileges and properties, progressing from frequent suits in the early thirteenth century to violence by the midpoint of the century. The chapters of Saint Germain and of the cathedral, being the best-endowed foundations, encountered the most difficulty. Bishop Conrad intervened in 1211 after many disturbances to decide between the burghers and Saint Germain's regarding rights of way on the church's property along the Rhine.[29] The payments to be rendered by the citizens at the Rhine tollstation belonging to Saint Germain's were the point of dispute in 1224.[30] The seeming amicability of the accord reached was betrayed in the following year when Bishop Beringer threatened the cathedral chapter's *censuales* with excommunication for continued tardy payment of their dues and accused the court of Speyer of deliberately dragging its heels in the adjudication of the chapter's complaints.[31] Similar conflicts arose in 1248 over the chapter's grinding mills and in 1260 over the payment of the minor tithe to the canons and the cutting of wood in their forest at Pfaffenau by the burghers.[32] The archiepiscopal court of Mainz, to which the cellarer of Saint Germain's had appealed a decision from Speyer, felt compelled in 1272 to repeat an earlier verdict (the date of which is not given) in favor of Saint Germain's requiring the prompt issuance of summonses to burghers.[33]

In the 1260s the intensity and character of the friction changed: The town council itself proceeded against bishop and clergy, and violence became the note of the day. The council ignored the exemption of the clergy and made it pay the *Ungeld* on wine, which the bishop in 1260 had allowed the town to collect for five years.³⁴ In 1262 the burghers forced the arbitration by outside parties of five disputed points with the bishop, who said he would not raise them again: the striking of Speyer coinage, the construction of the bridge across the Rhine, the ford over the Rhine at Ketsch, the *Ungeld,* and the oaths of seven persons given during the reign of Bishop Beringer.³⁵ The sources do not clear away the obscurity of this controversy, perhaps because Bishop Henry proved so pliant in the settlement. Henry's relations with the townspeople were so free of strife, in fact, that in 1258 he was asked to determine the number of members of the town council.³⁶ The secular clergy resident in Speyer, particularly in the four chapters, resisted more stoutly. The burghers retaliated by burning and pillaging various possessions of the chapters.³⁷

The canons had little but their own wits and resources to rely on to defend themselves. The counts of Leiningen and Eberstein and other princes frequently acted as mediators, but they offered little more, and the solutions they brought about amounted to little more than truces.³⁸ Count Simon of Zweibrücken in fact had sheltered certain criminals of Speyer.³⁹ Although Bishop Henry allied with his brother Emicho, count of Leiningen, to suppress the disruptions of 1265,⁴⁰ he otherwise evinced little interest in futile attempts to preserve his hold over the formidable town. He would in any event have gotten little support from the outside powers. Pope Alexander IV showed his sympathies without hesitation by denying Henry the see of Würzburg⁴¹ and by confirming the liberties and privileges of Speyer.⁴² In 1267 the imperial chamberlain Philip von Falkenstein attested that "the burghers of Speyer are subject to the empire and hence cannot be seized for the lord bishop of Speyer for any reason."⁴³ Actually, from time to time during the late Middle Ages, bishops contested, often with military campaigns, the independence of the town, and later emperors chose to maintain the equivocal situation rather than resolve the issues one way or the other. Nevertheless, the effective autonomy of the town by the middle of the thirteenth century was revealed in the way in which Bishop Henry yielded to the council on so many issues, as just indicated; in the fact that the bishops resided less and less in Speyer as the thirteenth century progressed; and in the fact that, from the later part of the century at the latest, the bishops could not enter the town without leave of the council.⁴⁴ In short, the bishop ordinarily could do little to aid his clergy in the town, even if he had wanted to. Still, Bishop Henry could have done much more, as the activity of his successor showed.[45]

In the absence of help from their bishop or other princes, the members of the four collegiate chapters therefore established a common protective association sometime in 1264 against the collection of the excise tax from the clergy. This pact was to last ten years and was concluded, they declared, "not for our own private advantage, but for the common good of all the clergy and people."[46] In October of the same year, they met and elected seven of their number to press home their suit against the town for the malicious destruction of some of their buildings and vineyards and "other enormities."[47] One month later the canons forbade conferral of any canonry or benefices in the city or the diocese on burghers of Speyer or their relatives within the fourth degree until the town made reparations for damages inflicted. To insure solidarity of opposition, the chapters in addition required every canon to swear to uphold these articles under pain of forfeiture of the right of participating in capitular deliberations, and they decreed that a prelate or canon would also lose the income of his prebend should he now abandon his post.[48]

The ban on the granting of benefices to citizens of Speyer was lifted in 1272.[49] This indicates, perhaps, the relaxation of tension between the clergy and the laity, but it could also point to a successful application of pressure by the magistracy. This suggestion is supported by the reassertion of the injunction just the year before by the ecclesiastical court to the town council to come to terms with the clergy,[50] and by the noteworthy insistence in the electoral capitulation of 1272 on the bishop's obligation to protect his clergy against the townspeople. The chapter's reading of the situation was correct, for during Bishop Frederick's pontificate the struggle in Speyer grew even more acrid and occupied most of the chapter's attention, as the capitulation of 1302 so starkly reveals.[51]

IV

The great transformation of Speyer in the High Middle Ages was a measure of the magnitude of change in the character of the empire. The most striking feature of that change was the breakdown of central authority and its converse, the rise of territorial principalities. When did these begin to appear, when did they come into full bloom? The answer depends partly on semantics, obviously, but it also turns on answers to other questions, none of them easy of resolution: When did imperial power really begin to decline? Were certain policies pursued by the later princes strictly "territorial"? If so, which ones? How and why did they contribute to the downfall of the empire? When did the emperors lose control over their subordinates, and why? All these problems have been the subject of heated debate for well over a century.

The question is not necessarily any easier to solve when put to a particular territory. Much depends on the relative weight one assigns to the various elements involved. Some historians look carefully at evolving terminology as signs of changing realities. The word *territorium* in reference to the lands of the bishops of Speyer occurs several times in the first half of the twelfth century. The first local usage dates from 1163 in a charter of Bishop Ulrich I concerning "Mulenbrunnensi monasterio, quod in sante Spirensis ecclesie et territorio et fundo constructum. . . ."[1] Otto of Freising in his *Gesta Frederici* had earlier written of the castle of Limburg in the "territory of Speyer."[2] The most interesting usage of all in view of its date and source appeared in a letter written by Wldalricus, monk of Cluny, to Abbot William of Hirsau in 1110: "Heaven forbid that anyone believe God to be local, so that what He does in France He cannot do in the territory of Speyer."[3]

The argument for a "territory of Speyer" can be pushed back to the eleventh century. Bosl saw the territorialization of Germany taking place between 1000 and 1050.[4] Actually, the privilege of immunity, first granted by King Childerich II ca. 664–66, renewed by the Carolingian and German kings, and last confirmed in 1061, provided a potential bedrock of episcopal power by forbidding royal officials to enter the lands of the church of Speyer and thus implicitly conferring great responsibility on the bishops.[5] The extensive imperial donations of rights and lands to the see in the tenth and especially the eleventh centuries considerably increased the bishops' powers and holdings, particularly the extensive Lusshard forest (1056/63), six abbeys (1032, 1065, and 1086–87), and, for a time, two counties (1086).[6] Much of this was eventually lost, however, and the bishops had to carve out their territory by developing their residual rights and lands (especially forests) and by relying on monasteries, all of which deserve full study. During the eleventh century the bishops began to acquire the most solid bases of their future power—castles, which served as centers of both administration and defense. Some were donated to the bishopric by the emperors, e. g., Berwartstein in 1152, or by bishops, e. g., Meistersel by Bishop John I in 1100 or Bruchsal by Bishop Ulrich II around 1189;[7] but most were built or bought by utilizing the resources of the *mensa episcopalis*.

Still, one cannot speak meaningfully of an ecclesiastical principality of Speyer before the thirteenth century, when imperial power over the prince-bishops shriveled up within a few decades. Whatever independence other emergent principalities enjoyed before then, imperial control over the bishopric of Speyer continued through the first quarter of the thirteenth century. Donations of royal rights, lands, and monasteries may have formed the nucleus of the later bishopric, but they also tied the church of Speyer more closely to the *Reichskirchensystem*. The emperors felt free, in return for their largesse, to rely heavily on the church for troops, administrators, and money. Henry IV in particular regarded Speyer as "our special church"[8] and worked closely with Bishop John, who was a close relative and perhaps a nephew of the emperor, to promote a joint policy of gaining control over monasteries.[9] Henry V considered his consent necessary for a valid exchange of property by the bishop and chapter,[10] and he also held a castle with the bishop as late as 1112.[11] This suggests that he maintained firm control over the church of Speyer. The fate of imperial sway after his death is not known. Whether his successors retained direct control, delegated it to local counts, or lost it to them has been much debated, but on the basis of evidence insufficient to furnish a conclusive answer.[12]

The loss of the advocacy, if it occurred at all, was only temporary. Even before they attained the crown, the Staufens had dedicated themselves to extending and consolidating their possessions in southwest Germany. The county of Forchheim (near the modern city of Karlsruhe), which Henry IV had ceded to the bishops in 1086, passed out of episcopal hands by 1102 and eventually came into the hands of the Staufens.[13] With many such counties, with fiefs from ecclesiastical foundations, and with advocacies over bishoprics and monasteries, they steadily achieved predominance in the heartland of the empire. With such materials, they carved out, for instance, the future Electoral Palatinate, which they held in the critical years 1155 to 1214.[14]

As already noted in chapter one, Frederick Barbarossa not only resumed direct imperial authority over the bishopric, which he usually exercised through ministerial subadvocates, but he, and even more so his successors, also elevated it to a pivotal position in the imperial territorial complex in southwest Germany. For decades, the see supplied the empire with troops, administrators, diplomats, and a chancery.[15]

Friction surfaced from time to time. Bishop Gunther, after considerable pressure exerted by King Conrad III, finally granted him a certain fief from the church of Speyer, complaining that "we had no way of evading" the request.[16] The cathedral chapter in 1184 sued before Barbarossa certain ministerials, whom Frederick had delegated to exercise the *Vogtei* over the bishopric, for their failure to fulfill their obligations as vassals of the chapter.[17] These incidents only underscore all the more the extent of imperial domination of the see until the end of the century, when the tide began to run against the emperors, who had more and more to purchase the loyalty of their followers. Henry VI ceded to the cathedral chapter the right to consent to all changes in the coinage struck by the bishops, thus ignoring the clauses in the imperial privileges of 1111 and 1182 obliging the bishop to consult the burghers on such matters.[18] Philip of Swabia accorded the burghers substantial liberties in return for their aid in 1198.[19] Although Bishop Conrad of Scharfenberg appears not to have taken as full advantage of his position as he might have, he did secure concessions from three successive rulers: from Philip of Swabia, the leveling of an imperial castle being built on the lands of the bishop (1206); from Otto of Brunswick, the chancellorship (1208); and from Frederick II, the see of Metz (1212).[20]

Conrad's role in the formulation of the celebrated *Confoederatio cum principibus ecclesiasticis* of 1220 is a moot point,[21] as is the exact import of the *Confoederatio* for the emergence of the ecclesiastical principalities. Erich Klingelhöfer has most recently joined historians like Kirn and Schrader in stressing that the significance accorded the privilege has been exaggerated.[22] They ignore the fact that the *Confoederatio*, even though it did nothing more than recapitulate a whole range of concessions made to individual German churches (Klingelhöfer's argument), also generalized all those privileges for the whole German church. In this light, especially when considered together with Frederick II's other policies in Germany, the act takes on substantially more than symbolic significance.

The *Confoederatio* marked the beginning of the ecclesiastical principality of Speyer. Unlike other German prelates, the bishops of Speyer had obtained no major concessions from the emperors before 1220 aside from the cessation, mentioned above, of construction of a castle on the bishop's lands in 1206. There is no evidence to support Bosl's inclusion of Speyer on the list of sees that forced Philip of Swabia and Otto of Brunswick to renounce many of their fiefs.[23] Hence the *Confoederatio* represented for the bishopric a genuinely major step toward autonomy, although its provisions were fully implemented only gradually during the next three decades as the imperial grip on the see slackened and was finally broken.

Not without leaving scars, however. Besides relying on the church as a source of money and talented administrators, the Staufens also cut sharply into its landed wealth by forcing the conferral of fiefs on members of their family and their adherents. The see of Speyer was among the more heavily exploited in this respect, although the scanty sources yield only a partial list of these fiefs: Ilsfeld, Eschwege, Oberdertingen, Waiblingen, the advocacies of most of the monasteries dependent on the bishops and of church lands at Lussheim, Specterbach, Dernbach, and many other places.[24] Some of these reverted to the bishops, but many and perhaps most did not. Whereas a few such as Eschwege remained permanently in royal hands,[25] many had been subinfeudated to nobles and ministerials and thereby generally passed irretrievably from royal and ecclesiastical control. These implications of the feudal system were recognized early. The charters of the eleventh and twelfth centuries invariably equated enfeoffment with alienation of church property.[26]

Much better documented was the more serious problem of church fiefs held directly by the local nobility and by ministerials who formed the core of the future knightly class. They were not only more numerous than those to the crown; they also quickly became heritable in broadly defined ways (i.e., with rights of succession for females and collateral branches of the family), so that many reverted to the bishopric, if at all, only in the seventeenth or eighteenth centuries. These fiefs counted among the greatest losses of property to the bishopric in its history, and they were granted primarily in the twelfth and thirteenth centuries. The first relatively complete list of those fiefs, which dates from the middle of the fourteenth century, shows how extensive those losses were, although it is possible here to present only a few examples. The Electors Palatine held the town of Neustadt and the castles of Wersau and Wolfsberg; the count of Nassau, the advocacy of Lahnstein and numerous tithes; the count of Sponheim, the town and castle of Kreuznach and the castle at Tan; the burgrave of Nuremberg, one castle and two advocacies; the counts of Solms, a dozen tithes and the patronage rights to two churches; the counts of Eberstein, the town

of Gernsbach, two Rhine fords, and ten villages; and the lords of Lichtenberg, the town of Neuburg a. Rh. Most astounding of all were the fiefs
held by the counts of Leiningen, who were prominent in the Palatinate in
the High Middle Ages and dominated the see between 1235 and 1336:
the honorary office of episcopal chamberlain with its three appurtenant villages, two more villages, and the patronage rights to no fewer than seventy-
two churches, which far exceeded the number to which the bishop had the
right of collation (twenty-one churches and chapels, and twenty-one
benefices).[27]

Some of these were inevitably lost because of their distance from Speyer
and hence from the effective reach of the bishop. The emperors had made
many such donations: Kreuznach near Mainz, the abbeys of Kauffungen
and Naumberg in Saxony and of Schwarzach near Strasbourg, and, presumably, Lahnstein on the Lahn, to name but a few.[28] Whether close or far,
however, the bishop had to provide for the administration of his lands and
for his military needs by enfeoffing his rights and properties. Heritability
of tenure, which by the early thirteenth century had been extended to ministerials,[29] undermined quickly his meaningful rights over fiefs. A great
many were undoubtedly gained through pressure or force, although explicit evidence to that effect in the sources is scarce. It is clearest in the case
of the monasteries over which the bishops had so freely disposed in the
eleventh and twelfth centuries but which slipped more and more away from
their grasp.[30] It was more subtle in other instances, as in 1276 when the
Elector Palatine Louis, who had already bought one half of the castle of
Wersau and its two appurtenant villages from episcopal vassals, secured the
other half as a pawn and fief after exerting his influence at the imperial
court.[31]

Hence the cathedral chapter expressed understandable concern over the
fiefs granted by the bishops. Two articles of the 1272 oath were devoted
to the problem, according to which the bishop was not to alienate, recon-
fer, or exchange fiefs without the consent of the chapter.[32] Even before
then, however, for well over half a century, the chapter had worked, frequently with bishops, to recover fiefs for the bishopric, as noted in chapter
one,[33] but this was expensive business. The cathedral chapter paid 340
marks for a single plot at Rödersheim, 140 marks for a manor at Bühl,
£60 Heller for a *fief-rente* of £6 Heller per annum, and 80 marks for one
half the forest at Ketsch.[34] Buying out residual rights to fiefs was no less
costly. Bishop Henry II had to indemnify Frederick, burgrave of Nurem-

berg, with 100 silver marks for his renunciation of all future claims to the Bienwald, the extensive episcopal forest on the left bank of the Rhine. Count Simon of Zweibrücken received 100 marks for a similar renunciation in 1264 with respect to the castle at Lauterburg.[35] The large sums involved in this program imposed severe limitations on it. The chapter wisely acted to prevent or at least minimize further abuses by obliging the bishop to seek its consent to his dispositions of fiefs.

This was but one kind of problem associated with the rise of the ecclesiastical principality with which the chapter had to contend. Several other articles in the capitulation bound the bishop to obtain the consent of the chapter to any changes in the coinage and to dispense justice fairly.[36] The number of articles dealing strictly with the principality was deceptively small, five or six out of forty-three. Lest it be thought that the chapter's interest in its problems was correspondingly minimal, it ought to be noted that the three aspects of government to which it addressed itself—enfeoffments, coinage, and high justice—counted among the major prerogatives of the prince-bishops and that, in a way, the whole capitulation had very much to do with the bishop as prince, especially since no fine distinction can ordinarily be drawn between his activity as bishop and as prince so far as it concerned the clergy. It is easy to impute selfishness and myopia to the chapter in its preoccupation in the capitulation with the rights and prerogatives of the clergy. It is also easy to forget that the oath represented a reaction by the chapter to what the bishops had and had not done. Judging from the points stressed in the capitulation, which are often verified by other evidence, they had failed to render the clergy their due and had not adequately protected them in their persons and their rights against the burghers of Speyer, the archbishop of Mainz, and other aggressors; on the other hand, they had taken great liberties with the clergy, particularly in the confiscation of the estates of intestate clerics, in various arbitrary exactions, and in attempts to dispose over benefices. The precipitous decline in the imperial position in the thirteenth century, and the consequent removal of a controlling mediator between the bishops and the clergy, was important for the timing of the capitulation, for the chapter had thereby been forced to assume the leadership in the principality in bridling the bishop's excesses and forcing him to fulfill his obligations.

The emergence of a largely autonomous principality came at the worst possible time so far as its finances were concerned. This helps to explain the predicament in which the bishops found themselves and hence some of the measures to which they resorted to overcome it. A glance at the incomes and the expenditures of the prince-bishops in the thirteenth century reveals the great crisis confronting the principality. No exact figures or balance sheets can be drawn up before the late fourteenth century, but it is possible to compare the declining sources of revenue with the substantial outlays necessary for the maintenance and growth of the territory.

The most striking impression one receives from the documents is the virtual cessation of donations to the bishopric by the thirteenth century, a problem experienced by older ecclesiastical foundations in general.[37] The see of Speyer appears not to have owned much allodial property in the early Middle Ages,[38] so it was on the basis of the extensive imperial donations of lands and public rights in the tenth and eleventh centuries that the bishops later built up their territory.[39] By contrast, only one imperial donation is recorded for the twelfth century, the castle of Berwartstein in 1152.[40] Not only did imperial largesse wither away, but the emperors also began to take from the bishopric, to demand fiefs for the construction of their own territories. The emperors also undercut the bishop's exercise of public rights over large areas. Of the two counties granted by Henry IV to Bishop Rüdiger in 1086, the first, Forchheim, appeared in the possession of the margrave of Baden as early as 1102 and later in Staufen hands;[41] the second, Lutramsforst (on the left bank), was superseded in the later twelfth century by an imperial landgrave (*Landgraf*) and in the thirteenth century by the *Landvogtei* of Speyergau.[42] Bishop Henry II attempted to revive the long-eclipsed title to this county, but to little avail.[43]

Donations by twelfth-century bishops from their patrimonial holdings partly offset the effects of this drastic alteration in imperial policy. Bishop John, in 1100, gave the bishopric the castle and village of Meistersel.[44] In 1190 Bishop Ulrich II ceded the castle he had built at Bruchsal "at onerous expense" after he had bought back the advocacy of Bruchsal from the count of Calw for 400 marks.[45] These donations hardly counterbalanced the disappearance of imperial grants and the increasing exploitation of the see, however, and in any case, the bishops of the twelfth century preferred to endow monasteries. Bishop John himself lavished far more on his family monastery of Sinsheim (founded in 1092) than on his own see; Bishop Gunther in the mid-twelfth century gave all to the Cistercian abbey at Maulbronn.[46]

In the same period, the bishopric suffered substantial losses due to massive enfeoffment of its possessions, a great many of which slipped irrevocably away. The situation was exacerbated by the elimination or reduction of the bishops' revenues from Speyer, one by one, just as the town was expanding most rapidly and experiencing its greatest prosperity: in the twelfth century, mortmain, tolls, and arbitrary exactions from the burghers; in the thirteenth, excise taxes, coinage, justice, the Jews, and some tolls.[47] Because, other than Speyer, the bishops ruled over only villages until the later Middle Ages, the end of their lordship in Speyer constituted an even greater blow to their power than it normally might have. The comparative strength of Speyer and the meagreness of the bishop's resources was dramatically illumined by the imperial levies of the fifteenth century, when in many instances Speyer and the prince-bishop were expected to furnish roughly comparable amounts of money and troops.[48]

Tithes, undoubtedly once a great source of episcopal income, had by the end of the twelfth century been transformed from an ecclesiastical revenue to a form of real property in which all trafficked and which the bishops enfeoffed in order to secure vassals.[49] The bishop had two great forests, the Lusshard on the right bank and the Bienwald on the left, as well as other smaller ones, but it is impossible to estimate before the fifteenth century what cash profits he actually derived from them, although there can be no question of their great value.[50] Tolls are, for different reasons, equally difficult to evaluate. It cannot be easily determined what tolls the bishop had before the cession of the great imperial toll privileges of the fourteenth century.[51] That they yielded large sums can be seen in the amount for which Bishop Frederick pawned the episcopal tolls and fords around Speyer to the cathedral chapter in 1290: £3,300 Heller.[52] The pawn provided only temporary relief for the bishops, however, and in fact they never regained these tolls.

As their main source of revenue, therefore, the bishops had to fall back on the produce of their demesnes and the enforcement of their seignorial rights. Although general figures on these are available only from the middle of the fourteenth century, the bishop's receipts in money and kind were extensive. One of the principal levies was the so-called *Bede*, the equivalent of the *taille* in France. According to Karl Zeumer and Georg Waitz, it originated as a "voluntary" aid rendered by townsmen and peasants at the request (*Bitte, Bede*) of strong lords, which from the end of the twelfth century had come to be considered the customary right of a territorial prince.[53] How large it bulked in the bishop's earnings cannot be reckoned before ca. 1338.[54] It is extremely risky to extrapolate backwards from these figures, for the *Bede* appears frequently in the episcopal charters only from the last quarter of the thirteenth century, and as late as 1204 Bishop Conrad had damned it as "that wicked custom."[55]

Such revenues were in any event totally inadequate to underwrite the enormous expenditures of the bishops. The establishment and maintenance of castellanies constituted the largest single item in the normal budget. The castellany—a castle occupied by soldiers and administrators to protect and govern the lands and subjects of the lord in its environs—was the stable heart of the territorial system; it was also a major drain on princely resources. The construction of the castle at Bruchsal toward the end of the twelfth century entailed "onerous expenses,"[56] and as immediate or feudal lord, the bishops of Speyer disposed over a great many castles by the third quarter of the thirteenth century: Graben, Madenburg, Dankenstein, Weiher, Kisslau, Wachenheim, Rietburg, Urach, Hornberg, Krobsberg, Leimersheim, Lindenberg, Horremburg, Alttan, Neutan, Kestenburg, Rotenburg, Lauterburg, Wersau, Beckelnheim, Zuzenhausen, Steinach, Schauenburg, Kirrweiler, and Spangenburg, to mention but a few in addition to those already mentioned.[57] Most were not normally under the bishop's effective control. An imperial confirmation of the principality's liberties in 1366 listed eighteen castles, six towns, and sixty-six villages as being in the immediate possession of the bishop of Speyer.[58] The repair and maintenance of these castles helped reduce the princely coffers still further.[59]

The conduct of war imposed heavy financial burdens on the bishopric, and the bishops were engaged in wars and feuds from the tenth century down to the Napoleonic era. The bishops contributed troops to the imperial armies, e.g., twenty knights to the Italian expedition of 981–83.[60] Their obligation continued long after the passing of the Staufens. Seventy wagons, as well as an unknown number of soldiers and horses, from the see accompanied King Adolf in 1293 in his expedition against Colmar and Burgundy.[61] Bishop Gerhard sent fully fifty armored knights on the imperial campaign against Eltvil in 1350 and another fifty in the attack on Zurich in 1355, and in consequence of the heavy losses sustained by his contingents, had to pawn several possessions.[62] In the fifteenth century, the see was required to supply eight cavalry and fifteen infantry for the first Turkish expedition of 1471, and in 1489, ten horsemen and forty on foot for wars against France and Hungary.[63]

During the second quarter of the thirteenth century, the onerousness of military expenditures was multiplied severalfold by various factors: relatively, by the decline in donations; and absolutely, by expenses incurred in support of the papal cause, by the personal ambitions of Bishop Henry II, and by feuds with neighboring princes. The first has already been treated; it would have been enough to precipitate a financial crisis even if Bishops Conrad von Eberstein and Henry II had not taken the side of the papacy in the last and most bitter phase of its struggle with the Staufens. For his activity on behalf of the church, Bishop Henry obtained 500 marks from the monastery of Weissenburg alone, for which Innocent IV indemnified the monastery.[64] The popes sought to retain the allegiance of the bishops and reward their efforts in other ways, too. Gregory IX allowed Bishop Conrad to retain those benefices he held before his elevation.[65] Innocent IV ceded a large number of privileges and dispensations to the bishop and the chapter, including exemption from extraordinary taxation of the provincial clergy by the archbishop of Mainz in 1244, so that the bishop of Speyer might collect a subsidy from his clergy.[66] Innocent also tried to promote Henry's election, successively, to the see of Mainz, to "any rather wealthy archbishopric or bishopric," and to Würzburg.[67] Henry was on the verge of gaining Würzburg when Alexander IV, shortly after his elevation, rejected Henry's candidacy (1255–56). This came about only after Henry had waged a long and costly war against the rival candidate costing no less than 3,000 fl. Alexander ordered the bishop of Würzburg to restore this amount to Henry and the see of Speyer. Whether it was all paid back is questionable, inasmuch as part of the debt was still outstanding in 1265, two years after it was to have been canceled.[68]

Henry's other activities increased the strain on the bishop's precarious financial resources. His business as imperial chancellor and as prince-bishop, he noted, often drew him off to Spain and Italy.[69] When at home he was no more peaceful than when battling for a more prestigious see, although the turbulent times gave him little choice in the matter. With his brother Emicho he undertook a campaign to suppress the disturbances at Speyer in 1265.[70] In his vigorous assertion of the rights of the see, he often challenged the local nobility. Whereas many of these controversies were settled by arbitration,[71] others led to war. In execution of the imperial peace (*Reichsfrieden*), Henry in 1270 set out to destroy the illegal Rhine tolls erected in the bishopric at Germersheim and Udenheim and also the castle of Eschesheim.[72] The last five years of Henry's pontificate were taken up in feuds with the margrave of Baden and the Elector Palatine, which were ended only by Bishop Frederick.[73]

The principality's financial straits worsened noticeably as a result of all these combined pressures. At every turn, the sources point to a deepening financial crisis from the late 1230s on, whereas before then financial troubles are only vaguely attested in the eleventh century.[74] These charters also indicate some of the measures taken by the bishops to deal with the situation. Some lands and rights were sold outright: an allod and various incomes to the chapter in 1241, and a forest to Maulbronn Abbey in 1249.[75] Kreuznach was sold to the counts of Seyn in 1241 under the condition that they continue to hold it in fief from the bishop.[76] Another expedient employed by the bishops in succeeding centuries also came to the fore at this time: the pawn. In August 1248, in return for 100 marks, Bishop Henry pawned to his brother Emicho an income of 100 measures of wheat and five cartloads of wine per year as long as the loan remained outstanding.[77]

In this transaction, Henry failed to procure the consent of the chapter, nicely circumventing it instead by pleading pressures put on him to do so by King William and the archbishop of Mainz. The chapter, whose assent canon law required in all alienations of church property appurtenant to the *mensa episcopalis,* was justly concerned about Henry's attitude, especially because he did not always consult it on other matters as well. It consequently inserted in the capitulation sworn by his successor the clause obliging him to seek the chapter's compliance on such matters.

Around this same time—the second quarter of the thirteenth century— in their efforts to cope with financial stress, bishops began to tap another source that very much touched the chapter and the associated collegiate churches of Speyer: the secular clergy, who had, until then, remained largely untouched in the diocese of Speyer, if one can draw this conclusion from the silence of the documents. The bishop had instead relied primarily on the monasteries under their temporal and spiritual jurisdiction, so heavily, in fact, that the monasteries frequently raised outcries and lodged appeals at Rome.[78] During the thirteenth century, however, they ceased to be a main pillar of episcopal policy and finance. The older Benedictine foundations were suffering from financial woes themselves,[79] and most had long since fallen under the sway of other lords.[80] The newer reformed monasteries and the mendicant orders were theoretically exempt from episcopal exactions. Whereas they never completely successfully resisted the considerable dual pressures brought to bear by the bishop as lord temporal and spiritual, they and the Benedictine houses were never, in the late Middle

Ages, exploited to the extent to which monasteries had been in the eleventh and twelfth centuries.[81]

The bishops turned by way of compensation to their own diocesan clergy, who, insofar as they lived in the principality, were doubly subject to the bishop, as lord and as pastor. On his part, the bishop was fully cognizant of the wealth of the clergy and of his power over them. It is not surprising, therefore, that in Speyer, as in many other German dioceses, the main burden of extraordinary levies down to the sixteenth century fell on the clergy.[82] From the electoral capitulation of 1272, it is clear that the bishops sought to dispose of benefices and their incomes, seized the property of deceased clerics, extracted money and services from the clergy, and violated their liberties in other unspecified ways. Before the fourteenth century, the sources cite few concrete instances to substantiate these allegations, but their constant recurrence in later capitulations, backed up by well-documented cases, points to problems of long standing about which the chapter was justifiably disturbed, however little we may know in detail about them in the thirteenth century. Pope Innocent IV, for example, had, in 1244, granted the bishop permission to collect a twenty percent tax on all ecclesiastical revenues from his clergy.[83] The sources do not indicate whether the tax was actually collected or, if it was, whether the clergy was consulted. Difficulties over such extraordinary levies arose later, however, when they became a regular credit entry in the bishop's ledgers. The collegiate churches of Speyer responded by directing some of their later unions not only against Speyer but against the bishop as well,[84] and in 1321, by setting limits to what the bishop could request of his clergy at any one time.[85] The cathedral chapter's demands in 1272 foreshadowed more collective and more successful efforts to temper the bishops' abuse of their prerogatives over the clergy.

Finally, the cathedral chapter had good reason to express anxiety over the changing attitudes of the bishops as well as over their particular acts; this too can be traced back to the conjunction of various factors, not the least of which was the sudden evaporation of the imperial presence. As long as the bishopric was subordinated to the empire, it retained a highly cosmopolitan character. Its bishops and canons came from many parts of the empire and worked on its behalf, and the emperors in their turn tried, according to their means, to look out for the best interests of the see. The relationship had unpleasant features, to be sure, which eventually soured the German church toward the empire, but the localism and chaos that followed were scarcely better. Most ecclesiastical foundations and positions became instruments for the advancement of the ambitions of noble families, high and low, and pawns in the seemingly interminable struggle between the papacy and the empire. Whereas these tendencies had been present for two centuries and more, they could not triumph so long as the emperors remained in control and held the loyalty of the imperial church. They ceased to do so by the second quarter of the thirteenth century. The situation of the German church thereafter steadily worsened, reaching a nadir in the fourteenth century, when prelates accumulated benefices and offices, when bishops used one see as a stepping stone to another, and when the church was buffeted about in every other conceivable way.

A corresponding change of tenor can be discerned among the bishops of Speyer in the twelfth and thirteenth centuries. Bishops John I, Gunther, and Ulrich II were all steadfastly loyal to the crown and lavished their personal wealth on the bishopric or on monasteries. Bishop Conrad III of Scharfenberg appears in distinct contrast to them: a nonnoble who donated nothing to the see and used his position to obtain the imperial chancellorship and the diocese of Metz. At first glance, he closely resembles Bishop Henry II, who also held the chancellorship and tried to gain another see, albeit unsuccessfully. The comparison is misleading, however. Conrad II stood closer to his predecessors than to Henry von Leiningen. He was fiercely loyal to the Staufens throughout, and his elevation to Metz in 1212 was probably a stopgap employed by Frederick II to quash Philip Augustus' efforts to bring that bishopric into his realm.[86] Although Conrad did procure the chancellorship from Otto of Brunswick, he seems otherwise to have taken little advantage of his position and to have had no hand in the making of the *Confoederatio*.[87]

Henry II represented something entirely different. The most obvious point of divergence was his frank espousal of the papal cause, although Bishops Beringer and Conrad IV had already adopted a neutral stance toward the empire and Conrad V had openly broken with it. Henry attended the elections of Henry Raspe and William of Holland, and the support he rendered the anti-imperial faction provoked King Conrad IV's retaliatory pillaging of the village of Deidesheim and its environs.[88] All this might have passed muster so far as the cathedral chapter was concerned, had it not been for some disturbing aspects of Henry's attitude toward the bishopric of Speyer. Although he did assert and defend the principality's rights during his reign of twenty-seven years, he generally conducted himself in imperious wise. He often ignored or circumvented the chapter's consultative rights. He paid no attention to repeated papal injunctions to receive episcopal consecration until 1259 or 1260.[89] Without compunction, he used the principality's troops and money in a war to wrest the see of Würzburg for himself, and without a doubt would have continued to do so had the opportunity presented itself. This is revealed from his free-wheeling disposition in his testament of January 1272 over the imperial villages of Hassloch and Böhl, which had been pawned to the bishopric in 1252 by William of Holland.[90]

When all this is considered together with the threats facing the clergy in the politically chaotic mid-thirteenth century and Henry's failure to protect them, the chapter's response in 1272 becomes even more intelligible. In the absence of a firm imperial hand, it alone could act effectively to restrain episcopal excesses, force the bishops to live up to their obligations and respect the rights of their subjects, and look out for the best interests of the principality. There were precedents for such responses. When it seemed, in the later ninth century, that the property of the church might be swallowed up wholesale in the disintegration of the Carolingian empire, cathedral chapters divided the cathedral's wealth into the *mensa episcopalis* and the *mensa capitularis,* the latter to be used for purely ecclesiastical purposes. The distinction lapsed, however, and only from the middle of the eleventh century onward was it permanently institutionalized.[91] Whether the chapter at Speyer would be any more immediately successful in its reform effort of 1272 was by no means certain.

Chapter 3

A Succession of Crises, 1272-1396

I

The century and a quarter between the accession of Bishop Frederick of Bolanden and the death of Bishop Nicholas of Wiesbaden constitutes an intelligible period in the history of the bishopric. In brief, it was characterized by constant disruption and near collapse. This was true for most of Europe in the fourteenth century. Wars raged everywhere, dynasties shook, banks folded, peasants rose in revolt, and the population fell by a good third. The principality of Speyer was no exception. Its financial status grew ever more precarious, leading to the pawning of the entire bishopric to the famous archbishop of Trier, Baldwin of Luxembourg, in 1331. Only imperial intervention in 1337 and 1349 saved it from total bankruptcy. The crisis was brought on partly by a string of notorious bishops who were "elected" through local pressure or appointed by the papacy, partly by the bishops' inability to close the widening gap between expenditures and receipts, and partly by certain widespread economic and demographic trends. Although the chapter had little or no control over any of these, it did struggle against them, sometimes at the expense of the bishopric, but on the whole, to its advantage. As its parliamentary consciousness slowly developed, so too did its share and importance in the government of the principality.

It stood most helpless before the profound alterations in the general social and economic patterns of life experienced by most of Europe. The single most important cause of these changes was the Black Death, which, beginning in 1348–9 and continuing in some places as late as the seventeenth century, swept away one fourth to one half of the population, depending on the region considered.[1] Several decades of bad weather, crop failure, and famine had preceded the Black Death and already eliminated thousands of people from a population that, in the view of many historians, lived dangerously close to the margin of its resources.[2] The *Chronicle of Sinsheim,* composed in the fifteenth century, wildly estimated that nine thousand died in Speyer alone during one such epidemic in 1313.[3] Already, in 1300, Bishop Frederick had inserted in a lease of lands a clause requiring prompt payment of all dues, "hailstorms, armies, crop failure, fire, or any other fortuity notwithstanding."[4]

Curiously, the Black Death left few clear tracks in the records of the bishopric. Of the decimation of the population and the consequent rise in peasant wages, the abandonment of whole villages, and the attempts to cope with the situation, they say nothing directly. Still, some of its effects can be discerned, above all on the episcopal manors. A sharp decline in population entailed a loss in manorial revenues and difficulties in cultivating, harvesting, and leasing the bishops' demesne lands. The resulting shortages of income in kind were felt most sharply in 1375–76, when Bishop Adolf was forced to borrow 2,812 fl. on short term to buy grain, oats, and wine.[5] That proving insufficient, he confiscated by force wine and grain dues of the monastery of Eusserthal, stored at Landau, worth 2,000 fl., for which he had later to pay the abbey damages.[6] Adolf's military campaigns at the time might account for his resort to such extreme measures, but such loans were undertaken normally to secure troops, not to victual them, and there is no parallel example in the history of the bishopric in the late Middle Ages.

The problem persisted for some time. Only in the latter part of the fifteenth century were the bishops again able to lease their lands on a large scale.[7] This may conceivably have represented a new policy, but in fact it was a resumption of a practice that dated back to the thirteenth century. It had lapsed because the population decline had appreciably reduced the pressure on the land, and peasants consequently had no great need to take episcopal lands, which usually carried a high rate of return to the bishops, in contrast to lands held under ordinary heritable tenure. In one of the few leases made during the long reign of Bishop Raban von Helmstadt (1396–

1438), Hensel Liechtenstein, the bailiff at Kirrweiler, in 1438 let out to the peasants at Venningen a pasture there that, he noted in passing, had been abandoned and untended for some time.[8]

A different feature of economic life that proved more problematical in the long run, yet also more susceptible of treatment, was financial policy. During the fourteenth century the bishops borrowed heavily from Jews. Loans in general tended to be short term and to carry high interest rates, although conditions improved later in the century. Because these loans therefore provided minimal relief, the bishops sought more effective remedies. A fair amount of property and rights was sold, but this was even more self-defeating: in return for one lump sum of money the bishops lost permanently a piece of territory or the exercise of certain rights which in the long run were worth much more to them than the immediate gain involved. Pawns obviated that danger, only to raise others. Raising enough money to redeem them was always difficult, yet it had to be done periodically to prevent further alienation of the property in question or the growth of heritable claims to it. Finally, the bishops, of necessity, looked more and more to extraordinary taxation as a regular means of supplementing their incomes.

The cathedral chapter and the clergy, in the fourteenth century, assumed a large place in the finances of the bishopric. Specifically, the chapter, acting corporately or through individual canons, loaned the bishops money, bought episcopal lands and rights, and received them in pawn. It and its members were wealthy enough to participate in all these activities to a significant degree. It was legally and practically obliged to aid the bishopric as far as it could, and because its larger interests were identical with those of the bishopric, it offered the bishops certain advantages as general banker to the principality. On more than one occasion in the thirteenth and fourteenth centuries, the bishops noted how much safer it was to borrow from or sell or pawn to the chapter than to outside institutions or people, on whose loyalties and fickleness one could never depend.[9] For its part, the chapter fully realized the implications of the power of the purse, which it used, not only to set down strict conditions for financial transactions, but also to extend its rights in the governance of the bishopric as well.

In the bishopric of Speyer, as in every other state or principality of Europe in the fourteenth century, extraordinary taxation became common as a principal way of dealing with chronic deficits.[10] The chapter's position in voting these levies was somewhat complicated. Down to 1404, according to the records, the clergy alone bore the entire burden of extraordinary taxation in the principality. By times, some monasteries negotiated individually with the bishops to determine their contribution, and in the 1380s the margrave of Baden began to interfere with episcopal taxation of diocesan clergy resident on his lands. On the whole, however, the clergy of the entire diocese, not merely of the principality, had to pay, and in general they were represented before the bishop by the four united collegiate churches of Speyer, the seats of the four archdeacons, which demanded that they give their collective consent to all such taxes. The consent of the cathedral chapter alone appears never to have sufficed in this, the most important business of any diet. This constituted a major modification of its activity as the "parliament" of the principality.

The chapter's success, too, was limited, despite its intention and efforts, mostly for extrinsic reasons. Finance had not yet evolved to the point at which a stable public debt based on long-term, low-interest loans could be established, nor could a stable public debt develop as long as confidence was wanting. The turbulent fourteenth century gave little reason for such hopes. Extraordinary levies helped supply the defect to some extent, but not enough to keep Bishop Walram von Veldenz from pawning the principality in 1331. Even a somewhat provident bishop like Gerhard von Ehrenberg (1336–1363) was plagued by the ever-present need to contract new debts to cancel those contracted but a few weeks or months before.

With a few exceptions, the bishops in this period only aggravated these problems by their extravagance, irresponsibility, belligerence, and lack of regard for the bishopric. Most gained the miter through outside intervention. Of the nine bishops who ruled between 1272 and 1396, no fewer than six obtained the see through papal provision. For three of these, Speyer was nothing more than a stepping-stone to a prestigious see—Strasbourg in two cases, Mainz in the third. Small wonder, then, that the chapter vigorously opposed these nominees who endangered its own electoral rights.

Things were not quite so black and white, however. The chapter's intransigeance sometimes led to ruinous wars in which the peasants and the finances of the principality suffered most of all. Its bitterly hostile attitude toward the nonnoble Nicholas of Wiesbaden delayed the introduction of sorely wanted reforms. Nicholas also proved that a bishop appointed from the outside need not represent a disaster for the principality, whereas Bishop Emicho von Leiningen (1314–1328), whose election from within doubtless had much to do with the fact that his brother Joffried was

Landvogt of Alsace and his brother-in-law George von Veldenz was *Landvogt* of Speyergau, was by far the most disgraceful of the nine bishops.[11] On the other hand, Gerhard von Ehrenberg, and more so Nicholas of Wiesbaden, ruled well; Nicholas had secured his position by the grace of the pope, Gerhard by that of Louis the Bavarian.

Still, on balance, it must be said that the massive influence exerted by external powers on the affairs of the bishopric was decidedly deleterious. The Leiningens and other local potentates had squeezed, and continued to squeeze, much from the church of Speyer, but they were soon outstripped by powers to whom they were forced to turn to preserve their hold—the popes and the emperors. Whether in conflict, as under Louis the Bavarian, or in cooperation, as under Charles IV, the popes and the emperors disposed over most of the German church, over its benefices, offices, sees, and revenues.[12] Few elements of the German church managed to remain untouched; Speyer numbered among the more heavily exploited sees. Papal provisions to the episcopate have already been mentioned. Papal and imperial nominations to canonries and prebends in the cathedral and collegiate churches may not have been proportionately as numerous; yet they constituted incursions into the cooptative rights of the chapters.[13] The motives involved—extending control over the church and rewarding loyal followers—were not of the sort to enhance the quality of the upper German clergy, although aristocratic control of the German church had not produced a clergy noted for its piety or learning.

Lastly, papal and imperial tithes and crusading taxes further drained churches unable to make their own way. Between 1312 and 1418, fourteen papal and imperial or territorial tithes were imposed that fell on all or part of Germany.[14] It is very difficult to arrive at a comprehensive understanding of how great a burden they formed. In the end, the popes received only about forty percent of the sums taken in; most of the remainder went to the emperors or the princes. Resistance to them ran high, and collection was difficult.[15] Thirty-three years after the Council of Lyons levied a tithe in 1245, Nicholas III was still issuing exhortations to the dioceses of Mainz, Speyer, Worms, Strasbourg, Augsburg, and Würzburg to pay their allocated shares.[16] In 1360 the pope was denied permission to sequester the incomes of benefices then vacant and falling vacant during the next two years in the diocese of Speyer.[17] These considerations plus the paucity of documentation make exact calculations of sums handed over very risky. Speyer was called upon to render 1,200 fl. in the tithe of 1373–4, and in the tithe of 1418/22 it actually did hand over more than 7,800 fl., a sum far greater than that paid by the dioceses of Strasbourg, Passau, Basel, or Halberstadt.[18] Little information is available aside from these few figures, but it is worth noting that the 7,800 fl. nearly equalled the normal annual revenues of the bishops.

The cathedral chapter and the clergy could and did resist some of these demands and impositions, especially the crusading tithes, but resistance in the long run to papal provisions was hopeless and bound to become self-destructive, as indeed it did every time the chapter refused to accept a papal nominee. The see was too small, the costs of opposition too great. Instead, the chapter, in the long run, was compelled to work with the given situation. With this attitude, it set out to establish, as far as possible, orderliness in finance, in the administration of the bishopric during vacancies, and in the bishops' regular consultation with the chapter to insure observance of the best interests of the principality and its subjects. This inevitably resulted in a slow but perceptible increase of the chapter's share in the government of the principality.

II

The chapter met its first real test in the person of Bishop Frederick of Bolanden, the youngest canon of the chapter, upon his election on 4 March 1272. He was the youngest son of the imperial high steward Werner IV of Bolanden and of his first wife, Kunigunde von Leiningen, sister of the late bishop Henry. The family was well represented in the aristocratic German church. Frederick's uncle Henry held a canonry at Worms and an archdeaconry in the diocese of Trier. His brother Gerhard was provost at Erfurt, his sister Guda a nun at Kirschgarten, his younger half brothers Peter and Henry canons of Speyer (where Peter later became provost), and Frederick himself provost of Saint Stephan's in Kamberg.[1]

Frederick's aggressive and abrasive temperament embroiled him in strife with nearly everyone with whom he came into contact. In 1276 Wolfram, lord of Fleckenstein, took Frederick captive and held him at his castle. The reason for the seizure is not known, although it has been conjectured that Frederick had refused to honor Wolfram's claims on him for unpaid services. King Rudolf, then at Hagenau, marched to Fleckenstein and freed Frederick when he heard of it.[2] Nine years later Rudolf himself had reason to move against Frederick. Rudolf besieged the bishop's town of Lauter-burg and took it after six weeks, drove Frederick from the bishopric, put him under the ban of the empire, and committed the administration of the principality to Archbishop Henry of Mainz. The causes of the falling out are not readily apparent. Remling marshalled the various opinions without attempting to resolve them. Lehmann ventured to say that Frederick had offended Rudolf by ostentatiously kissing his wife in public, but he offered no evidence to support this touchingly romantic surmise. More recent work done by Ludwig Litzenburger came to the sounder conclusion that Frederick, originally an adherent of Rudolf, took up with the Rhenish electoral princes when the king began making solid progress in his revindication of imperial rights and possessions in southwest Germany and thereby incurred Rudolf's hostility.[3] Frederick was again taken prisoner near Mainz and held for ransom by Count Gerhard von Katzenellenbogen while returning from the provincial synod at Aschaffenburg.[4] Frederick even had troubles with his own kinsmen. On two separate occasions, in 1278 and 1292, he and his uncle Frederick von Leiningen had to appoint arbiters to settle their frequent disputes.[5]

Frederick's relations with his clergy were equally turbulent. Pope Gregory X, in 1274, ordered several prelates of the Strasbourg cathedral to investigate the complaints of the monastery of Denkendorf concerning the bishop's usurpations of its incomes from the Church of the Holy Sepulchre at Speyer.[6] Nicholas III in 1279 appointed new judges-delegate to review litigation between the bishop and the monastery of Saint Lambrecht. Frederick was accused of seizing the monastery's church at Steinweiler and had appealed the decision of the court of first instance against him.[7] One of the many charges laid to Frederick by the burghers of Speyer in 1294 was his unlawful detention of a monk of Sinsheim Abbey and deprivation of the abbot of Klingenmünster of his seal and other rights.[8]

Frederick crossed the cathedral chapter as well, and under him the canons began to discover to their discomfort the practical limitations on their ability to keep him in check. It was he no doubt who moved Nicholas IV to condemn his electoral capitulation in 1288.[9] No fewer than five of his important legal acts that are directly attested bore no mention of the chapter's consent.[10] That many more such violations occurred is evident in the electoral capitulation of 1302, in which the chapter bound Frederick's successor to recover all alienations made without its assent, particularly Bishop

Frederick's grant in fief of revenues at Dürkheim to the count of Leiningen.[11] The first article of the same oath touched on another area of conflict: the exercise of ecclesiastical jurisdiction. The chapter specially demanded that the bishop appoint a canon as his *officialis*.[12] Frederick had followed the lead taken by the archdeacons and instituted an *officialis* to exercise his jurisdictional powers as ordinary.[13] Trouble brewed for the next two decades, and it finally broke forth in open conflict in 1300 that had to be settled by the archbishop of Mainz. He found against both parties. He forbade all conspiracies and mutual oaths among the clergy. The archdeacons and their *officiales* he ordered to obey the bishop, not to obstruct the execution of his lawful orders or appeals made to him, and to desist from extortions from the clergy subject to them. The bishop he enjoined to afford all protection possible to the clergy, to render the chapters of Speyer their customary dues, to appoint a canon as his *officialis,* and to defer any visitation of his subjects for at least one year except in case of emergency, and then only with the archbishop's permission.[14]

Such unions of the clergy, specifically of the four chapters of Speyer, against Frederick had been common for two decades, although in some instances they were not clearly directed at him, in others not at him alone, and in any case were revivals of the original union of 1264 against Speyer. The first was the vaguest. A fragmentary charter records only that in 1281 the four collegiate churches united to protect their rights and property against the incursions of wicked men.[15] A renewal of the union in 1284 was no less vague except to establish in great detail the methods of common discussion and collective action.[16] The alliance of 18 August 1296 is much better documented. Although it was phrased in proleptic terms as a defensive measure against various possible violations of their rights, the specific misdeeds listed clearly referred to real problems in the past. The chapters of the cathedral, Saint Guido, and Holy Trinity (Saint Germain's is, curiously, not mentioned) pledged themselves to common action should Frederick try to seize the property of any chapter or of any of its dependent clergy, summon any of them to one of his courts, deny them justice or block the execution of decisions, or seek an extraordinary levy in any of the archidiaconates.[17] The union drawn up on 2 May 1299 had a wider scope, according to which all four chapters proclaimed a common front against all who infringed in any way their possessions or liberties.[18]

Like virtually every other prince in the late Middle Ages, however, Frederick found his arbitrariness ultimately restricted by his financial difficulties. On several occasions, he spoke of the great debts of the church of Speyer which "we cannot pay except with grave injury to us and to our church."[19] A great fire that gutted the cathedral in 1289 exacerbated the problem.[20] Some of the solutions with which Frederick tinkered seemed only slightly less ruinous. Taking loans from usurers scarcely helped.[21] In 1286 he granted in fief to Henry of Herbortsheim and his heirs the castle and town of Zuzenhausen in return for £800 Heller. Although Henry promised to serve the bishops as their vassal and never to alienate the fief, Zuzenhausen in fact never reverted to the immediate possession of the bishops.[22] Individual positions as castellans could be pawned too. Over these the bishops retained far greater control, and for them they could obtain real services. These posts entailed disadvantages, too, not the least of which was the relatively small amount of money they could command. To cite but one instance, in 1301 Bishop Frederick confirmed that Rudolf of Ottersbach had become his castellan in return for 40 silver marks. Rudolf was to reside at Lauterburg, according to the custom of the castellans there. The post remained heritable until redeemed, and until such time, Rudolf and his successors were to receive 40 measures of wheat per year.[23]

To judge from the frequent outcries, Frederick fell to despoiling the clergy, but the clergy, not yet ready to fund chronic episcopal indebtedness, resisted firmly. Frederick therefore had to sell lands and rights. How best to gain the maximum financial advantage without permanently losing properties? By selling to the cathedral chapter. Remarkably, despite the general tension between them for roughly thirty years, the bishop and the chapter cooperated to a significant degree on just such a policy. Frederick once indicated that he appreciated the advantages involved.[24] The chapter realized its paradoxical position: no matter how independent the bishop, it was obliged on constitutional and practical grounds to aid him.[25] The chapter at Speyer in the 1290s proved unusually sensitive in responding to the bishop's distress. In 1290 it paid him £3,300 Heller for all his rights to the tolls and Rhine ford at Speyer. The chapter furthermore agreed to return the administration of the whole complex to the bishop once it had received £300 Heller in revenues (approximately a year's income) plus £48 Heller in *servitia* from the bishop and £28 Heller from the bishop's fisheries. The bishop said he would protect these possessions, the chapter that it would observe this contract.[26] Two years later, the canons bought lands at Bellheim from the bishop for £300 Heller.[27] In March 1294 they sold back to Frederick the village of Eschelbronn in exchange for all the episcopal fisheries and fishing waters around Speyer.[28]

The transactions of 1290 and 1294 concerning the tolls and fisheries around Speyer must be considered more carefully, however, for they give the lie to any hasty conclusion that the bishops enjoyed the superior position. On the contrary, the chapter inevitably did. The canons had in fact driven a hard bargain. In 1290 the bishop was compelled to resume the administration of the tolls and the ford after a certain point. He had to bear this cost without collecting a single pfennig for himself; all the profits went to the chapter. Frederick furthermore foreswore for himself and all later bishops any attempt to regain possession. Every member of the chapter similarly swore under oath to the same effect should he at some time become bishop.[29] The 1294 sale was just as carefully thought out. The bishop said that he would in no wise alienate the tolls nor appoint a ferryman (*conductor*) who did not promise to the cathedral dean to render the customary *servitia* to the churches of Speyer. The chapters of the cathedral and Saint Guido also extracted from Frederick the concession that no harvests could be undertaken in the bishop's villages of Hagenbach and Deidesheim without the express permission of the chapter's missives (*nuntii*) there. The wine tithes were also to be divided equally among the bishop and the two chapters.[30]

The chapter seems to have brought successful pressure to bear through its power of the purse on wider matters as well. Specifically, during Frederick's reign the corporate notion of the bishopric was much more strongly expressed than it had ever been before. The chapter made some headway in securing to itself several important rights of participating in the ruling of the bishopric. Archbishop Gerhard of Mainz, in his concord of 1300, acknowledged openly that, in accordance with custom, the fortifications of the principality automatically passed under the control of the chapter upon the death of the bishop, "oaths made to the contrary notwithstanding, which we rescind by these presents."[31] During his absences from the see, Frederick had already been represented in 1295 by the cathedral dean and the schoolmaster, in 1296 by the dean and by Canon Sigibodo of Lichtenberg, who was also provost of Saint Guido.[32] As far back as 1273, two canons and a prebendary of the cathedral adjudicated, as episcopal arbiters, a dispute between two episcopal villages concerning meadow rights.[33] The dean and chapter in 1287 lent their approval to Frederick's extension of the feudal rights of inheritance, in one case to the daughter of a vassal.[34] The idea of the bishopric as consisting of the bishop and his chapter was pushed still further. A certain vassal of the principality in 1299 significantly alluded to "my reverend lords, to wit the venerable lord bishop and the chapter of the church of Speyer."[35] Most striking was the chapter's unilateral reenfeoffment of part of the castle of Krobsberg held "from us and from our church of Speyer." This phrase, which recurred three more times in the same charter, is peculiar in that, had the castle belonged solely to the chapter, it would not have added "and from our church of Speyer." The absence of the bishop's assent to this is commentary sufficient on the advancing position of the chapter.[36]

One factor that may, paradoxically, help to account for both the growth of the corporate character of the bishopric and the chapter's inability to keep firm reins on Frederick was the twofold threat to both from without. The archbishop of Mainz presented the less formidable and long-lived of the two, although it was regarded as serious enough at the time to elicit a strong reaction. The problem revolved around Archbishop Gerhard's visitations of the diocese between 1293 and 1296, which, the four chapters of Speyer charged, were conducted not to reform abuses but to extort money. The four chapters, acting on behalf of the entire diocesan clergy, responded by formally allying with the representatives of the diocesan clergy of Strasbourg, the chapters of the cathedral and of Saint Thomas' and Saint Peter's collegiate churches in Strasbourg, to resist Gerhard's exactions for six years. Both parties were to contribute money and procurators as necessary to carry their appeals forward.[37] The upshot of the whole affair is not recorded, but it is reasonable to infer from the archbishop's successful imposition of a tax on the diocese in 1302, among the collectors of which appeared the provost of Saint Guido's, that the opposition in the end turned out to be futile.[38]

By far the more serious of the threats came from the burghers of Speyer. The thirty years of Bishop Frederick's episcopate formed the bloodiest and most savagely contested period in the history of the relations between the town and the clergy. It put the bishop and his clergy very much on the defensive and forced them to draw closer to each other. It also so preoccupied the chapter that it had little time or energy left to deal effectively with the bishop. The struggle progressed on two different levels: The first centered on the nature and extent of episcopal lordship over the town; the second, on the privileged status of the clergy within it. Although the two issues sometimes became intertwined, it is easier to consider them separately.

It appeared at first that Bishop Frederick would follow his predecessor's indifferent policy towards Speyer. In 1280 he confirmed the liberties of the town—the first bishop to do so.[39] Lehmann asserted that Frederick fought with the town council between 1280 and 1292 with regard to his homage and his ceremonial entrance into the city.[40] Nothing supports this opinion. Indeed, two charters issued by Frederick from Speyer in 1281 lead one to believe that the issue had already been settled.[41] Open conflict is first documentable only in the 1290s. In 1293, Speyer, Worms, and Mainz signed a treaty to aid each other should any one of them be attacked, especially by the emperor or by their bishops.[42] In the following year, the council of Speyer notarized a list of grievances against Bishop Frederick that centered on his attempts to strangle the secular court of Speyer and to restore full episcopal jurisdiction in the town. When the bishop then threatened to excommunicate the citizenry, the council appealed to the pope, adding for good measure that Frederick had imprisoned a monk of Sinsheim and ejected the abbot of Klingenmünster from his office. Six arbiters appointed by the pope effected a settlement. Their judgment went overwhelmingly against the bishop, which is the more surprising considering that five of them were clerics. The bishop promised to desist from all exactions levied on the burghers and their property throughout the bishopric, to appoint to the courts and the offices of the town only those named by the council (thereby reducing his right to a pro forma function), to establish no special ecclesiastical judge outside Speyer to try burghers so long as they submitted to the jurisdiction of his *officialis,* not to arrest any layman or cleric in the town or its suburbs unless already convicted, and to submit to review by the papal legate and the abbot of Himmerod his excommunication and expulsion from Speyer of a priest living irregularly. (The latter sentence was reversed.) Several particularly sensitive points were deliberately left unresolved.[43] On the whole, however, the settlement dealt an effective blow to the final remnants of episcopal power in the town, and many historians have rightly emphasized that Speyer attained real independence from the bishop in 1294.[44] To be sure, numerous minor points of dispute remained and provided material for endless contention and litigation between the bishops and burghers until well into the early modern period. Moreover, at least three distinct attempts were made by the bishops in the fourteenth and fifteenth centuries to reconquer the town (1375, 1422, and 1466). They all failed, and the wrangling that dominated the intervening decades revolved around relatively insubstantial issues. The real focus of attention shifted now to the internal struggle for control of the town between the patricians and the guilds.[45] In narrating this conflict in the sixth book of his chronicle, Lehmann significantly scarcely mentioned the bishops at all.[46] The lack of prominence of the bishops in the charters contained in the cartulary of Speyer covering the first half of the fourteenth century is similarly noteworthy.[47]

The demands of the burghers on the clergy resident in Speyer, particularly in the four collegiate chapters, were not susceptible of such easy resolution and surfaced again and again in the late Middle Ages, although never again in such acrimonious form as during the latter part of the thirteenth century. There were three main issues: the clergy's privileges in the wine and grain trade, clerical exemption from secular jurisdiction, and the right of the burghers to use the cathedral chapter's commons at Pfaffenau. Although by times the tension between the burghers and the clergy eased and even gave way on occasion to cooperation,[48] undisguised hostility otherwise pervaded the atmosphere of the town.

It must be said in Bishop Frederick's defense that he acted promptly on behalf of the clergy when the burghers became even more belligerent than they had been in the 1260s. In July 1275 he excommunicated a magistrate (*camerarius*) of Speyer for summoning the dean and chapter before his court in prejudice of ecclesiastical liberty.[49] A dispute between the canons and a burgher in 1276 was adjudicated fairly,[50] but two major incidents occurred in 1277. In January, Pope John XXI commissioned the dean of Mainz to have the Speyer town council lift its ban on the export of grain from the city.[51] In October in a general synod, Bishop Frederick solemnly excommunicated those men, together with their accomplices, who had murdered the cathedral dean, Albert of Musbach, on Good Friday morning. The murderers were never caught.[52]

Events developed for the worse in 1279. Lehmann thought the bad winter of 1279 brought on the crisis by driving up the price of grain and wine. He alleged that the clergy took their produce out of the city only to sell it back to the hungry burghers at outrageous prices.[53] The charge would seem to be substantiated by the town council's prohibitions on such removals of goods for this purpose, on the purchase of the clergy's wine by burghers, and on their use of the chapter's mills in the city. Pope Nicholas III ordered the abbot of Maulbronn and the deans of Mainz and Worms cautiously to investigate the clergy's outcries against these measures.[54] The

town council disclosed the firmness of its intentions by building two towers
at the very edge of the chapter precincts in 1279, retaining John of Lichtenstein for a year's war service in 1280, and buying his share of the castle
of Lichtenstein and the right of free use (*Öffnungsrecht*) of his half of the
castle of Krobsberg in 1281.[55] It may have done all this to better the city's
defenses against marauders and predatory nobles, as Lehmann held,[56] but
the proximity of the two towers to the canons' quarters and the nervous
reaction of the four chapters in renewing their alliance in 1281 and 1284
incline one to suspect more offensive purposes.[57]

   These fears were soon realized. After the council again proceeded against
the clergy in 1283, Bishop Frederick ordered the clergy to leave the city.
The cathedral clergy withdrew to Bruchsal. Upon their departure, their
houses and some of the bishop's villages were plundered. In retaliation,
Bishop Frederick undertook similar reprisals against the holdings of the
burghers.[58] At this point, King Rudolf intervened to impose a peace. He
categorically rejected the council's claims to jurisdiction over the clergy and
their goods. Cleric and layman alike were permitted to take their wine and
grain out of the city and sell it to those whom they pleased, although they
could not export it from the area. The burghers were obliged to render the
chapter the lesser tithe. The mendicant clergy who had taken the burghers'
side were to be obedient to the bishop. On the other hand, the common at
Pfaffenau was declared open to all from the town and not the exclusive
property of the chapter. The two towers were to remain. Rudolf effectively
refused to solve the problem of ecclesiastical jurisdiction by saying simply
that custom ought to prevail. The settlement of future disputes was rele-
gated to a committee of three canons and three burghers.[59]

   Such an ambiguous peace, unsatisfactory to both sides, clearly could produce nothing better than an uneasy truce. The sale of wine by the clergy
again emerged as one of the areas of contention in Bishop Frederick's treaty
with Speyer in 1294, in which he pledged within a short time to issue an
ordinance to the advantage of the burghers.[60] At the Mardi Gras celebration
of 1296, a brawl broke out between some burghers and the household
servants of several canons. When Provost Peter of Fleckenstein rejected the
council's summons to the servants to appear before its judges, the council
sent armed citizens to the provost's house to force their surrender. The
provost yielded; the men were tried and packed off to jail. The council then
ejected Canon Richwin of Schonenberg from his quarters and confiscated
his vineyard. The bishop suspended the celebration of divine services in

the city, excommunicated the six councillors who, he believed, had fomented the violence, and summoned them to appear at his court at Deidesheim two weeks later. They duly showed up, but only to deny the bishop's competence in the matter.[61] Although the vineyard was eventually restored to Richwin for his lifetime, the legal questions at stake went unresolved. The four chapters prepared for the inevitable by reviving their alliance in 1299.[62]

Trouble flared up again in 1301. Bishop Frederick dispensed from the chapter's regulation depriving absentee prebendaries of the income of their benefices those canons, vicars, and prebendaries of the cathedral who left the town out of fear of the citizenry.[63] In 1302 the clergy was expelled from Speyer.[64] While the chapter resided at Lauterburg, Bishop Frederick died on 26 January at the monastery of Eusserthal, a lonely and embittered man. The chapter proceeded to the election of a new bishop. A majority voted for Sigibodo of Lichtenberg, the minority for Philip of Fleckenstein. For various political reasons, Boniface VIII, to whom the final decision fell because Sigibodo's election had failed of a two-thirds majority, provided Sigibodo to the see, even though he was under no compulsion to do so.[65]

Sigibodo, scion of a pro-Habsburg family in Swabia, had been provost of Saint Guido's and vicar-general as well as canon of the cathedral and had led the combined chapters in their struggle against Bishop Frederick and Speyer. The electoral capitulation he swore to in April reveals how much the troubles at Speyer played on the canons' minds and how much confidence they put in Sigibodo's qualities of leadership to resist the burghers' demands. Eight of its eighteen articles explicitly treated the clergy's relations with Speyer. They required of the bishop, among other things, that he grant the clergy refuge in his castles, maintain sixty horsemen for their protection, regain the right of appointing the members of the town council, denounce Bishop Frederick's concessions to the burghers, conclude no peace with the town without the assent of the majority of the chapter, revoke fiefs from all vassals of the church who stood with Speyer in the recent wars, and refuse admission to benefices to all clerics related to Speyer burghers within the fourth degree.[66]

Sigibodo lived up to the canons' expectations. Already in March he had spurned King Adolf's efforts at reconciliation. He now refused to promulgate the ordinance on the wine trade that Bishop Frederick had promised in 1294 or to confirm the town's privileges on the grounds that the council had tried to insert new clauses. When the town council countered by forbidding clerical trade in wine, he laid the city under interdict. Open warfare erupted, and for seven months each side pillaged the other's properties.[67] In October, the bishop and the four chapters realized the futility of further resistance and chose arbiters to act for them.[68] In contrast to the terms of King Rudolf's imposed peace of 1284, this treaty constituted a clear victory for Speyer. The clergy was allowed to sell wine only between Easter and Pentecost, otherwise not at all. The bishop and the clergy renounced all claims to damages incurred during the war. Although the burghers were held to their obligation to render the clergy all the usual dues, such dues and incomes as were captured by anyone suffering damages during the war could be retained. Finally, both sides withdrew their appeals to the pope.[69] In 1305 Sigibodo confirmed the privileges of Speyer and Frederick's concessions.[70] Thus ended many decades of strife. These decisions served as the basis of relations between the town and the clergy until the 1420s. Although the problem of ecclesiastical jurisdiction had been left conspicuously untouched and minor incidents took place from time to time,[71] tensions relaxed noticeably on the whole, and in the course of the fourteenth century a number of canons actually became burghers with the obligation of providing military service to the town.[72] In the future conflicts between the bishops and the towns, the chapter ordinarily preserved a neutral stance or at best tried to mediate between them.

Bishop Sigibodo did succeed in celebrating one substantial triumph over Speyer during his reign (1302–1314). In 1314 the town council conceded to the bishops their right to one half of all the fines collected by the secular court of Speyer.[73] Otherwise his years seem to have passed uneventfully. Aside from altercations over the *servitia* to be paid to the cathedral chapter and over the status of the Rhine tollstation at Speyer,[74] he got on well with the chapter and accepted the additions made to his electoral oath. Besides confirming Frederick's oath and privileges on four separate occasions (before and after his election and after both confirmation and consecration), he consented to render the chapter all dues, to refrain from seizure of benefices, to surrender all offices in the church within one month of consecration, and to attempt revocation of all enfeoffments and alienations made by Bishop Frederick without the concurrence of the chapter.[75] Sigibodo was probably not successful in trying to fulfill the last promise. He often cooperated with the chapter, especially to limit the rights of the reformed and mendicant houses of the diocese.[76] He also acted promptly to protect the canons at Speyer.[77] The chapter in turn loaned him an extra £1000 Heller on the Speyer Rhine toll to buy property for the bishopric.[78] The sources do not allude to any financial difficulties during his episcopate; although they doubtless existed, they probably in no way matched those of his predecessors and successors in office.

III

Conditions deteriorated rapidly under the next three bishops. Of Sigibodo's successor, Emicho von Leiningen (1314–1328), it was later written with considerable understatement that "he did not rule well."[1] The circumstances of his election are obscure,[2] but the reasons for it are easy to surmise. His relatives held high imperial positions both at court and in the area, as mentioned earlier,[3] and after his accession, Emicho roughly doubled the incomes of several of his relatives who held posts as castellans without the duty of residence.[4] His electoral capitulation is not extant, although he surely swore to one.[5] Most of the time he preferred to ignore it. Numerous charters having to do with enfeoffment, pawning, and augmenting the fiefs of his vassals bear not a trace of the chapter's consent.[6] He went far beyond this, however, and for years indulged in wholesale spoliation of the clergy and flagrant violations of its rights.

He did this partly for financial reasons. He purchased several villages, the chief of which was Udenheim, in 1316 from the Speyer burgher Henry of Cologne[7] and in 1324 gave Louis the Bavarian £5,000 Heller for the imperial town of Landau in pawn.[8] Besides maintaining his expensive retinue, Emicho labored in the cause of Louis, spending large sums and suffering the plundering of the principality,[9] for which the emperor rewarded him with pawns totaling £3,333 Heller on the imperial revenues from the burghers at Hagenau and the Jews both in Speyer and throughout the bishopric.[10] This was not easy to collect, however, and in any event, probably did not equal what Emicho had spent. He was unable even to maintain the fortifications of the principality[11] and consequently relied heavily on pawning to cover his expenses. In 1319 he pawned, with the consent of the chapter, various fishing rights with all appurtenances to Gottschalf Schaff zu der Ecke, burgher of Speyer, for £550 Heller.[12] The castle of Spangenburg in 1317 brought in another £300 Heller.[13] Three men were appointed castellans in return for a total of £240 Heller.[14] All this scarcely sufficed and furthermore entailed loss of revenue.

Emicho's high-handedness in dealing with the clergy had a deeper source in his arrogance, crudity, and intransigeance. Although at times it operated to the good of the bishopric,[15] his independence of mind and conduct on the whole resulted in perhaps the most shocking reign in the history of the bishopric. Three major statements of grievances against him reveal the scope of his horrors. Because they corroborate each other despite their difference of provenance, their essential veracity cannot be questioned.

The first and most complete was compiled anonymously about 1320, but it epitomized complaints going back to 1315. In that year he had his troops and cavalry march on Speyer, storm the chapter precincts, and batter down the door of the cathedral. Widely disliked for favoring the Jews and other usurers, he was alleged to have forced Christians to pay usury and in 1318 attacked the house of the Order of Jerusalem at Haimbach to compel it to pay the usury due to two Jews. He laid violent hands on two rural clerics, one of whom he imprisoned till he paid a large ransom, and excommunicated a third who refused to do the bishop's bidding against the monastery of Sinsheim and the papal legate. He was constantly in the company of soldiers who in fact ruled him; with them he played dice day and night. Little wonder, then, that the principality's debts mounted, heretics and heresies found a secure haven in the diocese, and churches and clerics were daily profaned. Not content with mere neglect, Emicho sequestered the endowment and incomes of prebends, deposed abbots, appointed unworthy men to benefices in contravention of papal provisions and reservations, disrupted chapter meetings, forced ecclesiastical judges to bend to his will, and, refused to appoint a canon as his *officialis*.[16]

In this light it is not surprising that, when Emicho apparently requested a charitable subsidy from the clergy of the diocese late in 1321, the four collegiate churches of Speyer convened to discuss the matter on behalf of the entire clergy. They professed their willingness to aid the bishops in all legitimate cases of financial distress, as canon law proscribed they should. They also declared they would not grant more than £1,000 Heller at any one time and proceeded to partition this amount in what appeared to have been a fair division. The cathedral chapter's share was £207.5.9; Saint Germain's, £43.3.8; Saint Guido's, £34.11⅔; and Holy Trinity's, £25.-18.2⅓. The parish priests attached to the four churches were to pay separately £22.8.0, making a grand total for the four chapters of £333.6.8. The diocesan clergy, divided into four archidiaconates and, within them, into fourteen rural deaneries, were responsible for £503.12.0. The remaining £205 were distributed among thirteen monasteries and priories, each of which contributed a fixed amount varying between £6 and £25.[17]

The third document makes it perfectly obvious that Emicho was not at all discouraged by these efforts to limit his arbitrariness. It was drawn up around 1324 to protest Emicho's latest outrages against the clergy. The list of seventeen charges adds little to what has already been enumerated. Under the guise of visitation and the exercise of his other prerogatives, the bishop had despoiled and imprisoned the clergy, trampled on the rights of the archdeacons and the rural deans, and extorted much more in charitable subsidies than the declaration of 1321 permitted.[18]

On Emicho's death in 1328, the chapter elected as bishop Provost Walram von Veldenz, who was also dean of Strasbourg. If it entertained hopes of better days, they were soon soundly dashed. What ensued can only be described as a most lamentable commentary on the state of the German church in the fourteenth century. Pope John XXII had already reserved the see of Speyer in 1326. The archbishop of Mainz, Mathias von Buchek, prevailed on the pope in 1328 to provide to Speyer his brother Bertold, master of the Teutonic Knights at Coblenz. Bertold was reluctant to devote the necessary money and troops to battle against Walram and his allies (including the count of Württemberg) for such a small bishopric. When Mathias died in the same year, Bertold tried in vain to get the see of Mainz. Meanwhile the bishop of Strasbourg had died, which see Bertold procured in November 1328 through the influence of Hugh von Buchek on John XXII, although Bertold had to take it by force from the rival candidate elected by the Strasbourg chapter. Bertold now began to take possession of several castles in the bishopric of Speyer, of which he called himself *administrator*. Walram nevertheless held out, and John XXII eventually acceded to the inevitable and, on 9 May 1329, named Walram bishop. Still Bertold refused to surrender his last bastions in the principality until the pope ordered him to on 1 January 1330.[19]

During these two years of warfare, the financial situation of the bishopric, already seriously weakened by Bishop Emicho's dissipation, became acute.[20] Bishop Walram in 1330 apparently solicited from the pope permission to levy an extraordinary tax in his diocese,[21] but nothing more is recorded about this. In April of the same year with the consent of the chapter, he pawned the castle and town of Udenheim, together with its appurtenant five villages and all rights, to Canon Hermann von Lichtenberg, the master of the cathedral school and chancellor of Louis the Bavarian, for £4,300

Heller (plus another £200 for repairs). The bishop and chapter carefully retained the right of using the castle and secured letters from Hermann and his brothers attesting the right of redemption. It was further stipulated that Hermann's officials and administrators there obey the cathedral chapter in the interval between his death and the arrival of his legal heirs.[22] Two months later, after consulting with the chapter, Walram pawned the castle of Rietburg and the two villages Weiher and Saint Martin to the widow of his late nephew, Count Fritschmann of Veldenz, for £3,000 Heller. Again the meticulousness of the bishop and chapter are evident in the clause denying the widow any claim to redress should the annual income fall short of £300 Heller.[23]

These measures were to no avail. In 1331, therefore, after deliberating with the chapter and his vassals and castellans, Walram handed over the church of Speyer with all its temporalities and spiritualities to Baldwin of Luxembourg, archbishop of Trier (1307–1354). The famous Baldwin, brother of the late emperor Henry VII, had already added the sees of Mainz and Worms in 1328 and 1330, respectively, to his own diocese of Trier.[24] From the resources of the churches of Mainz and Trier, which he had put on a stable footing through his financial acumen, he now loaned Bishop Walram and the chapter £30,000 Heller to be used for the amortization of the bishopric's debts. Walram was named administrator of the bishopric.[25]

Thus things remained for the next six years. In 1336 Walram died. The chapter, in November, chose to succeed him its youngest canon, Gerhard von Ehrenberg, not without reference to the wishes of Baldwin and Louis the Bavarian.[26] He faced his first major task shortly thereafter, for in 1337 Baldwin decided to give up the bishoprics of Mainz and Speyer. The £30,000 Heller fell due. Gerhard and the chapter, realizing the impossibility of swift repayment, negotiated with Baldwin. The following agreement was at length reached. The money was to be paid back at a rate of £3,000 Heller per annum, and elaborate conditions were laid down to discourage late payment. The active administration of the principality was now consigned to the nobleman Conrad "pincerna de Erpach," without whose knowledge and compliance nothing important could be done. The bishops could not contract other debts in excess of £1,000 Heller, nor could they pawn or pledge any property of the church without Baldwin's and the chapter's consent. The canons swore not to accept anyone as bishop who had not ratified these articles.[27]

At this pace it would have taken ten years of hard saving to cancel the debt. The bishopric was now blessed with a second stroke of luck. In recognition of the steadfast loyalty of the bishop and the chapter, Louis the Bavarian in 1337 abolished the threat of bankruptcy which Baldwin of Trier had averted in 1331. Louis allowed the £30,000 to be paid off in the following wise: Archbishop Baldwin was allowed to collect £10,000 from a tollstation at Coblenz; Archbishop Henry of Mainz, £10,000 from one created at Lahnstein; and Bishop Gerhard, the final £10,000 from a third station at Bingen with which he should cancel the unpaid difference to the two archbishops.[28] The amortization seems to have progressed without difficulty, and in 1345 Archbishop Henry of Mainz delivered up to Gerhard a receipt for the last of his £10,000.[29]

IV

With the return to solvency the principality was proffered the chance to reform and achieve relative stability. Bishop Gerhard (1336–1363) contributed to that effort. He compiled the first feudal registry of the bishopric[1] and the first tables of incomes, expenditures, and debts.[2] Thanks to these, we know far more in detail about his reign than about any previous one. He also successfully prosecuted the rights of the bishopric, whether against vassals who defaulted on their fiefs for neglect of duty[3] or against neighboring lords who sought easy gain at the church's expense[4] or against monasteries seeking to free themselves from subjugation to the bishops.[5]

His vigor can be seen in the upwards of forty privileges he secured from Louis the Bavarian and Charles IV. Naturally, some of these privileges merely described or confirmed rights the bishops already had[6] or else acknowledged as rights what the bishops had probably been doing for some time, e.g., enforcement of the *bannum* in forests and lordship over the imperial serfs living on the lands of the church of Speyer.[7] Nevertheless, they legitimized and rounded out the bishop's princely powers and gave him tangible legal proof of his right to exercise them. Other privileges greatly augmented his rights: to legitimize bastards, to ennoble, to create notaries in the name of the empire, to create tolls ad libitum, to quash appeals by his peasants to the imperial court, to demand services from the monasteries in the diocese, to negotiate with Jews in his territories concerning their taxation.[8] A few were more specific, permitting the fortification of Udenheim, Steinach, and Landau or the erection of tolls on the Rhine for certain lengths of time.[9] A final set of charters concerned imperial pawns to the bishopric. When Gerhard entered office, the two imperial towns of Waibstadt and Landau and the Jews within the lands of the church of Speyer had already been pawned to the bishopric.[10] Gerhard added the monastery of Odenheim in 1338,[11] and in 1349 he obtained from Charles IV the stipulation that all these could be redeemed only en bloc by an emperor.[12]

These pawns merit closer inspection lest they be misinterpreted. Like imperial donations under the Saxons and the Salians, they represented an addition to the holdings of a church and remuneration for services rendered and desired. There was a fundamental difference between the two, however. The emperor could increase the value of a pawn. This only made repurchase by a later emperor more costly. Beyond a certain point, the pawn ceased to be a real payment for services, nor did the increase necessarily reflect the true value of those services. The emperors, in short, enjoyed immense short-run advantages. The problem is best illustrated by several examples. The town of Waibstadt is first mentioned as being in the possession of the bishops of Speyer in 1331, the price of redemption having been set at £1,000 Heller. By 1349 Louis the Bavarian and Charles IV had more than tripled this to £3,200, and around 1470 Bishop Mathias Ramung calculated that the emperors in the course of time had raised the price of redemption to £34,400 Heller, 500 silver marks, and 27,000 fl.![13] By 1349 they had pushed to £7,000 Heller the price on the Jews in the principality whom Bishop Emicho had taken in pawn in 1315 for 1,333 silver marks and £1 Heller.[14] Episcopal revenues from these sources did not grow as a result (unless the bishop was able to extract it from them, which was difficult), and in fact only Landau was ever redeemed (in 1511/17), contrary to imperial assurances to repurchase pawned properties only in one great block.

The point of this digression is that this kind of "indemnification" was essentially nothing of the sort, for Gerhard very much devoted himself to the imperial cause and was not nearly as peaceful or as efficient as he has been portrayed.[15] For his service, he incurred excommunication in 1343 and 1346 and received papal confirmation only in 1350 and consecration in 1351 or 1352.[16] His origins, like those of most of the bishops and canons of Speyer, were military, and he reflected them at every turn. He fortified

Udenheim and Steinach and added a large tower to the walls at Bruchsal.[17] In July 1337 he joined the Upper Rhenish *Landfrieden*.[18] He sent fifty armored cavalrymen each to the sieges of Eltvil and Zurich and personally accompanied Charles IV to Italy for his coronation in 1355.[19] In the late 1350s he nearly went to war with Speyer over the collection of property taxes on the burghers' property in the bishopric.[20]

All this required money, perhaps more than most of his predecessors had spent, and the emperors were not really reimbursing him for his services to the empire. Gerhard soon had to borrow money from relatives, burghers of Speyer, and the Jews of Strasbourg, Speyer, and elsewhere. Interest rates were high, normally ten percent, and many loans, particularly from Jews, were contracted for short periods, forcing the bishop's financial officials into a vicious circle of keeping one step ahead of notes falling due.[21] Gerhard noted in 1349 the difficulty of alienating movable goods "on account of the sterility of the times."[22] On the other hand, the emperor again rescued the bishopric in 1349 from potential disaster by canceling all debts contracted by the bishops with the Jews, inasmuch as most of them had already been slaughtered in the Rhenish pogroms of that year.[23]

Gerhard also pawned fisheries, fiefs, petty incomes, the excise tax at Bruchsal, ground taxes, and forest revenues. He made special financial arrangements with the burghers of Bruchsal and the Jews of Landau. Among his more prominent creditors were the Speyer Jewess Jutha and his uncle Peter von Mur, provost of the collegiate church at Wimpfen.[24] A few examples should convey a sense of the constant urgency and essential futility behind these negotiations. In 1341 Gerhard pawned his horse to two Jews of Speyer for £50, with weekly interest payments scheduled to commence after one month.[25] To the Jewess Jutha of Speyer he pawned, by 1340, part and, in 1346, the whole of the property tax (*Bede*) from Bruchsal, the most important single item of revenue from the largest town in the principality.[26] A final case: The castle of Rietburg with its appurtenant two villages, which bishop Walram had pawned for £3,000 in 1330, was by 1344 on the verge of being lost to the bishopric. To prevent that, Bishop Gerhard, with the assent of the chapter, pawned the yearly income of 125 fl. from the Bienwald forest to a knight of Strasbourg, Eberhard von Kageneck, for 1500 fl., and also the fall property tax of £25 from Östringen to his uncle Peter von Mur for £250. With this money he redeemed the castle and immediately pawned it again to Peter for £1500 for six years, although Peter and his heirs could continue to receive grain and wine even after returning it to the bishopric. In 1349, a year before the expiration of the contract, Gerhard redeemed the castle and pawned it to the cathedral chapter for £3,000. Like some of his predecessors, he realized the desirability and utility of selling or pawning to the chapter as opposed to outsiders, but the resources of the chapter had shrunk too, owing perhaps to the immediate effects of the Black Death. In order to retain the castle, the chapter in 1358 had to borrow 1,700 fl. at an annual interest payment of 85 fl.[27] It is worth noting that the chapter paid here an interest rate of five percent in contrast to the ten percent for which the bishops usually had to contract.

Gerhard also requested extraordinary taxation of the clergy to help carry him through. Whether it was imposed in 1342 is not at all clear from the single possible piece of evidence, where Bishop Gerhard affirmed that, according to the 1321 declaration of the clergy, the abbot of Sinsheim should contribute £25, but that he would now be satisfied with £13.[28] A tax of £1,000 Heller was levied in 1344 on all the clergy in the diocese and collected by men deputed by the bishop. Failure to pay was punishable by interdict or excommunication. The rural dean at Hassloch doubted whether papal exemption covered Saint Lambrecht's, a former Benedictine monastery converted into a Dominican house in the thirteenth century. The bishop, on the advice of three experts consulted, ruled that exemption did apply. Nothing more is known about this subsidy.[29]

Negotiations for the second levy dragged on for more than six years. Possibly anticipating resistance, Gerhard, in 1351 and 1352, obtained bulls from Clement VI granting permission to exact a moderate tax from all secular and regular (but not exempt) churches and foundations and all holders of benefices. In protest against Gerhard's excessive spending, the four chapters representing the clergy rejected the request and appealed to Mainz, thus probably provoking Gerhard to secure papal condemnation of his electoral capitulation by Innocent VI in 1352. When the chapters lost their case at Mainz, they appealed to the pope in 1357. The outcome is not known.[30]

Gerhard had encountered the determined will of the chapter sometime before this. The chapter did not oppose him out of selfishness or narrow-mindedness. On the contrary, a series of measures instituted by the chapter during Gerhard's reign demonstrate its great desire to bring order and stability to the bishopric while still maintaining its territorial integrity. While the chapter could be overruled by superior powers such as the papacy, it effectively used the power of the purse to secure these ends to make some gains in its position in the principality.

The first clash went back to 1328 or 1329, when the chapter denied permission to Bishop Bertold to grant for life the castle and town of Obergrombach, together with the three villages in its bailiwick and a manor, to Ulrich of Württemberg, son of the count of Württemberg, canon of the cathedral, and provost of Saint Guido. Because Ulrich could not take possession without the written leave of the chapter, Bishop Bertold provided that he should hold Altenburg Castle near Bruchsal until he did receive this letter. In 1337 Ulrich still occupied Altenburg, the chapter having rejected similar requests from Bishops Walram and Gerhard. There is no indication that it ever yielded.[31]

The chapter attached stringent conditions to the bishop's financial arrangements. When maintenance costs forced Gerhard in 1344 to commit the administration of the castle of Steinach to his uncle Peter von Mur for life, the chapter stipulated that upon Peter's death the castle should pass under its control until the bishop restore to the chapter's funds the £200 he borrowed for repairs on the castle.[32] In 1347 the chapter dictated even stronger terms when Gerhard presented plans to retire £3,000 in debts. The chapter gave him permission to act provided that he not pawn or sell any castles, towns, or *Ämter;* that he pawn only with the consent of the chapter; that he redeem these pawns within the next ten years; that the episcopal *Amtleute* and bailiffs swear to abide by these conditions and obey the chapter; and that the chapter's lands and serfs be exempt from episcopal taxes.[33]

Two other documents illustrate how much the chapter advanced in other parliamentary capacities and prerogatives. In 1347 the magistrate, jurors, and inhabitants of Bruchsal promised to obey the chapter in the event of Bishop Gerhard's death or imprisonment and to remain obedient until Gerhard's return or the installation of a new bishop.[34] The chapter also extended its consultative rights in purely secular matters not specified in previous agreements or electoral oaths. When the village of Oberdeidesheim in 1360 petitioned Gerhard for elevation to the status of a town with the concomitant right to build fortifications, he granted the request after consulting with the chapter and ordered the levying of an *Ungeld* there to bear the cost.[35]

V

Strained though the chapter's relations with Bishop Gerhard might often have been, in retrospect the days of his rule seemed idyllic. On his death in 1363 the principality was immediately plunged for the next quarter-century into turbulence the equal of the chaos that had prevailed before his accession. The chapter elected as bishop the cathedral dean, Eberhard von Randeck, member of a family of the lower nobility settled near Mann-weiler in the principality of Mainz. But the pope, yielding to the impreca-tions of Duke Rudolf of Austria, awarded Speyer to the Alsatian Lambert von Born, abbot of the Benedictine monastery of Gengenbach and a col-lector of papal taxes, who received Speyer in compensation for Rudolf's having blocked his appointment to the see of Brixen because of his adher-ence to Charles IV. The deadlock issued in war between the rivals. Eberhard was supported by the chapter, Frederick von Leiningen, the princi-pality's soldiers and officials, and even by Speyer, although the town de-manded that, if it be laid under interdict or the ban of the empire, Eberhard should not conclude a peace with Lambert without first securing the revoca-tion of the punishment. In the end, resistance proved useless. The emperor mediated the settlement at the request of both sides in 1365. Lambert be-came bishop. As indemnification, Eberhard was allowed to occupy the fortresses of Udenheim and Kestenburg and their appurtenances (includ-ing the Rhine tollstation at Udenheim) for the rest of his life. Lambert withdrew his officials from these places, but Eberhard's castellans rendered homage to Lambert and swore to alienate none of these possessions and to obey him on the death of Eberhard. In addition, for their expenses during the war, Eberhard and his brother Heilmann, canon of Speyer, accepted in pawn the castle at Obergrombach. The bishops held the exclusive right to redeem this from them at any time for 3,000 fl., with the further provision that on the death of both brothers the castle revert without cost to the bishopric. Lambert also accepted responsibility for other debts incurred by Eberhard to a maximum of 10,000 fl., as well as for 8,000 fl. contracted with Eberhard by Bishop Gerhard and, after his death, by his *Amtleute*. All the bishop's towns, subjects, and castellans were directed to do homage to Lambert. Peter von Mur, provost of Wimpfen and the uncle of the late bishop, was appointed to oversee the execution of these mandates.[1]

The enormous costs of the war fell, it goes without saying, on the princi-pality, not to mention the great suffering it caused. Lambert procured in

1365 from Urban V a bull authorizing the exaction of a ten percent *subsidium caritativum* from all the clergy and foundations, exempt and non-exempt, in the diocese.[2] The chapter met this threat to its prerogatives in an ingenious way. It loaned Lambert 8,000 fl. without interest charges to discharge immediately some of the principality's debts and then, to facilitate repayment of the loan, voted a ten-year levy on the clergy at the usual rate of £1,000 Heller per annum.[3]

Lambert spent most of his time in the company of the emperor. He deputed his brother Henry, canon of Speyer and Basel and provost of Zoningen, to administer the principality in both temporal and spiritual matters.[4] He did secure a number of imperial privileges for the bishopric. Some signified little or nothing;[5] others represented real concessions, such as the right to mint gold and silver money, exemption from all tolls on the Rhine and freedom to establish tollstations anywhere in the principality, and revocation of the lord of Weingarten's charter to collect tolls at Rheinzabern.[6] He also signed a protective union with the Elector Palatine in 1365.[7] This treaty marked the beginning of nearly two centuries of close association between the bishopric and the Palatinate in which the Electors more and more blatantly encroached on the rights of the bishops and gradually reduced the principality to the status of a satellite, which they freely exploited. Lambert's indifference to the dangers implied in this alliance and to the bishopric of Speyer in general was strikingly demonstrated in his apparent lack of response when Elector Rupert II won the right of free use of the castle of Dalburg from the community there in 1367 and had this right explicitly denied to the bishop of Speyer, the feudal lord of the castle![8] Lambert's concern was to move on to a more prestigious prelacy, which he did in 1371 when the pope translated the bishop of Strasbourg to Mainz and appointed Lambert to Strasbourg. Four years after that, Lambert gained the see of Bamberg, where he died in 1398.[9]

His successor at Speyer was no less ambitious and decidedly more ruthless. Adolf von Nassau, nephew of the Elector Palatine and of the late Archbishop Gerlach of Mainz, was only eighteen years old when he was elected bishop of Speyer in 1371 but had already set his sights on Mainz. In the same year, some canons of the Mainz chapter had voted for him only to have their candidate rejected by the papacy at the behest of Charles IV. When the new archbishop died in 1373, the Mainz chapter unanimously postulated Adolf. Again he was rejected by the pope, who appointed the bishop of Bamberg, Margrave Louis of Meissen, to the electoral see. Gregory XI tried to appease Adolf by conferring on him Strasbourg. Adolf was not placated, prepared for war against Louis and his family in May 1374, and delegated the administration of the principality of Speyer to his uncle, Craft von Hohenlohe. A truce was reached in September 1375, and in the Rothenburg *Landfrieden* of May 1377, Adolf was acknowledged to be the de facto ruler of the principality of Mainz. Papal recognition was not forthcoming until Adolf in 1378 sided with the Avignonese Pope Clement VII, who conferred the pallium on Adolf in the following year.[10]

Adolf retained the administration of the bishopric of Speyer. Although after elevating Adolf to Mainz, Clement VII provided his brother John, canon of Würzburg, to Speyer, John was shortly thereafter taken prisoner in one of the numerous feuds conducted by the Nassau family, and Clement soon returned the governance of Speyer to Adolf. But, in 1382, the Roman Pope Urban VI named Nicholas of Wiesbaden, a burgher's son, custodian of the Worms chapter, and archdeacon of Deventer. Adolf and the majority of the Speyer chapter refused to accept the provision and war broke out. Despite support for Nicholas from the emperor, the pope, the Elector Palatine, and the margrave of Baden, Adolf adamantly held on to Speyer. Only in March 1389 did he cede the principality to Nicholas, and even then Adolf insisted on retaining the title of administrator of the bishopric and on keeping in his hands the castles then in his control. He died in the following year.[11]

To some extent the chapter at Speyer had anticipated this trouble. A full six weeks before Charles IV conferred the regalia on Adolf in October 1371, the chapter won from Adolf promises that he would appoint no *Amtleute* or other officials who failed to swear to submit to the chapter in the event of the bishop's death or imprisonment and to spend no more than 300 fl. in administration during such a vacancy, although they might use up to 10,000 fl. to ransom the bishop.[12] In 1381 Adolf arranged to transfer the governance of the bishopric to the chapter in the event of his death or translation. The chapter managed to squeeze this concession from him by permitting him to raise, by pawning, 6,000 fl. at an average interest rate of no more than ten percent, in order to be able to repay the chapter that amount during the next four years.[13]

It would be quite erroneous to infer from these negotiations Adolf's subservience to the chapter. On the contrary, Adolf simply ignored the chapter much of the time and got away with it. Most of the loans and pawns he undertook do not mention the consent of the chapter,[14] nor did he refer to the chapter in 1374 when he gave his uncle Craft von Hohenlohe full power to govern the bishopric in his absence.[15] When he wanted advice, even on the most serious matters affecting the bishopric, he turned to his relatives, friends, and noble councillors.[16] The negotiations of 1381 discussed above underline how dependent the chapter was on him. It will be remembered that in 1365 Lambert had borrowed 8,000 fl. from the chapter to cancel various debts and that the chapter had consented to a ten-year levy on the clergy to help liquidate the loan. By 1371 only 2,000 fl. had been repaid. Adolf pledged to pay the remainder from the sum collected during the next four years of the levy. In 1377 Adolf still owed the chapter the full 6,000 fl. The chapter forced him to hand over the town of Lauterburg to its administration until the amount was paid off from toll incomes at Udenheim and from pawns. In the interim no other possessions were to be pawned to anyone else.[17] The sources do not indicate whether the entire debt was actually paid, but it is possible that the detailed negotiations of 1381 concerning Adolf's repayment of 6,000 fl. to the chapter were but another round in this protracted episode.

Adolf's skillful manipulation of factionalism in the chapter partly accounts for his success in handling it. When Adolf requested in 1375 the chapter's consent to his allowing the Speyer town council to determine the levels of the wine trade there for eight years, the chapter refused. Adolf nonetheless granted Speyer the permission in return for a loan of 2,500 fl. to be repaid in equal installments over the next eight years without interest. Adolf then asked six canons of the chapter to act as guarantors for the loan. They assented and affixed their seals to the loan. Such defections from corporate decisions inevitably undermined the chapter's power.[18] Later, after war had erupted between Adolf and Nicholas in 1382, five canons (including four of the above six) concluded an accord with Adolf, pledging him their support in return for his protection of their persons, benefices, and properties.[19] Nicholas bought some support among the canons as well, but massive opposition to him among the clergy compelled him in 1384 to imprison clerics, drive them from their benefices, and interdict prebendal incomes. Such were the levers at the disposal of a bishop.[20]

Throughout his pontificate, Adolf without compunction used the resources of the bishopric of Speyer to serve his own ends. His military campaigns could only imperil its already tenuous financial position. He not only warred to gain Mainz and retain Speyer; he also became enmeshed in feuds and wars with other princes, including the Elector Palatine and the bishop of Würzburg, who plundered the principality.[21] In 1376 Adolf undertook a massive effort to conquer Speyer by siege, but failed.[22] The conduct of war was then no less expensive than at any other time in history. In 1382, for example, Adolf signed on forty-two retainers at a yearly fee of 30 to 90 fl. per man for a total of 2,270 fl.; in 1385, twenty-one men for a total of 1,010 fl.[23] Horses cost 60 to 150 fl. apiece.[24] Some of the sums involved in victualing his forces were cited at the beginning of this chapter.[25] Claims for expenses and for damages to persons, horses, and equipment ran very high and had to be satisfied with fiefs, castellanies, or whatever else was available. For instance, Adolf owed his nephew John von Ochsenstein, dean of Strasbourg cathedral, 280 fl. for lost horses.[26] Adolf's uncle Craft von Hohenlohe demanded no less than 5,400 fl. for his first two years as administrator of the bishopric, and Craft's nephew Ulrich (who succeeded his uncle in 1381) submitted a bill for 1,590 fl.[27]

To fund his campaign, Adolf resorted to the usual expedients. Judging from the chapter's complaint in 1377, narrated above, he appropriated to himself the £4,000 Heller collected from the clergy between 1371 and 1375.[28] He pawned many smaller offices, fiefs, and incomes, principally to meet claims for services rendered to the bishopric.[29] From Speyer Jews and burghers, from his bailiffs and relatives, from nobles and clerics, he borrowed thousands of gulden, individual loans varying in size between 300 and 3,500 fl. The loans tended to be of two types, neither of them designed to promote financial security: long-range loans carrying ten percent interest, or short-term notes at high rates requiring cancellation before a specified terminus within six months or a year. Several large loans from Jews were taken out for Adolf by relatives or officials, indicating, perhaps, general lack of confidence in Adolf,[30] and in contrast to the ten percent rate he had to pay, the town of Lauterburg, with his consent in 1384, borrowed 720 fl. at eight and a third percent.[31]

Nicholas was also driven to heavy expenditures to enforce his legitimate claims to the bishopric and, later, to protect the principality against its enemies. In his fight against Adolf, to cite a few instances, he purchased the support of the margrave of Baden for 3,000 fl. and of various other nobles for retainer fees of 250 to 500 fl.[32] It is worthy of note that Nicholas included in these contracts the proviso that these men could not petition for payment until he had taken possession of the bishopric of Speyer. Such care was characteristic of Nicholas, particularly in trying to put the principality's finances in good order. Yearly interest payments in 1390 amounted to 1,900 fl.[33] To ease the financial burdens of the principality, he arrived in office with 4,000 fl. to undertake necessary redemptions and amortizations.[34] His pawns were far fewer in number than Adolf's and were often made to relatives (especially to Hans Contzemann, *Amtmann* of Pforzheim) or else under the condition that the pawned property revert automatically to the bishops on the death of its holders.[35] He also contracted few short-term loans,[36] and whereas some of his many long-term loans carried an interest rate of 10 percent, others were arranged at rates of eight and a half,[37] eight and a third,[38] eight,[39] and in one case, seven and a seventh percent.[40] By taking loans at lower rates, he was able to liquidate loans made at higher rates and still save money.[41] He canceled many loans going as far back as Bishop Lambert's time.[42] He also managed to persuade many holders of notes to grant him a reduction in the interest rate or to allow a change in the form of the contract, particularly to nonheritable annuities, which he very much favored.[43]

Till the day of his death in 1396, Nicholas manifested this concern for the true interests of the principality in all areas of administration and governance. He was without question the best bishop of Speyer in two hundred years. He had drawn up elementary statements of indebtedness and income.[44] He improved the fortifications at Bruchsal and added a tower to the castle at Rotenberg.[45] He obliged his officials to swear to dispense justice fairly and govern according to the needs and customs of his subjects.[46] He went to great lengths to insure firm control over his serfs.[47] He brought suit against Speyer for redress of various grievances, for which the town eventually paid him 3,000 fl.[48] To pressures from the outside, he offered stout resistance. In 1391 at his request the pope exempted the diocese of Speyer from the latest papal tax,[49] and in 1396 the demands of the margrave of Baden for money to enforce the *Landfrieden* were firmly rejected.[50]

Ironically, few bishops of Speyer experienced so much opposition from the cathedral chapter as did Nicholas. The reasons are not far to seek. Nicholas had been provided by the pope, but what was far more infuriating was the fact that he was a burgher, a nonnoble. The town of Speyer also took the greatest offense in him. Remling accurately observed that not one of Nicholas' hundreds of charters was issued from Speyer.[51] Not only is there no evidence of Nicholas' ceremonial entrance into the town, but after his death the town council caviled so much over his burial in the cathedral that the body was secretly brought over the wall one night and quietly interred.[52]

Nicholas met the chapter's resistance head on. His resort to bribes, threats, and confiscation of the chapter's incomes to force its compliance with the papal will has already been described. He dickered long and hard in 1390 with the chapter over his electoral capitulation of fifty-one articles, the longest ever submitted to a bishop in the late Middle Ages. Besides incorporating the clauses of previous oaths and promises to abide by contracts concluded with the chapter by Bishops Frederick and Emicho, the chapter added new and significant articles guaranteeing orderly governance by the chapter during vacancies, enfeoffment of reverted fiefs only after consultation within the chapter, residence by castellans, and exemption of the chapter and its property from the guarantors of loans and pawns contracted on the *mensa episcopalis*. Nicholas objected to the phraseology of many articles, and in almost all instances the chapter gave way to him.[53]

Nicholas and the chapter clashed also on the matter of extraordinary taxation of the clergy. In 1391 he asked the four chapters of Speyer what sum the abbot of Sinsheim was accustomed to contribute in charitable subsidies. When they replied £12½ Heller, Nicholas let his displeasure with the amount be known. It is not clear from this charter whether a levy was voted in that year,[54] but he did request one in 1395. The chapter rejected the petition, saying that Nicholas instead ought to cancel debts in accordance with previously made arrangements. A deadlock resulted over this and other points of dispute. It was broken finally through the mediation of the Elector Palatine Rupert. The arbiters decided in favor of a three-year levy on the clergy. The bishop in turn was to drop the suit he had filed against the chapter, to render all customary dues, and to exempt the lands of the chapter and its canons from the *Bede*.[55]

Various documents suggest that the main source of contention was the chapter, not Nicholas. Certainly he went farther than any previous bishop to insure that his officials take oaths to obey the chapter during vacancies, fulfill their obligations, enforce the bishop's rights, and take care for the well-being of his subjects.[56] He also followed the chapter's advice on many matters, including rescinding from Hans Contzemann (the husband of his niece Katherine), whom he had appointed to office in the principality, the right to hold in pawn various possessions of the bishopric.[57]

Nicholas' reign in many respects resembled more that of his successors than of his predecessors in the increasing dependence of the bishops on the

Elector Palatine (with whom he renewed the protective treaty in 1392),[58] in his determined enforcement of episcopal rights, in his search for sounder methods of funding the principality's debts, and in his reliance on the chapter as the principal consultative body of the principality (despite the chapter's treatment of him). The chapter's rights and responsibilities had grown considerably during the fourteenth century, even though by times it had acted selfishly or found itself helpless before wilful bishops. Within the limits imposed on it and inherent in its structure and position, it had successfully dealt with the great challenges of the fourteenth century.

Chapter 4

The Palatine Protectorate, 1396-1552

I

The election of Raban von Helmstadt as bishop of Speyer in 1396 is a watershed in the history of the bishopric in the late Middle Ages. Like the century and a quarter preceding it, the century and a half following his elevation can be seen as a coherent whole, but one whose distinguishing features were rather different. By and large, peace and stability reigned. Only twice did the bishops become involved in major wars, one of them to gain control of the see of Trier, and both of which proved financially disastrous. Normally the bishops concentrated their efforts on restoring and extending their territories and rights, strengthening administration, and putting their finances on a good footing.[1] Of the nine bishops, six were interrelated, as the chart on page 120 shows.[2] Three of them came from the von Helmstadt family and ruled a total of eighty-six years. That all save one were from the lower nobility stands in sharp contrast to the dominance of the higher nobility in the episcopate through the rule of Adolf of Nassau.[3] Even more striking is the fact that not one of the nine bishops effectively owed his elevation to the emperor or the pope.[4]

Peace enabled the bishops to establish much wanted financial order. In general, they emphasized economy at court and in the administration and kept military expenditures to a minimum, so much so that their castles fell quickly in the Bundschuh of 1502 and the Peasants War of 1525, prompt-

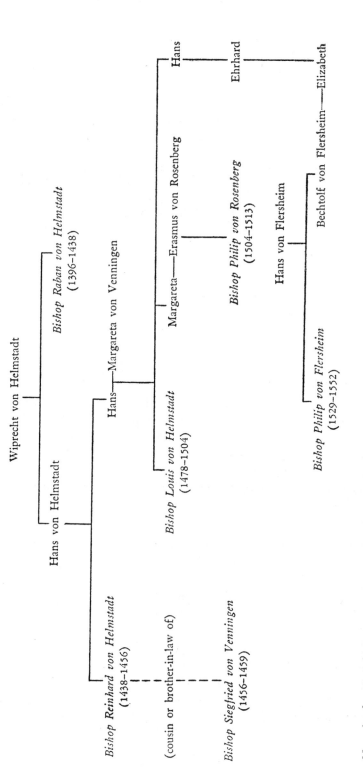

The Bishops of Speyer, 1396–1552

Wiprecht von Helmstadt

Bishop Raban von Helmstadt (1396–1438)

Hans von Helmstadt

Hans——Margareta von Venningen

Bishop Louis von Helmstadt (1478–1504)

Margareta——Erasmus von Rosenberg

Hans

Bishop Philip von Rosenberg (1504–1513)

Ehrhard

Hans von Flersheim

Bishop Philip von Flersheim (1529–1552)

Bechtolf von Flersheim——Elizabeth

Bishop Reinhard von Helmstadt (1438–1456)

(cousin or brother-in-law of)

Bishop Siegfried von Venningen (1456–1459)

Not related to these bishops were Bishops John Nix von Hoheneck zu Entzberg (1459–1464), Mathias Ramung (1464–1478), and George, count palatine of the Rhine and duke of Bavaria (1513–1529).

ing the Elector Philip's sarcastic recommendation in 1502 that the bishop should garrison his fortresses with a few nobles and cavalry men.[5] In time they reduced the general interest rate on their loans from ten or eight percent, to five and later four percent. The majority of these were taken with ecclesiastical foundations (including the chapter), nobles, burghers, relatives, and the bishop's *Amtleute*.[6] In addition, more and more were long term, many being retired only in the late seventeenth or the eighteenth centuries, nor was it any longer necessary, as a rule, to pledge property in pawn to secure money.[7]

Now it is true that all these were common trends in the fifteenth century, and to that extent the achievement of solvency cannot be ascribed to the bishops alone. Still, their accomplishment should not be slighted in view of what happened when they waged war. Bishop Raban von Helmstadt fought between 1430 and 1437 to take control of the archbishopric of Trier, to which he had been provided by the Holy See. To underwrite his campaigns, he was forced to pawn many possessions of the bishopric (having done so only twice since 1399) and to raise money through short-term loans or by appointing creditors as retainers of the bishopric (at an annual fee of 60 to 90 fl.) without the obligation to fight outside its borders. Despite the restraining efforts of the chapter he left the principality burdened with thousands of gulden in debts. In 1462 Bishop John II joined the imperial coalition against the Elector Palatine and Diether von Isenberg, archbishop of Mainz. John too had to employ many measures similar to those used by Raban to obtain money, and the chapter had to borrow money for him. The defeat of the coalition at Seckenheim caused many creditors of the principality to demand repayment of their loans. The resulting financial crisis moved John's successor, Mathias Ramung, to a savage indictment of the cathedral chapter's ineptitude in letting this happen.[8]

Extraordinary taxation to carry the bishops through became common, not only during such crises, but even when circumstances were not so pressing. The clergy continued to carry a large portion of the burden, but it was becoming increasingly difficult to expect them to bear the entire load. Inflation and depredations gradually cut sharply into their revenues, and the rise of anticlerical feeling made collection of their remaining incomes, particularly tithes, more difficult.[9] Neighboring princes assumed more and more control over the clergy in their lands and, in numerous cases, either encouraged opposition to episcopal levies or denied the bishop the right to tax clergy not subject to him as temporal lord. As a result, the bishop's burghers and peasants were slowly called upon more and more to contribute to *Schatzungen,* although only rarely were both the clergy and the laity included in the same tax. *Schatzungen* imposed on the burghers and peasantry seem sometimes to have been collected only from certain *Ämter* or villages rather than the entire population. Moreover, on occasion they took peculiar forms, in one instance as so-called *Freundschaftsgeld* ("friendship money"), and several times during Mathias Ramung's reign, in the doubling of the fixed *Bede* either in the fall or in the spring.

This succession of good bishops and the peace that allowed them to devote themselves to domestic affairs was very much connected with the growing dependence of the bishopric on the Electoral Palatinate, "the leading principality of the Empire in the fifteenth century."[10] Protective treaties had already been concluded between the bishops and the Electors in 1365 and 1392. In 1396 the chapter at Speyer split in its election of a new bishop. A majority cast votes for Gottfried von Leiningen, a minority for Raban von Helmstadt. The decision fell automatically to the pope. It is probable that the Elector Rupert II (1390–1398), standard-bearer of the Roman papal cause in Germany during the Great Schism, used his influence on the pope to have Raban appointed.[11] Raban became chancellor of the empire when the Elector Rupert III was chosen king (1400–1410) and was privy councillor to Elector Louis III (1410–1436). He was but the first of many such bishops of Speyer and Worms who came from the Palatine nobility and served the Electors as advisers and officials, as did many canons of both cathedral chapters.[12] When Bishop John II was forced to resign in 1464, two years after his defeat, Elector Frederick I, "the Victorious," (1449/52–1476) had the cathedral chapter elect his chancellor, Canon Mathias Ramung, to succeed him. Palatine influence on the bishopric reached its high point in 1513 in the election of Elector Louis V's brother George (1513–1529). The see of Worms was even more strongly dominated by the Electors. Bishops of both sees participated in the meetings of the estates of the Electors, and in a memorandum to Elector Philip the Upright (1476–1508), they referred to themselves as "members of your principality."[13] There is no exaggeration, therefore, in Lossen's conclusion that "By the end of the fifteenth century things had developed to the point that the bishops of Speyer and Worms lived in almost complete dependence on the Palatinate."[14]

Close association with the Palatinate largely withdrew the bishopric from the arena of papal and imperial politics, although the strength of papal influence, particularly in the matter of provisions to canonries, ought not to be underestimated.[15] The bishopric was spared many of the agonies it had endured in the fourteenth century and, furthermore, enjoyed the protection of the Electors. It paid a price, however, for this protection, one that grew heavier in time, especially after 1464, and that was eventually found to be intolerable. Whereas the canons might originally have favored the relationship to create a buffer against the popes, the emperors, and the margraves of Baden,[16] there can be little doubt that it was the Electors who brought the bishops within their orbit, not vice versa. Already in 1392–93, when Nicholas signed the treaty with Rupert II, the list of grievances against Palatine incursions was substantial. Nicholas was forced to renounce, among other things, his right to exact services from monasteries, and he noted that he had begged in vain for Palatine help in a feud with Count Arnold of Homburg.[17] What is more, in 1396 a majority of the cathedral canons voted for a Leiningen, traditional enemies of the Electors.

These incursions into both the temporal and spiritual rights, prerogatives, and possessions of the bishops became steadily more extensive and flagrant in time, and from Mathias Ramung's pontificate onward (1464–1478) the Electors demanded money from the bishops and above all from the four collegiate churches of Speyer. Many of these violations have been catalogued and described elsewhere, although some have been exaggerated and others largely neglected.[18] They are consequently not discussed here except insofar as they bear on the principality's general condition and on the bishops' and canons' attitudes toward the Palatinate.

Sentiment began to turn against the Palatinate by the first quarter of the sixteenth century. The defeat of Philip the Upright in the War of the Bavarian Succession (1505) greatly weakened his hold on the nobility and the dependent ecclesiastical foundations. Bishop George's extravagance and his feeble resistance to his brother's outrageous usurpations and demands engendered dissatisfaction in the cathedral chapter and the peasantry. When he died in 1529, the chapter spurned the Elector's attempts to have his other brother Henry elected and instead chose Chanter Philip von Flersheim, doctor of canon and civil laws, former chancellor of Heidelberg University, and advisor to Emperor Charles V. Within a short time, Philip clashed with the Elector on various issues, but it was the introduction of the Reformation into the Palatinate and threat of possible secularization that finally drove Philip to break the tie with the Palatinate and to revive the long dormant imperial relationship.[19] The bishopric suffered great losses when the Reformation was introduced by most of the surrounding princes, and as Philip lay dying in 1552, Margrave Albert Alcibiades of Brandenburg was about to plunder the principality. More than a century of conflict and hard times lay ahead.[20]

How did the cathedral chapter fare during this time of respite between the disorder of the fourteenth century and the upheavals of the Reformation? How did it develop in its parliamentary activity, in safeguarding the general interests of the principality, and in restraining princely excesses? The answer is complicated, yet it can be said that the chapter reached a certain maturity it had lacked in the fourteenth century. When the canons divided in the election of a new dean in 1443, they appointed arbiters to make the final selection "in order to avoid war, energy, costs, rancor, and ruinous damage to the principality" that would have resulted from resolution by feud.[21] Although the canons often haggled with the bishops at great length over a *subsidium caritativum* or a *Schatzung*, I have found no evidence that they ever ultimately declined to grant one. The chapter used this power to increase considerably its rights in the government of the bishopric. Demands to this effect became much more numerous from the electoral capitulation of Mathias Ramung onward, and that the bishops acceded to them in time is made abundantly clear by the minutes of the chapter meetings that are extant from 1500 on. The canons insisted especially on the right to audit and review the accounts of the principality and on the bishop's responsibility to restrict spending, to try to cancel debts and keep the principality's creditors at bay "to prevent war against the land and its people,"[22] and to fulfill all obligations to the clergy and the laity.

At the same time, however, the chapter found itself less and less accepted by the clergy and the peasantry as their "representative" before the bishop. *Subsidia caritativa* voted by the four chapters of Speyer were no longer automatically accepted by the monasteries and the rural deaneries, nor did the three collegiate chapters of Speyer or the cathedral vicars and prebendaries submit without question to the domination of the chapter. When the peasants were taxed extraordinarily, negotiation with them or at least consideration of their reaction and interests was requisite; the chapter's simple consent did not suffice. In both the Bundschuh and the Peasants War, the peasants uttered strong sentiments against the exalted position of the chapter in the governance of the bishopric.[23]

To some extent, the explanation of this phenomenon must be laid to the growth of greater self-awareness on the part of most estates and groups and also of antiaristocratic and anticlerical feeling in the fifteenth century. In his report on the Bundschuh in the bishopric in 1502, George Brentz, the bishop's secretary, astutely noted that the peasants had ceased to accept the fundamental premise of society that "the upper clergy and the nobility should rule and the peasants should serve them."[24] In 1525, too, the peasants relentlessly destroyed castles and monasteries, the seats of the nobility.[25]

Yet it cannot be denied that the chapter had helped bring this about by its sometimes haughtily aristocratic attitudes. To be sure, such attitudes were already present in the thirteenth century, but in time they deepened and came more often to the fore, and did so just when rulers and the other estates were becoming less tolerant of them. The chapter's treatment of Nicholas of Wiesbaden will be recalled. One of the new articles in Mathias Ramung's electoral oath, for example, stipulated that, in his courts, the bishop take cognizance of the status (*Ansehen*) of the respective litigants.[26] In 1423 the chapter had decreed that vicarages and other minor benefices in the cathedral could be conferred on nonnoble holders of licentiates, first degrees, or doctorates in theology, law, or medicine.[27] Two years later, Pope Martin V overrode the chapter's petition for confirmation of its exclusion of nonnobles from canonries by putting these degree holders on an equal footing with nobles in admission to the chapter.[28] The end result of this and other kinds of pressure was that the aristocratic canons received a better education, not that the number of nonnoble canons increased appreciably. In fact, in 1424, a year before Martin V's ruling, the chapter decreed that henceforth all canons had to complete two years of formal study.[29] It has been calculated that only seven of the forty to fifty canons appearing on the lists of the cathedral chapters of Speyer and Worms in the last half of the fifteenth century were not aristocratic.[30] In 1438 the statutes of the chapter of Speyer issued in 1423 were renewed almost verbatim.[31] The revised statutes of 1473 acknowledged the equality of degree holders in theology or law,[32] but in September 1483 Sixtus IV confirmed the ban on nonnobles.[33] The chapter probably revived the older statute in reaction to the Elector Palatine's attempts to secure canonries for learned theologians and lawyers at Heidelberg University, and on at least one occasion, Philip the Upright had to compel the chapter at Speyer to cease snubbing Canon Dr. Peter Wacker by threatening to withdraw his protection from the chapter.[34] Although the Council of Trent (1545–63) decreed that graduates in theology or canon law had to fill at least half the canonries in all cathedral churches, the chapter at Speyer, like most others in the empire, ignored this requirement in the seventeenth and eighteenth centuries.[35]

In the protracted negotiations with the bishops over *Schatzungen* the canons frequently sought to escape payment by suggesting that the tax be imposed on the bishop's peasantry. Almost invariably the bishops replied that their peasants were too poor to contribute and that the clergy's wealth could sustain the burden; and many times the bishops forestalled a potential impasse over this issue by threatening to interdict the chapter's revenues if it refused to yield. From the peasants' viewpoint, this was a curious reversal of the roles of prince and "representative assembly"!

The chapter's complaint, however, was not entirely unreasonable. The real value of clerical incomes seems to have been declining, while the number of clergy normally contributing to extraordinary taxation dropped for reasons already discussed. The Reformation enormously aggravated this problem, because most of the neighboring princes introduced the new religion. In addition, from the 1470s, the Electors demanded large sums of "protection money" (*Schirmgeld*) from the four collegiate churches of Speyer, which also had to pay a large proportion of the imperial and papal taxes.[36]

The whole relationship with the Palatinate perplexed the chapter from the later fifteenth century onward. In their inability to cope with the Electors' demands, largely for want of effective means with which to strike back, the canons complained much but always gave way, even at the height of Palatine incursions under Bishop George. When Bishop Philip II was left no alternative but to sever ties with the Elector, the chapter still advised caution. This policy of temporizing failed in the end. The chapter lost extensive properties and revenues upon the introduction of the Reformation, above all, tithes, patronage rights, and the church at Esslingen. Its hold on the bishops was probably weakened as a result of its contracted economic base and the defensive position in which it was put, successively, by the dependence on the Electors Palatine, by the Reformation, and by the century of turmoil that ended only in 1648.[37] This is only an hypothesis, however, the investigation of which is properly the subject of another study.

II

The papal provision of Raban von Helmstadt to the see of Speyer in 1396, instead of the majority candidate Gottfried von Leiningen, signaled a decisive triumph of the Electors over their old enemies, the counts of Leiningen. The Leiningens reacted accordingly. In 1397 near the episcopal town of Lauterburg, Count Emicho captured three papal legates, whom Rupert II ordered released.[1] Count Frederick in 1399 plundered the bishop's villages of Hanhofen and Dudenhafen in violation of the *Landfrieden*. Bishop Raban protested to Philip, count of Nassau and Saarbrücken, who was charged to enforce the peace, and by the judgment of the Elector Rupert III, Frederick had to indemnify the bishop with 340 fl. and £1.[2]

Raban enjoyed the favor of the Electors and under King Rupert became chancellor of the empire. In 1401 he purchased a house and an estate in Heidelberg for 700 fl.[3] The affairs of state carried him to imperial diets, to imperial cities to collect taxes, and to Italy to deliver money to the pope, subjugate Verona, and negotiate loans on Rupert's behalf from Venetian merchants.[4] He consequently had little time to administer his see, as both Rupert and he noted.[5] He personally loaned Rupert 9,400 fl.[6] For his years of service as chancellor and as councillor to the Electors and to Archbishop John of Mainz, he earned more than 18,000 fl.[7] and won a number of imperial privileges, among them the personal right to confer the royal prebends in the cathedral (1398, 1411), the *privilegium de non appellando* (1402), the right to tax royal subjects living in the principality (1404), the *preces primariae* in the diocese (1411), and permission to erect fortresses anywhere in the bishopric (1422).[8] In 1410 Rupert increased the redemption value of imperial possessions pawned to the bishopric by 20,000 fl.[9]

Despite the severe limitations on his time, Raban did accomplish a great deal for the bishopric while chancellor. He won high praise from Mathias Ramung.[10] Peter Anton de Clapis, in his tract *De principatus conservatione* (which he had been instructed in 1466 by Frederick the Victorious to compose for the benefit of Charles the Bold of Burgundy), held up Raban as the model prince.[11] Upon his elevation, Raban instituted regular, semi-annual diocesan synods,[12] and his work in religious reform is evident in numerous charters[13] and in his *Liber spiritualis,* the first of a series of such copybooks that was continued until the dissolution of the principality.[14]

He was equally successful in the secular administration of the principality. He initiated another two series of copybooks, the *Libri contractuum* in which were inscribed all manner of legal transactions of the bishops,[15] and the *Libri feudorum*, which recorded every enfeoffment, new or renewed, of episcopal property.[16] He undertook various improvements on the land,[17] especially to regulate the flow of water and to build dikes against the meandering Rhine.[18] He entered a union with King Rupert and Margrave Bernhard of Baden to reform the coinage.[19] He built fortifications at Jockgrim and tried to construct a castle at Hanhofen near Speyer, but the burghers regarded it as a menace and destroyed it.[20] Between 1404 and 1408 he bought from the lords of Ochsenstein half of one castle, a fourth of another; half of sixteen villages, three-eights of two others, a fourth of another; and the *Vogtei* with all appurtenant rights in another village for a total of 12,900 fl.[21] At some time, he bought part of the villages of Ruppersburg (with the *Vogtei*) and Königsbach.[22] He also bought the serfs of other lords living in his territories and, in manumitting serfs, required indemnification for the loss involved to the bishopric.[23]

The principles by which he governed the principality he set down in writing in 1439 for the benefit of his nephew and successor, Reinhard von Helmstadt, who he believed showed little aptitude for ruling well. He strongly admonished Reinhard to rely at all times on the advice of the *Amtleute* of the principality and of others of great experience and to avoid becoming the lackey of the cathedral chapter, because, he warned, "the canons would gladly be lord and master" of the principality at the bishop's expense. He should maintain a small entourage to cut costs and not garrison many horsemen in the villages, for it always resulted in harm to the peasants. He should remain on good terms with his subjects by keeping to a minimum exemptions from the *Bede,* by treating rich and poor alike, and by dispensing justice fairly and quickly. It was his first duty as a bishop to protect his clergy, and to that end he ought to station four or five horsemen at the cathedral provost's quarters to remind the burghers of Speyer of his readiness to defend the clergy. He should not hunt to excess, nor should he mix with women, for there was little profit in that. In foreign affairs he must above all avoid wars, consult with only those whom he trusted, and treat other princes with great deference.[24]

The general tone of the document suggests a meek and conscientious bishop. This is half true. Raban was conscientious, but he was not meek. His obstinacy in granting and regranting fiefs aroused considerable litigation, particularly on the part of the counts of Eberstein.[25] He proceeded so vigorously to vindicate and consolidate episcopal rights over monasteries that outside arbiters had to settle various disputes.[26] He summoned men of long memory to give dispositions in order to quash the claims of merchants at Landau, of the Palatine *Amtmann* at Germersheim to various fishing rights, and of Palatine subjects to exemption from certain of his tolls.[27] He tolerated no nonsense from the burghers at Landau when they refused to render him homage in 1426.[28] Friction with Speyer grew appreciably from about 1404 on, primarily over the issues of taxation of the burghers' property in the bishopric and the burghers' refusal to observe the old agreements respecting clerical sale of wine and exemption from the *Ungeld* and from secular jurisdiction. In 1417 with the help of the margrave of Baden and the count of Leiningen, the burghers razed the castle at Hanhofen, which the bishop had begun building in 1414. Successive settlements offered by the Elector, King Sigismund, and the archbishop of Mainz (in delegation from the pope) accomplished nothing. When war appeared inevitable, the burghers leveled the collegiate church of Saint Germain, which was situated on a knoll just beyond the walls and therefore presented considerable advantages to an attacker. Two weeks later, on 15 June 1422, Bishop Raban declared war and laid siege to the town. King Sigismund again intervened and forced both parties to accept Archbishop Conrad of Mainz's decision of 1420. This was in fact very favorable to the clergy, and although its ruinous effects on the town's economy have been asserted,[29] no scholarly evidence to that effect has been adduced. The town was also to pay 8,000 fl. in damages to the chapter, 10,000 fl. to the bishop, and 15,000 to Saint Germain's.[30]

Despite Bishop Nicholas' strenuous efforts to establish financial stability, annual payments on outstanding loans and pawns exceeded the bishop's income by 850 fl. when Raban entered office.[31] Raban set out to create a sound foundation for the principality's finances and did so before he resigned as chancellor of the empire in 1410. He could not have succeeded, however, without the close support of the cathedral chapter and of the clergy of the diocese. During his reign, Raban received the equivalent of eighteen years of annual *subsidia caritativa* on the clergy,[32] and most of this money was collected during his first decade in office.

In 1395 the four collegiate churches had, after considerable opposition, granted Bishop Nicholas a three-year *decimatio*.[33] This was apparently continued after his death. When it expired, the four collegiate churches of

Speyer in 1398 voted, in view of the great debts of the bishopric, a nine-year *subsidium caritativum* on the clergy of the diocese. The amount of the yearly contribution was to be in accord with custom except in the first year, when double the normal tax was collected.[34] The peasants were included in 1404, and King Rupert allowed direct subjects of the crown living on the bishop's lands to be included.[35] When the four chapters conceded a new, one-year *decimatio* in 1405, Rupert allowed the bishop to collect from the diocesan clergy settled in the Palatinate.[36] When difficulties in the collection arose, Nicholas of Königstein, the bishop's *officialis,* warned the clergy to remit the full amount within thirty days or face suspension from benefice and possible excommunication.[37]

Raban used this money to satisfy the principality's creditors, redeem pawns, and raise loans at more favorable rates. In 1399 the cathedral chapter negotiated with Raban the conditions under which he was to act. To meet the demands of six major creditors, the chapter permitted him to raise up to 8,000 fl. in loans and pawns on the strength of the possessions of the principality. The castles, however, could not be pawned without the chapter's express consent, and nothing could be sold or pawned for the same amount paid for its redemption. Whereas the bishop might convert loans to annuities, he could not take new loans at rates higher than had been usual.[38]

Raban had already pawned the *Amt* of Ketsch to the provosts of Holy Trinity and Saint Guido in 1397 for 2,100 fl. for the duration of their lives,[39] and in 1398 he pawned the *Bede* at Bruchsal for 4,000 fl. under the condition that the creditors could call for repayment only after four years and then with one year's notice.[40] In executing his agreement with the chapter, Raban in 1399 redeemed: the castle of Waibstadt and certain revenues from Hans von Hirschhorn and pawned them to his brother Wiprecht von Helmstadt for 1,000 fl.;[41] the tolls at Udenheim and pawned them to another brother, Reinhard, for 3,000 fl.;[42] and all the possessions of the principality on the left bank and pawned them for 7,800 fl. to Frederick, count of Zweibrücken and lord of Bitsch.[43]

After canceling many debts (in December 1400 he returned to the four chapters 500 fl. Nicholas had borrowed),[44] Raban consulted with his *Amtleute,* who worked assiduously with him to contract more favorable loans.[45] The reform took some time. For years they had to borrow money at rates varying between ten and six and two-thirds percent,[46] and on one occasion at eleven and a ninth percent.[47] By 1406, however, Raban had achieved a normal interest rate of five percent on the principality's loans.[48] He abolished the haphazard system of guarantors of the fourteenth century by pledging as guarantors the three main towns of the bishopric, Bruchsal, Lauterburg, and Udenheim, a practice maintained through the mid-sixteenth century. He followed Bishop Nicholas' policy and the chapter's advice in converting loans into nonheritable annuities.[49]

For the next twenty years, Raban devoted himself to the internal affairs of the principality. Although the attempt to regain Speyer caused some temporary financial stringency, the 10,000 fl. indemnity the city had to pay the bishop probably more than amply compensated for his expenses.[50] Aside from this there is little sign of difficulty in the principality's finances. The clergy was taxed again in 1426, and the count of Württemburg graciously permitted the bishop to include the diocesan clergy resident in his territories.[51] Before Raban set forth in the next year to join the imperial army's offensive against the Hussites in Bohemia, he requested all his subjects to contribute to a *Schatzung* to support his contingent, and he delegated his majordomo and the *Oberamtmann* of Lauterburg to negotiate with them. The results are not recorded.[52]

After 1430 Raban nullified the gains he had so carefully achieved. In that year the chapter of the electoral see of Trier had split in an election. The majority chose Jacob von Sirk, the minority, Ulrich von Manderscheid. Ulrich refused to accept the vote and revolted with some nobles. Both sides appealed to Martin V who instead provided Raban von Helmstadt, quite probably at the recommendation of the Elector Louis III.[53] Far from accepting the decision, Ulrich seized control of the principality's towns and thereby brought an interdict on the whole land. Raban went to war, but the issue was fundamentally resolved only in 1438, when Ulrich died and Raban came to terms with his greatest opponent, the count of Virnenburg. Shortly thereafter, under pressure from the chapter at Trier and feeling the effects of old age, Raban resigned the bishoprics of Speyer (1438) and Trier (1439).[54]

The war shattered the finances of both sees. Gustav Knetsch estimated that Raban left Trier a debt of 400,000 fl.,[55] and Bishop Reinhard, Raban's successor at Speyer, spent many years trying to repair the damage wrought at Speyer, on which Raban had had to rely until he could take possession of the principality of Trier. The hiring of large numbers of troops entailed enormous expenditures for retainer fees, horses, forage, armor and equipment, and sizable damage claims. Crop failure in 1431 compounded

Raban's problems, forcing him to borrow 4,000 fl. on short term to buy grain and other provisions.[56]

In 1430 Raban informed the chapter at Speyer that he had pawned four castles for 18,000 fl., justifying it on the grounds that he had contributed to the improvement of the principality a considerable part of the 18,000 fl. he had earned in the service of the emperor and the archbishop of Mainz, and that his provision to Trier concerned the principality, the empire, the priesthood, and the whole of Christendom, not merely himself and Trier.[57] The chapter gave ex post facto consent,[58] but now treated the bishop warily. Although in 1431 it accepted in pawn the tolls at Udenheim for 1,000 fl. for one year,[59] in 1433 it assented to his raising 8,500 fl. through pawns only on the condition that he redeem them within two years of the feast of Saint Thomas (21 December). Failure to do so would entitle the chapter to seize properties of equivalent value in the bishopric of Trier.[60] The tolls at Udenheim it allowed to be pawned for 300 fl. in 1434, but for no more than two years.[61] In 1436 Raban borrowed 6,000 fl. from the town council of Strasbourg, with repayment due on Christmas day. The chapter met with the bishop at Udenheim and assumed total responsibility as guarantor of the loan only after Raban handed over to it the town, castle, and tolls of Udenheim until the cancellation of the loan.[62]

These examples give only a partial impression of the measures used by Raban to finance his campaigns. He had to fall back on nearly all of the inadequate policies that had characterized fourteenth-century finance. Between 1430 and 1438 he raised 47,551 fl. in thirteen separate pawns of the castles, offices, and revenues of the bishopric.[63] In 1434 his fortunes seem to have reached a nadir. Hans von Hirschhorn renounced his castellany at Kestenburg, held since 1428, because he had not once received the grain and wine due him for his service.[64] Raban had to pawn his horse and some of his silver to the cathedral chapter for 511 fl.,[65] and his cousins Wiprecht and Hans von Helmstadt, the two *Oberamtleute* of the bishopric, had to pawn their own silverware for 366½ fl. to provide Raban with winter clothing.[66]

The principality's entire financial system broke down. Most loans continued to be made at five percent, although one each was taken at eight and a third, six and two-thirds, six and a third, five and seven-tenths, and five and a half percent.[67] More serious was the fact that many could be contracted only with the concession of supplementary interest payments or of retainerships to be held for the duration of the loan, or even for the lifetime of the creditor.[68] Raban had also to be content with a large number of short-term loans.[69] By 1433–34 his credit had sunk so low that his relatives borrowed 4,505 fl. for him.[70] From them he borrowed 6,000 fl. at five percent in 1434 and 8,000 fl. in 1435.[71] His relatives also backed Raban as guarantors of his loans and pawns, because the system of regular sureties he had established collapsed (as witness the chapter's negotiations with Raban for the Strasbourg loan cited above). In 1434 his relatives alone backed in excess of 14,000 fl. in loans to him.[72]

Although disposition of the bishopric reverted automatically to the papacy in 1438 by virtue of Raban's resignation, Raban had already arranged with the chapter to secure the appointment of his nephew Reinhard von Helmstadt (1438–1456), provost of the cathedral, in order to keep the creditors of the principality at bay.[73] Before his death in 1439, he instructed Reinhard to liquidate the debts he had contracted,[74] and indeed Reinhard did just that for most of his reign. The chapter apparently felt it safe only in 1446 to accede to Reinhard's request to pay off, on demand of the chapter at Trier, Raban's debts to the archbishopric of Trier,[75] and not until 1451 did Reinhard redeem Raban's silverware.[76]

Reinhard set about his task immediately. He borrowed 2,600 fl. at five percent from the chapter's operating funds to discharge a loan of 1,800 fl. taken at five percent plus a retainer fee of 75 fl. per annum from Eberhard von Hagenbach—a real interest rate, in other words, of 9.17 percent.[77] To redeem the four castles pawned originally in 1430 for 19,300 fl., he asked for an extraordinary levy on the clergy and the laity of the bishopric in 1439. The four chapters in convocation granted a *decimatio* on the revenues of all ecclesiastical benefices in the diocese. Certain items forming part of their endowment or income, such as vineyards and church fabric, were explicitly excepted from the computation of revenues; and the value of incomes in kind was defined, 1 fl. being set as the equivalent of 2 measures of wheat, 4 measures of settled grain, or 216 litres of wine. After Reinhard consulted further with the chapter and his advisers, it was decided that the bishop's burghers and peasants should also be included, but only at the rate of five percent of a year's net income. The bishop and various officials acting in his stead rode to the chief towns in each of the *Ämter* where the peasants were assembled to hear the reasons for the levy and discuss the methods of its collection, which was deputed to the bishop's majordomo, an *Unteramtmann*, and the keeper of accounts.[78] The bishop may have taken in more than he had expected, for in the following year he was able to pay out 36,300 fl. to return four castles and the office of *Schultheiss* at Landau to the principality.[79]

In 1441 Reinhard redeemed the castle at Obergrombach with 1,000 fl. borrowed from the chapter of Holy Trinity, money that was to have been repaid within a few months but was not in fact until 1724.[80] Another extraordinary tax was deemed necessary in 1444, not to continue the restoration of the bishopric's properties, but to improve its fortifications in view of the roving bands of marauders abroad in the land. The cathedral chapter authorized the bishop to spend 4,000 fl. on the castles and, to that end, with the other three chapters, consented to another *decimatio* on the diocesan clergy, particularly on the possessions of the cathedral chapter. Half was to be paid in 1446, the other half in 1447.[81]

In 1448 the chapter granted another tax of five percent on the clergy's incomes to facilitate the redemption of the castle of Hornberg from Gerhard von Talheim for 5,500 fl. The clergy in eight rural deaneries in Baden and Württemberg refused to contribute, however, and appealed to the pope. Margrave Jacob of Baden, who may well have inspired the resistance (since many of the deaneries were in his lands) negotiated a compromise. The clergy paid 700 fl. and agreed to ignore the papal decision, but this was in no wise to be construed as a recognition of the bishop's right to such exactions.[82]

There seems to have been one final extraordinary tax during Bishop Reinhard's reign. The accounts of the bishop's treasury office in Udenheim list an income of 4,708 fl. in *Freundschaftsgeld* ("fruntschafftsgelt") for the year 1453. The contributions of each of the towns, villages, and *Schultheissen* in the bishopric are listed, ranging from 500 fl. from Bruchsal to 5 fl. from a number of *Schultheissen,* not all of whom paid. The nature of the levy and its manner of collection are nowhere discussed. Some of the uses to which it was put are mentioned, e.g., 40 fl. to the burghers of Udenheim to dig a ditch ordered by the bishop, 19 fl. for the vineyard at Kisslau castle, 59 fl. to buy oats, 84 fl. for wheat, 8 fl. for wine, and 18 fl. for oil. Most of the money was spent on interest payments and the wages of the bishop's officials.[83]

Reinhard restored the soundness to finance that his uncle had achieved before his quest for Trier. He raised few short-term loans, and he never paid more than five percent interest on loans, and in one case only four percent.[84] The chapter helped by letting him borrow from its treasury 11,400 fl. at five percent.[85] He pawned only three castles and was careful to retain the right of usage, to have castellans take an oath of obedience to him, and to forbid alienation to anyone except the bishop or the chapter of Speyer.[86]

Shortly before his death in 1439, Raban sent his nephew the memorandum mentioned earlier on the proper way to govern the bishopric.[87] Reinhard, it seems, had offended the *Amtleute* of the bishopric by not consulting them. Raban summoned Reinhard to meet with him. Reinhard came but gave little heed to his uncle's words, thereby moving Raban to send him the rebuke.[88] Reinhard does appear to have been unnecessarily ostentatious in entering the village of Iöhlingen with fully fifty horsemen to receive the oath of obedience from his subjects.[89] Otherwise there appears to be little to substantiate Raban's allegations, both open and implied. Either anger caused Raban to distort matters, or else Reinhard took his uncle's rebuke to heart. In any case, he won the commendation of one of his successors, Mathias Ramung, although Mathias said that Reinhard's friends and others had dominated him.[90] The sources do not confirm this picture of weakness. It is understandable that they would not, but on the other hand, Reinhard demonstrated no lack of firmness in dealing with Speyer on various issues,[91] in revoking fiefs from vassals who had failed to render homage and fealty,[92] or in recalling cases appealed illegally by his subjects to the imperial court at Rottweil.[93] He would appear to have instituted regular bookkeeping procedures at Udenheim castle,[94] and he gave receipts to his officials for the accounts they rendered.[95] He undertook repairs and improvements throughout the principality,[96] including the development of mines.[97] Although he engaged in feuds in 1441 and 1450,[98] he followed his uncle's advice and avoided wars, which is more than can be said for the man who dispensed such sage counsel.

Friction with the Electors began during Raban's reign,[99] and in the 1430s the Elector's subjects took advantage of the disorder in the bishopric to pasture their pigs in the bishop's forests without paying the requisite fee.[100] Reinhard complained to Louis IV about the same problem.[101] He nevertheless renewed the protective treaty with the Elector in 1442 for five years.[102] The Elector at that time requested and got from the bishop and the four chapters a loan of 3,000 fl. for two years, on which he promised to pay an unspecified rate of interest.[103] It is doubtful whether the bishop and the chapters received either the principal or the interest, for the entry in the copybook bears no annotation to that effect. Loans altered or canceled, no matter how much later, were ordinarily struck through in ink, frequently with an accompanying comment on the date of liquidation and the bearer of the note at the time. If the original charter were still extant (which it was not in this instance), it would be slit diagonally both ways. This was but the beginning of such Palatine exactions.

III

Reinhard was succeeded in 1456 by his cousin Siegfried von Venningen, the master of the cathedral school and provost of Holy Trinity. According to Remling, he was chosen on the fourth ballot. The first three canons elected had declined to accept, and the dean had declared he would rather resign his office and prebend than become bishop. Siegfried, too, objected, but was persuaded to accept.[1] The papacy had already reserved the bishopric, but Calixtus III accepted the election on the condition that Siegfried would not sell, pawn, enfeoff, or otherwise grant or alienate the lands and holdings of the church of Speyer without the consent of the chapter and consultation with the pope.[2] Siegfried paid a total of 326 fl. 13s. 7d. in fees to the apostolic camera.[3]

Siegfried died in 1459 after only three years' rule, which was nonetheless sufficient to elicit the praise of Mathias Ramung.[4] In the main, he continued Reinhard's policies. All loans were taken at five percent save one at 4.86 percent.[5] All were long term except two, both in 1459: 2,000 fl. from the cathedral chapter for his *ad limina* visit to Rome, to be discharged within two years; and 1,500 fl. at five percent from the three collegiate churches of Speyer to permit the redemption of Wersau Castle, to be repaid in one year.[6] A few documents also indicate the chapter's progress in winning more rights in the governance of the bishopric. Before his departure for Rome in 1459, Siegfried appointed four regents to administer in his absence. One was his brother-in-law Conrad von Helmstadt, one of the two *Oberamtleute*; another was his brother Diether; and the other two were the master of the cathedral school and the chanter, Canons Reinhard Nix von Hoheneck zu Entzberg and Dr. John von Lisura.[7] The chapter's right of consent had advanced so far that it now extended to minor details of administration. When Siegfried assigned to Hans Schwarzkopff a lifetime pension of 3 measures of grain and ca. 216 litres of wine per year in recognition of decades of service to the bishopric, he did so with the consent of the chapter.[8]

On his death, the chapter elected Canon John Nix von Hoheneck zu

Entzberg, who was also provost of Worms and dean of Mainz, and came, unlike the other bishops of the fifteenth and early sixteenth century, not from the Palatinate but from Württemberg.[9] It was his misfortune to take sides in the celebrated *Mainzer Stiftsfehde* of 1461–63, and the wrong one at that. Diether von Isenburg had been deposed as archbishop of Mainz in 1461 by the pope, who then named Adolf von Nassau to the see. Diether won the support of the Elector Frederick the Victorious at a high price. Bishop John of Speyer first fought on Frederick's side against his enemies, but in 1461 John succumbed to great papal and imperial pressures and defected to Frederick's opponents despite Frederick's warning to remain at least neutral. John need not have participated at all, for the bishop of Worms successfully maintained neutrality in the face of the same pressures. On 30 June 1462 Frederick decisively routed his enemies at Seckenheim near Schwetzingen.[10] The spoils of war he demanded were considerable. From the bishopric of Speyer he obtained the *Amt* of Rotenberg, the castle of Wersau, and the exercise of all rights of high jurisdiction (the *Wildbann*) in the Lusshard forest—all lands and possessions immediately to the south of his own territory. The bishop could regain all these possessions for 32,000 fl. Frederick refused to negotiate directly with Bishop John and received all these holdings from the four chapters only after they had been transferred to their control.[11] During the war, Frederick had also captured the castle and village of Asbach, which were later granted to his natural son Louis as a hereditary fief by Bishop Mathias Ramung.[12]

The costs of war were substantially greater than this, however. John had hired a great many retainers, and many retainerships had to be granted in order to obtain loans at five percent.[13] Creditors lost confidence, so that the chapters at Speyer had to borrow 19,300 fl. for the bishop.[14] The bishop's chief accountant received no pay for four years.[15] The cathedral chapter had already loaned John 1,000 fl. at five percent in 1459,[16] and in 1462 it allowed him to take 1,000 measures of grain from its warehouse for one year.[17] In 1464, to satisfy the immediate claims of creditors, he pawned the castle and *Amt* of Kisslau for 9,800 fl.[18] Bishop Mathias estimated that John had contracted 10,000 fl. in debts, to 7,600 fl. of which the chapter had given express consent.[19]

It was all too much for John. He had been so viciously pilloried in Speyer during the war that he laid the city under interdict.[20] Frederick the Victorious had plundered a number of his villages after the battle of Seckenheim. His defeat had brought on a run against the bishopric's outstanding debts. Frederick undoubtedly did all in his power to get John to resign, which he finally did in 1464. The cathedral chapter "elected" as his successor Canon Mathias Ramung, licentiate in canon law and chancellor to Frederick since 1459. Because John had resigned, however, the papacy had the right of provision. The pope named Mathias Ramung.[21] After protracted negotiations with Mathias and the chapter, Bishop John received as an indemnity the castles and towns of Bruchsal and Obergrombach plus an annual pension in money and kind worth more than 1,600 fl. He died in 1467.[22]

Before his election, Mathias promised the chapter to try to return Bruchsal and Obergrombach to his control as soon as possible and had to provide compensation for the lost income the chapter normally derived from the Bruchsal Bede.[23] The chapter also imposed a stiff electoral capitulation that reflected its concern with the state of the principality and its determination to enhance its position in the bishopric. In court, the status of the persons involved should be considered, and the bishop was not to reverse the decisions of his judges. Two canons were to be appointed judges in the ecclesiastical court of Speyer, another the vicar-general, and only cathedral canons could be named provost, chanter, and custodian of the chapter as well as chamberlain and chaplain to the bishop. Castellans were bound to fulfill residence requirements. Only with the chapter's consent could the bishop grant exemptions from the Bede, tax the clergy, conclude treaties with other princes, or concede the right of free usage of a castle (one of the Electors' principal ways of encroaching on the rights of other lords). All revenues from ecclesiastical fines and fees were to be used to discharge the debts of the principality. To that end, the bishop should restrict household expenses. Wages, interest payments, and similar disbursements should be paid promptly to preclude feuds and wars. Two canons were to audit yearly the accounts of the Ämter and of the bishop's head accountant. Money collected in Schatzungen was to be handed over to two canons. The bishop's Amtleute must observe their duty to protect all under their jurisdiction, including monasteries. Should the bishop be taken prisoner, his Amtleute were to confer with two canons to decide upon a course of action, and all officials should remain at their posts until the return of the bishop or the installation of a new one. Finally, the bishop was to do his utmost to regain Rotenberg and its appurtenances from the Palatinate.[24]

Mathias protested vigorously against a number of clauses, especially the canons' auditing episcopal accounts, the chapter's governing the bishopric during an interregnum, its exempt jurisdiction, and the prohibition on the enfeoffment of reverted fiefs without the chapter's consent. Mathias maintained that the oath was unreasonable, violated his rights, and harmed the principality. The chapter gave way on several points, but basically retained the substance.[25]

Mathias went on to charge that although he knew the principality was thoroughly in debt, he had not realized before his election that it was unable to pay even the interest on these debts. Many of its creditors, particularly the Elector and the counts palatine of Veldenz-Zweibrücken, were demanding immediate repayment of their loans. Disclaiming any personal responsibility for this situation, Mathias placed the blame squarely on the chapter, which had assented to the creation of these debts. He therefore submitted to the chapter an *Exhortatio et protestatio specialis* to assist the bishopric in this crisis and cited the help rendered to their sees under similar circumstances by the chapters at Mainz, Cologne, Würzburg, Basel, and elsewhere. When the chapter suggested the possibility of other solutions, Mathias rejected sales, pawns, and loans as well as taxation of the clergy or the laity, both being already impoverished. The chapter ignored his repeated requests for help and his offer to transfer to its control the greater part of the principality to prevent further ruination. After taking counsel with his advisers and friends, Mathias in 1465 threatened the chapter, if it persisted in this attitude, with complete interdiction of all its incomes and permission to the principality's creditors to seize the chapter's lands as recompense.[26]

He also accused the chapter of complete negligence in the fulfillment of its liturgical and religious obligations and set out to reform the celebration of divine services in the cathedral.[27] He imprisoned a malfeasant cathedral vicar. The chapter asserted its right to punish him, and after negotiation, Mathias finally released him to the chapter, although only after the vicar had promised to pay the bishop 400 fl.[28] Mathias was not cynically holding up the possibility of reform merely to extract money from the chapter; he had punished other clerics throughout the diocese for similar reasons in 1465, and his ecclesiastical work of reform was well known.[29] On the other hand, his skillful use of rhetoric, however laudable its end, did less than full justice to the truth. On his entrance to office, the chapter borrowed 6,000 fl. and loaned him 5,000 fl., for the partial liquidation of which he left 3,500 fl. in his will;[30] it negotiated with him to retain the *Amt* of Kisslau, which Bishop John had pawned to the chapter for

9,800 fl;[31] and in 1465 Canon Raban von Helmstadt had, at Mathias's request, taken possession of the castle at Hanhofen.[32]

Still, the chapter appears not to have been cowed by Mathias's excoria-
tion. No evidence is preserved in the sources to indicate that Mathias did let
the creditors loose on the chapter's lands or that the chapter immediately
donated any large sums to appease the bishop. Indeed, contrary to his
insistence that the clergy and laity could not tolerate another tax, both were
taxed in different ways several times during his reign. The burghers and
peasants, in varying *Ämter*, several times paid double the normal *Bede*
instead of an extraordinary levy. In 1476, for example, the bishop collected 1,588 fl. in this wise.[33]

The extraordinary income from the clergy was even more complicated.
The bishop's accounts of 1468 list 5,539 fl. received from the chapter. Of
this, 1,000 fl. was collected in a *decimatio* from the clergy, another 1,000
fl. was handed over by the cathedral vicars on behalf of the chapter, and
the rest was turned over to the bishop by the chapter at various times.[34]
No explanation is given, but perhaps the chapter had at least yielded to
Mathias's imprecations. In the same year, Mathias took in 1,072 fl. donated
principally by ecclesiastical foundations and clergy, but also by nobles and
individuals from Speyer and elsewhere. The fifty-four entries included
the monasteries of Eusserthal (200 fl.), Saint Lambrecht (20 fl.), and
Neuenburg (2 fl.); the minters guild of Speyer and the records keeper
of Oppenheim; and fifty-two priests.[35] Another *decimatio* from the clergy,
imposed in 1476, produced 4,062½ fl. and £56.8.4, including 40 fl. from
the cathedral chapter.[36]

Mathias also struck at the chapter indirectly. In 1468 the four archdeacons, all cathedral canons and provosts for the four chapters of Speyer,
lodged a long list of violations of their prerogatives by the bishop's vicar-
general and *Amtleute*. The former they accused of usurping their rights of
jurisdiction both in courts and in ordinary ecclesiastical administration.
The bishop's officials, they charged, had declined to honor the mandates and
dispensations issued by the archdeacons' court and had actually threatened
to drown its representatives. The two recent vicars-general, both of whom
had served as *officiales* of the archdeacons, were asked to arbitrate. Although they found largely against the archdeacons, Mathias for some reason allowed a settlement to be concluded that restored most of the rights
of the archdeacons. It is fascinating to speculate whether this sudden re-

versal was connected with the 5,539 fl. he received from the cathedral chapter in the same year, but this is only a conjecture.[37]

One should not infer from the strained relations between Mathias and the chapter that Mathias was not a good bishop. Quite the contrary, he was one of the most able and vigorous men who ever occupied the see of Speyer. In a phrase reminiscent of Frederick the Great, he styled himself "the highest servant of his principality."[38] His considerable accomplishments as bishop and prince became even more impressive when one recalls that during his entire episcopate (1464–1478) he remained chancellor of the Electors Palatine. His efforts at religious reform in the diocese have been studied by Franz Haffner.[39] In secular administration he commissioned surveys of the population, possessions, and rights of the bishopric.[40] He revived the *Liber spiritualium*,[41] dormant since Bishop Raban's reign, and founded another series of copybooks, the *Libri officiorum,* to preserve the records of the bishop's officials and workers.[42] The maze of ordinances that flowed out from his chancery to the *Amtleute* stressed responsibility, economy, and efficiency in administration and covered every conceivable topic, down to the proper maintenance of the kitchen at Udenheim Castle, the bishop's chief residence.[43]

Mathias Ramung was, nevertheless, the chancellor of the Elector, and this may have been one of the primary sources of the chapter's friction with Mathias. Whatever fears the chapter had about Palatine domination of the bishopric were in time borne out. The Elector Frederick the Victorious had his *Amtleute* accompany Mathias when he made the rounds of his lands in 1465 to receive the homage of his subjects.[44] The results of Mathias's first discussions with Frederick in 1465 concerning relations between their *Ämter* on the left bank were not prejudicial to the rights of the bishop,[45] but in 1466 Mathias placed the principality under the special protection of the Elector and actually placed in his hands the entire bishopric with the exception of its eight principal castles and towns.[46] In October 1467 Frederick conceded that his subjects from Heidolsheim should continue paying tolls to the bishop at Langenbrücken, but only as long as Mathias was alive.[47] The Elector's purposes became obvious four years later when the crop failed. Frederick summoned delegates of the four chapters of Speyer to Heidelberg and ordered them to deliver 2,000 measures of grain to the Palatinate and forbade them to take any of their grain or fruit elsewhere.[48] Bishop Philip von Flersheim (1529–1552) firmly maintained over fifty years later that Mathias held the bishopric only to prepare the way for Frederick's son of the same name.[49]

Mathias's high position at the court of Frederick significantly increased his leverage against the chapter. His independence of action and his attitude toward the chapter are strikingly illuminated by a case from his feudal register. Although George Goler von Ravensburg had failed to receive his family fiefs from the bishop of Speyer within the customary one year of coming into his inheritance, Mathias nevertheless conferred them on him. The cathedral chapter objected, because it had enjoyed the incomes from the fiefs in the interim, but Mathias ignored the canons' complaints and regranted the fiefs. He did this despite the fact that, according to the feudal registry, George's father Martin had not received the fiefs from the hands of Bishops Reinhard, Siegfried, or John, although the fiefs had been duly conferred sometime in the past. Mathias, in other words, was scarcely bound in feudal law to comply with George's request, yet he insisted on snubbing the chapter and got away with it.[50]

Mathias's position was, nonetheless, ambiguous. He was a dependent of the Elector, and so was the bishopric, and the dependence of both on Frederick grew appreciably as a result of Mathias's entanglements with Speyer. This complicated series of events between 1465 and 1472 cannot be recounted here.[51] Suffice it to point out that Frederick the Victorious gladly gave Mathias all kinds of promises and alliances in 1466 when Mathias was determined to force Speyer to submit by blockade, but that he had no intention of helping Mathias realize that ambition and barely enforced the terms of his agreements with him. After Mathias had put the bishopric under the special protection of the Elector, Frederick informed the town council of Speyer that the members of the cathedral chapter should henceforth be considered Palatine subjects, and in 1470 the council wrote to the emperor that Frederick's hold on the bishopric was so strong that it was almost his own principality.[52] What they failed to note was that, in playing off Mathias against Speyer, Frederick had extended his protection to Speyer, thereby pulling the town into his orbit as well.

IV

Four days after Mathias's death the chapter elected Louis von Helmstadt (1478–1504), canon of Speyer and brother of Ulrich von Helmstadt, provost of Speyer, and of Nicholas von Helmstadt, master of the cathedral school at Speyer and provost of Worms.[1] Perhaps the canons hoped to loosen the tie with the Palatinate. Louis was no great adherent of Philip the Upright (1476–1508), but he could do little to escape the domination and gradual encroachments of his powerful neighbor to the north. A treaty concluded with Philip on 24 November 1491 leaves no question as to the strength of the respective parties. Its many provisions included exemption for the Elector's subjects from all tolls between Neuenburg and Weissenburg and for his subjects at Germersheim from tolls in the bishopric, free access for the Elector to the bishop's fortresses at Udenheim and Rheinzabern, and cessation of construction of a new tower on the fortifications at Udenheim.[2] Almost daily, violations of episcopal rights or lands occurred, which are often mentioned in the minutes of the cathedral chapter.[3] In 1495 Philip requested the four chapters and other foundations to contribute to a *Schatzung* in his territories.[4] Bishop Louis promised but did not pay 4,000 fl. to Philip as an aid for the War of the Bavarian Succession, and after his defeat in 1505 Philip canceled the obligation.[5]

The bishopric of Speyer was simply too small to resist such incursions, and during Louis's reign it was not the Elector alone who caused problems for the principality. Imperial taxes were levied in 1482 and 1495, for which the bishopric rendered 575 fl. and £10.1.17, and 1,185 fl. 1s. 3¼d., respectively.[6] For the Turkish tax of 1482, the bishopric had furthermore to provide twelve cavalrymen and twenty-four infantry, which was changed to twenty of each when Bishop Louis protested to Emperor Frederick III— hardly the revision the bishop had expected![7] In 1490 the bishopric became accidentally embroiled in the ongoing maneuvering among the emperor, the Elector, and the lower nobility and had to pay 2,000 fl. in damages to the Swabian League for which the bishop was not responsible.[8] In the papal tax of 1502, the bishopric was assessed at more than 2,850 fl.[9] In the same year the Bundschuh broke out in the bishopric.

In 1482 Louis took the occasion of his dispute with the emperor over the regalia to express his frustration before the myriad problems of the bishopric. He wrote that the twelve cavalry and twenty-four infantry he had been summoned to provide were disproportionate to his resources. He had attempted to collect an extraordinary tax from his subjects but had not succeeded because of crop failures and the poverty of his subjects. Monasteries refused to contribute and neighboring princes did not allow him to collect from the diocesan clergy of their lands. He estimated the bishopric's losses as a result of Bishop John's defeat at 100,000 fl.—a high price, he thought, to pay for obedience to the imperial orders to fight against the Elector. Disbursements to the principality's creditors exceeded income by more than 1,000 fl. He closed by commenting on the emperor's pettiness in refusing the regalia over such an insignificant issue as the right of collation to a benefice in a religious confraternity at the cathedral.[10]

Louis realized, of course, that the real issue was the bishopric's dependence on the Palatinate, which Frederick III sought to break, and that the empire could not be assigned primary responsibility for the misfortune of the bishopric, yet much of what he said was true. Resistance to extraordinary taxation on the part of the clergy and the surrounding lords who governed them was rising. The principality was burdened with debts and with demands from both the emperor and the Elector, who were extremely hostile to each other; the outlook for extrication from this predicament was for the moment not cheerful. The quarrel with Frederick III lasted until 1489, when after repeated summonses Louis appeared at the imperial court and received the regalia, for which he paid 4,000 fl. The emperor then asked for another 1,000 fl. for his campaign in Flanders. Louis sent 500 fl. plus two cavalrymen and ten infantry. In 1491 he remitted another 600 fl. at the emperor's request.[11]

Louis worked successfully to maintain solvency. In 1501 he issued an ordinance designed to reduce expenditures at the castle of Lauterburg.[12] He converted more loans to annuities than had any previous bishop and secured reduction of the interest rate on many other loans.[13] Most of the money he himself borrowed was taken at four percent.[14] The chapter cooperated closely with him. Shortly after he took office it contracted for him a total of 15,200 fl. in loans at five percent. He assigned the income of 1,000 fl. from the *Bede* at Bruchsal to pay the interest and help discharge the principal.[15]

From its own treasury the chapter presented another 4,700 fl. at five percent, which was liquidated only in 1747.[16] In 1482 impoverishment had forced the monastery at Weissenburg to sell to the chapter of Speyer the castle and village of Edesheim, together with high jurisdiction, several villages, and all appurtenances, for 17,500 fl., all of which the chapter in turn sold to Bishop Louis in 1487 for 4,500 fl., for which he gave the canons a promissory note. The canons had evidently taken a loss of 13,000 fl. in the whole transaction.[17]

The joint efforts of bishop and chapter were not adequate. Indeed, the purchase of another castle and *Amt* could only aggravate problems, however necessary it may have been to buy it back to prevent another lord from using it to erode the bishop's rights in the area. The bishop therefore fell back during his reign on extraordinary taxation again and again to meet his needs. In addition to the imperial taxes of 1482, 1495, and 1502, his subjects contributed to episcopal taxes in 1479, 1493, 1495, 1500, and 1502. With the exception of 1493, the levies were collected only from the clergy, but little information is available on any of these before 1502. In 1479 a ten percent tax on clerical incomes yielded 1,195 fl. and £249.19.0.[18] To raise the 2,000 fl. awarded in damages to the Swabian League in 1492, the bishop exacted a tax from his subjects, the only record of which is a charter from Louis acknowledging receipt of 100 fl. from the village of Iöhlingen, which was subject to the cathedral chapter, and declaring to its administrator, Canon William Flach von Schwartzenberg, that the bishop had no right to this contribution and that this constituted no precedent.[19] In 1495 the four chapters granted Louis permission to collect another *decimatio* from the clergy, but this conflicted with the Elector Philip's call to the four chapters and other ecclesiastical foundations to aid him in a subsidy. The bishop said he would ask the Elector to withdraw the request and, at the petition of the four chapters, canceled a loan of 200 fl. he had made to them. The outcome is not recorded.[20] The bishop received, in 1497, 230 fl. from the custodian of the cathedral chapter from a *decimatio* on the clergy that was still outstanding and, in 1499, another 40 fl. for the same reason.[21] Whether this refers to the tax granted in 1495, or to one of 1497, or to two separate taxes passed between 1496 and 1499, is open to conjecture. Another tax was collected in 1500, from which the bishop derived 729 fl. 11½d.[22]

The written minutes of the cathedral chapter, available from 1500 to the end of the eighteenth century, enable us to follow in great detail most of the levies voted from that time onward. An extraordinary amount of negotiation was involved in a *subsidium caritativum* to which the four chapters had consented in November 1500 but which Bishop Louis was not allowed to collect until May 1502. The origin of the delay lay not in some difficulty between the bishop and the chapter, but between the chapter on the one hand and the three collegiate chapters and the cathedral vicars on the other.

The three chapters objected that the cathedral canons had not executed the precise terms of their union in assenting to the tax. Bishop Louis concurred and admonished the chapter to do so. This was a minor dispute, however, which began late in 1501 and lasted but a few months.²³ The vicars caused much more trouble. Their power in the chapter had grown steadily since the fourteenth century, when they were assigned the administration of the chapter's operating treasury. This included all donations to the chapter made since the endowment of forty separate prebends as well as incomes from tithes, vacant prebends, and all dues. From it were made the daily disbursements of grain, wine, and money to those prebendaries in residence and also most of the loans to the bishops, ecclesiastical foundations, and others. It was called the *communis massa quotidianarum distributionum praesentiarum* (in German, *Dompräsenz*). In 1336 the chapter, with episcopal consent, transferred administration of this fund to the vicars. In deciding a dispute between the canons and the vicars in 1472, Mathias Ramung ordained that the vicars (of whom there were about seventy at this time) should select six of their number who were to adminster the fund and who had to be consulted on all changes and policies affecting it. In 1490 Bishop Louis gave them the right to wear ermine.²⁴ It was they who, between 1500 and 1502, held up the subsidy with protracted discussions over the 200 fl. to be given from the common fund.²⁵

These minutes also give an extremely detailed picture of the place the chapter occupied in the structure of the bishopric at the turn of the sixteenth century. It not only gave its consent to such important matters as extraordinary taxation, alienations of any kind, and the appointment of high officials; its rights of consultation and consent also reached down to the most intimate details of the bishop's administration. Although the chapter did not manage episcopal finances from day to day, it did exercise ultimate supervisory control and ordinary veto power over most minor as well as major matters, including approval of loans, increases in wages, and the conferral of pensions on servants of the bishops. Naturally, the chapter had slowly won these rights in the course of the fourteenth and fifteenth centuries, and this should have become clear in the discussions of the extant electoral capitulations and of specific cases illustrative of the constantly advancing power of the chapter. For all his independence of attitude and his opposition to the canons' auditing of his accounts, Mathias Ramung could not in the end prevent the canons from reviewing his books²⁶ or from being present at the conferral of most fiefs.²⁷ A few specific examples from the early sixteenth century will serve to show the extent of the chapter's participation in the governance of the principality.

Peter Nagel von Dirmstein, *Oberamtmann* at Bruchsal, had received a fief from the bishop, but in November 1500 the chapter rejected his request that it be made heritable in the male line.[28] In April 1501 Bishop Louis asked for a loan of 1,000 fl., to which the dean responded that Louis should try to raise one on the surety of his grain revenues.[29] A few weeks later he obtained permission to confer a pension on Martin Buwman of 6 fl., 6 measures of grain, and 500 litres of wine per annum.[30]

V

During the forty years after Louis's death in 1504 a struggle developed between the emperors and the Electors over the bishopric of Speyer. It was not clear at the outset who would triumph, and there were several reversals of fortune as the conflict developed. Rather than a constant duel, it was more a series of incidents that revealed the emperors' intentions to bring the bishopric back under their sway by making further alliance with the Palatinate costly and intolerable. It was not imperial power, however much revived under the Habsburgs, but the Reformation, that finally resolved the impasse.

The major defeat suffered by Philip the Upright in the War of the Bavarian Succession in 1505 at the hands of Emperor Maximilian, the margrave of Brandenburg, the dukes of Upper Bavaria and Württemberg, and the landgrave of Hesse led to the loss of Alsace and many other territories and was the deciding factor in the decision of the knights of the Kraichgau (the hilly country between the Black Forest and the Odenwald) against mediatization by the Electors Palatine and for the attainment of immediacy. Philip's defeat also brought on "a severe financial crisis from which the principality did not recover for several decades."[1]

It also presented a great opportunity to those small territories, imperial towns, groups, and foundations subject to the Palatinate in a "protective" relationship to loosen if not break those ties. The lower nobility of the Kraichgau severed their formal dependence on the court of Heidelberg. It was not possible for Bishop Louis's successor, Philip von Rosenberg (1504–1513), to go that far, but he did take advantage of the situation.[2] In 1505 he obtained cancellation of the 4,000 fl. that Bishop Louis had pledged but had not yet paid to the Elector.[3] The Elector was so desperate for ready cash that he let Bishop Philip redeem Rotenberg and the jurisdiction over the Lusshard forest for 12,000 fl., whereas Frederick the Victorious in 1464 had set the price at 32,000 fl.[4] Moreover, when the bishop wanted to include Palatine subjects settled in his lands in an extraordinary levy in 1505 to help cover the costs of redemption, the Elector overruled the protests of his *Amtleute* and acceded to Philip's request.[5]

At the same time, Maximilian applied pressure to the bishopric. Bishop Philip suffered from the gout or arthritis and toward the end of his reign had to be carried about. When Maximilian failed in August 1510 to persuade the chapter of Speyer to name, as Philip's coadjutor, the brother of Maximilian's private secretary, Paul Ziegler von Ziegelberg, bishop of Chur, Maximilian proceeded to redeem the imperial town of Landau, which had been pawned to Bishop Emicho in 1324. This was a rare step for an emperor. Ignoring Bishop Philip's offer to allow an increase of 5,000 fl. on the value of the pawn, Maximilian on 19 April 1511 released the burghers of Landau from their oath of obedience to the bishop, although the actual redemption was not fully paid until 4 April 1517.[6] Maximilian also revoked from the bishop of Speyer the honor of presiding over the ecclesiastical bank in the imperial diet and conferred it on the bishop of Eichstätt, about which degradation the bishops of Speyer registered vain protests for more than a century.[7]

Bishop Philip's death in 1513, curiously, did not precipitate a direct confrontation between the emperor and the Elector. Between 7 and 12 February the eighteen canons in residence received the representatives of the Elector and of Maximilian, who was at that time nearby in Landau. A majority of the canons had already decided for Philip von Flersheim, but at length they were prevailed upon by the Elector and the emperor to elect the Elector's brother George, who was barely twenty-seven years old. He ruled until 1529, while his brother Henry occupied the see of Worms from 1523 to 1552. Under them, Palatine influence on the two sees reached its acme.[8]

Although much of the literature covering George's reign is polemical or at least prejudiced, it can be said in fairness that George was neither a good bishop nor a good prince. He was essentially a weak man unable to cope with the progress of the Reformation or the outrageous demands of his brother the Elector. When he did once object, he was curtly reminded that he was a count palatine first and bishop of Speyer second.[9] Thus in 1521, for example, the Elector won out in a dispute over the inheritance of bastards who died intestate. The bishop adduced an imperial charter of

1510 conceding the bishop the right of confiscation for all such cases arising in the bishopric, but the Elector had received a more recent privilege granting him the estate of bastards who died without issue and last will. According to the settlement, the bishop was to get only one-fifth of the estate, the Elector the remaining four-fifths, in such instances in the bishopric.[10] Another agreement negotiated on the same day concerned the Elector's right to establish tolls anywhere in the bishopric. Despite the protests from the bishop and the chapter, the arbiters ruled that those that the Elector had erected on the left bank should remain, while those on the right were to be dissolved.[11]

Far more blatant were the Elector's financial exactions from the clergy and the laity. The Turkish subsidy voted by the Reichstag in 1526 moved the Elector to demand 7,200 fl. from the four chapters of Speyer, which he increased to 8,200 fl. when the collegiate chapters protested.[12] After the Peasants War, the Elector demanded a total of 40,000 fl. from the bishop's peasants.[13] These were but some of the more noteworthy infringements and encroachments on the part of the Elector.

The increase of Palatine and imperial exactions, expenditures like the 14,000 fl. spent to buy the castle of Madenburg in 1517,[14] and both the losses of revenue and the expenses resulting from the Bundschuh of 1502 and from the Peasants War all combined to cause Bishops Philip I and George to petition the chapter frequently for extraordinary levies. In April 1505 Philip requested permission to tax the clergy to facilitate redemption of Rotenberg from the Elector and payment of the fees for confirmation of his election and reception of the regalia. He rejected out of hand any suggestion that the tax fall on the peasantry. Although the four chapters granted it within two weeks, negotiations dragged on until the end of 1506 over a number of related matters, among them the rural deans' insistence on the inclusion of the parishes incorporated into the cathedral chapter's operating fund.[15]

In 1510 Philip desired a *subsidium caritativum* from the clergy to help cover the more than 6,000 fl. the emperor had caused him to spend within a few years. The chapter asked whether the bishop's subjects were also to be taxed and whether the subsidy should be one of five percent, rather than ten percent. Philip replied that he wanted a full *decimatio* from the clergy alone. The four chapters at first demurred, but gave way before his intransigeance in November. Although the levy yielded 2,253½ fl. in 1511 alone, opposition to its collection arose in the following year. Three rural deaneries refused to contribute, arguing that the bishop had "no legitimate mandate" and that the tax imposed "an intolerable burden" on the clergy. The bishop appealed to the archiepiscopal court at Mainz and, after losing there, to Rome. The pope appointed the dean of Saint Paul's collegiate church in Worms to adjudicate the matter; he ruled in favor of the bishop.[16]

In November 1515 the four chapters consented to a *decimatio* on the clergy provided it be collected in two installments.[17] In February 1516 Bishop George wanted to buy the castle of Madenburg from the duke of Württemberg to prevent its falling into the wrong hands. To raise the necessary 14,000 fl. he requested a general *Schatzung* on the subjects of the principality, clerical and lay, or some alternative course. The chapter met with the bishop twice and, after using the occasion to discuss the household expenditures and to recommend immediate reception of the regalia, granted George permission to negotiate with the duke in secret and to raise loans that were later to be discharged with the revenues from the levy. The provost, Dr. Erph von Gemmingen, declared himself ready to lend the bishop 3,000 fl. if the castle and *Amt* of Obergrombach were granted to him for life. The chapter agreed to this arrangement together with 200 fl. per annum income for the provost on the condition that the *Amt* revert to the bishopric automatically upon his death. The chapter also showed itself willing to guarantee 5,700 fl. in loans raised in Frankfurt, and other loans were also taken. The chapter strongly emphasized that the levy be used only for this purpose and that it created no precedent. The bishop promised to exact it within three months after the conclusion of the sale, and three canons were deputed to collect it. It would appear from later references in the minutes that the tax was imposed on the clergy alone (because it was called a *decimatio*) and that the chapter closely supervised its usage and was still disbursing money to the bishop as late as June 1520.[18]

The costs of Bishop George's attendance at the imperial diet in Nuremberg and its assessment for the coronation of the emperor and for the maintenance of the *Reichsregiment* (the "imperial governing council") caused George in January 1523 to request taxation of the peasantry, although he also suggested that the clergy be taxed to prevent dissension among his subjects. The four chapters consented to the latter and collection began in February even while the cathedral chapter discussed exemption for certain of its lands. Two canons were instructed to hold the money until further notice.[19] Meanwhile the bishop rode out to the main villages in his lands on the left bank to present the reasons for the tax to the assembled peasants and burghers, hear their objections and grievances, and discuss with them the amount and mode of payment. The majordomo and other officials from the bishop's court undertook similar negotiations on the right bank.[20] Bishop George brooked little opposition. When the cathedral chapter attempted to obtain exemption of its lands not subject to the *Bede*, George imprisoned some villagers of Gernsheim, one of the places in question. Although he released them a week later at the chapter's request, he remitted only one half their assessment.[21] The assertion of the dean and the chapter of the aristocratic collegiate church at Bruchsal (formerly of Odenheim) of their freedom from such levies elicited a threat from George to use force to enforce his rights. The chapter quickly offered to pay 50 fl.[22] The rural deaneries in the margravate of Baden (at Durlach, Gernsbach, and Pforzheim) also refused to pay, but they too were required to contribute according to a decision rendered against them in 1530 by the court of Mainz.[23]

On 13 January 1529 Bishop George appeared before the chapter with the provost and his majordomo and chancellor to present a statement on the deepening financial problems of the principality. After all disbursements on the outstanding debt of the bishopric, he contended, he had scarcely 3,000 fl. remaining to maintain his princely position. (Actually, this sum greatly exceeded normal court expenditures by the bishops, and the chapter had had to reprimand George frequently for his excessive household budget.) Many buildings were delapidated and wanted repairing, and the fortifications at Udenheim needed substantial improvements. The spread of the Reformation had resulted in the loss of many revenues, in particular of more than 1,000 fl. ordinarily derived from the exercise of ecclesiastical jurisdiction. Moreover, expenses for imperial assessments of all sorts had amounted to more than 30,000 fl., and a delegation sent to the emperor in Spain cost more than 700 fl. alone. He therefore requested a *decimatio* from the clergy of several years duration. The four chapters granted it in July, but shortly thereafter George began to foresee difficulties in collection in Württemberg. He proposed that the four chapters instead put at his disposal 500 fl. per annum for four years. They did this, but a four-year levy on the clergy was still voted. They also accepted George's suggestion that they investigate the responsiveness of the rural deaneries.[24]

George died on 28 September. His premonition proved correct. His successor experienced a great deal of opposition from several quarters to the collection of this tax.

VI

The election of Philip von Flersheim (1529–1552) by the cathedral chapter marked a decisive shift away from dependence on the Palatinate.[1] Elector Louis V (1508–1544) had tried to secure the election of another member of the family to the see but was soundly rebuffed. Unlike Bishop George, who had had in his entourage two Lutheran sympathizers and whose suffragan bishop and personal chaplain had gone over to the new persuasion,[2] and who had been consequently severely warned by the cathedral chapter in 1528,[3] Philip was a solid churchman as well as a learned humanist and was highly respected by Johannes Eck and Cardinals Vergerio, Morone, and Poggio.[4] Moreover, he had reason to bear ill feelings toward the Palatinate. The Elector's influence had prevented his election at Speyer in 1513 and at Worms in 1523, where Philip had been named coadjutor with the right of succession with papal and imperial approval. In 1523, in crushing the revolt of the imperial knights under Ulrich von Hutten and Franz von Sickingen, Louis had dealt harshly, not only with the von Sickingen family, but also with the von Flersheim family who, as next of kin, were dismissed en masse from Palatine offices and fined 1,000 fl. Philip's efforts to moderate these penalties had been unavailing.[5]

Nonetheless, Philip proceeded cautiously in his relations with the Elector for some time. As late as 1541, Cardinal Morone considered him "an ally and almost a subject of the Palatine Elector."[6] Philip's secretary, George Brentz, had written to Philip: "I see very well that Heidelberg will not rest until it has gobbled up the little principality of Speyer."[7] Philip realized this perfectly well,[8] but he also knew he could do little except resist where possible. On entering office, he declined the Palatine offer, which Bishop George had accepted, to buy the village of Ruppersburg in exchange for 5,000 fl. of the 40,000 fl. exacted from the bishop's subjects after the Peasants War.[9] In 1532 he expelled Palatine officials by force from two villages in the bishopric after repeatedly demanding their withdrawal.[10] Ordinarily, though, he was in no position to reject the Elector's demands. In 1529 Louis seized the estate of Bishop George at Mainz (where George had retained the office of provost) and answered Philip's protestations with a demand for 700 fl. for the return of George's horses, clothes, silver, and jewels.[11] The protective treaty was renewed in 1531 and 1544.[12] In 1532 Louis demanded 4,500 fl., subsequently lowered to 1,500 fl., from the cathedral chapter on the basis of the decision of the diet at Augsburg permitting him to tax his subjects to raise money for the Turkish campaign.[13] In 1536–37 4,000 fl. was "borrowed" from the bishopric, but there exists no record of its ever having been repaid.[14] The Elector also obtained in 1537 complete exemption for his subjects in the lordship of Guttenberg from four of the bishop's tollstations.[15]

The Elector also opposed participation by the diocesan clergy in his lands in the four-year tax voted in 1529, which Philip inherited from Bishop George. In 1530 Philip met with Louis at Germersheim to express his resentment over this and mentioned that during Bishop George's reign neither the Elector nor the duke of Württemberg had obstructed the collection of levies from the clergy and that resistance in the margravate of Baden had recently been defeated after seven years of litigation. He received only a vague reply from Louis' majordomo.[16]

Philip, in the first decade of his reign, concentrated on imperial affairs and the improvement of the principality. He attended ten imperial diets between 1529 and 1537 and served as advisor to Charles V and his brother Ferdinand.[17] Between 1529 and 1541 he spent, by his own reckoning, 8,076½ fl. 7s. 4d. on imperial diets and 7,943 fl. on subsidies against the Turks.[18] In the bishopric he worked to improve conditions and especially episcopal incomes. Shortly after taking office he summoned representatives of the clergy to Bruchsal to discuss the four-year subsidy granted in July and, despite the opposition of the Elector and of the rural deaneries in Württemberg, he took in a total of 8,110 fl. 14s. 1d.[19] A *Schatzung* in 1532 to meet the assessment in the latest Turkish levy brought in 8,468 fl., of which Philip remitted only 3,975 fl. to the empire.[20] He also spent considerable sums on improvements of all sorts, considerably increased incomes of grain and wine,[21] conducted a census in 1530,[22] and commissioned surveys of the whole situation of the principality in 1531 and 1541.[23] The interest rate on loans he maintained at the four to five percent prevalent under Bishops Philip I and George.[24] The chapter, mindful of George's extravagance and company, had inserted in Philip's capitulation clauses to the effect that the bishop should heed reproofs from the chapter concerning household expenses and should appoint only two canons to adminster the bishopric should he be absent more than fourteen days.[25] The number of canons assigned to oversee the principality's debts and disbursements was also increased from two to six.[26]

At no time had Philip forgotten the progress and the problem of the Reformation. But whereas the margrave of Baden broke openly with the church by 1525, the Elector Louis V chose not to act so precipitately. Although he harbored Lutherans at his court and promulgated a very strong reform ordinance in 1538, he dared not take the final step. Only in his son Frederick II (1544–1556) was the gauntlet finally thrown down to the emperor and, more pertinently, to Bishop Philip.[27] The Reformation snapped the tie between the Palatinate and the bishopric, because the bishop and the chapter had to act to obviate the threat of secularization or mediatization. It has been argued that, even in the fifteenth century at the height of their power, the Electors would have had great difficulty mediatizing the bishopric, primarily because the diocese extended into the margravate of Baden, the duchy of Württemberg, and many other smaller territories. Nevertheless, the bishopric had been effectively mediatized for a good seventy-five years, and secularization, to the extent of expropriation of ecclesiastical lands, incomes, and rights within the Palatinate, was not merely possible but was carried out. Philip foresaw the danger and secured imperial confirmation of all episcopal privileges and possessions in 1541.[28]

Events moved quickly after Frederick II declared himself on the side of the Reformed. He seized the collegiate church (formerly abbey) of Weissenburg, and Philip prevented its total secularization only by buying it and all its lands from Frederick in 1546 for 36,000 fl., although Frederick had originally wanted 45,000 fl.[29] In 1546, Frederick, still technically "protector" of the bishopric, aided the duke of Württemberg in raiding the bishop's villages.[30] By 1548 Frederick had extracted from the bishopric, by Philip's estimate, a total of 100,000 fl.[31] This plus a host of undisguised violations and usurpations of his rights finally moved Philip to file a lengthy statement of grievances against the Elector at the Reichstag of Augsburg in 1548. Frederick, in 1551, reproached Philip for being more hostile to the Palatinate than any bishop had been for over a century, and he reminded him of the fate of Bishop John II, whose deposition Frederick I had secured.[32] A year later he occupied and plundered many villages in the principality, ostensibly to defend them against Margrave Albert Alcibiades.[33]

Philip's financial reforms correspondingly suffered a decided setback in the 1540s. Revenues were hurt by the Reformation, which was introduced into nearly all the surrounding territories; by the duke of Württemberg's attack in 1546; and above all by the invasion of Albert Alcibiades in 1552, who demanded 117,000 fl. from the bishopric.[34] Meanwhile, imperial requisitions had increased substantially, and Philip thought them, though necessary, too heavy for the bishopric. The emperor and his brother requested 4,000 fl. in 1544, 6,000 fl. for the Schmalkaldean War, 4,500 fl. in 1548, and 13,000 fl. in 1552 for the league against the Protestant princes. For just the imperial tax against the Turks, Philip had paid out nearly 8,000 fl. between 1529 and 1541 and another 11,500 fl. thereafter.[35] Simultaneous taxation of his subjects for the needs of the empire and of the principality was necessary but seems not to have garnered much. Negotiations with his subjects over a *Schatzung* voted by the Reichstag in 1541 proved bootless.[36] Saint Guido's contributed a mere 100 fl. to each of the *subsidia caritativa* of the clergy in 1542 and 1545, although it did give the bishop 661 fl. in 1548.[37] On the basis of the recess of the Reichstag of Augsburg in 1549, all parishes and religious houses in the diocese were to pay another tenth, but the bishop as usual had great difficulty collecting it.[38] In 1567 the villagers of Neibsheim argued before Bishop Marquard that theirs was the only community taxed in 1551 by Bishop Philip, who had promised that they would be spared in the next levy.[39]

Just as he had anxiously watched developments in Heidelberg in the 1530s before seeking protection from the emperor in the 1540s, Philip refused to act decisively against the progress of the Reformation until the 1540s. For nearly a decade, the cathedral chapter had demanded severe punishments for peasants withholding tithes. Philip, justifiably nervous about the peasantry after the Peasants War, which had swept across southern Germany in 1525, submitted the case to Worms and Heidelberg for review.[40] In 1542, however, he finally issued a strong ordinance in which he declared harsh penalties for failure to render tithes to the four chapters of Speyer and ordered his *Amtleute* to execute this decree rigorously.[41] Stiefenhöfer ascribed Philip's change of policy to the chapter's threat not to contribute to the Turkish levy if he did not yield.[42] One might suggest that Philip had already undergone a change of heart, as evidenced by the imperial confirmation of the see's liberties and holdings in 1541 (which included a detailed listing of the properties of the church of Speyer) and by the determined steps Philip took in 1542 to extirpate heresy from his lands.[43]

How did Philip get along with the chapter on the whole? The evidence is complicated. Philip proved unable to force the chapter to alter some terms of his electoral capitulation, which contained several innovations described earlier.[44] As in most previous episcopates, the chapter continued to tighten its grip on episcopal administration, though largely in the interests of the principality. In 1538, for instance, the oath of Hans Blicker Landschad von Stein to the chapter contained promises to protect and defend the clergy under his care, to inform the chapter if the bishop contracted a loan or pledged a town or castle of the principality as guarantor for a loan, and to accept as his substitute while on vacation no one who could not produce a signed and sealed certificate from the dean and chapter of Speyer.[45] Philip was by no means a weak man, however. He sharply rebuked the chapter of Saint Guido in 1530 for rejecting his nomination to a prebend there,[46] and he rejected the cathedral chapter's claim to exemption from the four-year levy conceded in 1529.[47] In a dispute with the chapter in 1541 over the use of a prebend to supply part of the income of his suffragan bishop, Philip finally compelled the chapter to bow by suggesting he would punish the provost for nonresidence and resort to the papal legate and the imperial diet.[48] The chapter also complied with his wish in not selling its tithes at Esslingen until 1550 for 3,000 fl., whereas it could have received 24,000 fl. for them in 1530.[49]

How did the Reformation affect the bishop and the chapter and their relationship? Clearly it placed them on the defensive. By mid-century all the monasteries and nearly two-thirds of the churches and benefices in the diocese had been lost,[50] and the bishopric was surrounded by Protestant princes eager to gobble up the remainder. Ironically, the Reformation compelled the bishop to be more concerned than ever before with the "secular" and the "political" (to use common but quite misleading terminology), for he could effectively maintain Catholicism only in areas he governed temporally. The Reformation also forced the bishop and the chapter closer together, despite their frequent difficulties, especially since the chapter remained firmly Catholic and, unlike the highly aristocratic chapter at Strasbourg, did not divide into Catholic and Protestant factions. The loss of its revenues and properties in the Reformation seems to have made the chapter more dependent on the bishop, at least so far as their protection and collection were concerned, and may well have weakened its place in the principality simply by making it less able to play a leading role in its finances. It does not lie within the scope of this study, however, to answer this question or the question of whether the Catholic princes' position vis-à-vis their estates was enhanced by the Reformation,[51] for it becomes very difficult to distinguish the consequences of the Reformation as such from those of the Thirty Years War and, later, the rise of absolutism.

By 1552, a long chapter in the history of the bishopric had come to an end, and entirely new circumstances had to be faced: dangers from without, wars, extortionate demands on the bishopric, costly levies, and the problem of a standing army to defend the bishopric. The chapter would have to devise new solutions to these problems in the following centuries.

Chapter 5

The Representation of the Other Estates

I

The activity and development of the cathedral chapter as the functioning diet of the principality of Speyer between the thirteenth and the mid-sixteenth century have been studied, in the last three chapters, against the background of the general history of the bishopric; the complex reasons why the chapter achieved such a preeminent place in the structure of the bishopric were discussed in chapter one. Admittedly, the cathedral chapter took full advantage of its position to safeguard and extend its rights and privileges and was often at odds with the bishops over such issues, but in fairness it must also be emphasized that the chapter devoted much energy to the major problems of the bishopric in the late Middle Ages: frequent episcopal recklessness and squander, preservation of the territorial integrity of the bishopric, maintenance of a stable financial system, and provision for uninterrupted governance during interregna. Although limited in its viewpoint, its resources, and its power, it grappled with these predicaments, and, on balance, did so successfully. It insisted consistently on the bishops' observance of the general interests of the principality and their accountability to the chapter therefor. To that end, it devised procedures for the smooth assumption of control during vacancies or absences of the bishops, effectively forbade sales and lengthy pawns of episcopal properties, required its assent to virtually all significant acts of the bishops, loaned the bishops great sums of money and negotiated other loans when necessary, and agreed to an uncommonly large number of heavy extraordinary taxes.[1] Furthermore, it ordinarily contributed a significant portion of the amounts collected in these levies. Although at times it sought to shift the burden of a particular tax from the clergy to the peasantry, it does not appear to have rejected the bishops' requests in the end except in 1351 and 1395, when it was overruled, respectively, by the pope and by outside arbiters.[2] It never claimed general exemption from *subsidia caritativa,* unlike the cathedral chapters at Eichstätt in 1259, Halberstadt in 1311, Bamberg in 1328, and Würzburg in 1495.[3]

The canons, needless to say, were hardly as public spirited or as selfless as their actions might imply. The diverse origins of their ever stronger role in the government of the bishopric were analyzed in chapter one: the definition of a bishopric, by the ecclesiastical reformers of the twelfth and thirteenth centuries, as a corporation consisting of a bishop and his chapter alone; the great rights and responsibilities conferred on the chapter in consequence; the increasingly aristocratic composition and character of the chapter and the accentuation of a natural drive toward greater power; and the significant degree of coincidence between the interests of the chapter and those of the bishopric. This last aspect is rather important, for the chapter often had no choice except to help the bishops so far as it could, nor were the bishops always the villains of the piece. Their conduct and their outlook were often wholly admirable in contrast with those of the canons; yet it was almost always the bishops who, for whatever reason, precipitated the crises. The bishops, in other words, initiated policies, while the canons reacted to them. Other difficulties grew out of the limitations inherent in late medieval finance, the structure of bishoprics, and the like. The chapter confronted problems of both sorts and, to reiterate, devised reasonable solutions to them. In this respect it makes little difference what its motives were so long as it responded and with success. The chapter existed permanently; it was willing and obliged to act for a variety of reasons; and it was capable of acting effectively. The bishopric was fortunate in having such an institution.

The similarities between the work of the chapter and that of formally convened diets in late medieval Germany are striking. According to Carsten, the main purposes of these assemblies were to aid princes in overcoming chronic financial difficulties and to check warfare among the members of the ruling house and the deleterious effects flowing from it.[4] The latter condition did not obtain in the strict sense in ecclesiastical principalities, which were not technically heritable and were indivisible in canon law, but analogous situations in the form of contested elections frequently occurred and were often financially disastrous. To be sure, differences between the chapter at Speyer and the ordinary diet existed in both form and function. The chapter was a permanent, independent institution that met as it desired; the diet depended on convocation by the prince. Unlike many diets, the chapter never assumed full responsibility for the debts of the principality, and consequently did not take over the episcopal financial administration to handle princely indebtedness.[5] In the enormous number of *subsidia caritativa* and *Schatzungen* it granted, it did, however, implicitly acknowledge the duty of the country (*Land*) and especially of the clergy to support the bishops. It also exercised an extensive and thoroughgoing control over episcopal finance, and in fact over the whole government and administration of the principality, the like of which was to be found in no ordinary diet.

It is therefore not inappropriate to paraphrase the old question of German parliamentary historiography: Did the cathedral chapter at Speyer "represent" the *Land*? The answer depends, of course, on what one means by "represent." Max Weber distinguished four different kinds of representation according to the organization of authority in corporate groups: appropriated representation, as in monarchies; representation by estates; instructed representation; and free representation.[6] It is necessary to draw even further distinctions, particularly in the case of a principality in which the work of a formally constituted parliament was largely executed by the cathedral chapter and which consequently partook of some features of "appropriated" representation.[7] It is essential to ask who was represented by the activity and decisions of the chapter and to differentiate what interests were represented, whether they were those of the *Land* as a whole or those of one or more particular estates. The subjective questions should also be considered, i.e., to what extent the chapter viewed itself as "representing" the other estates and, conversely, to what extent the estates regarded the chapter as competent to act for them and accepted its decisions as binding. Finally, one must ask what other institutions, procedures, and customs in the bishopric served to represent particular estates and hence to complement or, perhaps, to counterbalance the work of the cathedral chapter.

It should be clear from the foregoing chapters that the cathedral canons very much acted for, defended, and advanced the common interests of the estates of the bishopric of Speyer in the late Middle Ages, above all those affecting the preservation of territorial, financial, and administrative stability and the restraint of princely excesses. It should be no less evident that it was not competent to vote extraordinary taxation on its own authority. From the earliest days, the granting of a *subsidium caritativum* or a *decimatio* was a matter for the common action of the four chapters at Speyer. The cathedral chapter's relations with the three collegiate churches were occasionally strained, and during the fifteenth century their right to act for the clergy of the diocese was increasingly questioned by monasteries and by the prebendaries in the rural deaneries. The members of three such deaneries in 1511 openly denied the competence of the four chapters "acting for and representing the whole of the clergy of the city and diocese of Speyer," asserting that they had "no legitimate mandate" to do so.[8]

Schatzungen on the bishops' nonclerical subjects were not consented to by the four chapters, but again the cathedral chapter's approval did not suffice. Whereas the evidence in most cases is too scanty to support the conclusion that the burghers and the peasants were always consulted in such matters, they were directly consulted on certain major levies, as in 1439 and 1523,[9] and the minutes of the cathedral chapter indicate that the bishop and the chapter often tried to assess their possible responsiveness and reaction to these requests.[10] More often than not, the bishops refused to countenance suggestions from the chapter that the peasantry be taxed instead of the clergy.[11] For their part, the peasantry had no deep affection for the chapter, as became evident in the Peasants War.

Despite its far-reaching hold over the administration of the bishopric, the cathedral chapter had nothing to do with the dispensation of justice in the secular courts of the bishops except that canons sometimes sat with trained jurists and nobles, both informally as arbiters and also as judges on the supreme court (*Hofgericht*).[12] This lack of involvement in the judicial system was also true of most diets in the empire,[13] but it is nevertheless interesting to compare this with the importance of judicial activity in the English Parliament, the Aragonese Cortes, and the Polish Sejm. The petitionary process, again so significant in the rise of Parliament, affected the cathedral chapter at Speyer only insofar as the bishop might solicit the chapter's advice, but as a rule he seems not to have been bound to do so.

Indeed, the cathedral chapter capped a complex network of institutions and practices that had evolved to insure adequate representation of the various estates before the bishops and to insure preservation of the estates' legitimate interests and rights. The chapter occupied a decidedly ambiguous middle position between the bishops and the estates, a problem that came to the fore in other ecclesiastical principalities when formal estates general were convened. Although in most principalities the cathedral chapter sat as one of the estates, it stood with the princes over against the estates in Mainz and also in Trier, except in 1542–44.[14] In the bishopric of Speyer, the question never arose, but the peasantry in 1502 and 1525, according to reports written on their revolts, regarded the cathedral canons as part of the ruling order.[15]

How were the other estates represented before the bishop in the ecclesiastical principality? How did they defend their rights and privileges and seek redress of grievances? These questions are best examined by separate consideration of the different estates of the bishopric—the nobility, the clergy, the towns, and the peasantry—and of their roles in the life and government of the principality as they changed and developed in the course of the late Middle Ages.

II

The nobility enjoyed a preeminent and powerful place in the bishopric in the High Middle Ages. They not only held a great many fiefs from the church of Speyer, which were for the most part eventually lost to the bishopric, but they also served as episcopal advisers and councillors and appeared at diocesan synods. A charter of 1203 indicates that some nobles as well as ministerials were in some way subject to the bishop, although possibly as nothing more than vassals.[1] They were in any event overshadowed by the high nobility, particularly by the counts of Leiningen and Eberstein. Although it was for a long time thought that more bishops of Speyer in the twelfth century were Leiningens than was in fact the case,[2] they and their relations dominated the see until the second quarter of the fourteenth century, when the emerging knights began to place members of their families on the episcopal throne. The counts, however, saw the principal threats to their control of the see in papal and imperial appointments (hence Frederick von Leiningen's supporting Eberhard von Randeck against Lambert von Born in 1363)[3] and, later, in the Elector Palatine's subjection of the bishopric to his effective control. With the election of 1396, the sway of the comital nobility in the principality came to an end until the eighteenth century, when counts were elected bishops again.

In terms of the internal governance of the bishopric, both the counts and the ministerials had already been displaced in the thirteenth century by the cathedral chapter, but contrary to what one might expect, no conflict seems to have resulted. Whereas ministerials in other bishoprics revolted when they were excluded from episcopal elections, the chapter at Speyer dictated in the electoral capitulation of 1272 that the bishop's chamberlain be a canon or a ministerial, from which one may infer that the chapter experienced either no difficulties with the ministerials or opposition sufficient to force it to give way.[4] It is most probable that the former is true, inasmuch as both the counts and the ministerials retained much power and influence in the bishopric despite the new place accorded the cathedral chapter in canon law. From their ranks came the bishops and the canons, whose attitudes reflected their backgrounds and who could be expected to be sympathetic to the claims of their fellow aristocrats, although it would be an oversimplification to assume complete congruity of interest and an injustice to say that the canons put the interests of the aristocracy before those of the bishopric. Nevertheless, the cathedral chapter contemned the only nonnoble bishop of the late Middle Ages and sought to exclude nonnobles from membership, and Bishop Raban in 1401 accepted the decision of his castellans at Kestenburg that only nobles could be appointed castellans.[5]

The nobility actively participated in the government of the principality insofar as it affected them. As vassals, they stood under feudal law and under the jurisdiction of the bishops' feudal court. As castellans, they frequently spoke the law at the request of the bishops, and their findings were binding.[6] The bishops appointed relatives and friends as *Oberamtleute*, *Amtleute*, majordomos, and the other higher officials in their administration; conferred with them often; and at times used them as a counterweight to the power of the cathedral chapter. During the later fifteenth century a formal privy council (*Hofrat*) came into existence, the minutes of which are extant from 1527 on.[7] The bishops also relied heavily on a wider circle of knights settled in and around the bishopric as "friends and councillors" (*frunde vnd rete*) whom they consulted both informally and as judges who adjudicated cases together with canons from the collegiate churches and trained jurists.[8] They also loaned large sums of money to the bishops at prevailing rates.[9] The bishops in turn often arbitrated disputes between nobles or between nobles and nonnobles. Bishop Louis's register of legal decisions is filled with many such cases, which he took, he said, to spare both sides the expense of litigation involved.[10]

If all this sounds like rather limited participation for the nobility, it was nonetheless commensurate with their status in the principality. For in the late Middle Ages, there appears to have been no nobility technically *landsässig* in the principality, that is, directly subject to the bishops as their territorial lord. The sole possible reference to a nobility subject to the bishops in more than a purely feudal capacity occurs in the charter of 1203 mentioned above. A charter of 1402 from King Rupert, which granted the bishop final jurisdiction over all his subjects, "be they noble or nonnoble, male or female," cannot of itself be construed to imply that the bishop actually did have noble subjects.[11] Bishop Mathias's inventory of the population on his lands ca. 1470 listed nineteen nobles as *husgessesen* (*hausgessesen*), i.e., settled on his lands.[12] Many knights did live in the principality,[13] but the word *husgessesen* does not necessarily imply their subjugation to the bishop, although it is not impossible that Mathias was attempting to establish some claim over them. In any case, Bishop Louis in 1482 complained to the emperor that "the principality has no nobility that will serve it without pay."[14] Bishop Philip II's population survey of 1530 included all the bishop's subjects, "noble and nonnoble, clerical and lay, young and old, male and female," but in fact no nobles were registered.[15]

The counts and the lords of the high nobility in this area of the empire never fell into this category, whereas the legal status of the ministerials who had become the backbone of the lower nobility remained most unclear for a long time. Although they attained immediacy only in the early sixteenth century, the King Sigismund had already, in the 1420s, attempted in vain to establish a union of the knights and the imperial towns, both to keep the peace and to offset the power of the princes. In the fifteenth century the self-consciousness of the knights in the Kraichgau, whence came most of the bishops, canons, and officials of the bishopric, developed quickly. In the 1480s another imperial effort to wrest them from the closing grasp of the Elector Palatine was launched and finally succeeded after the defeat of Philip the Upright in the War of the Bavarian Succession in 1505.[16] The bishops of Speyer were but bystanders in this struggle over the lower nobility.

The repercussions of these developments for the bishopric of Speyer were twofold. First, the principality commanded the primary loyalty of neither the high nor the low nobility. They were concerned with their own lands and, if they needed money, took employ with any one of the princes in the area, often transferring from the service of one to that of another.[17] Although the knights depended heavily on such employment, they proved unwilling to forfeit their independence, no matter how great the price.[18] Furthermore, Heidelberg, as the capital of the strongest principality in the region, especially under Frederick the Victorious and Philip the Upright, drew their attention. The knights of the Kraichgau attended the meetings of the estates of the Electors throughout the fifteenth century and were extremely influential in Palatine affairs.[19] It was not likely they would be much interested in the internal deliberations of a dependent bishopric like Speyer that seemed so much like an appanage of the Palatine house.

Second, the usual claims of the nobility to exemption from taxation, regular or extraordinary, were reinforced in the bishopric by their immediate status. From the later fifteenth century, the bishops sometimes tried to compel knights to render the *Bede* on their lands,[20] and other disputes, above all over hunting rights, arose again and again;[21] but Bishop Philip II's futile attempts in 1542 to halt Conrad von Helmstadt's purchase of lands in the principality that were subject to the *Bede* only underscores the strength of the nobility and the inability of the bishops to check it.[22] The sources indicate nearly complete exemption of the nobility from all regular taxation in the bishopric and complete freedom from *Schatzungen*. Only once, in 1468, did a bishop receive money from the nobility. This was "freely given" by various nobles and had no connection with any extraordinary tax.[23] The nobility, in other words, had no need to insist on a diet to preserve its freedom from princely exactions. The bishopric of Speyer was too small and too weak to force the issue, which was settled by the more powerful princes around it.

III

The clergy presented fewer problems to the bishop. Indeed, his power over most of the clergy was awesome. Opposition to his will could be quashed by interdiction of prebendal income, suspension or deprivation of benefice, incarceration in Mathias Ramung's prison at Udenheim (ironically called *Himmelreich*),[1] or excommunication. These courses of action were available to him as ordinary. The clergy subject to him also as territorial lord fell even more under his sway.

The church had, however, long been concerned to guarantee fair representation of legitimate rights and privileges within its hierarchical structure and had been instrumental in the spread of the Roman legal principle, *quod omnes tangit, ab omnibus approbetur.* Innocent III had summoned representatives of cathedral chapters to the Fourth Lateran Council in 1215 because matters affecting them were to be treated there.[2] In thirteenth-century England, the national and provincial ecclesiastical assemblies invited representatives of the lower clergy or, more often, consulted with them regarding the necessity of taxation.[3]

A comparable broadening of representation did not take place in the diocese of Speyer until somewhat later, but the bishop's relations with his clergy were still complex. They must be examined from three different directions: What was being treated? Who was concerned? And when did it take place? The last question is particularly important, for the once seemingly monolithic representation of the clergy by the four chapters of Speyer, above all in the matter of extraordinary taxation, gave way in the fifteenth century to a more fragmented order in which the diocesan clergy and the monasteries negotiated more and more directly with the bishop, if they did not simply refuse to contribute.

The four chapters acted on behalf of the clergy of the town and diocese of Speyer for two reasons that stemmed from the High Middle Ages. The first was that they were the seats of the four archdeacons of the diocese, who were regarded by the papacy in the twelfth century as "the eyes of the bishop," second only to him in rank and responsible for the supervision of the diocesan clergy entrusted to their care.[4] The second was the formal confederation of the four chapters, first attested in 1264 and initially directed against the burghers of Speyer, but which within a few decades expanded in scope to become the principal body defending the clergy and standing for it before all outsiders, be they the bishop, the archbishop of Mainz, or the townspeople of Speyer. Thus the four chapters in union drew up a document in 1321 determining exact contributions to any *subsidium caritativum* from all collegiate churches, rural deaneries, and monasteries in the diocese; declined to grant a *subsidium caritativum* in 1351; and negotiated under compulsion with Bishop Nicholas concerning taxation of the clergy in 1395.[5]

Disputes naturally flared up occasionally among the members of the union in the course of three centuries, most commonly between the cathedral chapter and the three collegiate chapters. In 1285 the three chapters brought suit before the bishop of Constance to win some control over the rich church at Esslingen donated to the cathedral chapter by Emperor Frederick II in 1220, but withdrew their case after inspection of the chapter's privileges.[6] From time to time the three collegiate chapters contested the custom that they select the provosts, who were also the archdeacons, from the members of the cathedral chapter and tried to elect one of their own canons; such incidents occurred in 1437, 1478–81, and 1513.[7] Although successful in the last instance, they were otherwise defeated, and in 1478 Sixtus IV directed that the old custom be followed unless the appointment happen to fall to the papacy.[8] The cathedral chapter by times violated the terms of the agreement by not consulting with the other chapters, as in 1346, 1502, and 1505, but invariably lost.[9] The union was renewed in 1446, 1462, and 1473[10] and continued well into the eighteenth century.[11] Collaboration lent a strength to the chapters in confronting threats from without that was too obvious to be discarded. The chapters also settled conflicts that arose in any one of the chapters.[12]

Their role as representative of the clergy was more and more implicitly questioned in the fifteenth century and openly attacked in the sixteenth, although one can legitimately ask whether the lower clergy ever accepted the union as "representing" them in the technical sense of the term. This was due partly to the gradual assumption of control over the clergy resident in their territories by the neighboring princes, primarily the Electors Palatine, the count (after 1495, duke) of Württemberg, and the margrave of Baden. They began, probably, by encouraging opposition by the prebendaries organized in rural deaneries, as in 1448,[13] and later either negotiated with the bishop over the sum to be rendered or else flatly refused to let the bishop collect any money at all.[14]

Another reason was the hostility of the lower clergy toward the privileged upper clergy, which was dominated by the nobility. In 1506 the rural deans notified the cathedral chapter that they wanted the parishes incorporated into its operating treasury to be included in the *decimatio* granted in that year.[15] In 1523 the pastor of Saint Martin's in Speyer published a bitter attack on the upper clergy at Speyer, especially on the chapter of Saint Guido for supplying inadequate incomes to its perpetual vicars, although he praised the cathedral chapter for creating sufficient revenues for its vicars.[16] A number of priests took part in the Peasants War in 1525, and two were decapitated in Bruchsal after the revolt was crushed.[17] Antipathy toward the nobility was, however, not the only source of bitterness at this time, perhaps not even the most significant one. The Reformed doctrines spread rapidly in the diocese of Speyer. As early as 1522, Bishop George complained to the chapter about the disobedience and heresy rampant among the diocesan clergy.[18]

Resistance to *subsidia caritativa* had first appeared a century earlier, however, and perhaps the most important single reason for it was the number and burden of taxes levied on the clergy. They had become steadily more common in the last half of the fourteenth century. During his forty-two year rule, Bishop Raban collected from the clergy the equivalent of eighteen years of *subsidia*.[19] Mathias Ramung was attacked in a contemporary chronicle of Speyer for draining the lower clergy with fiscal and other exactions.[20] What is therefore surprising is not that resistance developed, but that it arose late and slowly. Only in 1405 was the vicar-general first moved to threaten the recalcitrant with suspension from benefice and excommunication.[21]

Such methods worked easily enough against individuals but not against collective resistance by the members of the rural deaneries, which became the centers of opposition to extraordinary taxation of the clergy in the fifteenth century. Although they had existed in the diocese since the mid-eleventh century and had attained corporate status by the early thirteenth century, they were primarily liturgical organizations that executed the mandates of the bishops and the archdeacons.[22] Now they demonstrated greater aggressiveness and forced the bishops to negotiate directly with them on such matters, although it is possible that the bishops initially encouraged such direct bargaining in order to undermine the power of the archdeacons and of the cathedral chapter.[23] In the end they ordinarily had to come to terms with the bishop unless they enjoyed the protection of a higher power such as a secular prince, but they could secure reduction of their share or delay payment by lengthy litigation. In 1511 three deaneries explicitly denied the ability of the four chapters of Speyer to act for them and hence the legitimacy of Bishop Philip I's right to exact a *subsidium*. The ecclesiastical court of Mainz sustained their objection, but Philip appealed to Rome and won.[24] A full seven years elapsed before several deaneries in the margravate of Baden lost their suit against the tax levied in 1523.[25] Bishop Philip II in 1530 found himself powerless before the refusal of the rural chapters in Württemberg to pay more than a nominal sum in the *subsidium*.[26] Resistance had become so widespread and successful in the sixteenth century that the bishops had even to consult and negotiate with individual pastors in several instances. Bishop Philip I in 1506 had to request one pastor to contribute to an aid,[27] and in 1524 the complaint of the pastor at Barbelrode to the cathedral chapter about unjust apportionment of the *decimatio* was referred to the bishop or his vicar-general.[28]

The monasteries in the diocese and those subject to the bishops showed similar tendencies in the fifteenth and sixteenth centuries. They had played an important part in episcopal policies in the High Middle Ages; although many fell eventually under the lordship of other rulers, the bishops continued to extract as much as possible from them, particularly hospitality rights and services. Emperor Charles IV in 1355, in contravention of the privileges of their order, directed the Cistercian monasteries in the diocese of Speyer to render their customary services to the bishops.[29] The Elector Palatine required Bishop Nicholas in 1393 to renounce such rights over all monasteries.[30] Nevertheless, even though more and more monasteries were taken into the protectorate of the Electors and other princes during the fifteenth century,[31] the bishops steadfastly enforced their established rights as much as practicable. Bishop Raban's *Amtleute* were so zealous in the pursuit of episcopal rights, went one deposition, that they snatched out of the frying pan at the monastery of Saint Lambrecht a fish caught illegally in the bishop's waters.[32] Raban's determined assertion of dormant rights over this monastery led to outside arbitration in 1404.[33] In their concern to consolidate and round off their territories, his successors firmly established their lordship over monasteries and collegiate foundations lying within their lands, over the lands of the four collegiate chapters, and over the manors and other holdings in the bishopric that belonged to foundations elsewhere (e.g., the manor of Maulbronn Abbey at Ketsch).[34]

Almost invariably the bishops treated with the monasteries on an individual basis. Complaints and grievances on the part of the monasteries against the bishops were frequently lodged before any number of princes: the emperor (if the foundation enjoyed immediacy), the pope, the archbishop of Mainz, the Elector Palatine, the duke of Württemberg, or the margrave of Baden.[35] It has been suggested that the abbey of Saint Lambrecht willingly subjected itself to the protectorate of the Elector Palatine to escape episcopal exactions.[36] There is little to support this as a general proposition, and there is even less to confirm the insinuation that conditions were better under secular rulers. Like the princes, the nobles, and the towns, the monasteries of southwest Germany sought above all to preserve their independence at any cost. In forsaking episcopal rule, they frequently acquired more ruthless masters who may have been capable of offering better protection (which they did not always do) but who were also the more able to subjugate the monasteries to their will.[37]

With respect to extraordinary taxation of the clergy, the monasteries followed essentially, but more slowly, the same course taken by the diocesan clergy. Thirteen monasteries and collegiate foundations were represented by the union of the four chapters in 1321, although their low assessments were undoubtedly arrived at after negotiation with the chapters of Speyer.[38] Bishop Gerhard in 1342 reduced Sinsheim's share from £25 to £13.[39] This was accepted by the four chapters, who gave that figure to Bishop Nicholas in 1391 when he wanted to know Sinsheim's customary contribution.[40] The monasteries for their part seem to have accepted the authority of the four chapters throughout the fourteenth century, but in 1427 the abbot of Hirsau successfully refused to participate in a *subsidium*. Trithemius said that the other six Benedictine houses in the diocese followed suit, but there are several reasons for doubting this lone report. Such massive opposition would very probably have been noted somewhere in the episcopal records; it was obviously to Hirsau's advantage to have such precedents to support future claims; and Trithemius was often strikingly inaccurate.[41]

Bishop Louis, in his letter to Emperor Frederick III in 1482, bemoaned the fact that the monasteries gave nothing in *subsidia caritativa*.[42] Whether they actually did or not cannot be proved from the extant sources. One suspects hyperbole, however, upon reading the minutes of the cathedral chapter, which indicate that monasteries did contribute after hard bargaining with the bishops. From at least 1510 on, monasteries as well as rural deaneries came to terms individually with the bishops. The cathedral chapter sometimes mediated and normally approved these covenants. Bishop Philip I concluded a treaty with Sinsheim Abbey in 1512 but experienced greater difficulties with the collegiate church of Odenheim.[43] In arranging for collection of the four-year *decimatio* granted in 1529, Bishop Philip II had his representatives negotiate with the rural chapters in Württemberg, the church at Backnang, and the monasteries. The diocesan clergy remained obstinate. Although the foundations contributed, their donations were not generous, when one considers that it was a four-year tax, and they apparently demanded receipts.[44]

The regular clergy constituted an exception. Most orders established houses in the town and the diocese of Speyer during the thirteenth and early fourteenth centuries. Those in Speyer, above all the Dominicans and the Franciscans, quickly incurred the hostility of the bishop and of the canons of the four collegiate churches over questions of ecclesiastical jurisdiction and the dispensation of the sacraments. They always allied with the burghers in the wars with the bishops and, on the basis of their privileges, celebrated divine services in spite of interdictions. The other houses of regular clergy in the diocese, together with those of the crusading orders, appear very little in the sources. There is no indication that any of these orders ever contributed to episcopal taxation of the clergy.[45]

In brief, as episcopal taxation of the clergy grew heavier and more frequent from 1395 on, representation of the clergy on such matters became much more complex and, one might argue, more equitable. This is not to imply that the four chapters had failed in their original task, but merely to say that increased taxation, coupled perhaps with greater self-consciousness among organized groups, led to a breakdown of the old system.

Negotiation on so many levels clearly entailed much more work for the bishops. Whether they ever considered convening representatives from all the different branches of the clergy to expedite matters is nowhere suggested in the sources. A convocation of this sort might well have operated to the advantage of the bishops, yet it could also have served as a rallying point for opposition to taxation. The bishops were doubtless aware of that possibility, one that was particularly likely in a meeting of a single estate. If the bishops did propose it, the cathedral chapter or the four chapters united at Speyer could have rejected it as a threat to their prerogatives. The rest of the clergy might also have declined to participate for any number of reasons: inconvenience, cost, or loss of protection afforded by other princes. It is worthy of note that the clergy in late medieval Germany were usually the last of the three major estates to participate in diets and the first to withdraw.[46] Finally, the peculiar historical development of southwest Germany must again be emphasized. In 1517 the Elector Palatine Louis V desired the formation of an estates-general in the Palatinate, for he attributed the recovery of the archbishoprics of Cologne and Mainz, the bishopric of Würzburg, and the duchy of Württemberg to the establishment of diets there.[47] The request fell on deaf ears, and even if it had not, there would have been no nobility attendant, and the only large town would have been Heidelberg.

IV

Legally, the towns in the bishopric fell into two different classes: imperial towns (*Reichsstädte*) and territorial towns (*Landstädte*). This distinction is not altogether satisfactory in a discussion of the actual relations between the bishops and their towns. The problem arises in the case of the imperial towns that were pawned to the bishopric, Landau (1324–1511/17) and Waibstadt. Throughout the period of its subjugation to the bishops, Landau retained its proudly independent traditions, whereas Waibstadt was never redeemed and was soon scarcely to be differentiated from the territorial towns. The bishops' relations with the towns in the bishopric was not all of a piece. Of them, Bruchsal, Udenheim, and Lauterburg dominate the records. They were the largest towns and probably also the most tightly under episcopal control. Waibstadt, Rotenberg, Deidesheim, Steinach, and Obergrombach were all technically towns, i.e., they were fortified and had market rights, but they figured less prominently because of their smaller size and their distance from the geographical center of the bishopric.

Speyer was the most important town on the Rhine plain between Strasbourg and Worms. Its population was about 6,000 before 1348 and 7,230 in 1536, and was thus moderately high by the standards of medieval northern Europe, for the town prospered as a center of trade and of cloth production.[1] Some rough idea of its wealth may be formed from imperial demands in troops and money in the late Middle Ages, which ordinarily equaled or exceeded those made on the bishops.[2] The town achieved practical independence of the bishops in the last half of the thirteenth century, and episcopal attempts to reconquer it in 1375, 1422, and 1466 came to nothing. The bishops nonetheless never surrendered any of their claims to lordship over the town. Occasionally they won out on some point, major or petty. Thus Bishop Adolf restored the policy of taxing the burghers' lands in the bishopric,[3] and Mathias Ramung won from Emperor Frederick III the concession that appeals from the decisions of the municipal court had to go first before Mathias's supreme court before they could be carried to the imperial court at Rottweil.[4] Normally, though, endless friction, contention, and litigation over relatively insubstantial issues prevailed, with neither side willing to admit or concede anything. The emperors refused to resolve the problem because they did not wish to or because they could not have compelled acceptance of a decision. The Elector Frederick the Victorious deliberately pitted bishop against town to make both more dependent on him. The town itself was, however, more than capable of defending its independence and of keeping the bishop at sufficient distance.

Landau fared less well because it was smaller and also because it could fall back on less legal protection at the imperial court than could Speyer. The terms of the pawn to the bishopric empowered the bishops to govern in full stead of the emperor.[5] From time to time they exercised this prerogative. In 1361, 1397, 1401, 1424, and 1433 they intervened to broaden the composition of the town council by compelling the patricians to include representatives of the other elements of the population, always reserving the right to do so at their pleasure.[6] The bishops also appointed the *Schultheiss* and the castellans; yet, from at least 1329 on, the bishops always took oaths to the burghers to observe their rights and privileges and never to increase the customary *Bede* of £200 or erect new fortifications. The *Schultheiss* was to pronounce the decisions of the court, but never to alter them. In changing the organization of the council, the bishops did violate their oath, but otherwise they seem to have observed its provisions.[7] The burghers normally had direct and ready access to the bishops, unlike many of his subjects. Difficulties sprang up from time to time, but the *Bede* was never increased, nor was the town subjected except once to the *Schatzungen* collected from the bishop's peasantry.[8] Mathias Ramung tried in vain to get the burghers of Landau to transport stone from a nearby quarry for the construction of the castle at Hanhofen in 1464.[9] J. G. Lehmann, a liberal nineteenth-century historian of the Palatinate, offered no evidence to support his belief that Landau suffered hardship and humiliation under ecclesiastical lordship.[10] Mone correctly pointed out that the bishops derived little financial advantage from their possession of the town.[11] He might also have noted that the bishops' reforms of the council were apparently not self-serving and possibly led to better representation on the council.

The bishops exerted considerably more authority over their territorial towns, so much so, in fact, that their burghers in virtually all respects were scarcely different from the bishops' peasants, for which reason both are considered together in the next section. Some points should be noted here, however. Bruchsal, Udenheim, and Lauterburg were the principal towns of the principality and were the most closely supervised of all. The bishops resided in Udenheim, their two *Oberamtleute* in the other two towns. The three towns served throughout the fifteenth century as the ordinary guarantors of episcopal loans. What practical effect this had on municipal finances has yet to be determined, but it is safe to deny Drollinger's suggestion that the burghers had to pay the interest on the bishops' outstanding debts in addition to the *Bede* and other dues rendered to the bishops themselves.[12]

Bruchsal could make the only real claim to being a town in an economic sense. It had a population of ca. 2,075 in 1530, only slightly larger than its population in 1464.[13] Many of its burghers were artisans in a variety of trades. In addition to weekly markets, larger fairs were held here, which grew in number from two to five per year between 1366 and 1541.[14] Nevertheless, most of its burghers were peasants who tilled the land, and the town was in this respect like all the towns subject to the bishop. They can best be described as *Ackerbürgerstädte*, "peasant towns," which grew the grains, vegetables, fruits, and livestock to supply their own needs and those of Speyer, the bishops, and those who had a right to demand tithes and other dues.[15] Despite its size and importance, furthermore, Bruchsal's communal institutions were not more advanced than those of the other territorial towns. The council was not distinguishable from the jurors (*scabini, Schöffen, Richter*) until the later fifteenth century, and even then the *Oberamtmann* sat as a member.[16]

V

Besides the clergy, the bishops had a second major group of dependent subjects: burghers and serfs. By southwest German standards, the bishops were no petty lords. In 1366 they owned 18 castles, 6 towns, and about 66 villages.[1] By 1541 this had increased to 24 castles and around 115 villages and towns owned in whole or in part, although the number of villages only partly ruled by the bishops was considerable.[2] Mathias Ramung's survey of 1470 registered 4,760 independent households in the principality. Of their occupants, 168 were priests, 20 were nobles, 5,300 were serfs (*Leibeigene*) living within the territory, and another 1,414 were serfs living without. About 1,400 Palatine *Leibeigene* also resided on the bishop's lands, as well as a considerable but unspecified number of serfs of other lords.[3] Children were not counted in this census, but for reasons discussed in appendix two, one can estimate that they numbered perhaps as many as 11,000.[4]

On the basis of the sources, one can paint two quite different pictures of the bishops' relations with their subjects in the late Middle Ages. At one extreme, one can emphasize the oaths of obedience taken in 1298 and 1362 by the Bruchsal burghers, who acknowledged their absolute dependence on the will of the bishops;[5] or the bishops' assertion of their right to increase the *Bede* or institute arbitrary exactions at any time;[6] or their reservation of the right to alter guild statutes at their pleasure.[7] On the practical level, one could depict as typical the gradual limitation of the peasants' use of episcopal forests throughout the fifteenth century,[8] the close supervision of communal and all other affairs exercised by the *Amtleute* and the village ordinances issued by the bishops,[9] or the doubling of the *Bede* several times during the later fifteenth century and the early sixteenth century.[10] At the other extreme, one could stress the limited nature of servitude in the fifteenth century, the annual pronouncements of custom and of the rights of the bishops and the peasants by the village jurors,[11] the villagers' right to sue their bishop, even before the emperor,[12] the compacts entered into by the bishops with their subjects over such matters as services on episcopal lands,[13] or the bishops' withdrawal of proposals deviating from custom in the face of stout peasant resistance.[14] One could point out in favor of the bishops that their forests were so endangered that ordinances to preserve them were necessary,[15] that on the whole the bishops sought to spare the peasantry the burden of extraordinary taxation,[16] that their establishing of grain reserves in the event of crop failure[17] and their issuing of *Bede* ordinances[18] demonstrated real care for their subjects, and that despite their absolutist claims the bishops were in fact bound in many ways by tradition and custom.

Where does the truth lie? Clearly somewhere between these extremes, but it is exceedingly difficult to pinpoint precisely the climate of relations between the bishops and their subjects. The problem is greatly aggravated by the perspective thrust upon historians by the peasant disturbances in southern Germany and Switzerland from the later fifteenth century on, culminating in the Peasants War of 1525. It is not easy to avoid the pitfalls of underestimating both the planning and the spontaneity behind the uprisings in many places, of presenting an implicitly deterministic explanation, of positing a simple causal relationship between peasant demands and lordly oppression, or of assuming that what the peasants said was necessarily true. The standard work on the Peasants War by Günther Franz falls to some degree into each of these traps.[19]

There are certain other assumptions that need to be examined critically in considering such questions. First, fifteenth-century society was not democratic, but estatist and hierarchical in organization. By common consideration, serfs were not entitled to participate in estates-general; in general, only in mountainous and coastal areas did they enjoy direct representation. The revolts of the early sixteenth century attacked this aristocratic conception of society as well as the nature of lordship itself, but the new views did not succeed or command wide acceptance.

Second, many historians of southwest Germany tend to have a certain implicit bias against territorial lords and for the independence or "freedom" of the imperial towns and knights—in short, against the legitimacy of the organized, large state. They ignore the disadvantages that accompanied this "freedom": parochialism of viewpoint, internal conflicts over the division of power, and the consequent dissipation of energy in the pursuit of superficial ends. By comparison, territorial lordship offered distinct advantages: wider perspective on the best interests of the land and its subjects and economic benefits derived from membership in a relatively large society. Bruchsal, Lauterburg, and Udenheim were never torn by the internal struggles over power that plagued Speyer after the expulsion of the bishops, and only the intervention of the bishops seems to have spared Landau similar strife.

The third point is closely related. Consideration of the relations between a lord and his subjects should focus squarely on the *legitimate* interests and demands of both parties. It is true that the bishops of Speyer during the fifteenth century restricted more and more the rights of the peasants to timber and pannage in their forests, but it is also true that the forests were being damaged by excessive use and by the overflowing of the Rhine and that they had to be systematically replanted in the sixteenth century. It is true that the bishops imposed sharp limitations on sales, by the peasants, of land subject to the *Bede*; yet it is also true that this was partly for the good of the peasants, inasmuch as the bishop collected the full fixed *Bede* from a community no matter how little land might be subject to it: The less land available, the higher the individual assessment. Bishop Louis and his successors forbade appeal of many minor cases to the episcopal supreme court, but only, they said, to save their litigious subjects onerous legal expenses disproportionate to the merits of the cases involved.[20] Evidently the episcopal courts were being swamped, and to remedy the situation intermediate courts (*Landgerichte*), particularly at Jockgrim, began to be established. One could enumerate various other instances in which seeming episcopal arbitrariness was designed for the advantage of the subject. To be sure, there were many cases of real arbitrariness and injustice on the part of the bishops, but not every peasant complaint or demand represented a true presentation of reality or a realistic appraisal of the possibilities for change. One should also bear in mind the tenacious conservatism of the peasant, which has been much noted by modern sociologists but which also captured the eye, for example, of Nicholas of Cusa when he was bishop of Brixen (1450–1464).[21]

This is not the place to present a complete history of the relations between the bishops and their subjects in the later Middle Ages or to discuss the background of the Peasants War in all its aspects—political, economic, social, religious, and psychological.[22] One thing, however, is certain: the Peasants War was not fundamentally about representation or representative government. True, virtually the only common denominator among all the varied demands of the peasants was that for local self-governance, and in a number of territories they sought greater control of the government by the estates. Otherwise the demands of the peasants both fell short of and transcended this question. Nearly everywhere they cried out for the abolition of servitude, tithes, and ground rents and the restoration of custom and "the good old law." In some places (e.g., Speyer), the peasants desired the vesting of full power in one lord of the land and the elimination of intermediate lords, clerical and lay. A few territories saw calls for the destruction of the existing regime and the creation of a peasant state.[23] Great hatred was directed against ecclesiastical lordship in particular, but Hussitism, the achievement of Swiss independence, and above all the Reformation significantly fanned the anticlerical feelings that tend to emerge naturally under a government of priests, and it has yet to be demonstrated in scholarly fashion that ecclesiastical lordship was inferior to secular rule. From the peasants of the Black Forest and the Upper Rhine came a maxim in the eighteenth century: "Life is good under the crosier" (*Unter'm Krummstab ist gutes Leben*). This may not have been true in the sixteenth century, but life was not necessarily bad then, either. Probably the principal failing of ecclesiastical lordship was its efficiency, as a cursory glance at the minutes of meetings of the chapter of Speyer quickly reveals.

A second indication that the Peasants War had essentially nothing to do with representative government was the geographical pattern of the revolts. Basically, the Peasants War was a series of uprisings by the peasantry, sometimes joined by knights, burghers, and members of the lower clergy, which swept Upper Germany, including Austria, between the springs of 1525 and 1526. Bavaria, where peasants did not participate in diets, did not experience such eruptions, whereas the archbishopric of Salzburg, the Tyrol, and the abbey of Kempten, where peasants were directly represented, and the duchy of Württemberg and the margravate of Baden, where they were represented by *Ämter,* suffered some of the most serious outbreaks. The peasants were, in fact, the only estate in the territory of Kempten, and those in the archbishopric of Salzsburg had been invited to the meetings of the estates since 1456, partly with a view to preventing such trouble.[24] In short, the earliest and most severe revolts occurred in lands where the peasants enjoyed, rather than lacked, representation.

However deficient his analysis of events in the bishopric of Speyer in 1502 and 1525,[25] Günther Franz's general discussion of the causes of these disturbances demonstrated how much more important other causes and problems were. In seeking to explain why the Peasants War broke out in southern but not northern Germany or Bavaria, he pointed to the concentration of population, the dominance of the nobility and the clergy, the servitude and tenuous legal position of the peasants, the small plots of land resulting from excessive partitions, and the princely dependence on the peasants for their income in all the areas disturbed. He also stressed the strength of community life and communal consciousness in the south and the consequent swiftness of reaction to any abridgment of custom.[26]

All these conditions obtained in the bishopric of Speyer. By the fourteenth century, strongly developed representative institutions existed there already. Despite professions by its burghers of complete subjugation to the bishops in 1298 and 1362, the town of Bruchsal possessed its own seal by 1265.[27] Pronouncements of the law and custom, on which the bishops sometimes relied heavily, were common from the second quarter of the fourteenth century at the latest.[28] One of the earliest extant petitions to the bishops dates from the 1360s.[29] Those submitted covered all subjects, including the elevation of small churches to the status of parishes to minimize inconvenience for the peasants, and a great many were granted.[30] Protests registered in the fifteenth and sixteenth centuries over episcopal alterations of customary rights and procedures often achieved the retreat of the bishops from their new demands.[31] In chapter four it was shown how often the bishops rebuffed the cathedral chapter's request that the peasants be taxed instead of the clergy. One cannot affirm or deny on the basis of the few extant sources that the peasants were always consulted those few times when they were taxed extraordinarily, but in 1438 and 1523, occasions of important levies, the bishops and their officials made the circuit of the principality to discuss the *Schatzung* with their subjects.[32]

What was the attitude of the peasants in the Bundschuh and the Peasants War? It was ambiguous towards the bishops, to judge from the reports, but decidedly hostile to the cathedral chapter, the upper clergy in general, and the nobility. George Brentz, secretary to Bishop Philip I, observed in his brief report on the Bundschuh of 1502 that the revolt was directed against the upper clergy and nobility, but he also noted with distress that nearly everyone in the principality knew the revolt was about to take place yet said nothing.[33] The conduct of Bishop George has much to do with the course of the Peasants War in the bishopric of Speyer. He appears to have been a haughty man who failed to deal adequately or fairly with the peasants' complaints in 1523[34] and who rejected the initial overtures of the rebels and the offers of the other peasants to crush the rebels.[35] Later, according to one report, he met with the peasants and agreed to their demands that the Gospel be preached without commentary in the bishopric and that he be the sole master of the bishopric.[36] Another account, an anonymous letter, said that the peasants demanded that George marry and be the only lord of the peasants, otherwise the bishopric should be dissolved and be annexed to the Palatinate.[37] The common point of these divergent stories was the antipathy of the peasants toward the cathedral chapter, which they shared with many members of the lower clergy.

VI

A brief recapitulation is in order. Representative institutions and practices in the principality of Speyer were many and varied, and became increasingly complex during the fifteenth century. All of the estates accepted the leadership of the cathedral chapter less and less, even though it had never been the only body to act for the principality or its members before the bishops. The higher estates—the nobility, the upper clergy, and the two most important towns—normally treated with the bishops directly as the need arose, although the monasteries began to do so on taxation only in the fifteenth century, and the cathedral chapter often served as intermediary between the bishops and the town of Speyer. The lower orders of society—the lower clergy, the burghers, and the peasants—nurtured more and more resentment against the cathedral chapter and the upper estates generally, and they also came to negotiate with the bishops on numerous questions, above all on extraordinary taxation.

The diversity of these levels of governance and the hostility toward the chapter should not blind one to the valuable work the canons had done and continued to do on behalf of the principality, no matter what the motives were that inspired them. The power of the chapter had, as a result, mounted considerably over the three centuries, but so had its responsibilities. This was not of itself an evil thing or a good thing; that depended on the way in which that power was exercised. The men associated with any institution are limited in their perspective and generosity. They are capable of using power for good or ill. All this was true of the cathedral chapter at Speyer. Certain aspects of its structure and attitudes, especially its aristocratic character, became more pronounced in the fifteenth century; yet in the same century, it acted less irresponsibly and more maturely toward the principality in many respects than it had during the troubles of the fourteenth century. Kloe held the chapter at Speyer responsible for the generally unfortunate state of the bishopric in the later Middle Ages.[1] On the contrary, the chapter served throughout the period as the chief restraint on princely excesses and as the principal guardian of the common, and hence the highest, interests of the principality.

Conclusion

The highly complicated relations of the bishops of Speyer with their cathedral chapter and their subjects during the later Middle Ages can perhaps be best reviewed by asking a different kind of a question that will focus on the central issues raised in this study: Why did a formally constituted diet fail to appear in the ecclesiastical principality of Speyer?

The setting of a negative question is fraught with methodological hazards. It is sufficiently difficult for a historian to determine exactly what happened and then to assign reasons, ordered according to their relative importance, to explain why it happened. The great dangers of imposing rationality where none existed, of explaining events away so convincingly as to posit implicitly some form of determinism, and of greatly underestimating or even eliminating the operation of chance, individual choice, or error in history assume even greater magnitude when one attempts to account for a course *not* taken. A fruitful inquiry can nonetheless be undertaken, provided one bears constantly in mind these qualifications about the ultimate inability of the historian to unravel completely the mysteries of the past. In this instance the comparative history of representative institutions in the empire and Europe in the late Middle Ages provides a number of different vantage points from which to examine the question.

Why did parliaments and diets appear in so many states of Europe from the thirteenth century onward? According to many proponents of the *parliamentarian* point of view,[1] the principal reason in almost all cases was the financial distress of kings and princes. *Landtage sind Geldtage,* ran the German maxim. Rulers turned to their subjects for aid and, after experimenting a great deal with various techniques of negotiating with them over voluntary subsidies, found in many cases formally convened assemblies of the estates the most convenient and expeditious method of obtaining these grants and of managing their debts.[2]

Before the fifteenth century, the bishops of Speyer had no need to consider such possibilities, for the entire burden of extraordinary taxation, as in many other ecclesiastical principalities,[3] fell entirely on the clergy, whose interests, to judge from the absence of dissension in the sources, were for a long time adequately defended by their archdeacons and the four chapters of Speyer acting in confederation. In 1321 the united chapters fixed the amounts to be rendered; in 1351 and 1395 they declined to vote *subsidia*. In the fifteenth century the frequency of taxation of the clergy resulted in considerable opposition from monasteries and above all from the rural chapters of the diocesan clergy. For this and other reasons, the bishops' burghers and peasants were also occasionally taxed. The bishops negotiated either directly or through representatives with the recalcitrant clerical organizations, and by the sixteenth century this almost became a matter of course. Information on taxation of the peasantry is scarce, but on at least two major occasions, 1438 and 1523, the bishops and their officials met with the peasants assembled by *Ämter* to discuss the proposed levies. The sources give no sign that the bishops ever thought of convening a formal diet. Perhaps, in experiencing the resistance of the clergy, they imagined that such an assembly would only serve to unify opposition. Both the clergy and the peasantry would doubtless have regarded the costs of sending representatives undesirable, and in any case the bishopric was small enough to permit the bishops to bargain with them directly. The complete round of the principality for new bishops receiving the oaths of obedience from their subjects lasted but a few days.

The second major reason for the rise of diets and their antecedents in the empire, unions of estates (*Einungen*), according to Carsten, was the need to curb the internecine warfare within the ruling houses, their endless partitions of principalities, and alienation of possessions and sovereign rights.[4] Ecclesiastical states experienced somewhat similar upheavals from time to time over contested elections or provisions to sees, but the problem was nowhere nearly as great as in the secular principalities. Alienation of possessions as a means of coping with persistent deficits did, however, pose a serious threat to ecclesiastical as well as secular states. Canon law forbade any alienation of church property but, bending to reality, decreed that, if it were necessary, it could be undertaken only with the consent of the members of the ecclesiastical corporation. In a monastery this was the community of monks; in a bishopric, the cathedral chapter. The chapter at Speyer throughout the late Middle Ages executed this responsibility conscientiously by requiring its consent to all alienations and by setting strict conditions on the nature and length of pawns. To circumvent these difficulties entirely, it also lent the bishops large sums of money at rates equal to or more favorable than those generally prevalent, and it also borrowed for the bishops when their credit had come into disrepute. As a result, with one exception, no property of the church of Speyer was permanently lost in the late Middle Ages through sales or pawns necessitated by shortage of funds. The exception was the lands bought from the von Ochsenstein family in the first decade of the fifteenth century by Bishop Raban and then sold in the 1430s because of his costly wars to gain the see of Trier.[5]

The third reason for the appearance of parliaments was to achieve redress of grievances of all sorts, and this was more and more coupled with supply. Again, there were complex analogues in the bishopric of Speyer. The *Einungen* of the four chapters, on behalf of the clergy, from the second half of the thirteenth century represented attempts to protect the clergy against arbitrary conduct by the bishops. The electoral capitulations taken thereafter by all new bishops were much more positive and efficacious, and they redounded to the good of the principality as well as to the good of the clergy and the cathedral chapter. Furthermore, each of the estates in the principality, down to the smallest community of peasants, had a variety of means at its disposal to secure justice. The higher estates could appeal to outside powers in addition to negotiating with the bishops, and even Bruchsal carried a case to the emperor in 1512.

The size of the bishopric, too, was important here. Although rather large by comparison with many states in southwest Germany, it was not yet so large as to preclude the possibility of personal confrontations between the bishops and their subjects. Indeed, appeal of even the most insignificant suits to the episcopal supreme court was so easy and common that it had to be restricted from the 1480s on. Size affected relations in another way. The bishops were simply not powerful enough to coerce their subjects, whose collective consciousness and strength on every level was formidable, to do their bidding. To be sure, the bishops won back many old rights and established new ones in the course of the fifteenth and early sixteenth centuries, but it was a slow process, and one for which they inherited the wind in 1502 and 1525.

One can take a different tack in analyzing why no diet existed in the ecclesiastical principality of Speyer. The corporatist historians tend to emphasize the initiative taken by the estates in the formation of assemblies as opposed to the initiative of the princes. Georg von Below, Hans Spangenberg, and Robert H. Lord all agreed that the nobility and the larger towns were the most crucial estates in the convocation of assemblies and that the clergy, even the upper clergy, only joined later, attended less often, and frequently dropped out completely.[6] The nobility and the larger towns were, in contrast, precisely the estates lacking in the principality of Speyer. The high nobility was never subject to the bishops. The status of the lower nobility remained vague until the early sixteenth century, when they became immediate. They never contributed to any extraordinary taxes and were active in the government of the principality only to the extent to which they were directly concerned. As for the towns, the only major one was Speyer, which wanted nothing to do with the bishopric. Landau tenaciously resisted the bishops at every turn. Bruchsal was probably just as large as Landau,[7] but it had no great economic leverage and, far from having a long tradition of independence like Landau, was firmly controlled by the bishops from the early thirteenth century at the latest.[8] The other towns of the bishopric were at best large fortified villages and cannot be counted among the "politically active classes"[9] in any meaningful sense.

One can, with the more traditional parliamentarians, stress princely initiative, and indeed no diet could be legally convened without a mandate from the ruler. It cannot be said whether the bishops ever contemplated summoning representatives to an assembly, or whether it would have served their advantage to do so. One should remember that the principality, during the period of subjugation to the Palatinate, experienced, to use modern jargon, a kind of identity crisis. The bishops attended the meetings of the estates in the Palatinate throughout the fifteenth century. The bishopric soon came to be regarded by many as a dependency, if not an appanage, of the Palatinate, and in any case attention was riveted on Heidelberg. One can legitimately ask whether this had any bearing on the bishops' attitudes toward a diet in their principality under such circumstances and, more importantly, on the responsiveness of the various estates toward one. The nobility was probably affected,[10] but the views of the other estates require further study.

Finally, to return to the principal contention of this study, a diet did not appear in the ecclesiastical principality largely because of the work of the cathedral chapter. Although the chapter used its position for self-aggrandizement, and although it came to be widely disliked and its leadership to be less taken for granted, there is no denying the great significance of its efforts on behalf of the principality between the thirteenth and the sixteenth centuries. Through electoral capitulations, oaths and agreements exacted from the bishops and their *Amtleute,* loans, and grants of extraordinary taxation, it helped bring the principality safely through perilous times. Continuity of government during vacancies and absences of the bishops, efficiency of administration, financial solvency, restraint of episcopal extravagance, preservation of the territorial integrity of the principality, supervision of foreign relations in the interests of the bishopric—all these were the achievement of the cathedral chapter acting in cooperation, or at loggerheads, with the bishops. Throughout the troubles of these centuries it remained the center of stability in the see of Speyer.

It is very important to understand the reasons why the chapter devoted so much concern to these tasks and how it attained the position it held. One German historian attributed the decline of the estates in the bishopric of Osnabrück to the *Egoismus* of the cathedral chapter.[11] Hans Spangenberg believed the chapter there had achieved its prominence as a result of its exclusive electoral rights or its control of the archdeaconries.[12] Georg von Below came much closer to the truth in looking to canon law, but he failed to press home this suggestion.[13] Whereas the chapter's independence, permanence, and resources enabled it to intervene effectively in the affairs of the bishopric, and its most vital interests compelled it to do so, canon law imposed on it the duty of helping the bishops rule the see. The reformers and canonists of the twelfth and thirteenth centuries cut through the great mass of often vague and contradictory laws and customs and conferred on the cathedral chapter the sole right of electing bishops and of governing during vacancies, and heavy responsibility for the good state of the bishopric. The bishop was obliged to consult with his canons and to obtain their consent to a whole range of acts, which they in time broadened. The bishops tended to regard the chapter as a nuisance at best, a hindrance at worst, and so have the great majority of German historians, particularly those of the early modern period.[14] Whatever the soundness of this charge for the seventeenth and eighteenth centuries, whatever the faults and weaknesses of the chapter in the execution of its responsibilities, there can be little doubt either of the excellent intentions of the reformers of the High Middle Ages or of the necessity and success of the work of the cathedral chapter of Speyer in the later Middle Ages.

Appendix I

The Chapter and Its Meetings

In 1375 Bishop Adolf of Nassau took advantage of evident division within the cathedral chapter by persuading six canons to affix their seals to a loan from the town council of Speyer, even though the chapter as a whole had refused its assent.[1] This is one of the very few occasions before the sixteenth century when the chapter does not appear to be a monolithic and inaccessible corporation. Fortunately, from 1500 on, the minutes of its deliberations are extant and yield a detailed picture of its inner workings, its efficient administration of its own holdings, and its extensive powers in the governance of the bishopric.

The cathedral at Speyer had, originally, forty prebends. By the standards of the empire, where the number could vary between seventy-two (Cologne) and fourteen (Meissen), this was average.[2] By the thirteenth century, thirty of these were restricted to canons, but the actual number of canons at any one time fluctuated between about fourteen and nineteen for several reasons.[3] First, and most important, a canon elected to the chapter had to wait up to five years and thirty days before taking possession of his prebend, and he had no voting rights before he had secured his benefice. The income of such vacant prebends went during this period to enrich the operating treasury (*Dompräsenz*) of the chapter.[4] The number of resident voting or capitular canons might further be reduced for any number of reasons. A canon might be away for the conduct of some specific business, the administration of one of the seventeen *Ämter* of the chapter, the fulfillment of the statute requiring two years of formal study, or simply vacation (three regular fifteen-day vacations in addition to the official vacation of the chapter). Thus only ten canons attended the general session of the chapter on 3 November 1509.[5] Those absent without dispensation were subject to immediate loss of their incomes. All this must be considered in any examination of nonresidence on the eve of the Reformation.

The chapter did not meet during the vacation period of 10 September to 31 October unless it were absolutely necessary. During the rest of the year, it convened in quarterly general sessions, semiweekly on Wednesday and Friday, and at other times as the press of affairs dictated.[6] Extra sessions were frequent. In 1504 the chapter assembled 156 times, including 12 times during the fall vacation.[7] Outbreaks of plague, epidemics, or disturbances sometimes prompted the canons to reassemble elsewhere or not to meet at all. During the Peasants War in 1525, for instance, no minutes are recorded for the crucial period between 11 May and 14 June.[8] At these meetings the dean usually presided, provided he held a canon's prebend. Because the canons transacted a great variety of business, six fairly representative sessions have been chosen to illustrate the range of the chapter's responsibilities.

On 19 December 1500 the chapter considered a request from Esslingen (presumably the city council) for a loan of 1,000 fl. at four percent and from a burgher of Esslingen for one of 250 fl. Although the chapter decided to postpone its answer until it could obtain the advice of Vicar Hans Mayrhofer, the administrator of the *Amt* at Esslingen, it did declare that the rate could be not less than four and a half percent. On the advice of Vicar Jost Rube, the canons agreed to sell the grain stored at Löchgau (near Ludwigsburg) to the inhabitants there for cash and for two or three pennies per measure lower than the prevailing market price. Vicar Rube also reported that the *Schultheiss* of Östrigen would soon appear to discuss the problems of tithe collection there. Finally, the canons accepted estimates on the value of their grain at Edesheim and demanded prompt payment for the sale thereof.[9]

On 17 February 1504, through his chief clerk (*Landschreiber*), Bishop Philip von Rosenberg announced the receipt of an imperial mandate to furnish a military contingent (for the War of the Bavarian Succession). To secure dispensation from this order, the bishop requested the chapter to allow him to send either a canon or Vicar Mayrhofer on an embassy to Maximilian. He also reported that the *Schultheiss* at Landau had died and that he had named someone to the post for life. The chapter approved the appointment and agreed to send Mayrhofer to the emperor. The chapter then heard the executors of the estate of Canon Frederick von Nippenburg (d. 1502) demand repayment of an outstanding debt of 9 fl. from Canon John von Cronberg. Cronberg's procurator was ordered to liquidate the debt within two weeks. The session concluded with the chapter's warning to the pastor at Deidesheim not to carry out some action he had planned (which the minutes do not clarify).[10]

Exactly a week later the chapter acceded to the request of Canon Eberhard von Ehrenberg for a one-year leave to study at Tübingen or some other university. When Vicar Jacob Ungerer reported that the ferry-station at Rheinhausen was inadequately equipped with wood and ships, the chapter deputed the chanter and Canon Walter von Vilbel to negotiate with the canons of Saint Germain on the matter. Another canon and an official were then sent to Heidelberg to hear a judgment handed down by the Palatine supreme court in a case affecting the chapter. The canons ended the meeting by assigning Canon Thomas von Rosenberg responsibility for the granary.[11]

Episcopal finance and tithes constituted the agenda on 11 August 1512. The bishop received permission to borrow 800 fl. at four percent in Strasbourg. The lessees of the chapter's wine tithe at Utzingen (near Landau) petitioned for reduction of their dues, for the wine was going bad. The canons promised to answer after the wine had been inspected. Several people who refused to render tithes were told that the chapter would accept their claims to exemption only if they could adduce valid documents to that effect.[12]

The meeting of 19 March 1516 was part of a convocation of the clergy (i.e., the four chapters) called to consider the case of Melchior Pfintzing, who, despite royal backing, had not obtained a prebend in the cathedral. In the name of the bishop, the vicar-general solicited the advice of the clergy concerning a pension to idemnify Pfintzing. The cathedral chapter suggested either a single payment of 150 fl. or a pension of no more than 30 fl. per annum. The chapter then consulted with the other three collegiate churches, which declared themselves ready only to grant a flat 200 fl. from their common treasury.[13]

The chapter met on 11 March 1529 to resolve several questions arising from the recent death of Provost George von Schwalbach. It considered and approved a petition for the conferral of the vacated prebend on Otto Truchsess von Waldburg (later bishop of Augsburg and cardinal). A date was set for the election of a new provost. Four canons said they would communicate this information immediately to four nonresident canons (two of them counts) who had asked them to report without delay the vacancy of any prelacy in the chapter. Because Schwalbach had held also the provost-ships of Saint Germain's and Saint Guido's, the chapter decided to consider on the next day a proposal that the new provost should resign any other provostships he held.[14]

If, after reading these proceedings, the reader vaguely senses that he has entered the cloister but not the chapter house, that, in the end, the cathedral chapter remains a slightly mysterious monolith, he is right, and he would form the same impression if he read the eighteenth-century sources. The reasons are not hard to discern. The sources are, on the whole, impersonal, partly because of the men who wrote (or did not write) them, partly because of the business they transacted, and partly because of the way they, of necessity, conducted these affairs. As aristocrats, politicians, and managers, the canons had little time and less interest in revealing in writing to each other, much less to outsiders, any of those ignoble feelings and motives that form the stuff of gossip, factionalism, and so much of man's history. Although greed, hatred, ambition, and factionalism existed behind the facade, they elude almost completely any attempt to grapple with them and to assess their importance. Lest all this sound either too romantic or too sordid, it ought also to be clear from these summaries that what preoccupied the canons was not very high politics, but the petty details (*Kleinkramm*) of everyday life. This in itself is most instructive. No matter what other far-flung interests and connections the canons had, they were very much high-level estate managers and guardians of a corporation. These activities consumed much of their time as individuals and as members of the chapter in convocation. So, too, the minutes of their meetings were properly concerned with the affairs of the chapter as a corporation. Whoever jotted them down had no business recording anything except the affairs and decisions of the corporation. Exactly how and why many of those decisions were made, and so much other fascinating information, has unfortunately died with those men.

Appendix II

The Population of the Bishopric

It is simply hopeless to try to estimate the population of the principality or the number of the bishops' subjects before the later fifteenth century, but it is most fortunate that three censuses were taken between 1470 and 1530. In 1470 Mathias Ramung completed the first of them as part of a survey of the lands, subjects, incomes, and expenditures of the church of Speyer.[1] A second was undertaken in 1495 to facilitate collection of the new imperial tax, the Common Penny.[2] In 1530 Bishop Philip von Flersheim commissioned the third and most informative of these censuses.[3] They are not exactly comparable, however, for they do not all include the same places (including whole *Ämter*) or persons. A brief résumé of these variations is in order:

1. *Places.* The *Amt* of Rotenberg was pawned to the Palatinate between 1464 and 1505 and so appears only in the last census. Landau was redeemed by the emperor Maximilian in 1511/17 and figures only in the first two. Not listed in the 1495 rolls are the *Ämter* of Ladenburg, Landeck, and Edesheim. The latter, purchased by the chapter in 1482 and sold to Bishop Louis in 1487, naturally does not appear in the 1470 register, but the absence of the *Amt* of Deidesheim from the latter is inexplicable.

2. *Persons.* (a) Although all three censuses list the adult population in each place, only those of 1470 and 1530 record separately the number of the bishops' subjects. In addition, the 1470 register lists only the subjects

of the Elector Palatine living in the principality, not the "considerable number" (*merkliche zale*) of those belonging to other lords. It is frankly difficult to say exactly what adults were included in the 1495 list, i.e., whether the subjects of other lords were counted, although it would appear that they were. Only the census of 1530 clearly distinguished among the subjects of the bishop, the Elector, and all other lords. (b) Children were not counted in the 1470 census or in 1495, because the Common Penny was a head tax only on all those over the age of 15. The 1530 census did number children, but the totals do not distinguish between those of the bishop's own subjects as opposed to those of other lords domiciled on the bishop's lands. (c) Calculating the numbers of clergy is a tricky business, because their dependence on the bishop varied enormously according to order, institutional affiliation, and living.

All these hazards notwithstanding, it is still possible to formulate some very tentative conclusions about the number of the bishops' subjects, the population settled in the bishopric, and demographic changes during this period. They can only be tentative, not only because the evidence is complex and perplexing, but also because I cannot claim to be even an amateur demographer. Yet the temptation, indeed the responsibility, remains too great to bring to the attention of demographers another cubit of material on a period about which we know so little.

1. The population in 1530 is easy to determine, for Bishop Philip's officials performed their task fairly well. Settled on episcopal lands were 12,307 adults and 15,933 children (who presumably reached majority at fourteen or fifteen). Of the adults, 2,224 were subjects of the Elector, 242 of the emperor (150 of whom lived at Scheidt in the *Amt* of Lauterburg), and 2,104 of other lords. Thus, directly subject to the bishop were only 7,045 adults, while another 1,468 lived in the lands of other lords (so-called *Ausleute*), making a total of 8,513. Through simple calculation, one can estimate the number of their children at 11,046, which brings the total of episcopal subjects to 19,559.[4] To this figure must be added 268 people employed in various capacities in the bishop's castles and manors as well as 166 clerics listed in the census, which yields a grand total of 19,995. By comparison, the bishops of the eighteenth century ruled over 50,000 subjects. The Electors to the north governed somewhere between 100,000 and 200,000 subjects in the fifteenth century and 300,000 in the eighteenth.[5]

The 166 priests will interest Reformation historians as well as demographers. Save for the eleven members of the aristocratic collegiate church of Odenheim who had settled in Bruchsal in 1507 and who had assigned a twelfth benefice to support a preacher, 155 were evidently secular priests somehow engaged in pastoral work. They were distributed in seventy out of eighty-six places listed (excluding the five places in Madenburg *Amt,* the priests of which were unaccountably omitted from the census). If one considers all the people settled on episcopal lands and served by these priests, there was one secular priest for every 80 adults or, including children, for every 182 people. In the 1470 census, 164 secular priests were enumerated, which suggests a high degree of stability in the clerical population.

2. Was the lay population as stable? We know that in general the population of Europe regained by the second half of the sixteenth century its pre-1348 level and all its attendant problems. When exactly did the great upsurge begin on the Upper Rhine? The question takes on added interest in the light of a recent study that concluded that population increase and consequent demographic pressure helped to precipitate and shape the Peasants War in Upper Swabia.[6] Whether this was so in the bishopric of Speyer requires close consideration of the 1470 and 1495 censuses.

Unfortunately, neither is highly reliable. In 1470 episcopal officials demonstrated yet again their customary inability to add a column of figures correctly, partly because they continued to use Roman numerals well into the sixteenth century. Addition of their *Ämter* totals yields 7,422 subjects of Bishop Mathias on his lands and 1,512 *Ausleute,* but addition of all the numbers listed for each place produces 5,298 and 1,414, respectively! Which set of figures should one accept? For several reasons, the lower population figures appear more reasonable, which means that the number of episcopal subjects in the bishopric increased by about thirty percent between 1470 and 1530 (from roughly 5,300 to over 7,000). If the Elector had about 1,400 subjects in the bishopric in 1470 (but again much depends on how one adds), these increased by an astonishing fifty-nine percent in the same period. Serfs domiciled on former imperial lands at Scheidt (so-called *Königsleute*) rose from 82 to 150. In fact, comparison of the local figures for the episcopal subjects only confirms this overall impression and inclines one to accept the lower total calculations given above.

Episcopal Subjects Only

	1470	1530
Östrigen	101	150
Undenheim	153	212
Langenbrücken	76	121
Obergrombach	62	98
Untergrombach	144	213
Wiesenthal	80	91
Schifferstadt	106	181
Mingolsheim	98	183
Bruchsal	683	662
Lauterburg	364	261

Assuming, with great temerity, that Mathias Ramung's men counted both correctly and inclusively in 1470, we may conclude that the population increased significantly in the bishopric in these sixty years, especially the Palatine population.

3. When did the increase take place? In the decades immediately preceding the Peasants War, or earlier? The only relevant source, the 1495 census, is even less reliable than that of 1470. Episcopal subjects were not counted separately, which eliminates a crucial basis of comparison. Of course the census was not drawn up by episcopal officials for episcopal purposes, and indeed it was not really a census at all. It was instead a tax register of individuals who could (and would) pay 1 fl. or ½ fl. and of groups of twenty-four people who could collectively pay 1 fl. The comparable list for the bishopric of Constance shows how arbitrarily the tax was levied. Here it fell on the secular inhabitants of seven villages, the clergy in the forty deaneries of the diocese on German soil (and including the members of the University of Freiburg i. B.), and the monastery of Saint Gall, whose abbot was himself an imperial prince![7] Nor had the ability of bureaucrats to add improved in a quarter century. In the census of the bishopric of Speyer, they counted an adult population of 12,039, whereas I calculate 11,848.

The caveats are thus clear and impressive. What is nevertheless surprising is that comparison of the total and local population figures for 1495 and 1530 indicate demographic stabilization or actual decline during these years. The total figures are 12,039 (or 11,848) versus 12,307. A similar picture emerges at the village level.

Total Adult Population

	1495	1530
Östrigen	398	348
Undenheim	280	305
Langenbrücken	194	181
Obergrombach	120	112
Untergrombach	301	285
Wiesenthal	165	132
Schifferstadt	237	246
Mingolsheim	106	278
Bruchsal	1209	986
Lauterburg	468	328

In short, if all these figures are correct and can be validly compared, we may infer that, although the population of the bishopric climbed substantially between 1470 and 1530, it did so in the last quarter of the fifteenth century, not in the first quarter of the sixteenth. These conclusions, however, are but the tentative deductions of an amateur and deserve more careful examination by those trained in this new science.

List of Abbreviations

AMKG   *Archiv für mittelrheinische Kirchengeschichte*

APAE   *Anciens pays et assemblées d'état*

BEF   Bibliothèque des Écoles françaises d'Athènes et de Rome

CIC   *Corpus iuris canonici,* vol. 1, *Decretum Gratiani* (ca. 1140); vol. 2, *Decretalium collectiones* (of which I have used the *Decretales* of Gregory IX [1234], the *Liber sextus* of Boniface VIII [1298], and the *Extravagantes communes*). Emil Friedberg, ed. Leipzig, 1879–81.

COD   *Conciliorum oecumenicorum decreta.* 3d ed. Josepho Alberigo, Josepho Dossetti, Perikle Joannou, Claudio Leonardi, and Paolo Prodi, eds. Bologna, 1973.

CR   *Chorregal und jüngeres Seelbuch des alten Speierer Domkapitels.* 2 vols. Konrad von Busch and Franz X. Glasschröder, eds. Speyer, 1923–26.

Études   Études présentées à la Commission internationale pour l'histoire des assemblées d'états

FDA   *Freiburger Diözesan-Archiv*

GLA   Generallandesarchiv, Karlsruhe

HSA   Hauptstaatsarchiv, Munich, Rheinpfälzer Urkunden

Jaffé   Jaffé, Philip, ed. *Regesta pontificum Romanorum*. 2d
               ed. Ferdinand Kaltenbrunner, Paul Ewald, and Samuel
               Löwenfeld, eds. Leipzig, 1885–88.

Mansi   Mansi, Giovanni Domenico. *Sacrorum conciliorum
               nova et amplissima collectio*. 54 vols. Jean Martin and
               Louis Petit, eds. Florence, Venice, Paris, Arnheim, and
               Leipzig, 1759–1927.

MGH *Const.*   Monumenta Germaniae historica. *Leges,* sec. 4, *Con-
               stitutiones et acta publica imperatorum et regum*.
               Ludwig Weiland et al., eds., Hanover, 1893–1926.

MGH *Dipl.*   *Diplomata regum et imperatorum Germaniae: Die
               Urkunden der deutschen Könige und Kaiser*. Theodor
               Sickel, Harry Bresslau et al., eds. Hanover and Berlin,
               1879–.

MGH *Dipl. Karol. Germ.*   *Diplomata regum Germaniae ex stirpe Karolinorum*.
               Paul Kehr and Theodor Schieffer, eds. Berlin, 1955–63.

MGH *Epist. pontif.*   *Epistolae saeculi XIII e registis pontificum Romanorum
               selectae per G[eorg] H[einrich] Pertz*. Karl Roden-
               berg, ed. Berlin, 1883–94.

MHVP   *Mitteilungen des Historischen Vereins der Pfalz*

N.F.   *Neue Folge*

Potthast   Potthast, August, ed. *Regesta pontificum Romanorum
               inde ab anno post Christi natum MCXCVIII ad annum
               MCCCIV*. 2 vols. Berlin, 1874–75.

Protokolle   *Die Protokolle des Speyerer Domkapitels*. 2 vols. Man-
               fred Krebs, ed. VBW A, vols. 17 and 21. Stuttgart,
               1968–69.

Reg. Baden   *Regesten der Markgrafen von Baden und Hachberg,
               1050–1515*. 4 vols. Richard Fester, Heinrich Witte, and
               Albert Krieger, eds. Innsbruck, 1892–1915.

Reg. Pfalz	*Regesten der Pfalzgrafen am Rhein, 1214–1410.* 2 vols. Adolf Koch, Jakob Wille, Ludwig von Oberndorff, and Manfred Krebs, eds. Innsbruck, 1894–1939.
Remling	Remling, Franz X. *Geschichte der Bischöfe zu Speyer.* 2 vols. Mainz, 1852–54.
s.a.	sub anno
SAS	Staatsarchiv, Speyer
s.d.	sub dato
Stumpf	Stumpf-Brentano, Karl F. *Die Reichskanzler vornehmlich des X., XI., und XII. Jahrhunderts,* vol. 2, *Die Kaiserurkunden des X., XI., und XII. Jahrhunderts chronologisch verzeichnet.* Innsbruck, 1865–83.
UBS	*Urkundenbuch zur Geschichte der Bischöfe zu Speyer.* 2 vols. Franz X. Remling, ed. Mainz, 1852–53.
USS	*Urkunden zur Geschichte der Stadt Speyer.* Alfred Hilgard, ed. Strasbourg, 1885.
VBW A	Veröffentlichungen der Kommission für geschichtliche Landeskunde in Baden-Württemberg, Reihe A, Quellen
VBW B	Reihe B, Forschungen
WUB	*Wirtembergisches Urkundenbuch.* 11 vols. Stuttgart, 1849–1913.
ZGO	*Zeitschrift für die Geschichte des Oberrheins*
ZRG Germ.	*Zeitschrift der Savigny-Stiftung für Rechtsgeschichte, Germanistische Abteilung*
ZRG Kanon.	*Kanonistische Abteilung*

Notes

In the notes, a shortened form of citation is used for all books and articles included in the bibliography. The first time a work is cited, its author and title appear in full; in subsequent citations, the last name of the author and a shortened title are given. Some frequently cited works are further abbreviated in accordance with the list of abbreviations on pages 199–201.

PREFACE

1. This controversy continues to boil and bubble. See the lively discussions in *Pfälzer Heimat* 6 (1955): Ernst Christmann, " 'Speier' contra 'Speyer': Ein Vorschlag zu deutscher Schreibung," p. 108; Günther Groh, " 'Speyer' contra 'Speier': Ein Beitrag zur pfälzischen Ortsnamenforschung," pp. 28–29; and Karl Lutz, "Wenn Speyer, warum nicht Keyserslautern und Zweybrücken? Altertümelnde oder zeitgemässe Ortsnamenschreibung?" pp. 156–58.

INTRODUCTION

1. I have throughout used the terms "parliament," "diet," or "estates general" to refer to the formally convened assemblies of two or more estates or their representatives. The term "estates" I have reserved for the various orders of society, privileged and unprivileged: the nobility, the clergy, the towns, and the peasants.

2. On the historiography of the parliamentarian position, see Émile Lousse, *L'État corporatif au moyen âge et à l'époque moderne*, pp. 1–2, 6–34; Gavin Langmuir, "Counsel and Capetian Assemblies," p. 21. The discussions of English historians about the origins of Parliament have long been so complicated as to elude simple classification. See Edward Miller, *The Origins of Parliament*, pp. 3–8.

3. Helen Maud Cam, *Law-Finders and Law-Makers in Medieval England*, pp. 159–

63. For Lousse's works as of 1964, see the "Elenchus bio-bibliographicus Prof. É. Lousse," pp. 205–62, especially 218–36. German historians have long been corporatist in their viewpoint. See Lousse, *L'État corporatif*, pp. 1–2, 35–66; Herbert Helbig, "Ständische Einungsversuche in den mitteldeutschen Territorien am Ausgang des Mittelalters," pp. 187–88; Robert Folz, "Les assemblées d'états dans les principautés allemandes (fin XIIIe–début XVIe siècle)," pp. 164–69.

4. The first appeared in Paris in 1937. The succeeding sixty-one volumes (to date) have been published most frequently in Paris, Louvain, and Brussels. They are listed at the end of each number of *APAE*.

5. 1950 ff., variously published in Paris, Louvain, and Brussels.

6. Otto Hintze, "Weltgeschichtliche Bedingungen der Repräsentativverfassung," pp. 1–5. A translation of this essay is now available in *The Historical Essays of Otto Hintze*, ed. Felix Gilbert and Robert Berdahl (New York, 1975), pp. 305–53.

7. For a summary of recent work, see Lousse, "Gouvernés et gouvernants en Europe occidentale durant le bas Moyen Âge et les temps modernes," pp. 7–48.

8. Gerhard Buchda, "Reichsstände und Landstände in Deutschland im 16. und 17. Jahrhundert," pp. 193–226, criticized the applicability to the empire of the customary simple distinction between the "governing" and the "governed" (as in the previous note).

9. Severinus de Monzambano (Samuel von Pufendorf), *De statu imperii Germanici*, p. 167: "Nihil ergo aliud restat, quam ut dicamus, Germaniam esse irregulare aliquod corpus, & monstro simile, siquidem ad regulas scientiae civilis exigatur. . . ."

10. For surveys of their views, see Helbig, "Einungsversuche," pp. 187–92; Francis L. Carsten, *Princes and Parliaments in Germany from the Fifteenth to the Eighteenth Century*, pp. vii, 432–36, 444; Peter Blickle, *Landschaften im Alten Reich*, pp. 30–47, especially 44–45, whose own conclusions are uncommonly positive. Blickle is much influenced by Otto Brunner, who has strongly criticized the conceptual schemes and whole approach of German historians. See his *Land und Herrschaft*, pp. 146–64, 231–39, 358–59, 395–404, 413–40.

11. Herbert A. L. Fisher, *The Medieval Empire*, 1:9, said that Philip the Fair's celebrated councillor Pierre du Bois advised his king to revive the empire of Charles the Great and to compensate the German princes at the expense of the ecclesiastical principalities. On the mediatization of many formerly imperial bishoprics and abbeys, see Albert Werminghoff, *Verfassungsgeschichte der deutschen Kirche im Mittelalter*, pp. 59, 89, 92.

12. Fritz Hartung, *Deutsche Verfassungsgeschichte vom 15. Jahrhundert bis zur Gegenwart*, pp. 142–47; Walter Bruford, *Germany in the Eighteenth Century*, p. 49; and Klaus Epstein, *The Genesis of German Conservatism*, pp. 276–85, may all be regarded as presenting typical treatments.

13. Hans Erich Feine, *Die Besetzung der Reichsbistümer vom Westfälischen Frieden bis zur Säkularisation 1648–1803*, pp. 297–329; Hajo Holborn, *A History of Modern Germany: 1648–1840*, pp. 48–49.

14. Werminghoff, *Verfassungsgeschichte*, p. 72; Albert Hauck, *Kirchengeschichte Deutschlands*, vol. 5, pt. 1, p. 128. See the fine maps of the ecclesiastical principalities

in Hubert Jedin, Kenneth Scott Latourette, and Jochen Martin, eds., *Atlas zur Kirchengeschichte,* pp. 82–83.

15. An assembly of estates, according to Lousse, consisted only of the politically privileged orders or their representatives. See his "Assemblées représentatives et taxation," p. 27, and "Gouvernés," p. 31.

16. Until recently it was thought that in the empire the peasants constituted an estate with participatory rights only in the Tyrol, Vorarlberg, the imperial abbey of Kempten, the archbishopric of Salzburg, and the counties of Frisia and Mörs, but Blickle, *Landschaften,* passim, has considerably extended this list. In some other territories, such as the bishopric of Würzburg, the duchy of Württemberg, the Electoral Palatinate, and Ansbach-Bayreuth, the peasants' representatives were customarily the officials of the *Amt* in which they lived. See Carsten, *Princes,* pp. 424–25; Nikolaus Grass, "Alm und Landstände in Tirol," pp. 139–42; Folz, "Assemblées," pp. 174–76. In England, according to Gaines Post, "Serfs were not recognized as having such rights as had to be represented—except insofar as their masters represented them; as Helen M. Cam has said, the shire represented by knights was the community of all men under peers and above serfs" (*Studies in Medieval Legal Thought,* p. 112, n. 92). Precisely this argument was adduced to justify the dropping of the estate of the peasants from the Danish *Rigsdag* in 1627: Alec R. Myers, *Parliaments and Estates in Europe to 1789,* p. 28.

17. Werminghoff, *Verfassungsgeschichte,* p. 70.

18. Buchda, "Reichsstände," p. 196.

19. On the knights, see Gustav Knetsch, *Die landständische Verfassung und reichsritterschaftliche Bewegung im Kurstaate Trier, vornehmlich im XVI. Jahrhundert,* p. 136. On the imperial towns, see Karol Koranyi, "Zum Ursprung des Anteils der Städte an die ständischen Versammlungen und Parlamenten im Mittelalter," p. 53, who agreed with Hermann Aubin that these towns well deserved to be called "die Säulen der Reichsfinanzen," inasmuch as they paid well over half the military taxes of the empire even though they had only ten percent of its population.

20. Bryce Lyon, "Medieval Constitutionalism," pp. 155–83.

21. Helen Maud Cam, in her introduction to "Mediaeval Representation in Theory and Practice," pp. 349–52. A happy exception to the prevailing formalism and legalism among German historians is to be found in Blickle, *Landschaften.*

22. Hans Spangenberg, *Vom Lehnstaat zum Ständestaat,* p. v.

23. I am preparing in a long article a comprehensive survey of the estates in the ecclesiastical principalities of the Holy Roman Empire.

24. Ernst Schubert, *Die Landstände des Hochstifts Würzburg.*

25. Roger Ballmer, "Les assemblées d'états dans l'ancien évêché de Bâle," pp. 54–140.

26. Carsten, *Princes,* p. 423.

27. Helbig, "Einungsversuche," pp. 187–90; Spangenberg, *Vom Lehnstaat,* pp. 111–13.

28. See Werminghoff, *Verfassungsgeschichte,* pp. 73–74, for the considerable disparities in size between dioceses and principalities. The bishop of Constance ruled, for instance, the largest diocese but one of the smallest ecclesiastical territories in the empire: Hans Erich Feine, *Kirchliche Rechtsgeschichte,* p. 364. As territorial lord, the

bishop of Bamberg ruled only about half his diocese: Siegfried Bachmann, *Die Landstände des Hochstifts Bamberg,* p. 33.

29. The Latin documents throughout the period covered by this study always speak of the lands, castles, and subjects of the church of Speyer. Thus the monastery of Heilsbruck was to be founded in the bishopric in 1232 "sine ecclesie Spirensi preiudicio, in cuius fundaretur territorio" (Stephan-Alexander Würdtwein, ed., *Monasticon Palatinum,* 5:83–84). Thus a charter of Charles V in 1541 to Bishop Philip of Speyer: "suae ecclesiae accesserint interim alia [castra]" and "quidquid dicta ecclesia Spirensis in praesentarum licite possidet" (*UBS,* 2:538–39, no. 284). Analogously, the bishops in the fourteenth and fifteenth centuries thought of ecclesiastical benefices in feudal terms as fiefs (see SAS Kopialbuch 63; and Franz Xaver Glasschröder, "Die Pfründen librae collationis des Speyerer Bischofs im Mittelalter," pp. 155–68, and "Die Speierer Bistums-Matrikel des Bischofs Mathias Ramung," pp. 75–126). For these reasons I have deliberately used the equivocal term "bishopric" (*Bistum*) rather than the more precise words "diocese" (*Diözese*) or principality (*Hochstift*).

30. For a fairly recent statement of this old view, see Brian Tierney, *Medieval Poor Law,* pp. 2–3.

31. The literature on the aristocracy and the church is voluminous. See, for example, Aloys Schulte, *Der Adel und die deutsche Kirche im Mittelalter*; Albert Werminghoff, "Ständische Probleme in der Geschichte der deutschen Kirche im Mittelalter," pp. 35–64; Feine, *Besetzung,* pp. 297–329, and *Rechtsgeschichte,* pp. 149 ff.

32. Antonio Marongiu, *Medieval Parliaments,* pp. 37–41, sharply criticized the views advanced by Georges de Lagarde, "Les Théories représentatives du XIVe–XVe siècle et l'église," pp. 63–75, and held also by Dietrich Gerhard, "Assemblies of Estates and the Corporate Order," p. 289.

33. Only a few examples can be cited here. Maude V. Clarke, *Medieval Representation and Consent,* pp. 259–77, 296–310, concluded that "The Fourth Lateran Council put the representative principle into action on a scale and with a prestige which made it known throughout the whole of Western Europe" (ibid., p. 296). Ernst Kantorowicz, "Inalienability: A Note on Canonical Practice and the English Coronation Oath in the Thirteenth Century," pp. 488–502, suggested a strong connection between, on the one hand, the clauses of nonalienation in the coronation oaths of Henry III and Edward II and the abstract conception of the crown, and, on the other, the oaths of newly consecrated bishops to the pope as these oaths developed in the twelfth and thirteenth centuries. Post, *Studies,* pp. 415–21, argued rather that both had a common source, the revival of Roman law; but then he went on to underline the work of the popes, especially of Innocent III, in bringing about the widespread use of Roman law (ibid., pp. 66–67, 85–90).

34. In a letter of 25 September 1779 to Charlotte von Stein in his *Briefe,* selected and ed. Walter Flammer (Munich, 1961), pp. 62–63.

35. A brief and well-illustrated history of the cathedral may be found in Franz Klimm, *Der Kaiserdom zu Speyer.*

36. Ludwig Stamer, *Kirchengeschichte der Pfalz,* 2:54; Theodor Kaul, "Der Klerus des Domstiftes von Speyer im Jahre 1542," pp. 112–58, especially 114.

37. For the reasons, see pp. 68–69.

38. *UBS*, 1:645–51, no. 638.

39. Ibid., 2:538–42, no. 284.

40. Remling, 1:151–55; Werner Hacker, *Auswanderungen aus dem früheren Hochstift Speyer nach Südosteuropa und Übersee im XVIII. Jahrhundert*. The bishop of Münster, by comparison, controlled the largest ecclesiastical principality in the empire with over 4,300 square miles (11,250 km^2) and 360,000 subjects in the eighteenth century: Friedrich Keinemann, *Das Domkapitel zu Münster im 18. Jahrhundert*, p. 381. On the territories of the other ecclesiastical princes, see Hauck, *Kirchengeschichte*, vol. 5, pt. 1, pp. 66–129, and Bruford, *Germany in the Eighteenth Century*, pp. 333–36.

41. Rudolf Reinhard, "August, Graf von Stirum, Bischof von Speier, und die Zentralbehörden im Bistum Speier," pp. 165–68.

42. Blickle, *Landschaften*, pp. 124–26, noted that, although the subjects of the bishops often lodged suits against their lords in Vienna in the seventeenth and eighteenth centuries, their formal representation was confined to meetings of the *Ämter* (*Ämtertage*) convened only to assent to taxation. These meetings, however, seem to have been neither frequent nor important.

43. Let a few examples of this kind of argumentation suffice: Hans Spangenberg, "Beiträge zur älteren Verfassungs- und Verwaltungsgeschichte des Fürstentums Osnabrück," pp. 8–20, 24; Karl Wild, *Staat und Wirtschaft in den Bistümern Würzburg und Bamberg*, pp. 14–16; Gustav Schöttke, *Die Stände des Hochstifts Osnabrück unter dem ersten evangelischen Bischof Ernst August von Braunschweig-Lüneburg* (*1662–1698*), p. 7; Joseph Ohlberger, *Geschichte des Paderborner Domkapitels im Mittelalter*, pp. 13, 17, 85; Josef Oswald, *Das alte Passauer Domkapitel*, pp. 1–82; Konrad Lübeck, *Die Fuldaer Äbte und Fürstäbte des Mittelalters*, p. 241; Ulrich Herzog, *Untersuchungen zur Geschichte des Domkapitels zu Münster und seines Besitzes im Mittelalter*, p. 66; Bachmann, *Bamberg*, pp. 35–42; Schubert, *Würzburg*, pp. 21–26, 32–33, 185; Reinhard Renger, *Landesherr und Landstände im Hochstift Osnabrück in der Mitte des 18. Jahrhunderts*, pp. 50–67.

44. *Lexikon für Theologie und Kirche*, 9:963.

45. I shall argue this point in an article on the bishopric of Speyer as a "Renaissance state."

46. Manfred Krebs, ed., *Die Protokolle des Speyerer Domkapitels*. Vol. 1 covers the years 1500–1517, vol. 2 the years 1518–31.

Chapter 1, Part I

1. The text of the oath is in *UBS*, 1:324–29, no. 360. Appended to it are the names of the twenty-four prelates and canons.

2. Electoral oaths of bishops to the chapter were already customary, as a charter of Bishop Henry II in 1265 indicates, where he said that the canons "nullum in episcopum et pastorem eligant, nisi idem inter alia, que per iuramentum servare promittet, prius

iuret sentencias contra malefactores predictos editas inviolabiliter observare" (*UBS*, 1:309, no. 342). How long the custom had existed, however, cannot be determined.

3. Spangenberg, *Vom Lehnstaat,* pp. 45–56, 100–116; Carsten, *Princes,* pp. 425–28; Helbig, "Einungsversuche," pp. 187–92; Folz, "Assemblées," pp. 177–86, 191.

CHAPTER 1, PART II

1. MGH *Dipl. Karol. Germ.* Louis the German, no. 92. Franz Xaver Glasschröder, "Zur Frühgeschichte des alten Speierer Domkapitels," p. 481, found no earlier reference to the chapter.

2. MGH *Dipl. Karol. Germ.* Louis the German, no. 118.

3. Arnold Pöschl, *Bischofsgut und mensa episcopalis,* 1:4–5 and 2:63–174.

4. Ibid., 1:5, and vol. 3, pt. 1, passim.

5. MGH *Dipl.* Henry II, no. 125 (1007) (Stumpf, no. 1436); MGH *Dipl.* Conrad II, no. 4 (Stumpf, no. 1855); MGH *Dipl.* Henry IV, no. 426 (1091) (Stumpf, no. 2914).

6. MGH *Dipl.* Henry III, nos. 167–174 (1046) (Stumpf, nos. 2305–12); MGH *Dipl.* Henry IV, nos. 277 (1074) (Stumpf, no. 2783), 466 (1101) (Stumpf, no. 2950), 474–75 (1102) (Stumpf, nos. 2957–58).

7. MGH *Dipl.* Conrad II, no. 4 (Stumpf, no. 1855); MGH *Dipl.* Henry III, no. 173 (Stumpf, no. 2310).

8. MGH *Dipl.* Henry IV, no. 426; Stumpf, no. 2914.

9. *UBS,* 1:70, no. 70: "Omnes autem parochianas ecclesias ad eandem abbaciam pertinentes ab omni episcopali servicio absolvi, ut sicut Spirensium fratrum ecclesie ab omni census exactione sunt libere, ita et ab hiis nichil tributi ab episcopo queratur."

10. Glasschröder, "Frühgeschichte," p. 490.

11. MGH *Dipl.* Henry IV, no. 466; Stumpf, no. 2950. It was confirmed by Conrad III in 1140: *WUB,* 2:16, no. 314; Stumpf, no. 3409.

12. See chapter two, pp. 66–69.

13. Paul Hinschius, *Das Kirchenrecht der Katholiken und Protestanten in Deutschland,* 2:144, explained the striving of cathedral chapters towards independence as but one indication of the general medieval tendency toward corporate independence and exemption from local powers.

14. See Hans-Walter Klewitz, "Die Entstehung des Kardinalkollegiums," in his *Reformpapsttum und Kardinalkolleg,* pp. 9–134, especially pp. 11–14, 24, 46, 68–69, 106, 109–11.

15. On the legal characteristics of a corporation, see Post, *Studies,* pp. 29–30.

16. *UBS,* 1:90–91, 99–100, nos. 82 and 90. Cf. Glasschröder, "Frühgeschichte," p. 497, who hesitated to consider the seal referred to in the charter of 1137 as that of the cathedral chapter.

17. *UBS,* 1:90–91, no. 82.

18. Ibid., 1:146, no. 130.

19. *WUB,* 2:187, no. 410.

20. *UBS,* 1:124, no. 108.

21. Ibid., 1:155–56, no. 138; see also *USS,* p. 48, no. 58.

22. *UBS*, 1:156–57, no. 139.

23. Ibid., 1:326, no. 360.

24. Cf. ibid., 1:107–9, no. 97 (1159), with 1:162, no. 144 (1220), and 1:188–89, no. 181 (1230).

25. E.g., ibid., 1:221–22, no. 226 (1241).

26. *CR*, 1:9–14 (a decree of Bishop Philip I in 1510); Manfred Krebs, ed. in *Protokolle*, 1:x–xii; and chapter four, pp. 145–146.

27. *UBS*, 1:325, no. 360.

28. See pp. 19–20.

29. Friedrich Weber, *Die Domschule von Speyer im Mittelalter*, pp. 61–90; Friedrich Bienemann, *Conrad von Scharfenberg, Bischof von Speier und Metz und kaiserlicher Hofkanzler (1200–24)*, pp. 127–32; Stamer, *Kirchengeschichte*, 2:5–7; Karl Bosl, *Die Reichsministerialität der Salier und Staufer*, pp. 218–19, 231, 244, 276.

30. *UBS*, 1:230, no. 241 (1244). The other privileges were nos. 239–40, 242, 244–46, 249–50.

31. *Decretales*, 3.5.27 (*CIC*, 2:447 = Potthast, no. 5020).

32. Jean Guirard, ed., *Les Registres d'Urbain IV*, 3:265, no. 1712.

33. Ernest Langlois, ed., *Les Registres de Nicolas IV*, p. 185, no. 835 (a papal dispensation from pluralism granted in 1289 to one of King Rudolf's financial officials who held, among many other benefices and offices, canonries at Speyer, Mainz, and Trier); see also chapter three, pp. 88–89.

34. *UBS*, 1:623–24, no. 620 (in 1362 Charles IV agreed not to advance nonnobles to canonries in the chapter). On the so-called *preces primariae* of the emperors and territorial princes, see Werminghoff, *Verfassungsgeschichte*, pp. 65, 92, and Feine, *Rechtsgeschichte*, p. 387.

CHAPTER 1, PART III

1. Geoffrey Barraclough, "The Making of a Bishop in the Middle Ages," p. 284.

2. See, for instance, John A. Yunck, "Economic Conservatism, Papal Finance, and the Medieval Satires on Rome," for another aspect of the reaction.

3. But cf. André Desprairies, *L'Élection des évêques par les chapitres au XIIIe siècle*, pp. 7–14, who placed great weight on the initiative of the cathedral chapters in their struggle to exclude the laity from elections.

4. Otto Riedner, *Die geistlichen Gerichtshöfe zu Speier im Mittelalter*, 2:163–67, no. 43. Only vol. 2 (texts) of this work appeared.

5. Ibid., 2:3–48.

6. *UBS*, 1:328, no. 360.

7. See pp. 32–33.

8. MGH *Const.*, 2:8–10, 20–21, 57–62, nos. 8 (1203), 16 (1198), and 46–47 (1213).

9. Post, *Studies*, pp. 3–6, 14–16, 163–73, 415–33, 564. See also Hans Erich Feine, "Vom Fortleben des römischen Rechts in der Kirche," pp. 1–24.

10. See pp. 32–33.

11. Gratian himself noted the parallel in D. 63 *dictum post* c. 34 (*CIC*, 1:246–47): "Nunc autem sicut electio summi Pontificis non a Cardinalibus tantum, immo etiam ab aliis religiosis clericis auctoritate Nicolai Papae est facienda, ita et episcoporum electio non a canonicis tantum, sed etiam ab aliis religiosis clericis, sicut in generali sinodo Innocentii Papae Romae habita constitutum est." Gratian evidently here conflated the right of election with that of approbation. On the changes in the College of Cardinals, see Klewitz, "Entstehung" in his *Reformpapsttum*. Curiously, Georg von Below, *Die Entstehung des ausschliesslichen Wahlrechts der Domkapitel*, pp. 4–8, failed to note the significance of the 1059 decree. The definitive treatment of the growth of the electoral monopoly of cathedral chapters is by Klaus Ganzer, "Zur Beschränkung der Bischofs-wahl auf die Domkapitel in Theorie und Praxis des 12. und 13. Jahrhunderts." See also Robert L. Benson, "Election by Community and Chapter."

12. MGH *Const.*, 1:538–41, no. 382.

13. Mansi, 22:217–18 (= *COD*, p. 211): c. 1 of the Third Lateran Council of 1179.

14. MGH *Const.*, 1:159–61, nos. 107–8.

15. See Below, *Wahlrecht*, pp. 1–4, for a review of the older literature. On the problems raised in the empire by the Concordat, see Robert L. Benson, *The Bishop-Elect*, pp. 228–83, who stressed how little the agreement settled.

16. Most of the medieval and modern authorities cited by Below support this con-clusion. See also Feine, *Rechtsgeschichte*, p. 380. The elections at Cologne in 1132 and at Regensburg, Augsburg, and Basel in 1133 were all by "canonica electione Cleri et Populi": Johann Friedrich Schannat and Joseph Hartzheim, eds., *Concilia Germaniae*, 3:324–25, 327.

17. Below, *Wahlrecht*, pp. 4, 8–13; Hans-Walter Klewitz, "Das Ende des Reform-papsttums," in his *Reformpapsttum und Kardinalkolleg*, pp. 207–59, especially pp. 254 ff. Benson, *Bishop-Elect*, pp. 375–78, underlined the significance of the 1130 papal election as a turning point in the history of the reform movement, as did Herbert Bloch, "The Schism of Anacletus II and the Glanfeuil Forgeries of Peter the Deacon of Monte Cassino," pp. 159–74. Hinschius, *Kirchenrecht*, 2:602–3, on the other hand charged that the exclusion of the laity in the twelfth century had all along been the aim of the papacy, which for political reasons concealed its intents and proceeded very cautiously, "ja mit einer gewissen Schüchternheit."

18. Mansi, 21:533 (= *COD*, p. 203).

19. Below, *Wahlrecht*, pp. 5–6; Hinschius, *Kirchenrecht*, 2:603; Feine, *Rechts-geschichte*, pp. 380–81.

20. Desprairies, *Élection*, pp. 11–14. Either opinion would appear to be supported by the phraseology of Frederick Barbarossa's interventions in the elections of Cambrai and Regensburg in 1167: MGH *Const.*, 1:326–27, 329. Frederick addressed himself to the "venerabili clero, beneficiatis" of both churches, although at Regensburg the ministerials participated as well. See also n. 22 immediately below.

21. In support of these efforts Gratian cited, respectively, Popes Saint Leo I (440–461) and Celestine I (422–432) in D. 62 cc. 1–2 (*CIC*, 1:234): "Non sunt habendi inter episcopos, qui nec a clericis eliguntur, nec a plebibus expetuntur" and "Populus non debet preire, sed subsequi." But Gratian also incorporated the new outlook ex-pressed at the Second Lateran Council in 1139: see n. 11 immediately above.

22. Part of the text is given in Hinschius, *Kirchenrecht*, 2:603, n. 3.

23. Below, *Wahlrecht*, pp. 7–16; Desprairies, *Élection*, pp. 11–14. At Cumae three abbots gained the right to vote with the chapter: *Decretales*, 1.6.50 (*CIC*, 2:91–92). When Archbishop Conrad of Salzburg reformed the electoral procedure there in 1139, the abbot of Saint Peter's in Salzburg was allowed to participate in the capitular elections: Franklin Geselbracht, *Das Verfahren bei den deutschen Bischofswahlen in der zweiten Hälfte des 12. Jahrhunderts*, p. 135.

24. Desprairies, *Élection*, pp. 11–14.

25. Ibid.

26. Geselbracht, *Verfahren*, pp. 134, 136.

27. Cited in Desprairies, *Élection*, p. 14.

28. John A. Watt, "The Theory of the Papal Monarchy in the Thirteenth Century," pp. 212–13.

29. Clarke, *Medieval Representation*, pp. 296–98; Eric W. Kemp, *Counsel and Consent*, pp. 43–45; Post, *Studies*, p. 171; Raymonde Foreville, "Représentation et taxation du clergé au IVe Concile du Latran (1215)," pp. 63–74; Marongiu, *Medieval Parliaments*, pp. 33–35.

30. *Decretales*, 1.6.22, 36, 57 (*CIC*, 2:64–66, 82–83, 95–96); Barraclough, "Making of a Bishop," pp. 308–9.

31. Barraclough, "Making of a Bishop," pp. 286–92, 294–98.

32. *Decretales*, 1.6.16–33 (*CIC*, 2:55–79).

33. MGH *Const.*, 2:37, 58, nos. 31, 46–47.

34. *Decretales*, 1.6.22, 36, 57 (*CIC*, 2:64–66, 82–83, 95–96).

35. Mansi, 22:1011–14.

36. Barraclough, "Making of a Bishop," pp. 275–79.

37. *UBS*, 1:309, no. 342.

38. Ibid., 1:324, no. 360: "cum inter varios tractatus et diversas cogitaciones per nos habitas non solum de substituendo pontifice. . . ."

39. See Leo Santifaller, *Zur Geschichte des ottonisch-salischen Reichskirchensystems*, especially pp. 123–57, and Carlrichard Brühl, *Fodrum, gistum, servitium regis*, pp. 126–36, 202–3, 207–14, 767.

40. Bosl, *Reichsministerialität*, pp. 64, 94, 99–100; Johann Emil Gugumus, "Die Speyerer Bischöfe im Investiturstreit," p. 117; Brühl, *Fodrum*, pp. 134, 147–48.

41. Gugumus, "Bischöfe," p. 93, and *AMKG* 4 (1952):57 on Bishops Rüdiger (1075–1090) and John (1090–1104), both related to the Salians; and see n. 49 below.

42. Remling, 1:236–37, 239–43, 251–61, 397, 402–4, according to whom Bishops Gunther (1146–61) and Gottfried II (1164–67) died on Barbarossa's expeditions. The "Chronicon episcoporum Spirensium" in Stephan-Alexander Würdtwein, ed., *Nova subsidia diplomatica*, 1:144, noted that Bishop Ulrich I (1162–1163) also died in Italy, although it incorrectly listed the year of his death as 1164 (see Remling, 1:398).

43. Remling, 1:361, 368.

44. *UBS*, 1:125, no. 109.

45. Geselbracht, *Verfahren*, p. 41.

46. Ibid., p. 134; Hermann Krabbo, *Die Besetzung der deutschen Bistümer unter der Regierung Kaiser Friedrichs II.*, pp. 74–81, 84–98.

47. Georg Wolfram, *Friedrich I. und das Wormser Concordat*, pp. 72–73.

48. Wolfram, *Friedrich I.*, p. 73, incorrectly asserted that Bishop Rapodo (1167?–1176) was of the family of Rechberg. Actually he belonged to the Lobedenburg family: Remling, 1:400–407.

49. Remling, 1:408–9; Wolfram, *Friedrich I.*, p. 73.

50. Remling, 1:418.

51. See n. 29 immediately above, and Adam Fath, "Bistum Speyer, 1939–1950," p. 387.

52. Otto Riedner, "Das Speierer Offizialatsgericht im 13. Jahrhundert," p. 13, asserted that Bishop Conrad caused (*veranlasste*) Frederick II to grant the famous imperial privilege of 1220 to the ecclesiastical princes, although he admitted at the same time that the question needed further investigation. Erich Klingelhöfer, *Die Reichsgesetze von 1220, 1231/32, und 1235*, pp. 59–60, made no mention of Conrad in this context, but instead concluded that Archbishop Albert III of Magdeburg and Bishop Conrad of Regensburg were most responsible for the concession. Bienemann, *Conrad von Scharfenberg*, pp. 30–31, called Conrad of Speyer and Albert of Magdeburg "die beiden bedeutendsten Vertreter der staufischen Partei" and emphasized Conrad's great loyalty to the Staufens, although he did believe that Conrad demanded the chancellorship of the empire from Otto IV as the price of his support in 1208 (ibid., p. 31).

53. Ludwig Mazetti, "Die verfassungsrechtliche Stellung des Bistums und der Stadt Speyer zur Zeit des Bischofs Beringer von Entringen," pp. 6, 9, 16, 39–56.

54. Ibid., p. 58; Remling, 1:461.

55. Mazetti, "Beringen von Entringen," pp. 39–41, 49–53.

56. Fisher, *Medieval Empire*, 1:258–59 and 2:93–135; Charles C. Bayley, *The Formation of the German College of Electors in the Mid-Thirteenth Century*, pp. 3–18.

57. Bayley, *Formation*, pp. 10–11.

58. See Élie Berger, ed., *Les Registres d'Innocent IV*, nos. 613, 654, 790, 2055, 2672, 4480, and 6161.

59. Ibid., nos. 788, 948–49, 984, 1270–71, 2495.

60. See p. 209, n. 30 above, and also *UBS*, 1:243–46, 254, nos. 259, 261–63 (all 1249), and 274 (1253).

61. Berger, ed., *Les Registres d'Innocent IV*, nos. 787, 805, 1433, 2533, 2637, 3683, 4344, 4395, and 4577.

62. Remling, 1:479–620; Fisher, *Medieval Empire*, 2:133; Bayley, *Formation*, pp. 18, 36; Wilhelm Engel "Die Stadt Würzburg und die Kurie," pp. 303–5; and see chapter two, pp. 78–80, 82–83.

63. Stamer, *Kirchengeschichte*, 2:42.

64. Thus five counts of Berg reigned as archbishops of Cologne between 1132 and 1216, while in Mainz four counts of Eppstein ruled between 1220 and 1305 and four counts of Nassau between 1346 and 1475: Wilhelm Kisky, *Die Domkapitel der geistlichen Kurfürsten*, pp. 8–9, and Karl Demandt, *Geschichte des Landes Hessen*, pp. 237–42. See Werminghoff, *Verfassungsgeschichte*, p. 73, n. 3, for other examples.

65. See, for example, complaints against and condemnations of lay usurpations in Schannat and Hartzheim, eds., *Concilia Germaniae*, 3:266–67 (1105), 342–43 (1140), 422–24 (1180), 455–56 (1192), 488–91 (1208), 558–62 (1238), 586–87 (1256).

66. Philip Schneider, *Die bischöflichen Domkapitel,* pp. 129 ff.

67. Werminghoff, *Verfassungsgeschichte,* pp. 56, 59, 70.

68. Ibid., p. 59.

69. Johann Georg Lehmann, *Urkundliche Geschichte des gräflichen Hauses Leiningen-Hartenburg und Leiningen-Westerburg,* pp. 22–23, 40–42, 56, 58, 62–63, 67; Eduard Brinckmeier, *Genealogische Geschichte des . . . Hauses Leiningen und Leiningen-Westerburg,* 1:102; Albert Decker, "Die Benediktinerabtei Klingenmünster von der Merowinger- bis zur Staufenzeit," pp. 42–43, 53–54, 73 ff.; and the recent definitive article by Theodor Kaul, "Das Verhältnis der Grafen von Leiningen zum Reich und ihr Versuch einer Territorialbildung im Speyergau im 13. Jahrhundert," pp. 222–91, with a very good map at the end.

70. Hermann Schreibmüller, *Die Landvogtei im Speiergau,* pp. 32–86.

71. Georg H. Krieg von Hochfelden, *Geschichte der Grafen von Eberstein in Schwaben,* pp. 3–33, 50–51; Alfons Schäfer, "Waren die Grafen von Eberstein die Gründer der Stadt Neuenburg a. d. Enz oder der ehemaligen Stadt Neuburg am Rhein?," pp. 83–89.

72. Erwin Jacob, *Untersuchungen über Herkunft und Aufstieg des Reichsministerialengeschlechts Bolanden;* Bosl, *Reichsministerialität,* pp. 196–97, 260–74. Wernher II at the end of the twelfth century had no fewer than forty-five feudal lords.

73. *UBS,* 1:167–68, 184–85, 213–14, nos. 152 (1211), 175 (1229), 214 (1237); and Bienemann, *Conrad von Scharfenberg,* pp. 149, 153, 155, 157 for further examples.

74. *UBS,* 1:303–4, 307–11, 322–24, nos. 338 (1264), 342 (1265), 344 (1266), 358–59 (1270–71); *HSA* no. 1601 (1266); *USS,* pp. 84–86, no. 114 (1268); GLA 67/280, fol. 26r (1271).

75. See pp. 47–53.

76. Berger, ed., *Les Registres d'Innocent IV,* nos. 654, 788, 790–91, 948–49, 984, 1270–71, 2055, 2621, 6161.

77. Lehmann, *Haus Leiningen,* pp. 18–19.

78. See chapters two and three.

79. Hauck, *Kirchengeschichte,* vol. 5, pt. 1, pp. 20–23; Philipp Hofmeister, *Bischof und Domkapitel nach altem und nach neuem Recht,* p. 65; Barraclough, "Making of a Bishop," pp. 290–92, 294–98, 303–9.

80. Barraclough, "Making of a Bishop," p. 309.

CHAPTER 1, PART IV

1. Schneider, *Domkapitel,* pp. 4–19; Hofmeister, *Bischof und Domkapitel,* pp. 7–8, 30–31; and see pp. 25–27 below.

2. Unfortunately, there exists no scholarly treatment of this topic comparable to that of Klaus Ganzer on capitular electoral rights (see p. 20, n. 11 above).

3. See MGH *Dipl.* Henry IV, no. 466 (1101) (Stumpf, no. 2950); *UBS,* 1:104–6, 134, nos. 94 (1157) and 117 (1196); MGH *Const.,* 1:522, no. 374 (1196) (Stumpf, no. 5011); Schneider, *Domkapitel,* pp. 138–47.

4. MGH *Const.,* 2:37, 60, 68, nos. 31 (1209), 46–47 (1213), 56 (1213).

5. Ibid., 2:21–23, 37, 58, 67–70, 89, nos. 17 (1198), 31 (1209), 46–47 (1213), 56 (1216), 73 (1220).

6. See pp. 16–20.

7. Schneider, *Domkapitel*, pp. 18–19.

8. Ibid., pp. 50–52, 149–52 and notes. See also Edouard Fournier, *L'Origine du vicaire général et des autres membres de la curie diocésaine*.

9. See Santifaller, *Reichskirchensystem*, pp. 20–49.

10. The text of the Concordat of Worms is in MGH *Const.*, 1:159–61, nos. 107–8. See also the remarkable letter of Frederick Barbarossa to the cathedral chapter of Cambrai in 1167: "Licet enim, vobis discordantibus, de iure imperii quamlibet idoneam vobis subrogare possemus et quia iura imperii, qualem alibi nunquam iacturam vel ignominiam recepimus, apud vos nobis negata sunt, scilicet quod res episcopales decendente episcopo ad eamdem manum non redierunt de cuius munere eas constat descendisse" (ibid., 1:326–27, no. 231).

11. Fisher, *Medieval Empire*, 1:105–11, 258–59, and 2:72–74.

12. Werminghoff, *Verfassungsgeschichte*, p. 58.

13. See p. 25 and n. 4 immediately above as well as the following note.

14. Werminghoff, *Verfassungsgeschichte*, p. 58, doubted whether the renunciation was in fact absolute: "Doch scheint der Verzicht von 1216 nur das liegende Gut der Erzbistümer, Bistümer und Reichsabteien entlastet zu haben, während die Hoheitsrechte für die Dauer der Stuhlerledigung dm König verbleiben sollten."

15. See pp. 41–44.

16. *UBS*, 1:70, 84, nos. 70 and 76.

17. Remling, 2:830–31; Anton Wetterer, "Zur Geschichte des Speierer General-vikariats im 18. Jahrhundert," p. 97, pointed out that an unbroken succession of vicars-general began only under Bishop Raban (1396–1438).

18. Benson, *Bishop-Elect*, pp. 85, 106, 392.

19. *Decretales*, 3.9.2 (*CIC*, 2:501 = Potthast, no. 7794): "quum nusquam inveniatur cautum in iure, quod capitulum vacante sede fungatur vice episcopi in collationibus praebendarum. Nec in eodem casu potest dici potestas conferendi praebendas ad capitulum per superioris negligentiam devoluta, quum non fuerit ibi superior, qui eas posset de facto vel de iure conferre." Cf. Schneider, *Domkapitel*, pp. 413–15.

20. See Brian Tierney, *Foundations of the Conciliar Theory*, pp. 106–31, especially p. 130, on the slowness with which the development of formal theory proceeded.

21. Mansi, 21:533, and 22:1011 (= *COD*, pp. 203, 246).

22. C. 12 q. 2 cc. 38 and 45 (*CIC*, 1:699–701).

23. See n. 19 immediately above. Innocent III addressed his interdiction on change during a vacancy to the prior and chapter of Glastonbury: *Decretales*, 3.9.1 (*CIC*, 2:500–501 = Potthast, no. 2714).

24. Ibid.: "episcopali sede vacante, non debet super hoc aliquid innovari."

25. Tierney, *Foundations*, p. 128.

26. Ibid., pp. 127–31.

27. *Liber sextus*, 1.8.3–4; 1.17.1; 3.6.1; 3.8.1 (*CIC*, 2:974, 990, 1034–35, 1041–42).

28. Ibid., 1.6.42 and 1.8.4 (*CIC*, 2:967, 974).

29. Mansi, 21:282, c. 6 (c. 8 in *COD*, p. 191); 22:218–19, c. 3 (*COD*, pp. 212–13); 22:1014, c. 24 (*COD*, pp. 246–47).

30. *Decretales*, 3.10.4 (*CIC*, 2:502–3 = Jaffé, no. 11384): "Novit plenius, sicut credimus, tuae discretionis prudentia, qualiter tu et fratres tui unum corpus sitis, ita quidem, quod tu caput, et illi membra esse probantur. Unde non decet te omissis membris aliorum consilio in ecclesiae tuae negotiis uti, quum id non sit dubium et honestati tuae, et sanctorum Patrum institutionibus contraire."

31. Tierney, *Foundations*, pp. 117–27.

32. Foreville, "Représentation et taxation," pp. 57–59.

33. Post, *Studies*, pp. 3–5, 171; Tierney, *Foundations*, pp. 108–17.

34. Tierney, *Foundations*, p. 109.

35. See pp. 34–36.

36. Benson, *Bishop-Elect*, pp. 373–79.

37. Klewitz, "Entstehung," (in his *Reformpapsttum*) passim, but especially pp. 11, 13–14, 31–36, 46, 106, 109–11; and see the excellent article by Stephan Kuttner, "Cardinalis: The History of a Canonical Concept," pp. 129–214.

38. Mansi, 21:286, c. 22 (= *COD*, p. 194); *Decretum*, D. 24 c. 6 (*CIC*, 1:89) and C. 15 q. 7 c. 6 (ibid., 1:758), C. 12 q. 2 cc. 37 and 51–52 (ibid., 1:699, 703–4). For the textual tradition of the canons of this council, see *COD*, pp. 187–94.

39. Mansi, 21:286 (= *COD*, p. 194, and *Decretum*, D. 24 c. 6 [= *CIC*, 1:89]).

40. Mansi, 21:283, 285 (= *COD*, pp. 191, 194).

41. *Decretum*, D. 24 c. 6 and C. 15 q. 7 c. 6 (*CIC*, 1:89, 758).

42. *Decretum*, C. 12 q. 2 c. 53 (*CIC*, 1:704).

43. *Decretum*, C. 10 q. 2 c. 1 (*CIC*, 1:617).

44. See, for example, the variant textual readings given for "conniventia" in *Decretales*, 3.10.8 (*CIC*, 2:505).

45. Tierney, *Foundations*, p. 109. To appreciate Hostiensis's frustration one has only to read the relevant passages (*ad* C. 10 q. 2 and C. 12 q. 2) in the commentaries of some of the principal decretists: Roland Bandinelli (later Pope Alexander III), *Die Summa Magistri Rolandi*, ed. Friedrich Thaner, pp. 24, 26–27; Paucaplea, *Summa über das Decretum Gratiani*, ed. Johann Friedrich von Schulte, p. 80; *Summa "Elegantius in iure diuino" seu Coloniensis*, ed. Gérard Fransen and Stephan Kuttner; Stephen of Tournai (Stephan von Doornick), *Die Summa über das Decretum Gratiani*, ed. Johann Friedrich von Schulte; *The Summa Parisiensis on the Decretum Gratiani*, ed. Terence P. McLaughlin, pp. 143–46, 158–64.

46. *CIC*, 2:501–6.

47. c. 5: "mandamus, quatenus in concessionibus et confirmationibus et aliis ecclesiae tuae negotiis fratres tuos requiras, et cum eorum consilio, vel sanioris partis, negotia eadem peragas et pertractes. . . ."

48. In the same letter, Innocent went on to declare that "Irrita enim episcoporum donatio, venditio et commutatio rei ecclesiasticae erit absque conniventia et subscriptione clericorum."

49. See pp. 31–33.

50. *Decretales*, 3.13.5, 10 (*CIC*, 2:513, 515).

51. *Decretales*, 3.13.8 (*CIC*, 2:514).

52. *Liber sextus*, 3.6.1 and 3.8.1 (*CIC*, 2:1034–35, 1041–42).

53. Ibid., 3.9.2 (*CIC*, 2:1042).

54. See pp. 23–24, 27.

55. Kantorowicz, "Inalienability," pp. 488–502.

56. Mansi, 23:622–24, c. 13 (c. [1] in *COD*, pp. 293–95).

57. Hofmeister, *Bischof und Domkapitel*, pp. 144–45; *UBS*, 1:328, no. 360: "Item episcopus de possessionibus et aliis rebus episcopatus sive ad ecclesiam Spirensem pertinentibus de novo nullum infeodabit, neque alienabit since consensu capituli Spirensis."

58. *Extravangantes communes*, 3.4.1 (*CIC*, 2:1269).

59. Spangenberg, *Vom Lehnstaat*, pp. 45–56, 100–116.

60. Post, *Studies*, pp. 421–25.

61. MGH *Const.*, 1:204–6, no. 146.

62. Albert Hauck, *Friedrich Barbarossa als Kirchenpolitiker*, pp. 7–11; Post, *Studies*, pp. 421–25; Benson, *Bishop-Elect*, pp. 283–91; Peter Munz, *Frederick Barbarossa*, pp. 187–89.

63. MGH *Const.*, 1:425, no. 300.

64. Ibid., 2:80–81, no. 68.

65. Ibid., 2:391, no. 277.

66. Ibid., 2:229, no. 187.

67. Ibid., 2:443–44, no. 333.

68. Schannat and Hartzheim, eds., *Concilia Germaniae*, 3:600, c. 19.

69. Bosl, *Reichsministerialität*, p. 64, noted that Speyer was the only ecclesiastical foundation in the entire Rhine-Main area to receive extensive donations from Henry III.

70. MGH *Dipl.* Henry IV, no. 464 (1100) (Stumpf, no. 2946); *UBS*, 1:82–84, no. 76 (1103).

71. MGH *Dipl.* Henry III, no. 266 (1051) (Stumpf, no. 2400); MGH *Dipl.* Henry IV, nos. 411 (1090) (Stumpf, no. 2902), 464 (1100) (Stumpf, no. 2946), 489 (1105) (Stumpf, no. 2974): *UBS*, 1:68–69, 82–84, 89–90, nos. 69 (1099), 76 (1103), 81 (1114). Decker, "Klingenmünster," p. 41, n. 121, indicated that the bishops held their castle at Madenburg jointly with Henry V in 1112. See also Heinrich Büttner, "Zur Vogteientwicklung des Stiftes Hördt," pp. 343–44, 354, who maintained that Henry IV, determined to undermine the growing power of local lay families, had the advocacy of the collegiate church of Hördt transferred to the bishops of Speyer to keep it within imperial control (*UBS*, 1:82–84, no. 76 [1103]).

72. MGH *Dipl.* Conrad II, no. 41 (1025) (Stumpf, no 1894); MGH *Dipl.* Henry IV, no. 411 (1090) (Stumpf, no. 2902); *UBS*, 1:68–69, 85–86, nos. 69 (1099), 78 (1104), 81 (1114). In the last charter, an imperial confirmation of an exchange of properties between the bishop and the chapter, Henry V consented "quia absque nostro consensu et voluntate fieri non potuit. . . ."

73. *UBS*, 1:111–12, 120–21, nos. 99 and 105.

74. Ibid., 1:92–93, no. 84 (1147); *WUB*, 1:348–49, no. 276 (1122); 2:59, no. 335 (1152); 2:127–28, no. 370 (1160); 2:341, Nachtrag no. 38 (ca. 1100).

75. See chapter two, p. 71 and n. 12.

76. *WUB*, 2:254, no. 455 (1188).

77. Bosl, *Reichsministerialität*, pp. 144, 231, 276, 623–24.

78. Fisher, *Medieval Empire*, 1:258–59, and 2:74–76; Alexander Boss, *Die Kirchenlehen der Staufischen Kaiser*, pp. 24–25; Bosl, *Reichsministerialität*, pp. 151, 405–7; Wolfgang Metz, *Staufische Güterverzeichnisse*, pp. 41, 43, 47, 119. For a full discussion, see chapter two, pp. 71–73.

79. Bosl, *Reichsministerialität*, pp. 144, 276–77, 406–7. Clear evidence of imperial employment of episcopal ministerials is in *WUB*, 3:303, no. 808 (1232): "presentibus abbatibus, prepositis, decanis et universo clero, nostre dyocesis, in nostra generali synodo, constitutis, et nobilibus laicis: O. de Brusella, R. de Kyselowe, et ministerialibus tam imperii quam ecclesie, A. et A. de Lache, E. et C. de Altdorf, B. de Vlehingen, R. de Vbestat et aliis quam pluribus."

80. *UBS*, 1:126, no. 111.

81. Ibid., 1:133–34, no. 116.

82. On the importance of the issue of maintenance of coinage standards in the Burgundian estates general in the fourteenth century, see Peter Spufford, "Assemblies of Estates, Taxation and Control of Coinage in Medieval Europe," pp. 113–30.

83. *UBS*, 1:141, no. 124.

84. See n. 52 above in this section.

85. *WUB*, 3:289, no. 793.

86. MGH *Const.*, 3:1–5. The only advocacies of churches listed among the 104 entries are those of the abbeys of Kempten, Saint Gall, and Weissenburg. On Weissenburg, in Salian and then Staufen hands since the late tenth century, see Hans Werle, "Die salisch-staufische Obervogtei über die Reichsabtei Weissenburg," pp. 333–38.

87. MGH *Dipl.* Conrad II, no. 41 (1025); Stumpf, no. 1894; *UBS*, 1:25–26, 68–69, nos. 25 (1023) and 69 (1099).

88. *UBS*, 1:82–84, 92–95, nos. 76 (1103), 84 (1147), 85 (1148); *WUB*, 2:40–41, no. 324 (ca. 1147).

89. *UBS*, 1:96–97, no. 87 (1149); *WUB*, 2:123–24, no. 367 (1159), and 2:342–43, no. 521 (1203).

90. *UBS*, 1:99–100, no. 90 (1152); *WUB*, 2:252–54, nos. 454–55 (1188). There is much controversy concerning the exact comprehension of the term *familia* (*ecclesiae*). On the basis of German and Lotharingian charters of the eleventh to the thirteenth centuries, François L. Ganshof, *Étude sur les ministeriales en Flandre et en Lotharingie*, pp. 9–10, 39–60, concluded that the term meant only ministerials, who were unfree, and did not include *liberi*, whom he identified with *nobiles*. Leo Verriest, *Noblesse, chevalerie, lignages*, pp. 21, 24–25, 27, 51 n. 92, 68, sharply criticized Ganshof's findings. As for Speyer, *UBS*, vol. 1, nos. 70 (1100), 76 (1103), 78 (1104), and 79 (1105) do not help to resolve the question; but *WUB*, 2:252–54, nos. 454–55 (1188) seem to support Verriest. Here the bishop received the assent of "canonicorum quoque et ministerialium ac familia [sic] Spirensis ecclesie" to an exchange of lands. "Familia" probably includes the "hominibus beneficiatis" mentioned in the first of the two charters, but this is not absolutely clear.

91. *UBS*, 1:85–86, no. 78.

92. Ibid., 1:97–98, no. 88: "Assencientibus et ut hec fierent congruum esse attestantibus pocioribus de clero et ministerialibus ecclesie nostre. . . ."

93. *WUB*, 2:252-54, nos. 454-55.

94. *UBS*, 1:165-66, no. 150: "Quod hoc concambium placuit personis tam ecclesiasticis tam laicis ecclesie Spirensi attinentibus."

95. Ibid., 1:222-23, no. 227: "universarum ecclesiarum Spirensium cleri et ministerialium nostrorum consilio accedente. . . ."

96. Hauck, *Kirchengeschichte*, vol. 5, pt. 1, pp. 173-75. For a discussion of the meaning and comprehension of the term "synodales," see Franz Gescher, "Synodales: Studien zur kirchlichen Gerichtsverfassung und zum deutschen Ständewesen des Mittelalters," pp. 358-446.

97. *UBS*, 1:25-26, 96-97, nos. 25 (1023) and 87 (1149); *WUB*, 2:207, no. 421; 3:303, no. 808 (1232); Würdtwein, ed., *Nova subsidia*, 1:170 (1211). In 1176 such an assembly of clergy and laymen was called a "commune consilium": Franz J. Mone, "Urkunden über die bayerische Pfalz vom 12.-16. Jahrhundert," p. 167. Bienemann, *Conrad von Scharfenberg*, pp. 138, 141, said that similar synods were conducted in Speyer in 1202 and 1206.

98. Thus the arenga of a charter, issued by the chapter in 1225, in *WUB*, 3:179, no. 698: "rationabile est et iuri consentaneum, ut ecclesiastice persone invicem sua cognoscant negocia et alterutrum ydoneis peticionbus pium prebeant assensum."

99. See pp. 47-53.

100. See pp. 41-44.

101. GLA 67/448, fols. 45v-46r (= Würdtwein, ed., *Monasticon Palatinum*, 5:83-84, and *USS*, p. 43, no. 49).

102. See pp. 36-37.

103. *UBS*, 1:99-100, no. 90 (1152); *WUB*, 2:227, no. 435 (1183).

104. *UBS*, 1:133-34, no. 116.

105. Stephan-Alexander Würdtwein, ed., *Subsidia diplomatica*, 5:270-72; *UBS*, vol. 1, nos. 121 (1201), 141 (1220), 166 (1226), 178 (1230), 189 (1232), 229 (1242), 256 (1249), 278 (1254), 310 (ca. 1260), 314 (1260), 324 (1262), 349 (1267), 358 (1270); *USS*, p. 40, no. 45 (1230); *WUB*, 3:411-12, no. 909 (1238); 3:433, no. 930 (1239); 4:51-52, no. 1001 (1243); 4:68-70, no. 1018 (1244); 4:184-85, no. 1120 (1248); 6:60-61, no. 1658 (1262).

106. *UBS*, vol. 1, nos. 127 (1209), 152 (1211), 202 (1235), 256 (1249). *WUB*, 3:155-56, no. 678 (1224); 4:68-70, no. 1018 (1244); 4:79-80, no. 1028 (1244). Eduard Winkelmann, *Jahrbücher der deutschen Geschichte: Philipp von Schwaben und Otto IV. von Braunschweig*, 2:518-19 (1209).

107. HSA no. 1150 (1221).

108. *WUB*, 2:342-43, no. 521 (1203); Winkelmann, *Jahrbücher*, 2:518-19 (1209).

109. *WUB*, 3:37, no. 584 (1216); Bienemann, *Conrad von Scharfenberg*, pp. 141, 144-76, gives other examples.

110. *WUB*, 4:406, Nachtrag no. 108 (1227). This charter dates from the reign of Bishop Beringer.

111. *WUB*, 2:343-44, no. 521 (1203).

112. *UBS*, 1:146, no. 130 (1213), and the notes following.

113. Ibid., 1:141-42, no. 125 (1207). Würdtwein, ed., *Subsidia diplomatica*, 5:267-69

(1207). *WUB*, 2:356–58, no. 532 (1207); 3:91, no. 623 (1219); 3:195–96, no. 713 (1226). *USS*, p. 38, no. 40 (1226).

114. Bienemann, *Conrad von Scharfenberg*, pp. 143–76, cited at least twelve instances.

115. Ibid., pp. 149, 153, 155, 157; *WUB*, 3:37, no. 584 (1216).

116. *UBS*, 1:238–39, no. 255 (1248).

117. Ibid., 1:250, no. 269 (1251).

118. *WUB*, 5:325–26, no. 1567 (1260), and 6:82, no. 1681 (1262).

119. *UBS*, 1:276–77, no. 304 (1258).

120. Ibid., 1:267–68, 271, nos. 292 and 297.

121. Ibid., vol. 1, nos. 256 (1249), 278 (1254), 310 (ca. 1260), 314 (1260), 324 (1262), 349 (1267), 358 (1270).

122. Ibid., 1:267–68, 297, nos. 292 (1256) and 330 (1262: in both cases the assent of King William of Holland); Würdtwein, ed., *Nova subsidia*, 12:175 (1256: that of the count of Leiningen and of the burghers of Speyer); *WUB*, 4:205–6, no. 1237 (1252: that of the four collegiate churches of Speyer regarding the advocacy, enfeoffed by the bishop to some ministerials, of the monastery of Maulbronn).

123. *UBS*, 1:250–52, 280–81, nos. 270 (1252) and 309 (1259).

124. In addition to the two cited in the preceding note, also *WUB*, 2:342–43, no. 521 (1203), and Winkelmann, *Jahrbücher*, 2:518–19 (1209).

125. *UBS*, 1:325–28, no. 360.

CHAPTER 1, PART V

1. GLA 67/462, 465, and 483. See also 67/479, a fifteenth-century copybook drawn up for the defense of the chapter's possessions in litigation.

2. M. Krebs, in his introduction to the *Protokolle*, 1:x–xi; Gustav Bossert, "Beiträge zur badisch-pfälzischen Reformationsgeschichte," *ZGO* N.F. 17 (1902):68–73, 253. Neither Glasschröder, "Frühgeschichte," pp. 481–97, nor A. Gnann, "Beiträge zur Verfassungsgeschichte des Domkapitels von Speyer," pp. 167–206, treat this aspect of the chapter's development.

3. MGH *Dipl.* Henry IV, no. 466; Stumpf, no. 2950.

4. *UBS*, 1:327–28, no. 360.

5. MGH *Dipl. Karol. Germ.* Louis the German, no. 118 (865); MGH *Dipl.* Henry III, nos. 167–74 (1046) (Stumpf, nos. 2305–12); MGH *Dipl.* Henry IV, nos. 11 (1057) (Stumpf, no. 2536), 12 (1057) (Stumpf, no. 2539), and 325 (1080) (Stumpf, no. 2824); *UBS*, 1:147–49, 312–13, nos. 132 (1213) and 346 (1267).

6. *UBS*, vol. 1, nos. 246 (1245), 259 (1249), 263 (1249), 274 (1253). These were all indulgences.

7. Ibid., vol. 1, nos. 221 (1239), 290 (1255), 313 (1260), 328 (1262).

8. Ibid., vol. 1, nos. 70 (1100), 109 (ca. 1190), 130 (1213), 135 (1216), 146–48 (1221), 150 (1221), 354 (1268).

9. GLA 67/448, fol. 60r (1235); Würdtwein, ed., *Subsidia diplomatica*, 5:280–81 (1235); *UBS*, vol. 1, nos. 195 (1234), 201 (1235), 207 (1236).

10. *UBS*, vol. 1, nos. 140 (1220), 192 (1233), 206 (1236), 220 (1239), 232 (1242), 264 (1249), 284 (1255), 336 (1264); *USS*, pp. 33, 59, nos. 32 (1220) and 74 (1249).

11. *UBS,* vol. 1, nos. 104 (1180), 118 (1197), 190 (1232), 356 (1269); *CR,* 2:40 (last decade of the twelfth century). See also Franz Xaver Glasschröder, ed., *Urkunden zur pfälzischen Kirchengeschichte im Mittelalter,* pp. 2, 4–5, nos. 3 (1195), 10–12 (1272–75).

12. *UBS,* 1:162, no. 144. Innocent IV confirmed this statute in 1245: ibid., 1:232, no. 244.

13. *Protokolle,* 1:xii–xiii.

14. *UBS,* vol. 1, nos. 158 (1223), 205 (ca. 1236), 208 (1236), 210 (1237), 228 (1241), 233–36 (1243), 258 (1249), 281 (1254), 294–95 (1256), 321 (1261), 331 (1263), 343 (1266), 354 (1268), 380 (1277); Würdtwein, ed., *Subsidia diplomatica,* 4:187–88 (1249), 5:295–96 (1249) and 300–301 (1251); *USS,* pp. 51–52, 95–96, nos. 63 (1241) and 131 (1276).

15. *UBS,* vol. 1, nos. 164 (1225), 254 (1248), 311 (1260).

16. Ibid., 1:147–49, no. 132.

17. Stamer, *Kirchengeschichte,* 2:7.

18. *WUB,* 6:381–84, no. 1987.

19. *UBS,* 1:211, 215, nos. 211 and 217 (1237).

20. *USS,* pp. 51–52, no. 63 (1241).

21. *UBS,* 1:89–90, 165–66, nos. 81 (1114) and 150 (1223); *USS,* pp. 71–72, no. 99 (1261).

22. *UBS,* 1:54–55, no. 137.

23. Ibid., 1:298, no. 331 (1263) contains the first clear reference to such *officia;* see also ibid., 1:327–28, no. 360 (1272) for a description of some of these administrative districts. The first reference to episcopal bailiffs (*amptlute, Amtleute*) occurs in 1318: ibid., 1:488, no. 518. An inventory of the bishop's incomes from his various castles and *Amter* compiled about 1338–41 is printed in [?] Reimer, "Zur Geschichte des Bischofs Gerhart von Speier," pp. 102–17.

24. *UBS,* vol. 1, nos. 174 (1229), 186 (1232), 251 (1247), 279 (1254).

25. Ibid., 1:81–82, no. 75.

26. Ibid., 1:104–6, no. 94. Remling, 1:385, thought the "instanti expedicione" referred to the Second Crusade, but I have accepted the undoubtedly correct interpretation of Wilhelm Bernhardi, *Jahrbücher der deutschen Geschichte: Konrad III.,* pp. 887–88.

27. *UBS,* 1:124, no. 108. Metz, *Staufische Güterverzeichnisse,* pp. 41, 119, indicated that the Boyneburgs were imperial ministerials who held the advocacy of the bishopric of Speyer in delegation from Frederick Barbarossa by 1184.

28. *UBS,* 1:52–53, no. 52 (1065), a donation of Kreuznach and all its appurtenances to the chapter by Henry IV was listed as a forgery by Dietrich von Gladiss in MGH *Dipl.* Henry IV, no. 167. Werner Vogt, *Untersuchungen zur Geschichte der Stadt Kreuznach,* pp. 64–73, 316–17, considered the forgery, the production of which he dated to ca. 1200, an attempt to replace the lost original of ca. 1045–50.

29. *UBS,* 1:222–23, no. 227: "Item allodium, quod habuimus in Ditensheim, . . . pro ducentis sexaginta marcis puri argenti securius ea vendi, quam bona preempta revendi censentes, maxime cum episcopatus per alium potentem bonorum prescriptorum que emimus posset opprimi possessorem."

30. On the great losses of church land by enfeoffment, see chapter two, pp. 73–77.

31. *UBS*, 1:145–46, 167–68, nos. 129 (1210) and 152 (1211); GLA 67/448, fols. 46v–47r (1214). Bishop Conrad also sought indemnification for fiefs subinfeudated or sold beyond the hope of recovery: *UBS*, 1:139–41, no. 123 (1204), and GLA 78/33 (1214).

32. *WUB*, 3:302, no. 807.

33. *UBS*, 1:193, no. 187.

34. Ibid., 1:206–7, no. 205.

35. Ibid., 1:223, no. 228.

36. Ibid., nos. 275 (1253), 278 (1254), 338 (1264), 341 (1265), 358 (1270).

37. Ibid., 1:298, no. 331.

38. Ibid., 1:269–70, no. 294.

39. Ibid., 1:261, no. 281. Bishop Henry confirmed the sale in 1255: ibid., 1:263, no. 285.

40. Ibid., 1:311, no. 343.

41. Ibid., 1:239–42, nos. 256–57; *WUB*, 4:187–88, no. 1123, and 5:112–13, no. 1347.

42. See MGH *Const.*, 1:346–47, no. 246, where Frederick Barbarossa in 1175 ordered the chapter and clergy of Würzburg to supply 350 marks to help their bishop join the expedition to Italy; and canon 16 of the diocesan synod of Utrecht in 1209: "Si episcopus gravatus fuerit, Ecclesia ei assistet auxilio, et consilio, et in expensis" (Schannat and Hartzheim, eds., *Concilia Germaniae*, 3:490).

43. Thus Hofmeister, *Bischof und Domkapitel*, pp. 12–14, 25–36, 144–45, 162–68; Below, *Wahlrecht*, pp. 17–34, 46–48; Schneider, *Domkapitel*, pp. 147–55.

44. *UBS*, 1:99–100, no. 90. The term "archdeacon" as such is not used here; but it is clear that the provost, who simultaneously held the office of archdeacon, performed the functions of that office.

45. Ibid., 1:70, 84, nos. 70 and 76. Franx Xaver Remling, *Urkundliche Geschichte der ehemaligen Abteien und Klöster im jetzigen Rheinbayern*, 2:22; Büttner, "Hördt," pp. 346, 351; and Gugumus, "Bischöfe," p. 75, n. 524, all mistook the *chorepiscopus* of these charters for the archdeacon. Eugen Baumgartner, *Geschichte und Recht des Archidiakonates der oberrheinischen Bistümer mit Einschluss von Mainz und Würzburg*, p. 81, did not, but he nevertheless believed that this was just another name for the archdeacon. There is no reason to assume the existence of archdeacons in the diocese of Speyer from a letter of 1078 from Gregory VII to Bishop Rüdiger which speaks generically of "archidiaconatus": Albert Brackmann, ed., *Regesta pontificum Romanorum: Germania Pontificia*, vol. 3, pt. 3, p. 94, no. 13. Even if this interpretation is correct, there exists no evidence to prove a connection between the archdeacon and the cathedral provost until the mid-twelfth century. On the *chorepiscopus*, which survived in some places in the West until the middle of the twelfth century, and whose duties were largely the same as those taken over later by the archdeacon, see Frank L. Cross and E. A. Livingstone, eds., *The Oxford Dictionary of the Christian Church*, s.v., and Theodor Gottlob, *Das abendländische Chorepiskopat*.

46. See Remling, 1:121; Franz Xaver Glasschröder, "Das Archidiakonat in der Diözese Speyer während des Mittelalters," pp. 114–16; Alois Seiler, *Studien zu den*

Anfängen der Pfarrei- und Landdekanatsorganisation in den rechtsrheinischen Archidiakonaten des Bistums Speyer, pp. 175–79.

47. Seiler, *Studien,* p. 177.

48. Ibid., p. 36. It was for a long time thought that about the year 1100 Bishop John translated the canons of the Sinsheim collegiate church to Saint Germain's, and the monks of Saint Germain's to Sinsheim, thereby changing the latter into a monastery: thus Remling, 1:125, and Stamer, *Kirchengeschichte,* 2:56. This view is now rejected in general: see Josef Semmler, "Sinshim, ein Reformkloster Siegburger Observanz im alten Bistum Speyer," pp. 339–47.

49. Stamer, *Kirchengeschichte,* 2:56.

50. Remling, 1:126.

51. See nn. 52 and 56 below.

52. See the witness lists in *UBS,* vol. 1, nos. 84 (1147), 86 (1148), 90 (1152), 99 (ca. 1164), 128 (1209), 130 (1213), 135 (1216), 141 (1220), 155 (1218), 159 (1224), 166 (1226), 179 (1230), 181 (1230); *WUB,* 2:343, no. 522 (1203); 3:156, no. 678 (1224); 3:419, no. 917 (1238); 4:188–89, no. 1124 (1249).

53. *Protokolle,* 1:xiv; and see chapter five, p. 168.

54. *UBS,* vol. 1, nos. 82, 84, 88, 90; WUB, 2:127–28, no. 370.

55. *UBS,* 1:100, no. 90.

56. *WUB,* 2:128, no. 370: "prepositura sancti Widonis, ad cuius archidiaconatum pertinere dinoscitur, in nostre potestatis esset arbitrio. . . ."

57. Glasschröder, "Archidiakonat," pp. 114, 123–28.

58. *Decretales,* 1.23.7 (*CIC,* 2:151–52).

59. This is the thesis of Heinrich Wirtz, "Donum, investitura, conductus ecclesiae," pp. 116–50.

60. See, for example, the five letters of Alexander III to various bishops "De excessibus episcoporum contra suos archidiaconos, et archidiaconorum contra suos episcopos" appended to the decrees of the Third Lateran Council (1179) in Mansi, 22:364–65.

61. See chapter three, p. 92, and chapter four, 140–141.

62. Riedner, *Gerichtshöfe,* 2:161–62, no. 41.

63. Ibid., 2:165, 169–70, nos. 43 (1238), 44 (1241), and 45 (1243).

64. Ibid., 2:173–74, 179–80, 182–83, nos. 47 (1248), 48 (1251), 52 (1260), 55 (1270).

65. *UBS,* 1:326, no. 360.

66. See Hauck, *Kirchengeschichte,* vol. 5, pt. 1, p. 157, n. 4; and Riedner, "Offizialatsgericht," pp. 39–40, who found the first *officiales* around 1270.

67. *UBS,* 1:439, no. 466. Riedner, "Offizialatsgericht," pp. 20–24, 69–70, curiously minimized the scope and importance of the struggle between the bishops and the archdeacons. He appears to have followed the opinion of Edouard Fournier, *L'Origine du vicaire général,* pp. 87–90, 159–60, who rejected the opinion of Paul Fournier, *Les officialités au Moyen Âge,* pp. 3–12, that the *officiales* were instituted by bishops to regain episcopal rights lost to the archdeacons. Whatever the case elsewhere, there certainly was such a struggle at Speyer.

68. See Wetterer, "Speierer Generalvikariat," pp. 99–100; and chapter four, pp. 140–141.

69. *UBS*, 1:76, no. 72: "Quicquid autem in rure, in beneficio, quod ab episcopo [a deceased canon] habuit, reliquit, in usum episcopi cedat."

70. Ibid., 1:135, no. 118 (1197); Würdtwein, ed., *Monasticon Palatinum*, 4:244 (1224), and 5:83–84 (1232); Glasschröder, *Urkunden zur pfälzischen Kirchengeschichte*, pp. 193, 196, nos. 454 (1208) and 464 (1234); Krieg von Hochfelden, *Grafen von Eberstein*, p. 36; Brinckmeier, *Haus Leiningen*, pp. 49–50; Mazetti, "Beringer von Entringen," p. 9.

71. GLA 67/451, fols. 127r–128r.

72. Cross and Livingstone, eds., *Oxford Dictionary of the Christian Church*, s.v. "Minor Orders."

73. Below, *Wahlrecht*, pp. 34–37.

74. *CR*, 2:40; on the history of this text, see ibid., 2:v–vi.

75. Würdtwein, ed., *Subsidia diplomatica*, 9:167, 171–73.

76. *UBS*, 1:332, no. 365.

77. Ibid., 1:232–33, no. 245 (Innocent IV's permission to do so).

78. Glasschröder, "Speierer Bistums-Matrikel," pp. 82–83.

79. *UBS*, 1:156–57, no. 139.

80. See the witness list at the end of the previous charter (ibid., 1:157): "G . . . subdiaconum, A. diaconum, vicarios. . . ."

81. Ibid., 1:292–93, no. 325 (1262).

82. Kaul, "Klerus des Domstiftes von Speyer," p. 114; *Protokolle*, 1:xi–xii.

83. *Protokolle*, 1:x–xi; and see chapter four, pp. 145–46.

84. Hinschius, *Kirchenrecht*, 2:55–58; Glasschröder, "Frühgeschichte," pp. 482, 490–91; Stamer, *Kirchengeschichte*, 2:108.

85. John C. Dickinson, *The Origins of the Austin Canons and Their Introduction into England*, pp. 14–21; cf. Hinschius, *Kirchenrecht*, 2:50–55.

86. See Hans-Walter Klewitz, "Königtum, Hofkapelle und Domkapitel im 10. und 11. Jahrhundert," pp. 102–56; and see this volume, pp. 26–29, 33, 37–39, 41–43.

87. One of the few historians to recognize this is Karl Otmar Freiherr von Aretin, *Heiliges Römisches Reich 1776–1806*, 1:37.

88. See Klewitz, "Entstehung," (in his *Reformpapsttum*) passim.

89. See the sensible remarks of Kathleen Edwards, *The English Secular Cathedrals in the Middle Ages*, pp. 20–22, 251, 318–25.

CHAPTER 1, PART VI

1. Schulte, *Adel*.

2. Santifaller, *Reichskirchensystem*, passim.

3. Schulte, *Adel*, p. 67. Schulte admitted the weakness of his evidence in many instances: see ibid., pp. 2–3, 32 n. 3, 36–38, 48–49, 96–113.

4. Gnann, "Domkapitel," p. 169; Glasschröder, "Frühgeschichte," p. 496.

5. MGM *Dipl.* Henry IV, no. 466: "unusquisque Spirensis ecclesie canonicus, sive nobili vel humili genere ortus. . . ."

6. *UBS*, 1:623–24, no. 620.

7. *CR,* 1:446, n. 3.

8. *UBS,* 1:304–5, no. 339.

9. *USS,* p. 90, no. 121.

10. *UBS,* 1:440, no. 466.

11. Ibid., 1:460–61, no. 487.

12. Hermann Schreibmüller, *Pfälzer Reichsministerialen,* pp. 27–33, 38–39.

13. *CR,* 1:87, n. 2; and see this volume, p. 48, n. 29, and p. 51. Peter Acht, "Studien zum Urkundenwesen der Speyerer Bischöfe im 12. und im Anfang des 13. Jahrhunderts," pp. 302–3, pointed out that Bienemann only assumed that Conrad was dean, which has since been shown to be incorrect.

14. *WUB,* 4:188–89, no. 1124; *UBS,* 1:252, no. 270; Bosl, *Reichsministerialität,* p. 357.

15. Würdtwein, ed., *Subsidia diplomatica,* 5:328–32; Bosl, *Reichsministerialität,* pp. 208, 221, 235–36, 338.

16. *UBS,* 1:169, no. 154 (1217): "Egeno de Muspach, ministerialis noster."

17. Bosl, *Reichsministerialität,* p. 221; *CR,* 1:560, n. 1.

18. Bosl, *Reichsministerialität,* p. 407. *CR,* 1:87, n. 2; 1:392, n. 1; 2:202. *UBS,* 1:193, no. 187 (1232).

19. Bosl, *Reichsministerialität,* p. 407.

20. Ibid., pp. 196–97, 203–4, 238–39, 260–74. *CR,* 1:295, n. 1; 1:544, n. 6; 1:610, n. 1. Franz J. Mone, "Urkundenarchiv des Klosters Herren-Alb vom 12. und 13. Jahrhundert," *ZGO* 1 (1850):237, 255, 374.

21. *UBS,* 1:312, no. 345.

22. Eberhard F. Otto, *Adel and Freiheit im deutschen Staat des Mittelalters,* pp. 211–433.

23. Bosl, *Reichsministerialität,* pp. 25–31: "eine besonders qualifizierte Oberschicht der Unfreiheit" (p. 28).

24. *UBS,* vol. 1, nos. 89 (1150), 94 (1157), 99 (ca. 1164). *WUB,* 2:134, no. 374 (1160); 2:211, no. 424 (1181); 2:245, no. 446 (1186); 3:122, no. 646 (1221). GLA 67/448, fol. 15v (1238). In 1238 the bishops of Speyer and Strasbourg with the consent of their chapters exchanged two families of ministerials: Franz Mone, "Urkunden über das Unterelsass," pp. 152–53.

25. Otto Imhof, *Die Ministerialität in den Stiftern Strassburg, Speier und Worms,* p. 51.

26. Bryce Lyon, *From Fief to Indenture,* pp. 183–84, 189–91, 271–72.

27. *UBS,* 1:151, no. 135.

28. Ibid., 1:158, 160, nos. 140–41.

29. *WUB,* 3:303, no. 808; *UBS,* 1:211, no. 211.

30. Ibid., 1:223, no. 227.

31. Ibid., 1:157, no. 140: "Cuonradus, miles de Sutzfelt, ministerialis ecclesie Spirensis."

32. Ibid., 1:271, no. 296.

33. Ibid., 1:206–7, 213–14, nos. 204–5, 214.

34. Mone, "Herren-Alb," pp. 237, 255, 374.

35. GLA 42/173 s.d.

36. *UBS*, 1:328, no. 360: "Item feoda tam a vasallis vel ministerialibus Spirensis ecclesie quite obtenta. . . ."

37. Ibid., 1:366, no. 401. Cf. Imhof, *Ministerialität*, p. 87, who believed ministerials continued to exist to the end of the fourteenth century.

38. *UBS*, vol. 1, nos. 414 (1286), 431 (1292), 468 (1302).

39. Ibid., 1:440, no. 466 (1302).

40. *WUB*, 11:526, no. 5668 (1268); *UBS*, 1:406, 410, nos. 438 (1294) and 444 (1295).

41. HSA no. 13: "Welher aber das ver libes not nicht gethun mecht, der salt eynen erbern edeln knecht mit gantzem wapen an sin stadt senden und stellen, der yne verwesen solt, glicher wyse als er selber da were."

42. Imhof, *Ministerialität*, pp. 51, 81–82, 84–89; and Karl Jordan and Karl Bosl in Herbert Grundmann, ed., *Gebhardts Handbuch der deutschen Geschichte*, 1:423–25 and 821–23, respectively, and the literature cited there.

43. See pp. 15–16, and chapter three, pp. 88–89.

44. *CR*, 1:187, n. 2, and 1:393, n. 1.

45. *UBS*, 1:405–6, no. 438 (1294).

46. Ibid., nos. 142 (1220), 187 (1232), 192 (1233), 203 (1235), 228 (1241), 277 (1253), 293 (1256).

47. Bienemann, *Conrad von Scharfenberg*, pp. 1–10.

48. See the witness list in *WUB*, 3:122, no. 646 (1221): "Ministeriales: Heinricus de Scharphenekke, Albertus camerarius, Bertoldus de Scharfenberch, Burchardus de Wachenheim, et ceteri quam plures."

49. Würdtwein, ed., *Nova subsidia*, 1:174.

50. *UBS*, vol. 1, nos. 152 (1211), 177 (1230), 185 (1232), 233 (1243); *USS*, p. 46, no. 54 (1235); Bosl, *Reichsministerialität*, pp. 221, 231, 233.

51. *USS*, p. 30, no. 28 (1212).

52. *UBS*, 1:158, 171, nos. 140 and 155.

53. Ibid., nos. 179, 185, 233.

54. Bosl, *Reichsministerialität*, pp. 196–97, 260–74; Jacob, *Reichsministerialengeschlecht Bolanden*, passim.

55. Bosl, *Reichsministerialität*, pp. 203–4; *CR*, 1:190, n. 1; 1:295, n. 2; 1:449, n. 1; 1:567, n. 2; 1:610, n. 1.

56. Bosl, *Reichsministerialität*, p. 254; *CR*, 1:36, n. 3; 1:176, n. 2; 1:211, n. 1; 1:349, n. 1; 1:473, n. 1; 1:483, 517, and 548, n. 1.

57. Bosl, *Reichsministerialität*, p. 208; *CR*, 1:48, n. 2; 1:74, n. 1; 1:95, n. 1; 1:203, n. 1; 1:577, n. 2.

58. *UBS*, 1:12, no. 13. See also MGH *Dipl.* Conrad II, no. 26 (1024); Stumpf, no. 1855.

59. *UBS*, 1:96–97, no. 87.

60. Ibid., 1:97–98, no. 88.

61. Ibid., 1:111–12, nos. 98–99 (1163–64). See also ibid., 1:102, no. 92 (1153).

62. Bosl, *Reichsministerialität*, pp. 144, 218–19, 230–33, 275–77, 406–7.

63. MGH *Const.*, 1:329, no. 234 (at Barbarossa's behest the clergy and ministerials of Regensburg in 1167 elected his choice as bishop); 2:70–72, no. 57 (1216: no

alienation of imperial principalities without the consent of the prince and his ministerials); 2:80–81, no. 68 (1219: upon the death of a bishop, all offices of the bishopric are automatically vacated except the four court offices, which in most German bishoprics under imperial sway were by this time in the hands of ministerials); 2:391, no. 277 (1222: the income of these four offices is to be alienated in no way without the consent of the cathedral chapter and the ministerials); 2:423, no. 310 (1231: fiefs held by imperial and ecclesiastical ministerials are declared heritable); 2:443–44, no. 333 (1240: renewal of the 1219 sentence regarding the four court offices during episcopal vacancies).

64. Geselbracht, *Verfahren*, p. 13.

65. Krabbo, *Besetzung*, pp. 74–81, 84–98.

66. MGH *Const.*, 1:182–85, no. 128 (1150: the *sententia contra temeritates ministerialium* of the monastery of Corbei) and 2:35–36, no. 30 (1209: alienations of allodial and feudal property by ministerials without the consent of their lords); Schannat and Hartzheim, eds., *Concilia Germaniae*, 3:367–68 (1151: Utrecht), 424–25 (1180: Gurk), 568 (1239: Eichstätt).

67. Monasteries subject to the bishops complained of outrages committed by episcopal ministerials, however: Semmler, "Sinsheim," pp. 343–44; Potthast, no. 8330 (1229: Maulbronn); *WUB*, 4:305–6, no. 1237 (1252); 6:65–67, no. 1663 (1262); 7:96–100, no. 2155 (1270: all three concern Maulbronn).

68. *UBS*, 1:222–23, no. 227.

69. Ibid., 1:326, no. 360.

70. Desprairies, *Élection*, p. 13.

71. Karl Bosl, "Die aristokratische Struktur der mittelalterlichen Gesellschaft," in his *Die Gesellschaft in der Geschichte des Mittelalters*, pp. 25–43.

72. Heinrich Dannenbauer, "Adel, Burg und Herrschaft bei den Germanen," *Historisches Jahrbuch* 61 (1941):1; my translation is from the revised article printed in Hellmut Kämpf, ed., *Herrschaft und Staat im Mittelalter*, pp. 66–67. It is most instructive to compare the somewhat timid rule of the nonaristocratic monks of Durham before 1541 with the great self-confidence of their aristocratic "reformed" successors: see David Marcombe, "The Durham Dean and Chapter: Old Abbey Writ Large?" in Rosemary O'Day and Felicity Heal, eds., *Continuity and Change: Personnel and Administration of the Church in England 1500–1642*, pp. 125–44, especially 135–40.

73. Heinrich Mitteis, *Der Staat des hohen Mittelalters*, pp. 13, 426–27.

74. On the conflicts among the orders of society, especially between the nobles and the towns, see Friedrich Baethgen in Grundmann, ed., *Gebhardts Handbuch*, 1:611–13; Lyon, "Medieval Constitutionalism," pp. 165–68; Carsten, *Princes*, pp. 423–24, 439.

75. Karl S. Bader, *Der deutsche Südwesten in seiner territorialstaatlichen Entwicklung*, pp. 171–72, who agreed with similar judgments expressed by Roth von Schreckenstein and Gerhard Ritter. Speyer was one of a number of sees (the others being Mainz, Worms, Würzburg, Bamberg, and, to a lesser extent, Trier) dominated by the imperial knights, who both served the empire faithfully and, in the early modern period, rather successfully parried the efforts of the great princely dynasties to reduce these bishoprics to the status of appanages. See Andreas Veit, "Geschichte und Recht der Stiftsmässigkeit auf die ehemals adeligen Domstifte von Mainz, Würzburg

und Bamberg," pp. 323–58; Sophie Matilde Gräfin zu Dohna, *Die ständischen Verhältnisse am Domkapitel von Trier vom 16. bis zum 18. Jahrhundert,* pp. 20–21, 59–70; Heribert Raab, *Clemens Wenzeslaus von Sachsen und seine Zeit,* 1:310–14; Max Domarus, "Der Reichsadel in den geistlichen Fürstentümern"; Aretin, *Heiliges Römisches Reich,* 1:76–89; and my article, "The Church as an Institution of the Reich," in James A. Vann and Steven W. Rowan, eds., *The Old Reich,* pp. 149–64.

CHAPTER 2, PART I

1. Feine, *Besetzung,* pp. 332–40: "das Staatsgrundgesetz des geistlichen Wahlstaates" (p. 338); Brunner, *Land und Herrschaft,* passim, but especially pp. 146–64, 231–39, 357–440, whose views and approach have superseded those of older treatments like that of Georg von Below, *Territorium und Stadt,* pp. 247–55.

2. Feine, *Besetzung,* pp. 333–35, 340; Knetsch, *Kurstaat Trier,* pp. 31–43; Jean Lejeune, "Les notions de 'patria' et d' 'episcopatus' dans le diocèse et le pays de Liège du XIe au XIVe siècle," p. 37.

3. Spangenberg, "Osnabrück," pp. 7–8, 107–114. For the later constitutional development of Osnabrück, see Renger, *Landstände im Hochstift Osnabrück.*

4. Feine, *Besetzung,* p. 334 and n. 5.

5. Below, *Territorium,* pp. 248–54; Folz, "Assemblées," pp. 186–91; Carsten, *Princes,* pp. 428–29.

6. Schneider, *Domkapitel,* p. 175 and n. 1; Feine, *Besetzung,* p. 332 and n. 1, and *Rechtsgeschichte,* p. 382.

7. Theodor Gottlob, *Der kirchliche Amtseid der Bischöfe,* pp. 1–11, 138 ff., Kantorowicz, "Inalienability," pp. 488–502; Benson, *Bishop-Elect,* pp. 169, 207 n. 11, 330–31.

8. Frederick W. Maitland, *The Constitutional History of England,* ed. Herbert A. L. Fisher, p. 99; Feine, *Besetzung,* p. 331, n. 1. See also Siegfried Haider, *Die Wahlversprechungen der römisch-deutschen Könige bis zum Ende des 12. Jahrhunderts*; Gerd Kleinheyer, *Die kaiserlichen Wahlkapitulationen*; and Daniel Waley, *The Papal State in the Thirteenth Century,* pp. 122–23, 139–40, 269.

9. *UBS,* 1:324–9, no. 360.

10. Ernest Langlois, ed., *Les Registres de Nicolas IV,* pp. 66–67, no. 362.

11. *UBS,* 1:350–52, no. 387.

CHAPTER 2, PART II

1. *UBS,* 1:326, no. 360.

2. Hinschius, *Kirchenrecht,* 2:144–50; Hofmeister, *Bischof und Domkapitel,* pp. 230–34, especially 232; Feine, *Rechtsgeschichte,* p. 384.

3. *UBS,* 1:325, no. 360.

4. Langlois, ed., *Les Registres de Nicolas IV,* pp. 66–67, no. 362.

5. On the exclusion of provosts from the cathedral chapters at Mainz, Regensburg, Speyer, and elsewhere, see Hauck, *Kirchengeschichte,* vol. 5, pt. 1, pp. 201–2. No

precise dates can be assigned to this development at Speyer, where it evidently varied from one church to another, but it did take place in the first half of the fourteenth century. It was already beginning at Saint Guido's in 1275, where the dean and the chapter renewed the statutes, "communicato igitur consilio et habita cum domino nostro preposito matura deliberatione . . ." (HSA no. 1774). This was premature, however, for the provosts participated in the union of the four collegiate churches of Speyer in 1299 (ibid., no. 1620), and the cathedral provost attended the episcopal election of 1302 (*UBS,* 1:438–41, no. 466). By contrast, the provosts were not involved in a dispute concerning the union of the four chapters in 1346 (HSA no. 1715), and in 1355 the provost of Saint Germain's rendered an oath to his chapter not to interfere in its affairs except in disputed elections: SAS Urkunden Sankt German und Moritz no. 2.

6. See Anton Doll, "Entstehung und Entwicklung der Pfarreien der Stadt Speyer."

7. *UBS,* 1:107–9, no. 97.

8. Thus ibid., 1:302, 425, nos. 337 (1264) and 454 (1300).

9. Similar control of the archdeaconries and of the provostships of the collegiate churches of the cathedral city by the cathedral chapters existed in Osnabrück, Utrecht, Trier, Hildesheim, Liège, Cologne, Worms, and elsewhere: Below, *Entstehung,* pp. 31–34; Spangenberg, "Osnabrück," pp. 8–20; Feine, *Rechtsgeschichte,* pp. 201–3.

10. *UBS,* 1:179–80, no. 168. This was confirmed in 1280: ibid., 1:365–66, no. 401.

11. GLA 67/448, fol. 35r (= Würdtwein, ed., *Subsidia diplomatica,* 5:318–20).

12. GLA 67/448, fol. 35.

CHAPTER 2, PART III

1. *UBS,* 1:156–57, no. 139.

2. Ibid., 1:389–91, no. 423.

3. Ibid., 1:457–58, no. 484.

4. Berger, ed., *Les Registres d'Innocent IV,* 1:105, no. 613.

5. *UBS,* 1:440, no. 466 (1302).

6. Ibid., 1:326, 328, no. 360. In the end, however, the bishop won out in the case of clergy who died intestate, as witness the statute of the synod of 1474 which decreed that in such instances the estate, including "patrimonialibus bonis aut industria propria acquisitis," fell to the bishop: *Collectio processuum synodalium et constitutionum ecclesiasticarum diocesis Spirensis ab anno 1397 usque ad annum 1720,* p. 217.

7. *UBS,* 1:326–27, no. 360: "Item aderit sibi, nobis et toti clero civitatis et diocesis Spirensis in appellacione facta supra visitacione contra dominum archiepiscopum Moguntinum et in eadem nos et predictum clerum suum non deseret. . . ." No mention of this visitation or the storm it stirred up occurs in Friedrich W. Oediger, Wilhelm Kisky, and Richard Knipping, eds., *Die Regesten der Erzbischöfe von Mainz im Mittelalter.*

8. *UBS,* vol. 1, nos. 139 (1220), 148 (1221), 160 (1224), 201 (1235), 282 (1255), 394–95 (1279), and 454 (1300).

9. Ibid., 1:412–15, no. 445. See chapter three, p. 95.

10. Ibid., 1:262, no. 283.

11. *WUB*, 6:78–79, no. 1676.

12. *UBS*, 1:307–10, no. 342.

13. *WUB*, 11:525–26, nos. 5667–68.

14. *UBS*, 1:11–13, no. 13; MGH *Dipl.* Otto I, no. 379 (969) (Stumpf, no. 473); MGH *Dipl.* Otto II, no. 94 (undated) (Stumpf, no. 864). The imperial privileges were confirmed in 989, 1003, 1027, and 1061 (Stumpf, nos. 927, 1362, 1963, 2559). Anton Doll, "Zur Frühgeschichte der Stadt Speyer," pp. 159–60, defended the often questioned authenticity of the 946 grant from Conrad the Red. On Conrad, see Robert Holtzmann, *Geschichte der sächsischen Kaiserzeit*, pp. 132, 141, 152–56, 159–62, 176.

15. Doll, "Frühgeschichte," pp. 164–71, 184–93, 197; Kuno Drollinger, *Kleine Städte Südwestdeutschlands*, pp. 78–79. There exists no single good history of the town of Speyer in the Middle Ages.

16. *UBS*, 1:57 (1084): "Cum ex Spirensi villa urbem facerem. . . .": MGH *Dipl.* Otto I, no. 379.

17. *UBS*, 1:57–58, no. 57 (1084); MGH *Dipl.* Henry IV, no. 411 (1090: imperial confirmation of these privileges); Doll, "Frühgeschichte," pp. 181–184.

18. Doll, "Frühgeschichte," p. 199; Drollinger, *Kleine Städte*, pp. 178–80. See *USS*, pp. 155–58, no. 199 (1298), where the cathedral chapter cooperated with the burghers of Speyer to establish the conditions of manufacture and sale of woolen cloth in Speyer.

19. MGH *Dipl.* Henry IV, no. 466.

20. *USS*, pp. 17–19, no. 14; Stumpf, nos. 3071–72. The text is presented in confusing fashion in *UBS*, 1:88–89, no. 80, and the following unnumbered charter.

21. *USS*, pp. 21–23, no. 18; Stumpf, no. 4341. The text in *UBS*, 1:121–24, no. 107, is very badly edited.

22. *USS*, pp. 25–26, no. 22. Of the town council of Speyer, Bosl, *Reichsministerialität*, p. 276, remarked that "er war der freieste aller rheinischen Stadträte."

23. The basis of the error seems to have been twofold. In the charter of 1111, the bishop was forbidden to alter the coinage "nisi communi civium consilio" (*USS*, p. 19). This may have been the basis for the opening clause in the following sentence of the 1198 charter: "Preterea secundum ordinacionem Heinrici felicis memorie imperatoris augusti, civitati tam auctoritate domini regis quam nostra indulsimus, ut libertatem habeat duodecim ex civibus suis eligendi, qui per iuramentum ad hoc constringantur, ut universitati, prout melius possint et sciant, provideant et eorum civitas gubernetur" (*UBS*, 1:137). Had Henry indeed made such a concession, it should presumably have been mentioned in the charter of 1182 from Frederick Barbarossa confirming the privilege of 1111. The mistake was taken up by the seventeenth-century jurist Christoph Lehmann, *Chronica der Freyen Reichs Stadt Speyer*, pp. 253–54, 261–63, 306–28, and repeated many times by later historians until it was corrected by Kolmar Schaube, "Die Entstehung des Speierer Stadtrates," pp. 445–61, who acidly observed of Lehmann: "Hier zeigt sich die wie in manchen anderen Punkten gedankenlose Kompilation Lehmanns" (p. 447). Lehmann may well have known what he was about, however; given his partisan stance, and the continuing hostility between the town and the bishops, he had every reason to try to date the independence of the burghers as far back in time as possible.

24. Würdtwein, ed., *Nova subsidia*, 1:144.

25. *USS*, pp. 26–27, 38–39, nos. 23 and 42.

26. *UBS*, 1:142, no. 125 (1207). Würdtwein, ed., *Subsidia diplomatica*, 5:267–69 (1207). *WUB*, 2:356–58, no. 532 (1207); 3:91, no. 623 (1219); 3:195–96, no. 713 (1226). *USS*, nos. 40 (1226) and 49 (1232). Würdtwein, ed., *Nova subsidia*, 12:175 (1256).

27. *UBS*, 1:141–42, no. 125.

28. GLA 67/286, fols. 108v–111.

29. *USS*, pp. 469–70, no. 534.

30. Ibid., pp. 35–36, no. 36.

31. *UBS*, 1:177–78, no. 164.

32. Ibid., 1:238, no. 254; HSA no. 44.

33. *USS*, pp. 90–91, no. 122.

34. GLA 67/280, fols. 61v–62r; *UBS*, 1:284–85, 298–99, nos. 314 and 332. C. Lehmann, *Chronica*, p. 568, said without offering any proof that the Emperor Henry (V?) had allowed the town council to collect the excise on the wine trade. Despite the possibly contradictory evidence in *UBS*, 1:321, no. 357 (1270), where Bishop Henry exempted the Cistercian monastery of Herrenalb "ab omni theloneo sive exactione, que volgariter dicitur ungelt, quod nobis ex eis de civitate nostra Spirensi et oppido nostro Brussel [i.e., Bruchsal] vel nostris successoribus provenire posset," Bishop Henry probably did in fact renounce his right to collect the excise in Speyer in 1262: *UBS*, 1:291, no. 324. This was the contention of C. Weiss, "Das Rechnungswesen der freien Reichsstadt Speier im Mittelalter," pp. 3–4, as opposed to that of Wilhelm Harster, "Die Verfassungskämpfe in Speier während des Mittelalters," p. 215.

35. *UBS*, 1:291–92, no. 324.

36. Ibid., 1:277–78, no. 305.

37. HSA nos. 1601 (1266) and 2295 (1264).

38. Ibid., no. 1601 (1266); *UBS*, 1:282–83, 311, nos. 311 (1260) and 344 (1266); *USS*, pp. 84–86, no. 114 (1268).

39. GLA 67/280, fol. 26r.

40. *UBS*, 1:307–10, no. 342, and see above, pp. 64–65.

41. Charles Bourel de La Roncière et al., eds., *Les Registres d'Alexandre IV*, nos. 102, 1093, 1238; MGH *Epist. pontif.*, no. 430; Potthast, no. 16226.

42. *UBS*, 1:285–86, nos. 315–17 (1260); *USS*, p. 69, no. 95 (1260). For similar developments at Würzburg and Worms, see Engel, "Stadt Würzburg und die Kurie," pp. 303–59.

43. *USS*, p. 83, no. 112: "cives Spirenses sunt imperio annexi, ita quod pro domino episcopo Spirensi pro nulla causa possunt ocupari."

44. In a union concluded in 1293, the cities of Speyer, Worms, and Mainz agreed not to admit their bishops until they first confirmed all the privileges and liberties of their towns and did homage to the town council: *USS*, pp. 134–35, no. 180. Bishop Frederick was the first bishop to render such confirmation, in 1280 (*UBS*, 1:363, no. 399), but according to C. Lehmann, *Chronica*, p. 328, his negotiations with the town regarding his entry dragged on until 1292. Remling, 1:484, thought it possible that the council had refused permission to a bishop to enter as early as 1249. On the withdrawal of most imperial ecclesiastical princes from their cathedral towns by the fourteenth century, see Bruno Dauch, *Die Bischofsstadt als Residenz der geistlichen Fürsten*.

45. See chapter three, pp. 96–101.

46. *UBS,* 1:298–99, no. 332.
47. HSA no. 2995 (= *UBS,* 1:302–3, no. 337).
48. *UBS,* 1:304–5, no. 339.
49. *USS,* p. 90, no. 121.
50. Ibid., p. 89, no. 119.
51. The text of the 1302 oath is printed in *UBS,* 1:438–41, no. 466.

CHAPTER 2, PART IV

1. *UBS,* 1:109, no. 98. The term "fundum" had been used earlier: *WUB,* 3:469, Nachtrag no. 8 (1143), and *UBS,* 1:93, no. 85 (1148). It is, though, a matter of some dispute whether the term can be equated with "territorium": Klingelhöfer, *Reichsgesetze,* p. 36, n. 4.

2. Otto of Freising, *Gesta Frederici,* 1:14, ed. Georg Waitz, Bernhard Simson, and Franz-Josef Schmale, p. 154: "Castrum Lintburc in territorio Spirensi situm. . . ."

3. Luc d'Achery, *Spicilegium,* 1:642: "Absit autem ut quisquam credat Deum esse localem, ut quod facit in Francia, non etiam facere possit in territorio Spirensi." I owe this reference to my friend, Professor Joseph H. Lynch.

4. Bosl, *Reichsministerialität,* p. 29.

5. *USS,* p. 2, no. 2; MGH *Dipl. Karol.,* no. 143; MGH *Dipl.* Otto I, no. 379 (Stumpf, no. 473); MGH *Dipl.* Otto II, no. 94 (Stumpf, no. 864); MGH *Dipl.* Otto III, no. 57 (Stumpf, no. 927); MGH *Dipl.* Henry II, no. 52 (Stumpf, no. 1362); MGH *Dipl.* Conrad II, no. 110 (Stumpf, no. 1963); MGH *Dipl.* Henry IV, no. 78 (Stumpf, no. 2599). On the significance of immunities in the growth of ecclesiastical lordships, see Brunner, *Land und Herrschaft,* pp. 192–93, 333.

6. MGH *Dipl.* Conrad II, no. 180 (1032) (Stumpf, no. 2030); MGH *Dipl.* Henry III, nos. 226 (1048) (Stumpf, no. 2358) and 370 (1056) (Stumpf, no. 2497); MGH *Dipl.* Henry IV, nos. 100 (1063) (Stumpf, no. 2619), 165–66 (1065) (Stumpf, nos. 1680–81), 382 (1086) (Stumpf, no. 2875), 384 (1086) (Stumpf, no. 2876), 396 (1097) (Stumpf, no. 2887).

7. *UBS,* 1:70, 100–101, nos. 70, 91, and 109.

8. MGH *Dipl.* Henry IV, no. 466 (1101): "precipue nostros speciales in nostra sancta speciali Spirensi ecclesia. . . ."

9. Büttner, "Hördt," pp. 342–54; Gugumus, "Bischöfe," pp. 57, 71–78; Semmler, "Sinsheim," pp. 339–47.

10. *UBS,* 1:90, no. 81: "Quod quia absque nostro consensu et voluntate fieri non potuit. . . ."

11. Decker, "Klingenmünster," p. 41, n. 121.

12. The controversy may be followed in Siegfried Rietschel, *Das Burggrafenamt und die hohe Gerichtsbarkeit in den deutschen Bischofsstädten während des früheren Mittelalters,* pp. 121–34; Schreibmüller, *Landvogtei im Speiergau,* pp. 13–15; Bosl, *Reichsministerialität,* pp. 144, 218–19, 275–77, 623–24; Hans Werle, "Studien zur Wormser und Speyerer Hochstiftsvogtei im 12. Jahrhundert," pp. 80–89; idem, "Staufische Hausmachtpolitik am Rhein im 12. Jahrhundert," pp. 249, 270, 288; Alfons Schäfer, "Das Schicksal des Weissenburgischen Besitzes im Uf- und Pfinzgau," p. 76,

232 NOTES, PP. 71–74

n. 37; idem, "Grafen von Eberstein," p. 94; and Anton Doll, "Vögte und Vogtei im Hochstift Speyer," pp. 245–73.

13. Schäfer, "Weissenburgischer Besitz," p. 82, and idem, "Staufische Reichsland-politik und hochadelige Herrschaftsbildung im Uf- und Pfinzgau und im Nordwest-schwarzwald vom 11.–13. Jahrhundert," pp. 182–83.

14. See Boss, Kirchenlehen; Hans Werle, "Die Aufgaben und die Bedeutung der Pfalzgrafschaft bei Rhein in der Staufischen Hausmachtpolitik," pp. 137–54; Henry J. Cohn, The Government of the Rhine Palatinate in the Fifteenth Century, p. 5.

15. See chapter one, pp. 15–20.

16. UBS, 1:104–6, no. 94.

17. Ibid., 1:125, no. 108. On these vassals, see Metz, Staufische Güterverzeichnisse, p. 41.

18. UBS, vol. 1, nos. 80, 107, 116.

19. Ibid., 1:137–38, no. 120.

20. Ibid., 1:141, no. 124; Bienemann, Conrad von Scharfenberg, pp. 29, 31, 53–57.

21. See p. 212, n. 52.

22. Klingelhöfer, Reichsgesetze, pp. 1–4, 60.

23. Bosl, Reichsministerialität, p. 407. Neither Fisher, Medieval Empire, 2:74–76, nor Klingelhöfer, Reichsgesetze, pp. 47–51, lists Speyer among the churches to which fiefs were returned. The texts of Otto of Brunswick's surrender of fiefs to the churches of Cologne and Magdeburg in 1198 and 1208, respectively, are in MGH Const., 2:21–23, 30–32, nos. 17 and 26.

24. Boss, Kirchenlehen, pp. 24–25; Werle, "Speyerer Hochstiftsvogtei," pp. 84–87, and "Die Landgrafschaft im Speyergau," pp. 72–73; Metz, Staufische Güterverzeich-nisse, pp. 41, 43, 56; Bosl, Reichsministerialität, pp. 276, 405–7.

25. Metz, Staufische Güterverzeichnisse, p. 41.

26. MGH Dipl. Henry IV, nos. 167–74 (1046) (Stumpf, nos. 2305–12), 466 (1101) (Stumpf, no. 2950), 475 (1102) (Stumpf, no. 2958); UBS, 1:69–72, 105, nos. 70 (1100) and 94 (1157); GLA 78/33 (1214).

27. These fiefs are listed in the fourteenth-century feudal register, SAS Kopialbuch 63, entitled "Feudorum et aliorum Friderici, Gerhardi, Lamperti et Emichonis epis-coporum registrum antiquum (1272–1367)." The benefices at the collation of the bishop are listed first. They have been edited by Franz X. Glasschröder, "Die Pfründen librae collationis des Speyerer Bischofs im Mittelalter," pp. 158–62. It is extremely difficult to date the original grant of most of these fiefs, which is worth a separate study in its own right, but that the church of Speyer effectively lost control over a large amount of property in the High Middle Ages through enfeoffments to the Staufens and to the high nobility is made perfectly clear in Schäfer, "Weissenburgischer Besitz," pp. 65–93, and "Grafen von Eberstein," pp. 81–96; Werle, "Speyerer Hoch-stiftsvogtei," pp. 80–89.

28. MGH Dipl. Conrad II, no. 41 (1032) (Stumpf, no. 1894); MGH Dipl. Henry III, nos. 169–70 (1046) (Stumpf, nos. 2308–9); MGH Dipl. Henry IV, nos. 10 (1057) (Stumpf, no. 2538), 167 (1065) (Stumpf, no. 2682), 277 (1074) (Stumpf, no. 2783), 325 (1080) (Stumpf, no. 2824), 380 (1086) (Stumpf, no. 2873), 382–84 (1086) (Stumpf, nos. 2875–76), 396 (1087) (Stumpf, no. 2887). On the donation of

Kreuznach, see this volume, p. 39 and n. 28. It would be well worth knowing whether imperial donations were ordinarily so widely scattered.

29. MGH *Const.*, 2:423, no. 310 (17 July 1231), accepted what was already an accomplished fact.

30. See pp. 80–81.

31. *UBS,* 1:342–43, no. 378.

32. Ibid., 1:328, no. 360.

33. See pp. 40–41.

34. *UBS,* vol. 1, nos. 205 (ca. 1236), 257 (1249), 294 (1256), 331 (1263).

35. Ibid., nos. 338 and 341 (both 1264).

36. Ibid., 1:325–26, no. 360. On the exercise of high justice and capital punishment by prince-prelates in the High and late Middle Ages, see the very careful discussion by Ernst Hoyer, "Gratian und der Blutbann der geistlichen Fuersten des mittelalterlichen deutschen Reiches," pp. 131–83, which goes down to the early modern period and avoids most of the facile generalizations common on this subject.

37. *The Cambridge Economic History of Europe,* vol. 1, *The Agrarian Life of the Middle Ages,* ed. Michael M. Postan, pp. 299–303.

38. See Franz Haffner, "Die Bischöfe von Speyer bis zum Jahre 913 (918)," pp. 357–59; Alois Seiler, "Die Speyerer Diözesangrenzen rechts des Rheins in Rahmen der Frühgeschichte des Bistums," pp. 258–59.

39. See p. 70.

40. *UBS,* 1:100–101, no. 91; Stumpf, no. 3650.

41. See the two Schäfer articles cited in n. 12 above in this section.

42. Schreibmüller, *Landvogtei,* pp. 13–19, 29–101, made no attempt to explain what happened to the bishop's rights as a result; see also Werle, "Landgrafschaft," pp. 71–75. Werle, "Staufische Hausmachtpolitik," p. 284, n. 150, believed that the immunities of the bishopric of Speyer and of the abbeys of Weissenburg and Klingenmünster effectively robbed the donation of these two counties of any practical significance.

43. King Alphonso in Burgos confirmed for Henry the donation of the county of Lutramsforst: *UBS,* 1:275–76, no. 303 (1257). See also the very complicated case of 1256 in Würdtwein, ed., *Nova subsidia,* 12:170–75, where the basis for Bishop Henry's cooperation with the *iudex provincialis* in settling a dispute is not at all clear.

44. *UBS,* 1:70, no. 70.

45. Ibid., 1:125, no. 109.

46. Ibid., nos. 70 (1100), 85 (1148), 90 (1152); *WUB,* 2:116, no. 363 (1158); 2:123–25, nos. 367–68 (1159); 2:132–34, no. 374 (1160). Another supposed donation of Bishop Günther to Maulbronn around 1147, printed in ibid., 2:40–41, no. 324, was shown to be a forgery by Acht, "Urkundenwesen," pp. 287–97.

47. See the discussion on pp. 66–68. For a more detailed examination of changes in various aspects of government in Speyer during this period, see [?] Eheberg, "Die Münzerhausgenossen von Speyer," pp. 444–80; Wilhelm Harster, "Versuch einer Speierer Münzgeschichte," pp. 1–166, and "Verfassungskämpfe," pp. 210–320; Karl Heinrich Korz, *Das Schultheissen- und Kämmerergericht von Speyer in den Jahren 1294–1689,* pp. 1–23. The Jews, over whom the bishops of the eleventh and twelfth centuries had had so much power (see *UBS,* 1:57–58, no. 57 [1084]), had by the

middle of the thirteenth century passed under the direct control of the royal fisc, as is evident in a charter of King William of Holland in 1255: "A iudeis Spirensibus, camere nostre servis . . ." (*USS*, pp. 64–65, no. 87).

48. In 1471 the bishop had to supply eight horsemen and fifteen foot soldiers; Speyer, six and sixteen, respectively (C. Lehmann, *Chronica*, pp. 893–95). For the *Landfrieden* of 1486, the bishop was taxed at 1,500 fl., Speyer at 4,000 fl. (ibid., pp. 913–14). In the following year, they were to pay 1,000 fl. and 1,500 fl., respectively (ibid., pp. 917–18). In 1489 their contingents for the imperial army numbered ten cavalry and forty infantry, seventeen cavalry and sixty-eight infantry, respectively (ibid., pp. 930–33).

49. On the problem in general, see Giles Constable, *Monastic Tithes from Their Origins to the Twelfth Century*, pp. 3, 307. For an early instance of such activity, see *UBS*, 1:25–26, no. 25 (1023). The authenticity of ibid., 1:1–2, no. 1, in which King Sigibert III, around 653, granted the church of Speyer the right to collect all tithes in Speyergau (one of the earliest known such royal grants, if not the earliest), has often been questioned. It was accepted by Duchesne and Brackmann, although parts of it may not be original. See Constable, *Tithes*, pp. 22, n. 4, and 28, n. 2, and Wolfgang Metz, "Die Urkunde König Sigiberts III. für das Bistum Speyer," pp. 9–19.

50. In 1344 the yearly income from the Bienwald was only 125 fl.: *UBS*, 2:18, no. 2. The Lusshard, together with Bruchsal, had been donated by Henry III in 1056 and greatly extended by a further grant in 1063: MGH *Dipl.*, Henry III, no. 370 (Stumpf, no. 2497); MGH *Dipl.* Henry IV, no. 100 (Stumpf, no. 2619). When and how the bishops came to possess the Bienwald is not known. It appears in 1265 in a charter where Frederick, burgrave of Nuremberg, renounced his rights to it, but it probably already numbered among the "forestis episcopi" mentioned in a document of 1197: *UBS*, 1:135–36, 306, nos. 119 and 341. For the history of the Lusshard and the smaller episcopal forests on the right bank of the Rhine, see Hans Hausrath, *Forstgeschichte der rechtsrheinischen Theile des ehemaligen Bistums Speyer*. Forests appear to have played a large role in the consolidation of the bishops' territory, but this is difficult to demonstrate before the fifteenth century. Hauck showed how important *Bannforsten* were in the development of the ecclesiastical principalities of Fulda and Prüm: Werminghoff, *Verfassungsgschichte*, p. 82, n. 3. The grant of the Lusshard had included the *Bann*, the right to punish wrongdoers and to summon the host.

51. See pp. 105–6, 111.

52. *UBS*, 1:389–91, no. 423.

53. Cited in Carl Stephenson, "Taxation and Representation in the Middle Ages," pp. 299–300. See also the important remarks of Brunner, *Land und Herrschaft*, pp. 273–78.

54. At this time, Bishop Gerhard von Ehrenberg had drawn up a rudimentary ledger of expenditures and receipts. It is contained in GLA 67/284, the so-called "Signatura Gebhardi," and was in large part printed by Reimer, "Bischof Gerhart," pp. 102–17.

55. Franz Mone, "Zur Geschichte der Volkswirtschaft," p. 306: "pravam illam consuetudinem."

56. *UBS*, 1:125, no. 109.

57. SAS Kopialbuch 63; *UBS*, vol. 1, nos. 70, 91, 105, 109, 129, 303, 338, 358, 360, 378, 408, 414, 494, 511, 513; *WUB*, 5: 57–58, 60–62, nos. 1293 and 1295; Würdtwein,

ed., *Subsidia diplomatica*, 9:194; [?] Reimer, "Das Todtenbuch des Speierer Domstifts," p. 433; Johann Georg Lehmann, *Urkundliche Geschichte der Burgen und Berg-schlösser in den ehemaligen Gauen und Herrschaften der bayerischen Pfalz*, 1:142; Maximilian Huffschmid, "Hochhausen am Neckar und die heilige Notburga," pp. 388–89; Franz Klimm, *Burg und Dorf Graben einst und jetzt*, pp. 17–18; Decker, "Klingenmünster," p. 41, n. 121; Günther Haselier, *Geschichte des Dorfes und der Gemeinde Weiher am Bruhrain*, pp. 61–63; Hans-Martin Maurer, "Die Entstehung der mittelalterlichen Adelsburg in Südwestdeutschland," pp. 325–28.

58. *UBS*, 1:645–51, no. 638.

59. This included both the costs of maintaining castellans and various officials, who were ordinarily paid in a mixture of money, grain, and wine (e.g., *UBS*, 1:303–4, 435, nos. 338 [1264] and 462 [1301]), and of keeping the castles in good condition, which was so expensive that throughout the fourteenth and fifteenth centuries the bishops were compelled either to pawn them or to grant them in heritable tenure on condition that the holder tend to this task at the cost of the bishop. Thus ibid., 1:482–84, no. 513 (1317: Spangenberg Castle); and see chapters three and four, passim.

60. Oediger, Kisky, and Knipping, eds., *Regesten der Erzbischöfe von Mainz*, 1:163, no. 533.

61. Ibid., vol. 3, pt. 2, p. 210, no. 3397.

62. GLA 67/279, fol. 49; *UBS*, 1:604–5, no. 605.

63. C. Lehmann, *Chronica*, pp. 893–95, 930–33.

64. Glasschröder, *Urkunden zur pfälzischen Kirchengeschichte*, p. 3, no. 7 (1250).

65. Lucien Auvray, ed., *Les Registres de Grégoire IX*, 1:1262, no. 2418 (1235).

66. See p. 21 and p. 81.

67. Berger, ed., *Les Registres d'Innocent IV*, nos. 2672, 4395, 4480.

68. La Roncière et al., eds., *Les Registres d'Alexandre IV*, nos. 102, 1093, 1238; MGH *Epist. pontif.*, 3:387–89, no. 430; *UBS*, 1:306, no. 341. Remling, 1:493, thought Alexan-der decided against Henry because he had not yet been consecrated bishop.

69. *UBS*, 1:358, no. 393 (1262).

70. Ibid., 1:307–10, no. 342.

71. Ibid., nos. 275, 278, 338, 341, 358–59; *WUB*, 4:305–6, no. 1237.

72. J. G. Lehmann, *Burgen*, 1:143; Remling, 1:513.

73. *Reg. Pfalz*, vol. 1, nos. 852 and 899; *Reg. Baden*, vol. 1, no. 470; Reinhard Merkel, "Studien zur Territorialgeschichte der badischen Markgrafschaft in der Zeit vom Interregnum bis zum Tode Markgraf Bernhards I. (1250–1431)," pp. 38–40. Its weighty title notwithstanding, this is a superficial study.

74. MGH *Dipl.* Henry III, no. 190 (1109) (Stumpf, no. 1512), where Henry III gave the bishops market and coinage rights "ad relevandam ex parte Spirensis ecclesie inopiam. . . ."

75. *UBS*, 1:222–23, 238–40, nos. 227 and 256.

76. Würdtwein, ed., *Nova subsidia*, 1:147.

77. *UBS*, 1:238–39, no. 255.

78. It is impossible to discuss here at length the *Klosterpolitik* of the bishops during the Salian and Staufen periods, for this would form an entirely separate chapter. Some indications of the bishops' heavy-handedness may be found in: Potthast, nos.

5339, 5801, 8330, 11322; Decker, "Klingenmünster," pp. 53–54; Büttner, "Hördt," pp. 358–64; Semmler, "Sinsheim," pp. 343–44, 346; *UBS*, vol. 1, nos. 70, 119, 176; *WUB*, 3:222, no. 736 (1228); *WUB*, 4:305–6, no. 1237 (1252); *WUB*, 11:535, no. 5680 (1274); A. Stauber, "Kloster und Dorf Lambrecht," pp. 74, 92; Mone, "Herren-Alb," p. 477; Brackmann, ed., *Germania pontificia*, vol. 3, pt. 3, pp. 127, 134–35; *Gerettete Wahrheit in einer diplomatischen Geschichte der Abtey Schwarzach am Rheine*, 1:37 and 2:14–15, 25–26.

79. *Cambridge Economic History*, 1:302.

80. Again, it is not possible here to give more than references to material for such a study: HSA no. 1157; Würdtwein, ed., *Subsidia diplomatica*, 5:266–67; idem., ed., *Monasticon Palatinum*, 2:25–27; GLA 67/283, fols. 93, 96–97; *WUB*, 5:212–13, no. 1447; *WUB*, 7:267, no. 2374; Remling, *Abteien*, 1:62, 65, 68, 123–24, 195–96; A. Neubauer, "Regesten des ehemaligen Benediktiner-Klosters Hornbach," p. 14; and the articles by Büttner, Decker, Semmler, and Stauber cited in n. 77 immediately above.

81. See pp. 170–72.

82. Knetsch, *Kurstaat Trier*, pp. 15–26, Barthold Witte, *Herrschaft und Land im Rheingau*, p. 170; Karl-Heinz Kirchhoff, "Die landständischen Schatzungen des Stifts Münster im 16. Jahrhundert," p. 118; Justus Lücke, *Die landständische Verfassung im Hochstift Hildesheim 1643–1802*, pp. 11–12; Richard Laufner, "Die Landstände von Kurtrier im 17. und 18. Jahrhundert," p. 299. Registers for the taxation of the clergy were thus frequently drawn up early: see *UBS*, 1:502–4, no. 528 (1321); W. Fabricius, "Taxa generalis cleri Trevirensis," pp. 1–52; Hans Goldschmidt, *Zentralbehörden und Beamtentum im Kurfürstentum Mainz vom 16. bis zum 18. Jahrhundert*, p. 55; Joseph Ahlhaus, *Die Landdekanate des Bistums Konstanz im Mittelalter*, p. 59; Georg Droege, *Verfassung und Wirtschaft in Kurkölin unter Dietrich von Moers (1414–1463)*, pp. 139–43.

83. Berger, ed., *Les Registres d'Innocent IV*, nos. 613, 653–54.

84. See pp. 91–92.

85. *UBS*, 1:502–4, no. 528.

86. Krabbo, *Besetzung*, pp. 30–31.

87. See p. 212, n. 52.

88. Remling, 1:487.

89. Ibid., 1:500.

90. GLA 42/139 s.d. 19 Jan. 1272 (= Würdtwein, ed., *Subsidia diplomatica*, 9:194); *UBS*, 1:252–53, 274–75, nos. 271 and 302.

91. My interpretation is similar to that of Pöschl, *Bischofsgut*, 1:4–5, and 2:63–174. The evidence from Speyer is insufficient to support either that of Hinschius, *Kirchenrecht*, 2:55–58, who regarded the introduction of the division as a symptom of the decline of the common life, or that of Hauck, *Kirchengeschichte*, vol. 5, pt. 1, pp. 185–86, who saw it as a result of the establishment of the common life!

CHAPTER 3, PART I

1. See Georges Duby, *Rural Economy and Country Life in the Medieval West*, p. 300, and Léopold Genicot's article in the *Cambridge Economic History*, 1:661–94, especially 674–75. A good popular account is by Philip Ziegler, *The Black Death*.

2. Duby, *Rural Economy,* pp. 294–302; *Cambridge Economic History,* 1:661–94. See also Henry Lucas, "The Great European Famine of 1315, 1316, and 1317," pp. 343–77.

3. Franz Mone, ed., *Quellensammlung der badischen Landesgeschichte,* 1:212. Such an estimate is most implausible, for Speyer before the plague had a population of perhaps only 6,000: Josiah Cox Russell, *Medieval Regions and Their Cities,* pp. 92–95.

4. *UBS,* 1:430–31, no. 456: "non obstante grandine, exercitu, sterilitate, incendio seu casu alio fortuito qualicunque."

5. GLA 67/286, fols. 9–10; 67/287, fols. 8v–10r, 14–15, 35v–36.

6. GLA 67/287, fol. 26.

7. Most of these are inscribed in the so-called *Libri contractuum,* which are continuous from the reign of Bishop Raban (1396–1438) and are lodged in the Generallandesarchiv in Karlsruhe, Abteilung 67, Kopialbücher nos. 289, 291–95, 297, 304, 310, and 312 (through the reign of Bishop Philip von Flersheim, who died in 1552).

8. GLA 67/289, fol. 417v: "vngebuwet, Wüste gelegen vnd nyemant bissher keinen nütz haben." In 1452 a priest, with the bishop's consent, sold a vineyard forming part of the endowment of his living because it had lain vacant for a long time: GLA 67/292, fols. 176v–177.

9. In 1241 Bishop Conrad V sold lands to the chapter "pro ducentis sexaginta marcis puri argenti securius ea vendi, quam bona preemta revendi censentes, maxime cum episcopatus per alium potentem bonorum prescriptorum que emimus posset opprimi possessorem" (*UBS,* 1:222, no. 227). Bishop Frederick in 1290 sold the tolls around Speyer to the chapter "cum longe nobis sit visum iustius, melius et decencius, quam extraneis vendisse . . ." (ibid., 1:389, no. 423). In 1349 Archbishop Gerlach of Mainz confirmed Bishop Gerhard's pawn to the chapter of Speyer of the castle of Rietburg because it seemed "longe decentius, securius, melius est et utilius, quod castrum et villae predictae cum suis juribus et attinentiis, ut praedicitur, alienanda, apud capitulum ecclesiae Spirensis remaneant sub forma praedicta, quam transferantur ad manus exteras, potentes dubias et incertas et a quibus rara vel difficilis earundem restitutio speraretur . . ." (ibid., 1:581, no. 590). The original contract in German expressed the same thought: GLA 67/450, fols. 105–6.

10. The term "extraordinary taxation" is actually rather misleading and is used only for convenience. "Taxation" anachronistically implies a regular taxing power of the state recognized by its subjects, which was not really the case. A better term might be "aids," which subjects were obliged to render to their lords in instances of demonstrable necessity. Subjects might not think such necessity existed, but where it did, they had the obligation, not the right, to grant an aid. Feudal custom usually specified such cases, but Roman law broadened the possibilities through appeal to the common good (*utilitas regni, necessitas rei publicae*). See Post, *Studies,* pp. 241–309, and the very sensible remarks of Brunner, *Land und Herrschaft,* pp. 270–72, 292–97.

11. Remling, 1:573–74.

12. See Johann Peter Kirsch, *Die päpstlichen Kollektorien in Deutschland während des XIV. Jahrhunderts,* and *Die päpstlichen Annaten in Deutschland während des XIV. Jahrhunderts;* Ernst Hennig, *Die päpstlichen Zehnten aus Deutschland im Zeitalter des avignonesischen Papsttums und während des grossen Schismas;* Guillaume Mollat, *La Collation des bénéfices ecclésiastiques sous les papes d'Avignon (1305–1378);* and

Geoffrey Barraclough, *Papal Provisions.* Many of the relevant sources have been published in the *Registres* and the *Lettres* of the popes by the Bibliothèque des Écoles
françaises d'Athènes et de Rome; by the Görres Gesellschaft and the Deutsches
Historisches Institut zu Rom in the series *Vatikanische Quellen zur Geschichte der
päpstlichen Hof- und Finanzverwaltung 1316–1378;* and, more particularly, by Heinrich V. Sauerland, ed., *Vatikanische Urkunden und Regesten zur Geschichte der
Rheinlande,* and Sigmund Riezler, ed., *Vatikanische Akten zur deutschen Geschichte
in der Zeit Ludwigs des Bayern.*

13. In addition to the works cited in the previous note, see also Michal Glaser, "Die
Diözese Speier in den päpstlichen Rechnungsbüchern 1317 bis 1560," pp. 1–166. It is
unfortunately not possible to develop this topic here.

14. See the table in Hennig, *Zehnten,* p. 82. Although he based his discussion on
Hennig's work, Wilhelm Schwickerath, *Die Finanzwirtschaft der deutschen Bistümer,*
p. 81, incorrectly spoke of thirteen papal and twelve imperial or territorial levies.

15. See Mollat, *Collation,* pp. 271–84; Schwickerath, *Finanzwirtschaft,* p. 81.

16. Jules Gay and Suzanne Vitte, eds., *Les Registres de Nicolas III (1277–1280),*
pp. 3–4, no. 3 (1278).

17. Remling, 1:626, no. 1649.

18. GLA 67/462, fols. 128–29; Guillaume Mollat, ed., *Lettres secrètes et curiales du
pape Grégoire XI (1370–1378) intéressant les pays autre que la France . . . ,* 1:258,
no. 1846; Hennig, *Zehnten,* pp. 82–85. The dangers of generalizing from such par-
ticulars are again made clear in Schwickerath, *Finanzwirtschaft,* p. 81, n. 409, who
asserted on the basis of figures compiled by Hennig on the tithe of 1418 that Speyer
was the third highest contributor in Germany for the entire fourteenth century!

Chapter 3, Part II

1. Remling, 1:520.

2. Ibid., 1:524.

3. Ibid., 1:537–38; Würdtwein, ed., *Nova subsidia,* 1:173; C. Lehmann, *Chronica,*
pp. 585–86; *Reg. Pfalz,* vol. 1, no. 1113; *Reg. Baden,* vol. 1, no. 550; Ludwig Litzenburger, "Die Besetzung des Speyerer Bischofstuhles im Jahre 1303," p. 301.

4. Remling, 1:533–34, gave 1282 as the date, which varies from those given in
Würdtwein, ed., *Nova subsidia,* 1:152 (1291), and C. Lehmann, *Chronica,* p. 586
(1292). Lehmann is correct.

5. *UBS,* 1:345–55, 396–98, nos. 390 and 431.

6. *WUB,* 11:535, no. 5680.

7. *UBS,* 1:362, no. 398.

8. *USS,* p. 139, no. 183.

9. Langlois, ed., *Les Registres de Nicolas IV,* pp. 66–67, no. 362.

10. *UBS,* vol. 1, nos. 381 (1277), 393 (1279), 414 (1286), 466 (1302).

11. Ibid., 1:440, no. 466.

12. Ibid., 1:439.

13. The bishop's *officialis* is first mentioned in 1278: ibid., 1:354, no. 388.

14. Ibid., 1:424–28, no. 454.

15. HSA no. 1777 (=UBS, 1:372–73, no. 407).

16. SAS Kopialbuch 81, fols. 50–51r. HSA no. 1519 records a union of 18 December 1284 among the three collegiate churches only.

17. HSA no. 1617 (=UBS, 1:417, no. 448).

18. HSA no. 1620 (=UBS, 1:421–22, no. 451).

19. UBS, 1:342, 389, nos. 378 (1276) and 423 (1290).

20. Remling, 1:539.

21. UBS, 1:389, no. 423 (1290): "Cum igitur usurarum vorago et grandia onera debitorum nos et nostram ecclesiam, variis ex causis et legitimis, in magna parte destruxerint et attenuaverint. . . ."

22. Ibid., 1:379–80, no. 414.

23. Ibid., 1:435, no. 462.

24. See above, n. 9.

25. See the arenga in UBS, 1:502, no. 528 (1321), issued by the four chapters of Speyer: "Attendentes sacrorum canonum statuta non sine rationabilibus et certis circumstantiis fore circumscripta et sapienter ordinata, perpendimus, quod videlicet idem canones non praecipuendo, nec jubendo, sed permissive sustinendo contendunt, quod possit episcopus a suis subditis precibus postulare, non exigendo exigere subsidium, non tantum quantumcunque, sed moderatum et id ipsum aliquotiens, non frequenter, nec ex coactione, sed ex caritate et tempore necessitatis et indigentiae emergentis. . . ."

26. Ibid., 1:389–91, no. 423.

27. HSA no. 66.

28. UBS, 1:406–7, no. 439. When the bishop had originally sold Eschelbronn to the chapter is not indicated.

29. Ibid., 1:390, no. 423.

30. Ibid., 1:406–7, no. 439.

31. Ibid., 1:426, no. 454: "Municiones ecclesie per eundem episcopum quibuscunque personis commisse post mortem eius in disposicione capituli remanere debent secundum consuetudinem ab antiquo servatam, iuramentis in contrarium factis non obstantibus, que nos presentibus revocamus."

32. Franz Xaver Glasschröder, ed., Neue Urkunden zur pfälzischen Kirchengeschichte im Mittelalter, p. 17, no. 14; UBS, 1:412, no. 445.

33. UBS, 1:335–36, no. 369.

34. SAS Urkunden Hochstift Speyer no. 117.

35. UBS, 1:323, no. 452: "reverendis dominis meis, videlicet venerabili domino episcopo et capitulo ecclesie Spirensis. . . ."

36. Ibid., 1:405–6, no. 438.

37. Ibid., 1:412–15, no. 445.

38. Ibid., 1:442–43, no. 469. On the violent opposition in Europe in the High and late Middle Ages to archiepiscopal visitations, which Innocent III had promoted for purposes of reform, see Joseph Dahmus, William Courtenay, Archbishop of Canterbury 1381–1396, pp. 107–111.

39. UBS, 1:363, no. 399.

40. C. Lehmann, Chronica, p. 528.

41. *UBS*, 1:368–71, nos. 404–5. Moreover, in the confederation formed in 1293 by Speyer, Worms, and Mainz, mentioned in the next note, the three cities stipulated that they would render homage and obedience to their bishops only after written confirmation of all their privileges.

42. *USS*, pp. 134–35, no. 180.

43. Ibid., pp. 137–40, no. 183.

44. E.g., Korz, *Kämmerergericht von Speyer*, p. 23: "Daraus lässt sich klar ersehen, dass durch diesen Vertrag dem Bischof alle Regentengewalt über die Stadt genommen war." In 1298 Bishop Frederick also agreed to pronounce no excommunications or interdictions over burghers of Speyer without first exhausting all other legal procedures against them: *USS*, p. 158, no. 200.

45. See ibid., nos. 277, 396–98, 424, 552.

46. C. Lehmann, *Chronica*, pp. 587–621, and his comment on the internal troubles in the town in 1304: "Die erste Veränderung des Raths ist geschehen Anno 1304, ohne Hülff und Zuthun Bischoffs Sibothi/ denn die Burgerschafft die Mittel selbst bey Handen gehabt/ dadurch sie sich der beschwerlichen Regierung entheben können" (p. 651).

47. *USS*, pp. 150–468.

48. Ibid., no. 199; *UBS*, vol. 1, nos. 401, 403, 411, 433.

49. GLA 67/448, fol. 5 (=*UBS*, 1:340, no. 375).

50. *USS*, p. 95, no. 130.

51. *UBS*, 1:345–46, no. 382.

52. Ibid., 1:350–52, no. 387; Remling, 1:627, n. 1331.

53. C. Lehmann, *Chronica*, pp. 568–70.

54. *UBS*, 1:356–57, no. 392.

55. *USS*, pp. 102–5, nos. 141 and 143; Remling, 1:530.

56. C. Lehmann, *Chronica*, p. 570.

57. HSA no. 1777; SAS Kopialbuch 81, fols. 50v–51r.

58. Remling, 1:534–35.

59. *USS*, pp. 109–12, no. 149. In 1285 King Rudolf ordered his judges to accept or adjudicate no cases lodged against the burghers of Speyer, because he personally would hear them: ibid., pp. 113–14, no. 152. On the Franciscans and Dominicans of Speyer and their almost invariable alliance with the burghers in quarrels with the bishops, see Konrad Eubel, "Zur Geschichte des Minoritenklosters zu Speier," pp. 675–98, especially 678–81.

60. *USS*, p. 141, no. 184.

61. Ibid., pp. 144–48, no. 188; C. Lehmann, *Chronica*, pp. 580–82; Remling, 1:545–46. On Richwin, see *CR* 1:263, n. 1.

62. *UBS*, 1:421–22, no. 451.

63. Ibid., 1:436–38, no. 465.

64. Würdtwein, ed., *Nova subsidia*, 1:174.

65. A full discussion of the intricate politics involved may be found in Litzenburger, "Besetzung," pp. 302–11. See also Georges Digard et al., eds., *Les Registres de Boniface VIII*, pp. 786–87, no. 5621, and Charles Grandjean, ed., *Les Registres de Benoît XI*,

pp. 85–86, no. 87, where Benedict XI disposed of the office of master of the cathedral school at Speyer vacated by Sigibodo's elevation.

66. *UBS*, 1:438–41, no. 466.

67. Harster, "Verfassungskämpfe," pp. 222–23; Remling, 1:557–58; C. Lehmann, *Chronica*, pp. 632–35.

68. *UBS*, 1:442, no. 468.

69. GLA 67/280, fols. 41–42 (=*USS*, pp. 169–71, no. 218).

70. *USS*, p. 175, no. 224.

71. See, for example, ibid., nos. 233, 346, 355, 489, and 492; HSA no. 134; GLA 67/448, fol. 41v.

72. *CR*, 1:36, n. 3 (Dean Eberhard von Randeck in 1352); 1:320, n. 1 (Canon Anselm von Duttweiler in 1348). See also *USS*, pp. 183–84, no. 233, and *UBS*, 1:494–96, no. 523.

73. *USS*, p. 225, no. 282.

74. Ibid., pp. 187–88, no. 241; *UBS*, 1:457–58, no. 484. The consent of the chapter is not mentioned in ibid., 1:465–66, nos. 492 (1310) and 494 (1312).

75. Ibid., 1:438–41, no. 466.

76. Ibid., 1:444–50, nos. 472–73, 475.

77. Ibid., 1:460–61, no. 487; *USS*, pp. 201–2, no. 262.

78. *UBS*, 1:457–58, no. 484.

Chapter 3, Part III

1. "None bene rexit" appears in a chronicle of the bishops of Speyer written about 1470 by John of Mutterstadt, vicar of the cathedral, at the instance of Bishop Mathias Ramung: Mone, ed., *Quellensammlung*, 1:188.

2. Ludwig Litzenburger, "Die Päpste und die Speyerer Bistumsbesetzung während der ersten Hälfte des avignonesischen Exils," pp. 596–98, did not really explain why Archbishop Peter von Aspelt of Mainz postulated Emicho, although it may well have had something to do with Emicho's being a minor: *USS*, p. 168, no. 334.

3. See pp. 88–89.

4. Remling, 1:575; Hermann Schreibmüller, "Reichsburglehen in dem Gebiete der Landvogtei in Speyergau (bis 1349)," p. 77.

5. Karl Kloe, *Die Wahlkapitulationen der Bischöfe zu Speyer (1272–1802)*, p. 30. Like most others of its kind, this book is too narrowly legal in approach, tends to evaluate the importance of capitulations by the number of articles they contain, and in general regards these oaths as obstructive. On page 8, for example, Kloe blamed the fact that relatively few princes of the church sought the bishopric of Speyer on the electoral capitulations and stressed the responsibility of the cathedral chapter for the sad state of the see, particularly its paltry revenues.

6. *UBS*, vol. 1, nos. 506–7, 511, 517–8, 531.

7. *USS*, pp. 238–39, no. 300.

8. GLA 78/1114 s.a. 1324; Johann Georg Lehmann, *Urkundliche Geschichte der ehemaligen freien Reichsstadt und jetzigen Bundesfestung Landau in der Pfalz*, p. 26.

9. In 1315 and 1320 by Leopold of Austria: Remling, 1:579.

10. *UBS,* 1:473–74, nos. 503–4; *USS,* pp. 230–31, 240, nos. 289–90, 302.

11. *UBS,* 1:482–84, no. 513 (1317).

12. GLA 67/283, fol. 101.

13. *UBS,* 1:482–84, no. 513. The castle was redeemable, however, for £ 600 Heller, because the holder, Dietrich Zoller, was authorized to spend £ 300 Heller for repairs. The bishop reserved the right of redemption to himself or, should he not wish to redeem it, to the cathedral chapter. Only if neither desired to redeem the pawn could Dietrich or his heirs sell it to whomever they pleased.

14. Ibid., 1:476–77, 487–88, nos. 507, 517–18.

15. See SAS Urkunden Hochstift Speyer nos. 118–24, where Emicho in 1327 and 1328 pressed home his rights as the feudal lord of the castles Alttan and Neutan.

16. *USS,* pp. 266–68, no. 334.

17. *UBS,* 1:502–4, no. 528. Note that the sums add up to something more than £ 1,000 Heller.

18. Cologne, Stadtarchiv, Auswärtiges no. 320, fols. 92v–93. The text is partially printed in Riedner, *Gerichtshöfe,* 2:51–53, but omits the complaints of the cathedral chapter.

19. Sauerland, ed., *Vatikanische Urkunden,* 2:247, no. 1715; C. Lehmann, *Chronica,* p. 691; Würdtwein, ed., *Nova subsidia,* 1:176; Litzenburger, "Päpste," pp. 600–603; Remling, 1:587–88; Mollat, *Collation,* pp. 275–76; August Schuegraf, *Die Bistumsvereinigungen in der deutschen Kirche während des 14. und 15. Jahrhunderts,* pp. 8–10; Merkel, "Studien zur Territorialgeschichte der badischen Markgrafschaft," p. 79. Bertold died in 1353 as bishop of Strasbourg.

20. See *UBS,* 1:510, no. 536, and 2:1, no. 1, in the arengas.

21. *Reg. Pfalz,* vol. 1, no. 6617.

22. GLA 42/280 and 281 s.d. 20 Apr. 1330.

23. *UBS,* 1:501–2, no. 536.

24. On Baldwin, see Alexander Dominicus, *Baldewin von Lützelburg, Erzbischof und Kurfürst von Trier,* and Edmund E. Stengel, *Abhandlungen und Untersuchungen zur mittelalterlichen Geschichte,* pp. 180–215. Although Baldwin protested the purity of his intentions in accumulating so many sees, he allegedly also said he would gladly have snatched up Cologne had it been available. Mainz was actually far more important, for it linked Baldwin with his nephew John, whose kingdom of Bohemia lay in the ecclesiastical province of Mainz, and Baldwin frankly acknowledged that his holding Mainz was an affair of the house of Luxembourg. See Stengel, *Abhandlungen,* p. 194, and Adam Goerz, ed., *Regesten der Erzbischöfe zu Trier von Hetti bis Johann II.,* p. 76. Baldwin's holdings formed an enormous wedge of territory in southwest Germany running from Trier south to Saarwerden, east to Lauterburg, north along the Rhine to Coblenz, and back down the Moselle to Trier. For these lands, he concluded the *Landfrieden* of Kaiserslautern in 1333: Carl Pöhlmann and Anton Doll, eds., *Regesten der Grafen von Zweibrücken,* p. 181, no. 560.

25. *UBS,* 2:1–18, no. 1. On Baldwin's very sound financial policies, exceptional in the fourteenth-century German church (or in all Europe, for that matter), see Stengel, *Abhandlungen,* pp. 190–91, and *The Cambridge Economic History of Europe,* vol. 3, *Economic Organization and Policies in the Middle Ages,* ed. Michael Postan, E. E. Rich, and Edward Miller, pp. 524–25. Baldwin evidently intervened little in the

governance of Speyer save to appoint Henry von Fleckenstein in 1336 as *Oberamtmann* on the left bank and as retainer in charge of sixty-two men (*knechte*) to garrison the bishopric: Coblenz, Staatsarchiv, 1A no. 4881.

26. Litzenburger, "Päpste," pp. 601, 604–6; Remling, 1:596–97.

27. *UBS*, 1:526–27, no. 548.

28. Ibid., 1:530–31, 536–37, nos. 553 and 559; Heinrich Troe, *Münze, Zoll und Markt und ihre finanzielle Bedeutung für das Reich vom Ausgang der Staufer bis zum Regierungsantritt Karls IV.*, pp. 271–72, 273 n. 1. The archbishop of Mainz was included because part of the original loan of £30,000 had been made on his principality.

29. GLA 67/284, fol. 25r.

CHAPTER 3, PART IV

1. SAS Kopialbuch 63 and GLA 67/285, fols. 147–62.

2. Much of this is printed in register form in Reimer, "Bischof Gerhart," pp. 81–117.

3. SAS Urkunden Hochstift Speyer no. 868; Reimer, "Bischof Gerhart," p. 97.

4. *UBS*, 1:587–88, 613–14, nos. 594 (1351) and 612 (1358); Remling, 1:627.

5. *UBS*, 1:539–45, 577–78, 606, nos. 562 (1339), 587 (1349), 607 (1355).

6. E.g., ibid., 1:574–75, no. 584.

7. Ibid., 1:528–29, 572–74, nos. 550 and 583.

8. Ibid., nos. 582, 587, 589, 601, and 607.

9. Ibid., nos. 553, 557, 560, 573, 586, 600, and 604.

10. GLA 78/1114 s.a. 1324; *USS*, p. 231, no. 290 (1315); Alois Kimmelmann, *Waibstadt: Geschichte einer verpfändeten, ehemals freien Reichsstadt*, p. 47.

11. *UBS*, 1:533–34, no. 556. The value of the pawn was set at £1,000 Heller. In 1369 Charles IV increased it by another 1,000 fl.: Strasbourg, Archives départmentales du Bas-Rhin, C 66 (37).

12. *UBS*, 1:569–71, no. 581. On the pawn or property gage, which was little known outside the empire, see Götz Landwehr, *Die Verpfändung der deutschen Reichsstädte im Mittelalter*, passim, but especially pp. vi–vii, 236–43, 258–64, 275, 387–90; for the older references, see Cohn, *Palatinate*, p. 43, n. 1. In the fourteenth century the emperors pawned about one third of the 105 imperial towns, and about half of these pawns were made to the Electors Palatine; but territorial princes, towns, and ecclesiastical institutions also relied heavily on pawning. See Götz Landwehr, "Die Bedeutung der Reichs- und Territorialpfandschaften für den Aufbau des kurpfälzischen Territoriums," pp. 155–96.

13. *UBS*, vol. 1, nos. 566 (1339), 579 (1347), and 581 (1349); GLA 67/296, fol. 302.

14. *USS*, p. 231, no. 290; *UBS*, 1:569–71, no. 581.

15. See the adulatory remarks of Reimer, "Bischof Gerhart," pp. 78–79.

16. Kloe, *Wahlkapitulationen*, p. 31; Litzenburger, "Päpste," pp. 604–6.

17. *UBS*, 1:537, 557–58, nos. 560 and 573; Otto Roegele, *Bruchsal wie es war*, pp. 10–12. Charles IV also effectively ordered Gerhard to rebuild the destroyed fortifications at Landau: *UBS*, 1:577, no. 586.

18. *USS*, p. 392, no. 442.

19. GLA 67/279, fol. 49; *UBS*, 1:604–5, no. 605; Reimer, "Bischof Gerhart," p. 98.

20. C. Lehmann, *Chronica,* pp. 715–16. For his other difficulties with Speyer, see *USS,* pp. 426, 435–37, nos. 475 and 489; GLA 67/284, fol. 41r; Speyer, Stadtarchiv, 1U nos. 284 and 645–46.

21. Many examples may be found in Reimer, "Bischof Gerhart," pp. 81–101. Guido Kisch, *The Jews in Medieval Germany,* pp. 224–25, found that the usual rate of interest on loans from Jews to Christians was forty-three and a half percent, although it could go as high as sixty-five percent. The loans contracted by the bishops of Speyer confirm these findings.

22. *UBS,* 1:581, no. 590: "nec bonis mobilibus, cum propter temporum sterilitatem non existant. . . ."

23. Ibid., 1:575–77, no. 585. On some of the reasons for the massacres of the Jews, see Séraphine Guerchberg, "The Controversy over the Alleged Sowers of the Black Death in the Contemporary Treatises on Plague."

24. Reimer, "Bischof Gerhart," pp. 81–101.

25. GLA 67/284, fols. 29v–30r.

26. Reimer, "Bischof Gerhart," pp. 85, 94.

27. Ibid., pp. 91, 98–99; *UBS,* 1:510–12, 581–82, nos. 536 and 590; GLA 67/284, fols. 38–39, 43v–44r.

28. Reimer, "Bischof Gerhart," p. 91.

29. *UBS,* 1:558–59, no. 574.

30. GLA 67/285, fol. 47; Vatican City, Archivio segreto Vaticano, Registri Vaticani 209, fols. 81v–82r. Clement VI in 1352 also granted Gerhard the collation of various benefices and the right of visitation (including of exempt houses) throughout the diocese: ibid., fols. 81v, 82. The papal charter of 1351 is printed in *UBS,* 1:588–89, no. 595; the condemnation of the capitulation, in ibid., 1:589–91, no. 596.

31. Ibid., 1:523–25, no. 546. On Ulrich, see *CR,* 1:130, n. 1.

32. GLA 67/450, fols. 127–28r. Another £200 was secured for repairs by the appointment as bailiff there of Trigel von Zolle with the consent of Peter von Mur. Trigel could not be removed from office until either the bishop or the chapter had returned the money: GLA 67/285, fols. 58–59r.

33. GLA 67/449, fol. 10r. The text is printed in Franz J. Mone, "Finanzwesen vom 13. bis 16. Jahrhundert in der Schweiz, Baden, Elsass und Bayern," pp. 288–89.

34. GLA 67/449, fols. 9v–10r.

35. SAS Urkunden Hochstift Speyer no. 182.

Chapter 3, Part V

1. Kirsch, *Kollektorien,* pp. xliii–xlv; Mollat, *Collation,* pp. 211–12; Remling, 1:630–35; *UBS,* 1:625–33, nos. 622–27. On Eberhard, see *CR,* 1:36, n. 3.

2. GLA 67/285, fol. 48.

3. GLA 67/287, fols. 39v–41r. Oddly, the cooperation of the three other chapters is not mentioned, although this is probably a simple omission. For later developments in this levy under Bishop Adolf, see p. 113.

4. GLA 67/285, fols. 71v–72r; Remling, 1:636. Lambert also appointed a close relative, Cosmos von Born, as *Amtmann* of Kestenburg.

5. *UBS,* vol. 1, nos. 628–30, 637, 640–41, 646.
6. Ibid., nos. 632, 638–39, 642, 644.
7. *Reg. Pfalz,* vol. 1, no. 3551.
8. Ibid., no. 5051.
9. Remling, 1:642.
10. Schuegraf, *Bistumsvereinigungen,* pp. 13–18; Remling, 1:643–56.
11. Remling, 1:656–63; *UBS,* 1:682–84, 686–87, nos. 660 and 663.
12. GLA 67/287, fol. 8 (= *UBS,* 1:669–70, no. 648).
13. GLA 67/287, fols. 103–4r.
14. Most of his charters were recorded in the copybooks GLA/286 and 287.
15. *UBS,* 1:673–74, no. 651.
16. GLA 67/287, fols. 38–39r, 63–65r, 102v.
17. Ibid., fols. 39v–41r, 79v–81.
18. GLA 67/280, fol. 122r; 67/286, fols. 4v–7.
19. GLA 67/287, fols. 45v–46 (= *UBS,* 1:682–84, no. 660).
20. GLA 67/288, fols. 12–15r, 243–44r.
21. *Reg. Pfalz,* vol. 1, nos. 4309, 4336, 4341, 4343, 4345, 4366, 4371, 4484, 4496, 4545, 4748.
22. C. Lehmann, *Chronica,* pp. 726–28; Remling, 1:651–52.
23. GLA 67/287, fols. 42v–43, 62–63r, 70v–71.
24. Ibid., fols. 4v, 10v, 25, 20v–30r, 48v–49r.
25. See p. 86.
26. GLA 67/287, fol. 30.
27. Ibid., fols. 38–39r, 67–68r, 106v; GLA 78/1567.
28. See p. 113.
29. GLA 67/286, fols. 16v–17, 18–23; 67/287, fols. 4v–5r, 6v, 12v, 23, 30, 42, 44–45, 48, etc.
30. Ibid., fols. 30, 48–49, 99v–100r.
31. Ibid., fols. 68–70.
32. GLA 67/288, fols. 15v–17r, 18–19r. Fols. 16–17r are bound at the front of the volume.
33. Ibid., fols. 77–78.
34. Ibid.
35. Ibid., fols. 61–62r.
36. Ibid., fol. 67 was one of these.
37. Ibid., fols. 129v–130, 232–35.
38. Ibid., fols. 52v, 57–59r, 135–39, 173–74, 191v–193, 195–96r, 288r, 303.
39. Ibid., fols. 85–89r.
40. Ibid., fols. 94–99.
41. Thus ibid., fols. 191v–193, 195–96r.
42. A list is given in ibid., fol. 196v.
43. Ibid., fols. 44–47r, 84 and the following unnumbered folio (r), 113–14r, 120–22, 123–29r, 149r, 178–81, 196v, 237–40. An example will illustrate what is meant. In 1353 Bishop Gerhard had borrowed 1,200 fl. from the Speyer burgher Siegfried Schalloff at a yearly interest payment of 120 fl. Bishop Nicholas in 1391 prevailed on

the heirs of this note to change the annual interest into an annuity that ceased when they died: Reimer, "Bischof Gerhart," p. 96, and GLA 67/288, fols. 113–14.

44. GLA 67/288, fols. 134, 216r, 217r.

45. Ibid., fol. 266v; Roegele, *Bruchsal*, pp. 10–12.

46. GLA 67/288, fols. 150v, 198. Such clauses were thereafter customary in the oaths of episcopal officials.

47. Ibid., fols. 207v–208r, 263v–264. In 1395 he purchased the serfs of another lord settled on the lands of the principality (GLA 42/72 s.d. 25 July 1395), thereby initiating a policy continued down to the eighteenth century. Many of the relevant documents are gathered in GLA 78.

48. GLA 67/285, fols. 69v–70; 67/288, fol. 89.

49. GLA 67/288, fol. 140v.

50. Ibid., fol. 172r.

51. Remling, 1:679, n. 1862.

52. Ibid., 1:682.

53. GLA 67/288, fols. 82v–83 (=*UBS*, 1:705–14, no. 676). The capitulation is discussed in Kloe, *Wahlkapitulationen*, pp. 35–36.

54. GLA 67/288, fol. 76 (=Franz Mone, "Kraichgauer Urkunden vom 12.–16. Jahrhundert," p. 330).

55. *Reg. Pfalz*, vol. 1, no. 5631.

56. GLA 67/288, fols. 74, 102v–103, 148–49r, 197v–198, 206v–209r, 252–54. One of these, that of an *Amtmann* at Rotenberg in 1396, is printed in Mone, "Kraichgauer Urkunden," pp. 166–68.

57. GLA 67/288, fols. 24v–25, 29, 80r, 107v–108, 144v–148r, 155–56r, 265, 292–94, 295–98.

58. Ibid., fols. 224–26 (=*UBS*, 1:692–95, no. 668).

Chapter 4, Part I

1. I shall discuss some of these questions more thoroughly in an article on the bishopric of Speyer as a "Renaissance state."

2. The chart is from Stamer, *Kirchengeschichte*, 2:230.

3. See pp. 55–56 for the practical bearing of the distinction.

4. Richard Lossen, *Staat und Kirche in der Pfalz am Ausgang des Mittelalters*, p. 48, oversimplified when he said there were no papal provisions to the sees of Speyer and Worms in the fifteenth century. There were, but these were all technicalities, and the Electors effectively disposed of these bishoprics down through the first quarter of the sixteenth century.

5. Reported by the bishop's secretary, George Brentz, in his report on the Bundschuh in GLA 67/304, fol. 450.

6. One is reminded of Chaucer's Reeve, who showed

> A better hand at bargains than his lord,
> He had grown rich and had a store of treasure
> Well tucked away, yet out it came to pleasure
> His lord with subtle loans or gifts of goods,
> To earn his thanks and even coats and hoods.

"The Prologue" to *The Canterbury Tales,* trans. Neville Coghill (London, 1951), pp. 35–36.

7. Cohn, *Palatinate,* p. 114: "A decisive point was reached in the finances of many German principalities when their credit became sufficient for them to obtain loans without pawning their revenues or lands; in Württemberg this point was passed about the year 1419." In the bishopric of Speyer, this had occurred at least a decade earlier, and shortly thereafter in the bishopric of Constance, but only about 1460 in that of Strasbourg: Franz Keller, "Die Verschuldung des Hochstifts Konstanz im 14. und 15. Jahrhundert," pp. 40–66, 73; Francis Rapp, *Réformes et Réformation à Strasbourg,* pp. 203–9.

8. GLA 67/339, fols. 71–76, 80–87. Fols. 82–83 are missing.

9. For some instances of such problems, see SAS Urkunden Allerheiligenstift Speyer no. 124 and Urkunden Hochstift Speyer nos. 258–59; GLA 42/113 s.d. 19 Mar. 1452, 277 s.d. 30 Aug. 1471, 299 s.d. 31 May 1486, 308 s.d. 18 Mar. 1457; GLA 67/420, fols. 133–35, 207; GLA 78/1268; GLA 229/77953; *Protokolle,* no. 8785; *Sammlung der Hochfürstlich-Speierischen Gesetze und Landesverordnungen,* 1:32–33.

10. Cohn, *Palatinate,* p. v.

11. Alois Gerlich, *Habsburg-Luxemburg-Wittelsbach im Kampf um die deutsche Königskrone,* pp. 105, 123.

12. Lossen, *Staat,* pp. 51, 59–65; Cohn, *Palatinate,* pp. 141–43.

13. Cited in Cohn, *Palatinate,* p. 143.

14. Lossen, *Staat,* p. 64.

15. Karl Rieder, "Die kirchengeschichtliche Literatur Badens im Jahre 1906 und 1907," pp. 333–34, criticized Lossen for not emphasizing enough the extent of the influence of both the Electors and the popes on the composition of the two chapters. Partial calendars of papal documents concerning Speyer have been edited by Glaser, "Diözese Speier," and Theodor Scherg, "Palatina aus dem Vatikan (1464–1484)," pp. 109–90.

16. That the threat posed to the bishopric from the south by the margraves of Baden helped drive the bishops into the arms of the Electors is a distinct possibility that has not been explored. The margraves had begun to interfere with the administration of ecclesiastical jurisdiction as early as 1336 (see *Reg. Baden,* 1:124–25, no. 1225). The family treaty providing for the division of the margravate in 1380 forbade even pawning of possessions to the bishops of Speyer and Strasbourg and to the count of Württemberg (ibid., 1:137, no. 1335). Margrave Bernhard I utilized the disorder in the bishopric in the 1380s to the fullest to extract 3,000 fl. from Bishop Nicholas: GLA 67/288, fols. 15v–17r, 153v–154, 172r, 228v–230.

17. GLA 67/339, fols. 104–5.

18. Lossen spends a disproportionate amount of discussion on infringements of ecclesiastical jurisdiction, and neither he nor Cohn devotes much attention to the Electors' heavy financial exactions.

19. Even more significantly, in 1581 Bishop Eberhard von Dienheim (1581–1610) sold to the Elector the estate in Heidelberg that Bishop Raban had bought in 1401 (GLA 67/322, fols. 274r–276), and in 1588 Eberhard rejected the claim of the Elector John Casimir that the bishopric still stood under the protection of the Palatinate. Eberhard explained that the protective relationship had always been valid only for the

lifetime of a particular Elector and that the treaty had not been renewed since the time of Frederick II (1544–56): GLA 42/3 s.d. 18 Feb. 1588.

20. Drollinger, *Kleine Städte*, pp. 114–21, stressed the catastrophic effects of the Thirty Years War on the bishopric of Speyer.

21. GLA 67/291, fols. 258v–259: "zu vermyden krieg arbeit kosten zweytracht vnd verderplichen schaden des Stiffts. . . ."

22. The clause "damit lant und luten keyn krieg entstehe" occurs in the electoral capitulation of Mathias Ramung in 1465: Kloe, *Wahlkapitulationen*, p. 46.

23. See p. 180 for a discussion of the peasants' attitudes toward the bishop and the chapter.

24. GLA 67/304, fol. 450v: "das die Obristen priester vnd der Adel regiret vnd die Buren dienen sullen." This report was published by Franz Mone, "Zur Geschichte des Bundschuhes, Bauern- und Revolutionskrieges," pp. 165–69, and Günther Franz, ed., *Quellen zur Geschichte des Bauernkrieges*, pp. 70–72.

25. For a brief review of the events, see Stamer, *Kirchengeschichte*, 2:277–78, and Günther Franz, *Der deutsche Bauernkrieg*, pp. 222–27. Daniel Häberle, "Die Wüstungen der Rheinpfalz auf Grundlage der Besiedlungsgeschichte," p. 48, estimated that 31 of the approximately 297 castles in the Rhenish Palatinate were destroyed in the Peasants War.

26. Kloe, *Wahlkapitulationen*, p. 45.

27. *UBS*, 2:136, no. 69.

28. Ibid., 2:153–56, no. 76.

29. GLA 67/456, fol. 37v. On the education of the various canons, see *CR*, 1:98, n. 3; 147, n. 1; 321, n. 2; 336, n. 1; 350, n. 3; 523, n. 1; 524, n. 2; 547, n. 1; 575, n. 3; 578, n. 2; etc. Saint Guido's, which like the other collegiate churches in Speyer did not exclude nonaristocrats, in 1476 went even further by ordering that all canons eventually had to graduate in theology: GLA 78/1774, fol. 4v. For a more general consideration of aristocratic response to the threat posed by educated men, see J. M. Fletcher, "Wealth and Poverty in the Medieval German Universities," p. 411; J. H. Hexter, "The Education of the Aristocracy in the Renaissance," in his *Reappraisals in History*, pp. 45–70.

30. Lossen, *Staat*, p. 51, n. 2.

31. *UBS*, 2:202–8, no. 101.

32. GLA 67/455, p. 3.

33. *UBS*, 2:405–7, no. 212.

34. Lossen, *Staat*, pp. 51–52.

35. GLA 67/458, p. 4, contains the undated remark that "Abolitis ijs [statutis], quae olim Circa Magistros, Sive Baccaclaureos formatos in Theologia, aut Doctores uel Licentiatos in iure Canonico uel Civili obseruabantur—quorum admissio eam a Ducentis annis cessat." Inasmuch as this volume is entitled and dated "Liber statutorum recentissimus, mit Personal-Listen (1309–1770)," the sentence probably dates from about 1770. See also Feine, *Besetzung*, pp. 19–24, and Aretin, *Heiliges Römisches Reich*, 1:46–51.

36. See, for example, the detailed list of money collected for the imperial Common Penny (*gemeiner Pfennig*) tax of 1495 in GLA 65/2171, which is a photocopy of the original in the Stadtarchiv in Frankfurt.

37. For a discussion of the complexities of the issues in question, see Carsten, *Princes*, pp. 436–41.

CHAPTER 4, PART II

1. *Reg. Pfalz*, 1:401–2, no. 6788.
2. GLA 67/289, fols. 46–47r, 181v.
3. Ibid., fols. 84–85r.
4. *Reg. Pfalz*, vol. 1, nos. 265, 392, 1142, 1761, 1968, 2108, 2159, 2376, 2854, 3127, 3174, 3230, 3302, 3638–40, 4240, 4664, 4667, 4830, 4857, 5036, etc.
5. *UBS*, 2:30, no. 7; Franz Mone, "Politisches Testament des Bischofs Raban von Speier, 1439," p. 201.
6. *Reg. Pfalz*, 2:231, no. 3304.
7. *UBS*, 2:180, no. 88.
8. Ibid., nos. 4, 7–8, 14, 65–66, 74; GLA D no. 535a; 42/92 s.a. 1416; 78/1116 s.a. 1398.
9. *UBS*, 2:72, no. 33.
10. GLA 67/302, fol. 24.
11. Stamer, *Kirchengeschichte*, 2:263.
12. The synodal decrees are recorded in the *Collectio processuum*. . . .
13. *UBS*, vol. 2, nos. 69–71, 78, 80–81, 101–2.
14. GLA 67/415. Raban's volume ended in 1413, however, and the next volume in the series (GLA 67/416) began only in 1465.
15. GLA 67/289.
16. GLA 67/364.
17. GLA 67/290.
18. GLA 67/289, fols. 19v–20, 303.
19. Ibid., fol. 166.
20. GLA 67/296, fols. 306v, 310–11; Friedrich J. Hildenbrand, *Schloss Marientraut*, pp. 4–5.
21. GLA 67/289, fols. 153–57r, 162–64r; 67/296, fols. 204–5r; 78/1114 s.a. 1404. SAS Urkunden Hochstift Speyer no. 1026.
22. GLA 67/289, fol. 336v; 67/296, fol. 306r.
23. GLA 42/72 s.d. 25 July 1395, 8 Aug. 1407, and 21 Dec. 1407; 42/168 s.d. 13 Feb. 1413 and s.a. 1421–24 (three charters), 183 s.d. 17 Feb. 1413, 280 s.d. 1 Sept. 1419, 302 s.d. 25 Nov. 1411, and 318 s.d. 13 Mar. 1411; 67/289, fols. 169–70; 229/34862.
24. GLA 67/302, fols. 123–79. This was edited by Mone, "Politisches Testament," pp. 193–201.
25. GLA 67/285, fols. 123–26, 165–70, 175r; 67/364, fols. 36v–37r, 59v–60r, 81, 130, 257r, 298r.
26. GLA 42/295 s.d. 17 Mar. 1403; 67/283, fols. 121–22, 130–31; 67/289, fols. 92, 183v–184; Klaus Conrad, *Die Geschichte des Dominikanerinnenklosters in Lambrecht*, pp. 26–27.

27. SAS Urkunden Hochstift Speyer nos. 564–67, 573, 844–49.

28. GLA 67/289, fol. 446r.

29. Wilhelm Harster, "Die letzten Veränderungen der reichsstädtischen Verfassung Speiers," pp. 443–73.

30. Remling, 2:27–41. *UBS*, vol. 2, nos. 36, 43, 48, 57–59, 61–63, 72. GLA 67/277, fols. 14–24; 67/286, fols. 49v–51; 67/289, fols. 247, 467–68; 67/451, fols. 34–40. SAS Urkunden Hochstift Speyer no. 1241. On 26 August 1423 Raban acknowledged receipt of 18,000 fl. from the town (which presumably included the 8,000 fl. due to the chapter): Speyer, Stadtarchiv, 1U no. 762.

31. Mone, "Politisches Testament," p. 194.

32. Ibid., pp. 197–99.

33. GLA 67/450, fols. 189–91r.

34. GLA 67/289, fol. 34.

35. *UBS*, 2:41, no. 14.

36. Ibid., 2:63–64, no. 25; *Reg. Pfalz*, 2:302, no. 4199; GLA 67/415, fol. 3r.

37. Ibid., fol. 43v. Some clerics also refused to pay the *cathedraticum* in 1411–12: ibid., fol. 93v.

38. GLA 67/289, fols. 32v–33r, 34v–35r.

39. Ibid., fol. 10.

40. Ibid., fols. 26–28r.

41. Ibid., fols. 57v–58r.

42. Ibid., fols. 36–38r.

43. Ibid., fols. 59–60r.

44. GLA 42/110 s.d. 23 Dec. 1400. He had in 1399 promised to discharge it: GLA 67/289, fol. 32r.

45. Mone, "Politisches Testament," pp. 195–96.

46. GLA 67/289, passim.

47. Ibid., fols. 3–5r (1397).

48. Ibid., passim.

49. Ibid., fols. 34v, 68v–69, 76–77, 88–89, 113–15, 124–25, 205–6, 209–10, 262–63, 286, 292–93, 296, 387–88, 414–17.

50. Ibid., fols. 453–54r, 467v–468.

51. GLA 78/1708. The count's concession was perhaps related to a judgment delivered against him in the same year by the Elector Palatine because of damage inflicted on clerical property in Württemberg: GLA 67/289, fol. 270v.

52. Ibid., fol. 280r. According to the register of the Reichstag, Raban was responsible for supplying thirty fully equipped knights. On 28 June 1428 he paid to the committee of the Reichstag 1,600 fl., but he was still listed as being in arrears in 1429: Albert Werminghoff, *Die deutschen Reichskriegssteuergesetze von 1422 bis 1427 und die deutsche Kirche,* p. 217. In 1422 and 1431, however, Raban contributed a total of only 16 fl. and 10 fl., respectively (ibid., pp. 136, 146).

53. The connection, originally suggested by Trithemius, was accepted by Lossen, *Staat,* p. 9 and n. 1, and is more fully discussed in the larger context of the expansionist policies of the Electors in Erich Meuthen, *Das Trierer Schisma von 1430 auf dem Basler Konzil,* pp. 63–65.

54. [?] Lager, "Raban von Helmstadt und Ulrich von Manderscheid—ihr Kampf um das Erzbistum Trier," pp. 721–70; Knetsch, *Kurstaat Trier*, p. 29; Schuegraf, *Bistums-vereinigungen*, pp. 19–21; Meuthen, *Trierer Schisma*, pp. 58, 63–65, 253–55; Morimichi Watanabe, "The Episcopal Election of 1430 in Trier and Nicholas of Cusa," pp. 299–316.

55. Knetsch, *Kurstaat Trier*, p. 29.

56. GLA 67/289, fols. 305v, 322v.

57. *UBS*, 2:180–81, no. 88. These possessions were redeemed in 1434 with money from the archbishopric of Trier: GLA 67/289, fols. 378–79r.

58. Ibid., fol. 323.

59. Ibid., fols. 207r–208r.

60. Ibid., fol. 339v.

61. Ibid., fols. 354v–355.

62. Ibid., fols. 399v–401.

63. Ibid., fols. 307–8r, 311–16, 351v–352, 362v–63r, 373–74r, 383, 408, 421r, 433r. I have counted only once possessions that were pawned several times, but I have calculated on the basis of the highest sum for which they were pawned.

64. SAS Urkunden Hochstift Speyer no. 618.

65. GLA 67/289, fol. 433r.

66. *UBS*, 2:191, no. 94.

67. GLA 67/289, fols. 304, 308v–309r, 320, 328–30, 355v, 366v–368.

68. Ibid., fols. 300, 319r, 352r, 355v, 362–65, 385, 392–96, 404–6, 408–10.

69. Ibid., fols. 320, 322v, 328–30, 333, 337r, 338–44, 351, 362r, 378r, 382, 384–86, 391r, 398–402, 410, 419–20, 427, 431r, 440v.

70. Ibid., fols. 328–30, 342v–344r, 358v–359r.

71. Ibid., fols. 385v, 432v.

72. Ibid., fol. 379.

73. GLA 67/291, fols. 58v–59r. When the pope provided Raban to Trier in 1430, he also named Adolf, count of Eppstein, as bishop of Speyer. Adolf died in 1433, however, and no documents of the bishopric bear his name.

74. Ibid., fol. 227r.

75. Ibid.

76. GLA 67/292, fol. 127v.

77. GLA 67/291, fols. 14v–16r.

78. Ibid., fols. 45r, 58v–60r. These texts were edited by Franz Mone, "Steuerbe-willigung im Bistum Speier, 1439–1441," pp. 163–69.

79. GLA 67/291, fols. 76–77, 81.

80. GLA 42/118 s.d. 30 Sept. 1441; 67/291, fols. 82v–84r.

81. GLA 67/291, fols. 269–70r. To cope with this problem, Reinhard also concluded mutual aid treaties with the regent of the Palatinate and the count of Württemberg in 1439 and 1443, respectively: ibid., fols. 66v–67, 255r; 67/358, fols. 9–12.

82. GLA 67/292, fols. 67v–68, 80r; 67/359, fols. 139–41.

83. GLA 62/7909 A.

84. GLA 67/291 and 292, passim. The loan at four and a third percent is inscribed

in 67/292, fols. 69–71. It was contracted with a cousin of the bishop in 1448 and had to be repaid by Christmas.

85. GLA 67/291, fols. 14v–16r, 34v–36, 258v; 67/292, fols. 139–40.

86. GLA 67/291, fols. 68v–69, 74v–75r; 67/292, fols. 134v–136, 169v–170, 267.

87. See p. 128.

88. Mone, "Politisches Testament," p. 193.

89. GLA 67/291, fols. 30v–31r.

90. GLA 67/302, fol. 24.

91. GLA 67/291, fols. 62–66.

92. GLA 67/365, fols. 51v–52.

93. GLA 67/292, fols. 9–11, 37v–38.

94. GLA 62/7909 A et seq.

95. GLA 67/292, fols. 262v–264.

96. GLA 67/291, fols. 74v–75, 87v–89r, 241v, 269; 67/292, fols. 19–22, 169–70, 267.

97. GLA 67/292, fol. 17; Franz Mone, "Zur Geschichte des Bergbaues von Nussloch bis Durlach von 1439 bis 1532," pp. 46–48.

98. GLA 67/291, fols. 92–93r, 120v–125r; UBS, 2:266–68, nos. 137–39.

99. GLA 42/4 s.a. 1431 (thirteen depositions) and 143 s.d. 3 Jan. 1415; 67/289, fol. 216r (a continuation of the lost fol. 215).

100. GLA 67/289, fols. 411–12.

101. GLA 67/291, fol. 150.

102. UBS, 2:235–36, no. 123.

103. GLA 67/292, fol. 39.

CHAPTER 4, PART III

1. Remling, 2:96. Remling cited no source in support of this account, however, and I have found nothing to verify it.

2. UBS, 2:280–81, no. 148.

3. Ibid., 2:281–82, no. 149.

4. GLA 67/302, fol. 87.

5. GLA 67/293, fols. 9–63, 65–122. The exception is on fols. 35–38.

6. Ibid., fols. 119–22r, 125v–126r; SAS Urkunden Allerheiligenstift Speyer no. 19.

7. GLA 67/193, fol. 129. On Reinhard, brother of the next bishop, see CR, 1:431, n. 2.

8. GLA 67/294, fol. 304v.

9. CR, 1:547, n. 2; Cohn, Palatinate, p. 141.

10. UBS, 2:299–302, 306–13, nos. 162–63, 165–67; Cohn, Palatinate, pp. 11–12, 47–49, 141; Lossen, Staat, pp. 33–40, 56–57; and Heiko A. Oberman, Daniel E. Zerfoss, and William J. Courtenay, eds. and trans., Defensorium obedientiae apostolicae et alia documenta, especially pp. 7–16.

11. GLA 42/76a s.d. 10 Aug. 1462; UBS, 2:314–17, no. 169. Although these possessions were redeemed only in 1505, the bishops apparently still received revenues from the Amt of Rotenberg, at least in 1477 and 1484: GLA 66/7079 and 7080.

12. *UBS,* 2:360–61, 379–81, nos. 191 and 200; GLA 67/369, fols. 166v–168.

13. GLA 67/295, fols. 19–23, 114–22, 200–205, 210–14, 227–29, 273–75; 67/339, fol. 61r.

14. GLA 67/302, fols. 98–99.

15. GLA 67/297, fol. 1r.

16. GLA 42/118 s.d. 17 Jan. 1459.

17. GLA 67/295, fol. 158r.

18. Ibid., fols. 244v–252.

19. GLA 67/302, fol. 110. For a list of his loans, see GLA 67/1499, fols. 20v–23.

20. According to the "Speierische Chronik" in Mone, ed., *Quellensammlung,* 1:470–71. Mone believed the author of this chronicle was probably a member of the town council of Speyer (ibid., 1:369).

21. Ludwig Litzenburger, "Papst Pius II. providiert 1464 die Speyerer Kirche mit Matthias von Rammung."

22. *UBS,* 2:339–40, no. 180; GLA 67/339, fol. 71v; 67/1499.

23. GLA 42/54 s.d. 22 June 1464.

24. Kloe, *Wahlkapitulationen,* pp. 45–48, printed most of the text found in GLA 67/339, fols. 50–58. The chapter inserted the new clause requiring its consent to the granting of the right of free usage of the principality's castles because this was one of the favorite means of Palatine territorial expansion: see Christian Schütze, "Ziele und Mittel der pfälzischen Territorialpolitik im 14. Jahrhundert," pp. 3–4. It is of interest to note that, during his disputes with Speyer, Mathias in 1466 demanded 32,000 fl. bail for the emissaries of the town who had been taken captive by the bishop's *Amtleute* at Udenheim. The sum was exactly the amount necessary for the redemption of the lands pawned to the Elector. In fact, the town did agree in 1466–67 to pay the bishop about 9,700 fl. and by January 1468 had handed over 10,900 fl.: Speyer, Stadtarchiv, 1U nos. 822, 825–26, 828, 830, 832–33, 836, and Maximilian Buchner, "Die Stellung des Speierer Bischofs Mathias Ramung zur Reichsstadt Speier, zu Kurfürst Friedrich I. von der Pfalz, und zu Kaiser Friedrich III.," pp. 51–52, 70–72, 75–76.

25. GLA 67/339, fols. 74v–76, 103v.

26. Ibid., fols. 71r, 72–74r, 80–87. Fols. 82–83 are missing. Maximilian Buchner, *Die innere weltliche Regierung des Speierer Bischofs Mathias Ramung (1464–1478),* pp. 28–29, seems to have inferred, quite wrongly, from the financial crisis that obtained upon Mathias's entrance into office that the principality's finances were habitually this desperate.

27. GLA 67/339, fols. 84–87.

28. GLA 67/416, fols. 6–11. I have followed the new foliation in this copybook.

29. Ibid., fols. 1–11, 13v–14r.

30. GLA 42/140 s.d. 3 Feb. 1477; 67/302, fol. 112.

31. GLA 67/297, fols. 257–60, 268–71.

32. GLA 67/298, fol. 36v.

33. GLA 62/7009 E (1466), I (1476), J (1477), K (1478). In "I" it is explicitly stated that this measure took the place of a *Schatzung*: "Inname zu zwyfaltiger Herbstbete vnnd vffgesetztem gelt im Stifft an Staat eyner Schatzung."

34. GLA 62/7909 F.

35. Ibid.

36. Ibid., I.

37. GLA 67/299, fols. 60–61; SAS Urkunden Kollegiatstift Sankt Guido zu Speyer no. 21; Glasschröder, "Archidiakonat," pp. 119–21. The agreement was informally renewed in 1473, and in the 1482 Bishop Louis conceded even more to the archdeacons. The decrees of the Council of Trent did not break the power of the archdeacons in the diocese of Speyer. Even in the eighteenth century the rural deans and clergy rendered their oaths of obedience to their archdeacons, not the bishop: GLA 67/486, fol. 3r.

38. Cited in Buchner, *Regierung*, p. 2.

39. Franz Haffner, *Die kirchlichen Reformbemühungen des Speyerer Bischofs Matthias von Rammung in vortridentinischer Zeit (1464–1478)*.

40. GLA 67/296, 301, and 302. The results were summarized by Buchner, *Regierung*, pp. 4–11, and partially edited by Glasschröder, "Speierer Bistums-Matrikel."

41. GLA 67/416.

42. GLA 67/298, 306, 309, 311, and 313. An index to these books was prepared by Manfred Krebs, "Die Dienerbücher des Bistums Speyer, 1464–1768."

43. GLA 67/298, fols. 27–37, 44–46, 53–56r, 57–59, 92v–93, 99v–104r, 141–43r, 145–47r, 159–65. The ordinance of 1470 concerning the duties and responsibilities of the *Amtleute* is printed in *Sammlung der . . . Landesverordnungen*, pp. 1–8.

44. Lossen, *Staat*, p. 63. An account of this circuit is printed in Mone, ed., *Quellensammlung*, 1:363–67.

45. GLA 67/339, fols. 78–79.

46. GLA 42/3 s.d. 28 June 1466; *UBS*, 2:346–47, no. 184.

47. GLA 42/199 s.d. 19 Oct. 1467.

48. GLA 78/2077. This is incorrectly dated 1571.

49. Stamer, *Kirchengeschichte*, 2:229.

50. GLA 67/369, fols. 183v–184.

51. Buchner, "Stellung," pp. 37–83. The cathedral chapter often acted as a mediator between Mathias and the town.

52. Cohn, *Palatinate*, p. 142.

CHAPTER 4, PART IV

1. Remling, 2:176; *CR*, 1:424, n. 2.

2. GLA 42/143 s.d.

3. See *Protokolle*, nos. 9, 58, 91–92, 102, 233, 249, etc.

4. GLA 67/416, fol. 145v.

5. GLA 67/307, fol. 57v.

6. GLA 62/7909 M and 65/2171.

7. GLA 42/6 s.d. 12 Dec. 1482.

8. GLA 42/218 s.d. 17 Jan. 1491; 67/301, fols. 455–72. Remling, 2:198–200. A. Gustav Kolb, *Die Kraichgauer Ritterschaft unter der Regierung des Kurfürsten Phillip von der Pfalz*, pp. 90–97.

9. *UBS*, 2:452–55, 458–59, nos. 237 and 239.

10. GLA 42/6 s.d. 12 Dec. 1482.

11. GLA 67/296, fol. 420v. See also GLA 78/1375.

12. GLA 67/306, fols. 196–98.

13. GLA 67/304, fols. 13–14, 33–36r, 78–81, 110–13, 165–68, 172–75, 196–99, 302–4, 390–91. This list is by no means complete. The *Libri contractuum* of earlier bishops (GLA 67/289, 291–95, and 297) contain many marginal notations recording alterations that Louis won in the terms of outstanding loans.

14. GLA 67/304, passim.

15. Ibid., fols. 16v–20, 29, 43–45.

16. Ibid., fols. 45v–48r; 42/119 s.d. 22 Apr. 1479.

17. SAS Urkunden Domstift Speyer nos. 150 and 153a; GLA 67/304, fols. 4v, 240–44r.

18. GLA 62/7909 L.

19. GLA 42/192 s.d. 20 Nov. 1493; 67/304, fols. 305r, 473r; 67/449, fol. 155r.

20. GLA 67/416, fol. 145v.

21. GLA 62/7910 B and C.

22. GLA 62/5251.

23. GLA 67/416, fols. 180v–181r; *Protokolle,* nos. 9, 379, 469, 507, 543–44, 553, 565, 600.

24. *CR,* 1:9, and 2:iii, ix–xviii; *Protokolle,* 1:x–xi, and no. 323; *UBS,* 2:419–23, nos. 220 and 222 (confirmation of the privilege of 1490 by Innocent VIII).

25. *Protokolle,* nos. 9, 56, 65, 91, 102, 212, 236, 296, 315, 323, 326, 338, 341, 379, 382, 397, 418, 424, 433, 438–40, 458–59, 466, 469, 491, 507, 513, 517, 537, 543–44, 549, 553, 712, 725.

26. See GLA 62/7909 D through K.

27. See GLA 67/298.

28. *Protokolle,* no. 18.

29. Ibid., no. 213.

30. Ibid., no. 248.

CHAPTER 4, PART V

1. Cohn, *Palatinate,* p. 15; Kolb, *Kraichgauer Ritterschaft,* pp. 146–54.

2. On Philip, see *CR,* 1:86, n. 2. The margrave of Baden had applied pressure on the chapter to elect his son bishop, but without success.

3. GLA 67/306, fol. 57v.

4. GLA 42/76a s.d. 11 Feb. 1505; 67/307, fols. 48v–50, 54v–55.

5. GLA 67/307, fols. 57v–58r.

6. Remling, 2:228–29. On the rarity of such a step and on Charles V's promise to the electoral princes in 1519 not to disturb imperial pawns in their possession, see Landwehr, *Verpfändung,* p. 95.

7. GLA 67/312, fols. 32–35; Remling, 2:308.

8. Remling, 2:231–33; Lossen, *Staat,* p. 64, n. 2.

9. Lossen, *Staat,* p. 61. George's way of dealing with his brother is illustrated by his

proposal to the cathedral chapter in 1518 that they pay the Elector not to erect tolls in certain places in the bishopric: *Protokolle*, nos. 5182–83.

10. GLA 42/1a s.d. 5 Dec. 1521. The imperial charter of 1510 is in *UBS*, 2:469–70, no. 246.

11. GLA 42/149 s.d.

12. GLA 78/2077.

13. GLA 78/979.

14. *UBS*, 2:484–88, no. 258.

15. *Protokolle*, nos. 1728, 1738, 1745, 1748, 1856, 1900, 1994, 2036, 2038, 2040, 2055, 2061, 2320, 2336.

16. Ibid., nos. 3228, 3231, 3239, 3241, 3265; GLA 67/307, fol. 225r; 67/417, fols. 258–63.

17. *Protokolle*, nos. 4408 and 4417.

18. Ibid., nos. 4471–72, 4551, 4588, 4640, 4646, 4921, 5331, 5338, 5442, 5784; GLA 67/310, fols. 72v–90.

19. *Protokolle*, nos. 5787, 5940, 5943, 5946, 5952, 5970.

20. GLA 78/1951. I am editing this text for publication in the *ZGO*.

21. *Protokolle*, nos. 5985, 5987, 6058, 6066.

22. GLA 67/418, fols. 97v–98r.

23. GLA 67/420, fols. 202v–203r.

24. *Protokolle*, nos. 7493, 7791, 7809, 7872, 7874, 7883.

CHAPTER 4, PART VI

1. I have relied heavily in this final section on the biography of Bishop Philip by Hermine Stiefenhöfer, *Philipp von Flersheim, Bischof von Speyer (1529–1552) und gefürsteter Propst von Weissenburg (1546–1552)*, which is solidly grounded on the sources and, despite its restricted perspective, is a fine work (hereafter cited simply as Stiefenhöfer).

2. See Bossert, "Reformationsgeschichte," *ZGO N.F.* 17 (1902):282, 401–5; Remling, 2:250–53.

3. Stamer, *Kirchengeschichte*, 2:321.

4. Ibid., 2:323; Stiefenhöfer, pp. 130, 138; Deutsches Historisches Institut zu Rom, ed., *Nuntiaturberichte aus Deutschland*, 1:503–4, 8:158, 11:137 and 143.

5. Stiefenhöfer, pp. 90–98.

6. Cited in ibid., p. 123: "confederato et quasi subdito del Palatino."

7. GLA 78/1740 and cited in Stiefenhöfer, p. 125: "Ich sehe wol, das Wesen zu Heidelberg wird keine Ruhe haben, es ess dann das kleine Wesen zu Speyer auf."

8. GLA 67/353, fol. 5, cited in Stiefenhöfer, p. 124: "Unnd hat die Pfalz nit aufgeheret vonn tag zu tag gegen denn Stift mit neuerungen fürzugehen."

9. *Protokolle*, nos. 7136 and 8226.

10. Stiefenhöfer, pp. 105–6.

11. GLA 78/1638.

12. GLA 67/312, fols. 37–38, and 42/3 s.d. 16 June 1544.

13. Stiefenhöfer, pp. 104–5.

14. GLA 67/312, fols. 85v–87r, 88v–89r.

15. SAS Urkunden Hochstift Speyer no. 1064.

16. GLA 67/312, fols. 5–16.

17. Franz Mone, "Phillip II. Bischof zu Speier," pp. 125–26.

18. GLA 78/1638. Stiefenhöfer, p. 149, calculated that Philip spent only 6,889 fl. on Turkish subsidies between 1529 and 1542.

19. GLA 67/1891; *Protokolle,* nos. 8113, 8186, 8205.

20. GLA 78/1638. Actually, at the request of the cathedral chapter, the name of the four-year *decimatio* was simply changed to *Türkenhilfe,* so that Philip was not really expropriating imperial revenues: *Protokolle,* no. 8783.

21. GLA 78/1638. The results of this survey, conducted in 1541, are discussed by Stiefenhöfer, pp. 16–17, 19–23.

22. GLA 67/314.

23. GLA 67/315 and 78/1638, respectively.

24. GLA 67/312, passim. The loans of Bishops Philip I and George are recorded principally in GLA 67/307 and 310.

25. Kloe, *Wahlkapitulationen,* p. 52.

26. Stiefenhöfer, p. 14.

27. Stamer, *Kirchengeschichte,* 2:289–96.

28. *UBS,* 2:538–42, no. 284.

29. Ibid., 2:557–72, nos. 291–94; Remling, 2:309–15. According to Johann Jacob Moser, *Von den Teutschen Reichs-Ständen, der Reichs-Ritterschafft, auch denen übrigen unmittelbaren Reichs-Glidern . . . ,* pp. 556–57, 566–67, the bishop of Speyer thereby achieved the unique status of being the only ecclesiastical member of the imperial college of princes with two votes, because the provostship of Weissenburg and the bishopric of Speyer were only personally united in the bishop (whereas Prüm, for example, was formally incorporated into the archbishopric of Trier in 1579).

30. Stiefenhöfer, p. 142.

31. Ibid., p. 108.

32. Ibid., pp. 99–100.

33. Ibid., pp. 166–67.

34. Mone, "Philipp II.," p. 142.

35. GLA 78/1638; 218/626; Stiefenhöfer, pp. 24, 148–51.

36. GLA 78/1638.

37. SAS Kopialbuch 77b, fol. 35.

38. GLA 78/39.

39. GLA 229/72051.

40. *Protokolle,* no. 8785; Stiefenhöfer, pp. 32–33.

41. *Sammlung der . . . Landesverordnungen,* pp. 32–33.

42. Stiefenhöfer, p. 33.

43. *UBS,* 2:538–42, 549–53, nos. 284 and 287.

44. Kloe, *Wahlkapitulationen,* pp. 52–53.

45. GLA 67/312, fols. 113v–115.

46. GLA 67/420, fol. 10v.

47. *Protokolle,* no. 8055.
48. Stiefenhöfer, pp. 171–72.
49. Ibid., p. 172.
50. *Lexikon für Theologie und Kirche,* 9:963. The right of princes to determine religious practice in their lands generally triumphed over the rights of individual patrons, according to Hermann Tüchle, "The Peace of Augsburg: New Order or Lull in the Fighting," pp. 161–64.
51. See Carsten, *Princes,* p. 431.

CHAPTER 5, PART I

1. In the Palatinate only six *Schatzungen* were imposed during the fifteenth century, and they were levied at the rate of five percent as opposed to the ten-percent exaction far more frequently laid on the clergy in the diocese of Speyer: Cohn, *Palatinate,* p. 107.
2. See pp. 108, 116.
3. Hofmeister, *Bischof und Domkapitel,* p. 203.
4. Carsten, *Princes,* pp. 425–27.
5. Ibid., p. 429.
6. Max Weber, *The Theory of Social and Economic Organization,* ed. Talcott Parsons and trans. A. M. Henderson, pp. 416–17.
7. See the judicious remarks of Cam, *Law-Finders and Law-Makers,* pp. 159–75.
8. GLA 67/417, fols. 258–63.
9. See pp. 133–34, 150–51.
10. *Protokolle,* nos. 1728, 3228, 3231, 5940, 5946.
11. See pp. 139, 149.
12. See GLA 67/299 and 303, passim.
13. But Below, *Territorium,* p. 261, stressed the importance of the diets as courts.
14. Renger, *Landstände im Hochstift Osnabrück,* pp. 38–39; Knetsch, *Kurstaat Trier,* p. 44.
15. See p. 180.

CHAPTER 5, PART II

1. *UBS,* 2:53, no. 18: "coram positis et audientibus hominibus nostris nobilibus et ministralibus in loco. . . ."
2. Thus the chronicle of the bishops of Speyer in Würdtwein, ed., *Nova subsidia,* 1:139.
3. See p. 10.
4. See p. 53.
5. SAS Urkunden Hochstift Speyer no. 4.
6. GLA 67/288, fols. 169–70; 67/289, fols. 177v, 180v–181r, 182r; 67/364, fols. 119–120r, 180, 210, 279v–281r, 297; 67/365, fols. 21r, 25r, 155v–156, 172–73r; 67/369, fols. 218–26; 67/370, fols. 256–57r. SAS Urkunden Hochstift Speyer nos. 4, 118, 122–

24, 808. But in no. 118 (1327) Bishop Emicho instructed a canon of the cathedral to disregard the judgment of the feudal court if it should award a particular fief to the widow of John von Tann.

7. GLA 61/11487 et seq. See also GLA 78/331, an eighteenth-century document entitled "Bestellungen der Hofräte," which begins with the reign of Mathias Ramung.

8. See GLA 67/299 and 303, the registers of cases of Bishops Mathias and Louis.

9. See GLA 67/302, 305, and 308, where the outstanding debts of the bishops are listed and divided according to (1) the dates on which interest payments fell due and (2) the three classes of bearers of the notes: nobles, ecclesiastical foundations, and burghers.

10. GLA 67/303, fols. 10, 11v–14, 26v–28, 29–30, 76v–78r, 83v–85r, 139–42r, 175–78, etc.

11. *UBS*, 2:30, no. 7: "denselben Rabans, siner nachkommen vnd stifftes zu Spire manne, burgmanne, diener, vndersessen, oder die yene zu verantworten seent, sie sient edel odern vnedel, mane oder wip, samentlich noch sunderlich. . . ."

12. GLA 67/296.

13. See Carl W. Stocker, *Der grossherzogliche badische Amtsbezirk Bruchsal*, pp. 32, 66–67, 84, 134, 139; Kimmelmann, *Waibstadt*, pp. 70–77; Julius Hagen, *Urkundliche Geschichte des Landauer Gebietes*, p. 122; and J. G. Lehmann, *Landau*, p. 79, for lists of the noble families settled around these towns.

14. GLA 42/6 s.d. 12 Dec. 1482: "Der stifft hat nit Adelss der ime one soltde dyene."

15. GLA 67/314. Below, *Territorium*, pp. 99–107, listed registry in an index as one of the requirements for being considered a knight.

16. For a complete discussion, see Kolb, *Kraichgauer Ritterschaft*, which is admirably summarized in Cohn, *Palatinate*, pp. 169–74. See also Franz Mone, "Verbreitung des landsässigen Adels am Oberrhein vom 13. bis 17. Jahrhundert in Baden, Elsass, Bayern und Hessen," pp. 385–406.

17. A brief history of one of these families may be found in [?] Gärtner, "Das Geschlecht der Ritter von Zeiskam," pp. 125–36.

18. Knetsch, *Kurstaat Trier*, p. 136, pointed out that the imperial knights in the principality of Trier were, by the end of the sixteenth century, paying to the empire much more in taxes than those who had remained subject to the archbishops.

19. Cohn, *Palatinate*, pp. 189–201.

20. Thus GLA 67/294, fols. 144v–145r (1498).

21. SAS Urkunden Hochstift Speyer no. 185; GLA 67/372, fols. 31–33r; 153/73.

22. GLA 67/312, fols. 97–99r, 102v, 143–47r, 224v–228; 67/420, fols. 169–71.

23. GLA 62/7909 F, under the heading "Inname geschenckt gelt." Brunner, *Land und Herrschaft*, pp. 280–90, 365, pointed out that, because a prince could rightfully demand an aid only from those he really protected, the nobility were logically exempt so long as they could "protect" themselves, which ordinarily was tantamount to maintaining their independence. It is therefore anachronistic to speak of the "privileged" position of the nobility before the sixteenth or seventeenth century, by which time nobles had lost most of their military supremacy and were rapidly falling under the suzerainty of princes.

CHAPTER 5, PART III

1. Hieronymous Nopp, *Geschichte der Stadt und ehemaligen Reichsfestung Philipps-burg*, p. 31.

2. See pp. 18–19.

3. Kemp, *Counsel and Consent*, pp. 73–77. Thirteenth-century canonists disagreed on the consultative rights of the diocesan clergy. Johannes Teutonicus (d. 1245/46), in opposition to Huguccio (d. 1210) and Laurentius Hispanus (d. ca. 1248), believed they had none, for in his view the bishop and the cathedral chapter alone constituted and managed the diocese. See Kenneth J. Pennington, Jr., "A Study of Johannes Teutonicus' Theories of Church Government and of the Relationship between Church and State . . . ," 1:214–16.

4. See pp. 44–45.

5. See pp. 102–3, 108, 116.

6. *WUB*, 9:7, no. 3417.

7. *UBS*, 2:197–99, nos. 98–99; SAS Urkunden Kollegiatstift Sankt Guido zu Speyer nos. 13 and 30; SAS Kopialbuch 77b, fols. 141–46; GLA 42/132 s.d. 16 Mar. 1478; 67/299, fols. 204–5; 67/303, fols. 40v–41r; 67/451, fols. 182–85r. Also *Protokolle*, 1:xiv.

8. GLA 78/1950.

9. SAS Kopialbuch 81, fols. 53v–56r; GLA 67/416, fols. 180v–181r; *Protokolle*, no. 1748.

10. SAS Kopialbuch 81, fols. 56–57; Urkunden Sankt German und Moritz nos. 14 and 23; GLA 67/451, fols. 173v–175.

11. GLA 78/1776 s.a. 1761.

12. GLA 42/303 s.d. 9 July 1377; 78/1776 s.a. 1504; SAS Urkunden Allerheiligenstift Speyer no. 23.

13. See p. 134.

14. See pp. 151–52, 153.

15. *Protokolle*, no. 2336.

16. Bossert, "Reformationsgeschichte," *ZGO* N.F. 17 (1902):68–73.

17. Mone, ed., *Quellensammlung*, 2:33–34.

18. Bossert, "Reformationsgeschichte," p. 68.

19. Mone, "Politisches Testament," p. 197; and see above, pp. 129–31.

20. Mone, ed., *Quellensammlung*, 1:493–94: "was anzihens und ungemachs er mit schindung der mynnern pfaffheit durch fyschales und ander."

21. GLA 67/415, fol. 43v.

22. Seiler, *Studien*, pp. 218–28. The regulations of the rural chapter at Maikammer are printed in *UBS*, 1:560–65, no. 576 (1345); those of the deanery at Hassloch in 1400 in Friedrich Kayser, "Aus dem Kapitels-Buche des Dekanats Haselach, Diöcese Speyer aus dem 15. Jahrhundert," pp. 236–42; and those of several others in Alois Seiler, "Mittelalterliche Landkapitelstatuten des Bistums Speyer," pp. 143–62. These regulations were ordinarily drawn up and promulgated by the members of the deaneries themselves. In only one case did an archdeacon (the provost of the cathedral in this

instance) issue the statutes of a deanery, and the vicar-general rescinded them in part eleven years later in 1411: Seiler, "Landkapitelstatuten," p. 144.

23. The bishops of Constance and Würzburg also came to deal directly with rural deaneries over taxation in the fifteenth century: Ahlhaus, *Landdekanate des Bistums Konstanz,* pp. 136, 281–82; Julius Krieg, *Die Landkapitel im Bistum Würzburg von der zweiten Hälfte des 14. bis zur zweiten Hälfte des 16. Jahrhunderts,* pp. 2, 31–34. Krieg believed the initiative in Würzburg came from the bishops, but the sources do not permit a firm conclusion one way or the other for the bishops of Speyer.

24. GLA 67/417, fols. 258–63.

25. GLA 67/312, fol. 9v; 67/420, fols. 202v–203r.

26. *Protokolle,* nos. 8113, 8186, 8205.

27. Ibid., no. 2320.

28. Ibid., no. 6147.

29. *UBS,* 1:606, no. 607.

30. See p. 123.

31. Lossen, *Staat,* pp. 65–78, 135–82; Cohn, *Palatinate,* pp. 146–49.

32. Stauber, "Lambrecht," p. 122.

33. GLA 67/289, fols. 183v–184r.

34. GLA 67/283, fols. 32–37, 68–74, 117–22, 130–32; 67/289, fol. 92; 67/294, fols. 290–91r; 67/296, fols. 234–39; 67/299, fols. 240v–241; 67/310, fols. 95v–98r; 42/235 s.d. 8 Mar. 1531.

35. This practice dated back to the earliest days of monastic subjection to the bishops: see pp. 80–81.

36. Conrad, *Lambrecht,* p. 28.

37. See GLA 67/283, fols. 59–60; R. Krebs, "Die Politik des Grafen Emich VIII. zu Leiningen und die Zerstörung des Klosters Limburg im Jahre 1504," pp. 1–24; Theodor Karst, "Pfälzische Klöster im Zeitalter der Reformation," pp. 36–58.

38. *UBS,* 1:502–4, no. 528.

39. Reimer, "Bischof Gerhart," p. 91.

40. GLA 67/288, fol. 76.

41. Johannes Trithemius, *Annales Hirsaugienses,* 2:372. I cast doubt on Trithemius's reliability because, for example, he said here that the tax was imposed because of Raban's difficulties with Speyer, even though these had been settled more than five years before; because he believed incorrectly that Louis the Bavarian and Frederick of Austria in 1314 had tried to present rival candidates for the see of Speyer (ibid., 2:141); and because he held that Lambert von Born ruled at Speyer eighteen years (ibid., 2:249).

42. GLA 42/6 s.d. 12 Dec. 1482: "Item der stifft hat keyn Closter das Ime dyene oder gebe Sunder sie sint andern vnderworffen. . . . Der stifft hat nit Closter die Ime Contribuieren oder geben."

43. *Protokolle,* nos. 3574, 3576, 3594.

44. Ibid., nos. 8113, 8186, 8205; GLA 67/420, fols. 14v–15, 60, 65, 70v–71r, 87v–88r.

45. Stamer, *Kirchengeschichte,* 2:16–22, 208–20; Eubel, "Minoritenkloster zu Speier," pp. 675–98.

46. Below, *Territorium*, p. 187; Spangenberg, *Vom Lehnstaat*, pp. 97–99.
47. Carsten, *Princes*, p. 344.

CHAPTER 5, PART IV

1. Russell, *Medieval Regions*, pp. 92–95; Doll, "Frühgeschichte," pp. 134, 137, 141, 169–71, 184–93; Drollinger, *Kleine Städte*, pp. 78–80, 85.
2. See 234, n. 48.
3. GLA 67/286, fols. 1–3r.
4. Buchner, "Stellung," p. 80.
5. J. G. Lehmann, *Landau*, p. 37.
6. GLA 67/289, fols. 1–2r, 88, 251–53r, 346v–347, 441. These alterations were discussed by Franz Mone, "Stadtordnungen, von Heidelberg und Landau," pp. 402–5.
7. *UBS*, 1:508–9, no. 533.
8. In 1443 the burghers were, after initial sharp resistance, finally persuaded by Hans von Helmstadt, *Oberamtmann* of Lauterburg, to grant Bishop Reinhard 600 fl. in return for a letter of nonprejudice of their rights: GLA 67/291, fol. 244r. Bishop Raban, hardly a man to shrink before combat, in 1439 exhorted his nephew and successor Bishop Reinhard not to have too much to do with the burghers of Landau because of their profound belligerence and obstinacy: Mone, "Politisches Testament," p. 199.
9. Hagen, *Landau*, p. 121.
10. J. G. Lehmann, *Landau*, p. 26.
11. Franz Mone, "Die Besatzung zu Landau vom 13. bis. 15. Jahrhundert," p. 303.
12. Drollinger, *Kleine Städte*, pp. 85–88.
13. Ibid., pp. 11–12, based on GLA 67/296, fols. 61–72r, and 67/314, fols. 211–23.
14. Drollinger, *Kleine Städte*, pp. 85–88.
15. Ibid., pp. 52–63, 78–85, 90, 103–9.
16. Ibid., pp. 32–38.

CHAPTER 5, PART V

1. *UBS*, 1:645–51, no. 638.
2. Ibid., 2:538–42, no. 284. A more detailed description of the bishops' possessions and rights may be found in Stamer, *Kirchengeschichte*, 2:78–87.
3. GLA 67/296, fols. 13–158. The figures cited in Buchner, *Regierung*, p. 9, n. 2, are most inaccurate, particularly the number of episcopal subjects domiciled on other lords' lands.
4. See pp. 194, 266, n. 4.
5. GLA 42/159 s.d. 28 June 1362 and 42/168 s.d. 22 Oct. 1298. These oaths are printed in Karl Koehne, ed., *Oberrheinische Stadtrechte*, pt. 1, *Fränkische Rechte*, pp. 843–46.
6. Thus the ordinances establishing an excise tax in Bruchsal in 1466, 1472, and 1500: ibid., pp. 856–63, 876–99.

7. See the statutes printed in ibid., pp. 863–68, 870–76.

8. See SAS Akten Hochstift Speyer nos. 179 and 194; GLA 67/289, fols. 411–12; 67/291, fols. 18–19r; 67/292, fols. 60–62; 67/296, fols. 217–18, 222–26, 228–33; 67/297, fol. 109v; 67/298, fols. 61–66, 92–93, 159–65; 67/306, fols. 63–70; 67/307, fols. 119v–120, 173–80; 67/310, fols. 60, 100, 141–43, 189; 67/311, fols. 115v–116; 67/313, fol. 33v.

9. See *Sammlung der . . . Landesverordnungen,* 1:1–8, 10–13.

10. GLA 62/7909 E, I, J, K. The peasants in 1523 also complained to Bishop George about recent doubling of the *Bede* (GLA 78/1951), and in fact, two years earlier the bishop had spoken of "das erbett vnd steygung der Bethe so durch vnsere Amptlute" from the lands of burghers of Speyer which lay in the bishopric: Speyer, Stadtarchiv, 1U no. 881.

11. GLA 42/222 s.d. 28 Nov. 1337, 254 s.d. 15 May 1330; 67/283, fols. 74–75; 67/291, fols. 274–75; 67/450, fols. 27–30r; 229/60322. SAS Urkunden Hochstift Speyer nos. 225–30, 431, 514, 527, 564, 572–73, 948.

12. In 1512 the burghers of Bruchsal sued before Emperor Maximilian, then residing at Weissenburg, to have their annual *Bede* of 1,000 fl. reduced. He at first agreed and recommended to Bishop Philip that it be lowered to 800 fl., but Philip argued forcefully against it and won restitution of the original sum: GLA 133/716.

13. Thus GLA 67/299, fol. 193; 67/312, fols. 76–78. Also *Protokolle,* no. 7809.

14. GLA 67/298, fols. 63–66; 67/304, fols. 264, 396v; 67/307, fols. 165–67, 224; 67/310, fols. 199–200; 67/312, fols. 30–32; 153/65–66; 218/18 and 89; 229/29168, 86501, and 89454.

15. In the sixteenth century the bishops undertook systematic replanting of trees in their forests, as did the archbishops of Trier. See Hausrath, *Forstgeschichte,* pp. 48–49, and Fritz Michel, *Forst und Jagd im alten Erzstift Trier,* pp. 9–10.

16. See pp. 139, 149.

17. GLA 67/304, fols. 306–10r (1493).

18. Some of these ordinances are printed in *Sammlung der . . . Landesverordnungen,* pp. 15, 27–29 (1527–28), and in Franz Mone, "Ueber die Bauerngüter vom 15. bis. 18. Jahrhundert in Baden und der Schweiz," pp. 286–88 (1517).

19. Franz, *Bauernkrieg.*

20. *Sammlung der . . . Landesverordnungen,* pp. 9–10, 13–14 (1483 and 1517).

21. Nikolaus Grass, "Zur Kontinuität im bäuerlichen Rechte der Alpenländer," p. 516.

22. I will discuss the Peasants War in the bishopric of Speyer more thoroughly in a future article.

23. Franz, *Bauernkrieg,* pp. 64–66, 222–27, and Horst Buszello, *Der deutsche Bauernkrieg von 1525 als politische Bewegung,* pp. 21–23, 30–31, 144–49. Many of the relevant texts have been edited by Franz in his *Quellen zur Geschichte des Bauernkrieges;* see especially pp. 70–76, 174–79.

24. Franz, *Bauernkrieg,* pp. 279–80, 290–91; Herbert Klein, "Die Bauernschaft auf den Salzburger Landtagen," pp. 51–78; Peter Blickle, "Die Landstandschaft der Kemptener Bauern," pp. 201–42; idem, "Ständische Vertretung und genossenschaftliche Verbände der Bauern im Erzstift Salzburg," pp. 131–92.

25. Franz, *Bauernkrieg,* pp. 62–68, 222–27. I take specific exception to his contentions

that (1) Bishop Louis squandered money; (2) the *Ungeld* in Bruchsal was an episcopal revenue (actually it was used to maintain the walls) and "wurde auch ungemein kleinlich eingetrieben" (p. 63); (3) the forest ordinances were extraordinarily petty; and (4) the clergy enjoyed even greater tax exemptions than the nobility. The clergy bore by far the burden of extraordinary taxation, and their lands were no longer automatically exempt from the *Bede*. See, for example, GLA 67/488, fol. 2v, where Bishop Philip I in 1507 in a treaty with the collegiate church of Odenheim, recently translated to Bruchsal, stipulated that any new purchases of land by the foundation would also be subject to the *Bede* if they already had been under the previous owner.

26. Franz, *Bauernkrieg*, pp. 279–94. On the substantial differences between the princes of eastern and western Germany in their sources of revenue at this time, see Georg Droege, "Die finanziellen Grundlagen des Territorialstaates in West- und Ostdeutschland an der Wende vom Mittelalter zur Neuzeit," pp. 145–61.

27. *WUB*, 6:217–18, no. 1822.

28. See n. 11 above in this section.

29. SAS Urkunden Hochstift Speyer no. 182.

30. GLA 67/289, fol. 189r; 67/296, fol. 96; 67/301, fol. 156; 67/304, fols. 307–8; 78/1951; 229/72051; and this volume, p. 176.

31. See the references in n. 14 above in this section.

32. Mone, "Steuerbewilligung," pp. 163–69; GLA 78/1951.

33. GLA 67/304, fols. 449–50 (=Franz, ed., *Quellen zur Geschichte des Bauernkrieges*, pp. 70–72).

34. See GLA 78/1951.

35. Mone, ed., *Quellensammlung*, 2:18–25.

36. Ibid., 2:26–30.

37. A. Adam, "Zwei Briefe über den Bauernaufstand im Bistum Speier 1525," pp. 699–700.

CHAPTER 5, PART VI

1. Kloe, *Wahlkapitulationen*, p. 8.

CONCLUSION

1. See Introduction, pp. 1–2.

2. See Robert Hoyt, "Recent Publications in the United States and Canada on the History of Representative Institutions before the French Revolution," in "Mediaeval Representation in Theory and Practice," pp. 356–77. The thesis, widely held among German historians, that representative assemblies arose primarily for reasons of taxation has been sharply criticized by Brunner, Bosl, and Blickle. See Blickle, *Landschaften*, pp. 432–33.

3. See p. 81 and n. 82.

4. Carsten, *Princes*, pp. 425–27.

5. See pp. 131–33.

6. Below, *Territorium*, pp. 176, 185–87, 212; Spangenberg, *Vom Lehnstaat*, pp. 54–55, 97–99; Robert H. Lord, "The Parliaments of the Middle Ages and the Early Modern Period," p. 127.

7. At the beginning of the reign of Mathias Ramung, there were about 505 independent households in Landau, 519 in Bruchsal: Buchner, *Regierung*, p. 9, n. 2; Drollinger, *Kleine Städte*, pp. 11–12.

8. See *UBS*, 1:125, no. 109. Bruchsal had originally been donated to the bishops by Henry III in 1056: MGH *Dipl.* Henry III, no. 370 (Stumpf, no. 2497).

9. The phrase is from Lord, "Parliaments," p. 127.

10. See pp. 165–66.

11. Schöttke, *Stände des Hochstifts Osnabrück*, p. 7.

12. Spangenberg, "Osnabrück," pp. 8–20, 24.

13. Below, *Territorium*, p. 277.

14. Thus, for example, Feine, *Besetzung*, pp. 336–37.

APPENDIX I

1. See p. 113.

2. Feine, *Rechtsgeschichte*, p. 385.

3. Feine, *Besetzung*, p. 12, incorrectly said the number of canonries at Speyer was fixed at sixteen.

4. Manfred Krebs, in his introduction to the *Protokolle*, 1:xii–xiii. In the cathedral chapter of Constance, the waiting period was only two years and thirty days: Manfred Krebs, ed., "Die Protokolle des Konstanzer Domkapitels," *ZGO N.F.* 100 (1952): 129.

5. *Protokolle*, no. 2885. At Constance the names of the canons present at meetings were regularly recorded, whereas at Speyer they were only occasionally listed.

6. M. Krebs, in ibid., 1:viii–ix.

7. Ibid., 1:127–67.

8. Ibid., 2:145.

9. Ibid., 1:11.

10. Ibid., 1:134–35.

11. Ibid., 1:135–36.

12. Ibid., 1:342.

13. Ibid., 1:432.

14. Ibid., 2:252.

APPENDIX II

1. GLA 67/296, fols. 13–158.

2. GLA 65/2171, a photocopy of the original in the Stadtarchiv in Frankfurt. This is one of the best of the few detailed records of the collection of the Common Penny.

3. GLA 67/314.

4. Episcopal subjects comprised 57.25 percent of the adults resident in the bishopric. This percentage multiplied by the total number of children yields 9,152. If the same ratio of 1.29 children per adult prevailed among the *Ausleute,* whose children were not tabulated, then they must have had about 1,894 children. Thus 9,152 + 1,894 = 11,046. The ratio was probably lower among the *Ausleute,* however, for many were evidently single and had found work outside the bishopric.

5. Cohn, *Palatinate,* p. 4.

6. David W. Sabean, *Landbesitz und Gesellschaft am Vorabend des Bauernkriegs.*

7. GLA 65/2149, also a photocopy of the original in the Stadtarchiv in Frankfurt.

Bibliography

UNPUBLISHED SOURCES

COBLENZ. STAATSARCHIV.
1A URKUNDEN KURTRIER.
COLOGNE. STADTARCHIV.
AUSWÄRTIGES NO. 320.
KARLSRUHE. GENERALLANDESARCHIV.*
ABTEILUNG D. SELEKT DER (JÜNGEREN) KAISER- UND KÖNIGSURKUNDEN. 1200–1518.
ABTEILUNG E. SELEKT DER (JÜNGEREN) PAPSTURKUNDEN. 1198–1302.
ABTEILUNG 42. URKUNDEN BRUCHSAL-ODENHEIM.
ABTEILUNG 61. PROTOKOLLE.
ABTEILUNG 62. RECHNUNGEN.
ABTEILUNG 65. HANDSCHRIFTEN.
ABTEILUNG 66. BERAINE.
ABTEILUNG 67. KOPIALBÜCHER. Vols. 277, 279–315, 322, 339, 358–59, 364–73, 415–18, 420, 447–51, 455–56, 458, 460–66, 479, 483, 486, 488, 867, 1004, 1490, 1499, 1891.
ABTEILUNG 78. AKTEN BRUCHSAL GENERALIA.
ABTEILUNG 133. AKTEN BRUCHSAL AMT UND STADT.
ABTEILUNG 153. AKTEN KISSLAU AMT UND STADT.
ABTEILUNG 172. AKTEN PHILIPPSBURG AMT.
ABTEILUNG 218. AKTEN PHILIPPSBURG STADT.
ABTEILUNG 229. SPECIALAKTEN DER KLEINEREN ÄMTER UND STÄDTE UND DER LANDGEMEINDEN.

* A more detailed inventory of the collections of the archive in Karlsruhe may be found in Manfred Krebs, *Gesamtübersicht der Bestände des Generallandesarchivs Karlsruhe* (Stuttgart, 1954–57).

MUNICH. HAUPTSTAATSARCHIV.
RHEINPFÄLZER URKUNDEN.
SPEYER. STAATSARCHIV.
AKTEN HOCHSTIFT SPEYER.
KOPIALBÜCHER 63, 68a, 69–72, 72a, 72b, 72c, 77a, 77b, 77c, 77d, 81.
URKUNDEN ALLERHEILIGENSTIFT SPEYER.
URKUNDEN DOMSTIFT SPEYER.
URKUNDEN HOCHSTIFT SPEYER.
URKUNDEN KOLLEGIATSTIFT SANKT GUIDO ZU SPEYER.
URKUNDEN VON LANDAU.
URKUNDEN SANKT GERMAN UND MORITZ.
SPEYER. STADTARCHIV.
1A AKTEN DER REICHSSTADT SPEYER.
1U REICHSSTÄDTISCHE URKUNDEN.
STRASBOURG. ARCHIVES DÉPARTMENTALES DU BAS-RHIN.
C 66 (37), G 109 (H), G 4733 (2), H 480 (2), 12 J 89, 12 J 1104,
34 J 62.
VATICAN CITY. ARCHIVIO SEGRETO VATICANO.
REGISTRI VATICANI 209.

PUBLISHED SOURCES

ACHERY, LUC D'. Spicilegium. 3 vols. 2d ed. Paris, 1723.
ADAM, A. "Zwei Briefe über den Bauernaufstand im Bistum Speier 1525."
ZGO N.F. 6 (1891):699–700.
ALBERIGO, JOSEPHO; DOSSETTI, JOSEPHO; JOANNU, PERIKLE; LEONARDI,
CLAUDIO; and PRODI, PAULO, eds. Conciliorum oecumenicorum decreta. 3d ed.
Bologna, 1973.
AUVRAY, LUCIEN, ed. Les Registres de Grégoire IX. 4 vols. BEF, 2d ser., vol. 9.
Paris, 1896–.
BANDINELLI, ROLAND (later Pope Alexander III). Die Summa Magistri Rolandi.
Edited by Friedrich Thaner. Innsbruck, 1874.
BERGER, ÉLIE, ed. Les Registres d'Innocent IV. 4 vols. in 5 pts. BEF, 2d ser.
Paris, 1884–1919.
BRACKMANN, ALBERT, ed. Regesta pontificum Romanorum: Germania pontificia.
3 vols. in 5 pts. Berlin, 1910–35.
BUSCH, KONRAD VON, and GLASSCHRÖDER, FRANZ X., eds. Chorregal und
jüngeres Seelbuch des alten Speierer Domkapitels. 2 vols. Speyer, 1923–26.
Collectio processuum synodalium et constitutionum ecclesiasticarum diocesis
Spirensis ab anno 1397 usque ad annum 1720. Bruchsal, 1786.
DEPREZ, EUGÈNE, and MOLLAT, GUILLAUME, eds. Clément VI (1342–1352):
Lettres closes, patentes et curiales intéressant les pays autres que la France
publiées ou analysées d'après les registres du Vatican. BEF, 3d ser. Paris,
1960–61.

DEUTSCHES HISTORISCHES INSTITUT ZU ROM, ed. *Nuntiaturberichte aus Deutschland*, pt. 1, *1533–1559*. 17 vols. to date. Gotha, etc., 1892–.

DIGARD, GEORGES; FANCON, MAURICE; THOMAS, ANTOINE; and FAWTIER, ROBERT, eds. *Les Registres de Boniface VIII*. BEF, 2d ser., vol. 4. Paris, 1884–1939.

FESTER, RICHARD; WITTE, HEINRICH; and KRIEGER, ALBERT, eds. *Regesten der Markgrafen von Baden und Hachberg, 1050–1515*. 4 vols. Innsbruck, 1892–1915.

FRANSEN, GÉRARD, and KUTTNER, STEPHAN, eds. *Summa "Elegantius in iure diuino" seu Coloniensis*. Vol. 1. Monumenta iuris canonici, ser. A, vol. 1. New York, 1969.

FRANZ, GÜNTHER, ed. *Quellen zur Geschichte des Bauernkrieges*. Munich, 1963.

FRIEDBERG, EMIL, ed. *Corpus iuris canonici*. 2 vols. Leipzig, 1879–81.

GAY, JULES, and VITTE, SUZANNE, eds. *Les Registres de Nicolas III (1277–1280)*. BEF, 2d ser., vol. 14. Paris, 1898–1938.

GLASER, MICHAL. "Die Diözese Speier in den päpstlichen Rechnungsbüchern 1317 bis 1560." *MHVP* 18 (1893):1–166.

GLASSCHRÖDER, FRANZ XAVER, ed. *Neue Urkunden zur pfälzischen Kirchengeschichte im Mittelalter*. Speyer, 1930.

——, ed. "Die Speierer Bistums-Matrikel des Bischofs Mathias Ramung: Mit Anhang." *MHVP* 28 (1907):75–126.

——, ed. *Urkunden zur pfälzischen Kirchengeschichte im Mittelalter*. Munich and Freising, 1903.

GMELIN, MORIZ. "Urkunden, Regesten und Nachweisungen zur Geschichte des Klosters Frauenalb." *ZGO* 23 (1871):263–342, and 25 (1873):321–88.

GOERZ, ADAM, ed. *Regesten der Erzbischöfe zu Trier von Hetti bis Johann II*. Trier, 1861.

GRANDJEAN, CHARLES, ed. *Les Registres de Benoît XI*. BEF, 2d ser., vol. 22. Paris, 1883–85.

GUIRARD, JEAN, ed. *Les Registres d'Urbain IV*. 4 vols. in 5 parts. Paris, 1901–58.

HILGARD, ALFRED, ed. *Urkunden zur Geschichte der Stadt Speyer*. Strasbourg, 1885.

JAFFÉ, PHILIP. *Regesta pontificum Romanorum*. 2d ed. Edited by Ferdinand Kaltenbrunner, Paul Ewald, and Samuel Löwenfeld. Leipzig, 1885–88.

KAYSER, FRIEDRICH. "Aus dem Kapitels-Buche des Dekanats Haselach, Diöcese Speyer aus dem 15. Jahrhundert." *Archiv für katholisches Kirchenrecht* 67 (1892):236–42.

KIRSCH, JOHANN PETER. *Die päpstlichen Annaten in Deutschland während des XIV. Jahrhunderts*. Paderborn, 1903.

——. *Die päpstlichen Kollektorien in Deutschland während des XIV. Jahrhunderts*. Paderborn, 1894.

KOCH, ADOLF; WILLE, JAKOB; VON OBERNDORFF, LUDWIG; and KREBS, MANFRED, eds. *Regesten der Pfalzgrafen am Rhein, 1214–1410*. 2 vols. Innsbruck, 1894–1939.

KOEHNE, KARL, ed. *Oberrheinische Stadtrechte*, pt. 1, *Fränkische Rechte*. Heidelberg, 1895–1922.

KREBS, MANFRED, ed. "Die Dienerbücher des Bistums Speyer, 1464–1768."
ZGO N.F. 57 (1948):55–195.

————, ed. "Die Protokolle des Konstanzer Domkapitels." ZGO 100
(1952):128–257; 101 (1953):74–156; 102 (1954):274–318; and the
Beihefte of 103–107 (1955–59).

————, ed. Die Protokolle des Speyerer Domkapitels. VBW A, vols. 17 and 21.
Stuttgart, 1968–69.

LANGLOIS, ERNEST, ed. Les Registres de Nicolas IV. BEF, 2d ser., vol. 5. Paris,
1886–93.

LA RONCIÈRE, CHARLES BOUREL DE; LOYE, JOSEPH DE; COULON, AUGUSTE; and
CERNIVAL, P. DE, eds. Les Registres d'Alexandre IV. BEF, 2d ser. 3 vols.
Paris, 1902–59.

LEHMANN, CHRISTOPH. Chronica der Freyen Reichs Stadt Speyer. 4th ed. Edited
by Johann Melchior Fuchs. Frankfurt a. M., 1711.

MANSI, GIOVANNI DOMENICO. Sacrorum conciliorum nova et amplissima collectio.
54 vols. Edited by Jean Martin and Louis Petit. Florence, Venice, Paris,
Arnheim, and Leipzig, 1759–1927.

MCLAUGHLIN, TERENCE, ed. The Summa Parisiensis on the Decretum Gratiani.
Toronto, 1952.

MOLLAT, GUILLAUME, ed., Lettres secrètes et curiales du pape Grégoire XI
(1370–1378) intéressant les pays autre que la France publiées ou analysées
d'après les registres du Vatican. 2 vols. BEF. Paris, 1962–65.

MONE, FRANZ J. "Kraichgauer Urkunden vom 12.–16. Jahrhundert." ZGO 13
(1862):1–44, 317–25, 417–38; 14 (1863):148–80, 311–35; 15 (1864):
171–91, 295–322.

————. "Politisches Testament des Bischofs Raban von Speier, 1439." ZGO 11
(1860):193–201.

————. Quellensammlung der badischen Landesgeschichte. 4 vols. Karlsruhe,
1848–67.

————. "Steuerbewilligung im Bistum Speier, 1439–1441." ZGO 1 (1850):
163–69.

————. "Urkundenarchiv des Klosters Herren-Alb vom 12. und 13. Jahrhundert." ZGO 1 (1850):92–128, 224–56, 354–84, 476–98; 2 (1851):99–
128, 216–56, 356–84, 449–81.

————. "Urkunden über das Unterelsass." ZGO 15 (1863):152–64.

————. "Urkunden über die bayerische Pfalz vom 12.–16. Jahrhundert." ZGO
19 (1866):163–94, 429–35.

————. "Zur Geschichte des Bundschuhes, Bauern- und Revolutionskrieges."
Badisches Archiv 2 (1827):163–91.

Monumenta Germaniae historica. Diplomata regum et imperatorum Germaniae:
Die Urkunden der deutschen Könige und Kaiser. Edited by Theodor Sickel,
Harry Bresslau et al. Hanover and Berlin, 1879–.

————. Diplomata regum Germaniae ex stirpe Karolinorum. Edited by Paul
Kehr and Theodor Schieffer. Berlin, 1955–63.

————. *Epistolae saeculi XIII e registis pontificum Romanorum selectae per G[eorg] H[einrich] Pertz.* Edited by Karl Rodenberg. Berlin, 1883–94.

————. *Leges,* sec. 4, *Constitutiones et acta publica imperatorum et regum.* Edited by Ludwig Weiland et al. Hanover, 1893–1926.

NEUBAUER, A. "Regesten des ehemaligen Benediktiner-Klosters Hornbach." *MHVP* 27 (1904):1–358.

OBERMAN, HEIKO A.; ZERFOSS, DANIEL E.; and COURTENAY, WILLIAM J., eds. and trans. *Defensorium obedientiae apostolicae et alia documenta.* Cambridge, Mass., 1968.

OEDIGER, FRIEDRICH W.; KISKY, WILHELM; and KNIPPING, RICHARD, eds. *Die Regesten der Erzbischöfe von Mainz im Mittelalter.* 4 vols. in 5 parts. Bonn, 1901–61.

OTTO OF FREISING, *Gesta Frederici.* Edited by Georg Waitz, Bernhard Simson, and Franz-Josef Schmale. Darmstadt, 1965.

PAUCAPLEA. *Summa über das Decretum Gratiani.* Edited by Johann Friedrich von Schulte. Giessen, 1890. Reprint. Aalen, 1965.

PÖHLMANN, CARL, and DOLL, ANTON, eds. *Regesten der Grafen von Zweibrücken.* Speyer, 1962.

POTTHAST, AUGUST, ed. *Regesta pontificum Romanorum inde ab anno post Christi natum MCXCVIII ad annum MCCCIV.* 2 vols. Berlin, 1874–75.

REIMER, [?]. "Das Todtenbuch des Speierer Domstifts." *ZGO* 26 (1874): 414–44.

————. "Zur Geschichte des Bischofs Gerhart von Speier." *ZGO* 26 (1874), 77–117.

REMLING, FRANZ XAVER, ed. *Urkundenbuch zur Geschichte der Bischöfe zu Speyer.* 2 vols. Mainz, 1852–53.

RIEDNER, OTTO. *Die geistlichen Gerichtshöfe zu Speier im Mittelalter,* vol. 2, texts. Paderborn, 1915.

RIEZLER, SIGMUND, ed. *Vatikanische Akten zur deutschen Geschichte in der Zeit Ludwigs des Bayern.* Innsbruck, 1891.

Sammlung der Hochfürstlich-Speierischen Gesetze und Landesverordnungen. 4 vols. Bruchsal, 1783.

SAUERLAND, HEINRICH V., ed. *Vatikanische Urkunden und Regesten zur Geschichte der Rheinlande.* 7 vols. Bonn, 1902–13.

SCHANNAT, JOHANN FRIEDRICH, and HARTZHEIM, JOSEPH, eds. *Concilia Germaniae.* 11 vols. Cologne, 1759–90.

SCHERG, THEODOR. "Palatina aus dem Vatikan (1464–1484)." *MHVP* 32 (1912):109–90.

SEILER, ALOIS. "Mittelalterliche Landkapitelstatuten des Bistums Speyer." *AMKG* 21 (1969):143–62.

STERN, ALFRED. "Regesten zur Geschichte des Bauernkrieges, vornähmlich in der Pfalz." *ZGO* 23 (1871):179–201.

STUMPF-BRENTANO, KARL F. *Die Reichskanzler vornehmlich des X., XI., und XII. Jahrhunderts,* vol. 2, *Die Kaiserurkunden des X., XI., und XII. Jahrhunderts chronologisch verzeichnet.* Innsbruck, 1865–83.

TOURNAI, STEPHEN OF (Stephan von Doornik). *Die Summa über das Decretum Gratiani.* Edited by Johann Friedrich von Schulte. Giessen, 1891. Reprint. Aalen, 1965.

TRITHEMIUS, JOHANNES. *Annales Hirsaugienses.* 2 vols. Saint Gall, 1690.

WEECH, FRIEDRICH VON. "Pfälzische Regesten und Urkunden." *ZGO* 22 (1869):177–215, 361–79, 409–17; 24 (1872):56–103, 269–326; 32 (1880):190–233.

WINKELMANN, EDUARD, ed. *Acta imperii inedita.* 2 vols. Innsbruck, 1880–85.

Wirtembergisches Urkundenbuch. 11 vols. Stuttgart, 1849–1913.

WÜRDTWEIN, STEPHAN-ALEXANDER, ed. *Monasticon Palatinum.* 6 vols. Mannheim, 1793–96.

————, ed. *Nova subsidia diplomatica.* 14 vols. Heidelberg, 1781–92.

————, ed. *Subsidia diplomatica.* 13 vols. Heidelberg, 1772–80.

SECONDARY WORKS

For works which appeared before 1963 on most aspects of the history of the cathedral and the bishopric of Speyer, see also Rolf Bohlender, comp., *Dom und Bistum Speyer: Eine Bibliographie,* Pfälzische Arbeiten zum Buch- und Bibliothekswesen und zur Bibliographie, vol. 5 (Speyer, 1963).

ACHT, PETER. "Studien zum Urkundenwesen der Speyerer Bischöfe im 12. und im Anfang des 13. Jahrhunderts. (Speyer in seinem Verhältnis zur Reichskanzlei)." *Archiv für Urkundenforschung* 14 (1936):262–306.

AHLHAUS, JOSEPH. *Die Landdekanate des Bistums Konstanz im Mittelalter.* Kirchenrechtliche Abhandlungen, vols. 109–10. Stuttgart, 1929.

ALDINGER, PAUL. *Die Neubesetzung der deutschen Bistümer unter Papst Innocenz IV. 1243–1254.* Leipzig, 1900.

ALTER, WILLI, ed. *Pfalzatlas.* Speyer, 1963–.

ARETIN, KARL OTMAR FREIHERR VON. *Heiliges Römisches Reich 1776–1806: Reichsverfassung und Staatssouveränität.* 2 vols. Veröffentlichungen des Instituts für europäische Geschichte, vol. 38. Wiesbaden, 1967.

BACHMANN, SIEGFRIED. *Die Landstände des Hochstifts Bamberg.* N.p., 1962.

BADER, KARL S. *Der deutsche Südwesten in seiner territorialstaatlichen Entwicklung.* Stuttgart, 1950.

BALLMER, ROGER. "Les assemblées d'états dans l'ancien évêché de Bâle." *Schweizer Beiträge zur Allgemeinen Geschichte* 20 (1962):54–140.

BARRACLOUGH, GEOFFREY. "The Making of a Bishop in the Middle Ages." *Catholic Historical Review* 19 (1933–34):275–319.

————. *Papal Provisions.* Oxford, 1935.

BAUMGARTNER, EUGEN. *Geschichte und Recht des Archidiakonates der oberrheinischen Bistümer mit Einschluss von Mainz und Würzburg.* Kirchenrechtliche Abhandlungen, vol. 39. Stuttgart, 1907.

BAYLEY, CHARLES C. *The Formation of the German College of Electors in the Mid-Thirteenth Century.* Toronto, 1949.

BELOW, GEORG VON. *Die Entstehung des ausschliesslichen Wahlrechts der Domkapitel: Mit besonderer Rücksicht auf Deutschland.* Leipzig, 1883.
————. *Territorium und Stadt.* Historische Bibliothek, vol. 1. Munich and Leipzig, 1900.
BENSON, ROBERT L. *The Bishop-Elect: A Study in Medieval Ecclesiastical Office.* Princeton, 1968.
————. "Election by Community and Chapter." *The Jurist* 31 (1971):54–80.
BERNHARDI, WILHELM. *Jahrbücher der deutschen Geschichte: Konrad III.* Leipzig, 1883.
BIENEMANN, FRIEDRICH. *Conrad von Scharfenberg, Bischof von Speier und Metz und kaiserlicher Hofkanzler (1200–24).* Strasbourg, 1887.
BLICKLE, PETER. *Landschaften im Alten Reich: Die staatliche Funktion des gemeinen Mannes in Oberdeutschland.* Munich, 1973.
————. "Die Landstandschaft der Kemptener Bauern." *Zeitschrift für bayerische Landesgeschichte* 30 (1967):201–41.
————. "Ständische Vertretung und genossenschaftliche Verbände der Bauern im Erzstift Salzburg." *Zeitschrift für bayerische Landesgeschichte* 32 (1969): 131–92.
BLOCH, HERBERT. "The Schism of Anacletus II and the Glanfeuil Forgeries of Peter the Deacon of Monte Cassino." *Traditio* 8 (1952):159–74.
BOSL, KARL. *Die Gesellschaft in der Geschichte des Mittelalters.* Göttingen, 1966.
————. *Die Reichsministerialität der Salier und Staufer.* 2 vols. consecutively paged. Schriften der MGH, vol. 10. Stuttgart, 1950–51.
————. "Zu einer Geschichte der bäuerlichen Repräsentation in dem deutschen Landgemeinde." In *Liber memorialis Antonio Era,* pp. 1–17. Études, vol. 26. Brussels, 1963.
BOSS, ALEXANDER. *Die Kirchenlehen der Staufischen Kaiser.* Munich dissertation, 1886.
BOSSERT, GUSTAV. "Beiträge zur badisch-pfälzischen Reformationsgeschichte." *ZGO N.F.* 17 (1902):37–89, 250–90, 401–49, 588–619; 18 (1903):193–239, 643–95; 19 (1904):19–68, 571–630; 20 (1905):41–89.
BRINCKMEIER, EDUARD. *Genealogische Geschichte des . . . Hauses Leiningen und Leiningen-Westerburg.* 2 vols. Brunswick, 1890–91.
BRÜCK, ANTON. "Die Vorreformation in der Kurpfalz." *AMKG* 17 (1965): 27–37.
BRUFORD, WALTER. *Germany in the Eighteenth Century: The Social Background of the Literary Revival.* Cambridge, 1935.
BRÜHL, CARLRICHARD. *Fodrum, gistum, servitium regis: Studien zu den wirtschaftlichen Grundlagen des Königtums im Frankenreich und in den fränkischen Nachfolgestaaten Deutschland, Frankreich und Italien vom 6. bis zur Mitte des 14. Jahrhunderts.* Cologne and Graz, 1968.
BRUNNER, OTTO. *Land und Herrschaft.* 5th ed. Vienna, 1965.
BUCHDA, GERHARD. "Reichsstände und Landstände in Deutschland im 16. und 17. Jahrhundert." *APAE* 36 (1965):193–226.

BUCHNER, MAXIMILIAN. *Die innere weltliche Regierung des Speierer Bischofs Mathias Ramung (1464–1478)*. Munich dissertation. Speyer, 1907. (Also printed in *MHVP* 29–30 (1907):180–255.)
———. "Die Stellung des Speierer Bischofs Mathias Ramung zur Reichsstadt Speier, zu Kurfürst Friedrich I. von der Pfalz und zu Kaiser Friedrich III.: Ein Beitrag zur Geschichte des ausgehenden Mittelalters." *ZGO* N.F. 24 (1909):28–82, 259–301.
BUSZELLO, HORST. *Der deutsche Bauernkrieg von 1525 als politische Bewegung*. Studien zur europäischen Geschichte, vol. 8. Berlin, 1969.
BÜTTNER, HEINRICH. "Zur Vogteientwicklung des Stiftes Hördt." *ZGO* N.F. 49 (1936):341–70.
CAM, HELEN MAUD. *Law-Finders and Law-Makers in Medieval England: Collected Studies in Legal and Constitutional History*. London, 1962.
CARSTEN, FRANCIS L. *Princes and Parliaments in Germany from the Fifteenth to the Eighteenth Century*. Études, vol. 19. Oxford, 1959.
CLARKE, MAUDE V. *Medieval Representation and Consent: A Study of Early Parliaments in England and Ireland, with Special Reference to the Modus tenendi Parliamentum*. London, 1936.
COHN, HENRY J. *The Government of the Rhine Palatinate in the Fifteenth Century*. Oxford, 1965.
CONRAD, KLAUS. *Die Geschichte des Dominikanerinnenklosters in Lambrecht*. Heidelberg dissertation, 1960.
CONSTABLE, GILES. *Monastic Tithes from Their Origins to the Twelfth Century*. Cambridge Studies in Medieval Life and Thought, n.s., vol. 10. Cambridge, 1964.
CROSS, FRANK L., and LIVINGSTONE, E. A., eds. *The Oxford Dictionary of the Christian Church*. 2d ed. London and New York, 1974.
DAHMUS, JOSEPH. *William Courtenay, Archbishop of Canterbury 1381–1396*. University Park, Pa., and London, 1966.
DAUCH, BRUNO. *Die Bischofsstadt als Residenz der geistlichen Fürsten*. Berlin dissertation, 1913.
DECKER, ALBERT. "Die Benediktinerabtei Klingenmünster von der Merowinger- bis zur Staufenzeit." *AMKG* 2 (1950):9–87.
DEMANDT, KARL E. *Geschichte des Landes Hessen*. Cassel and Basel, 1959.
DESPRAIRIES, ANDRÉ. *L'Élection des évêques par les chapitres au XIIIe siècle*. (*Théorie canonique*.) Paris, 1922.
DICKINSON, JOHN C. *The Origins of the Austin Canons and Their Introduction into England*. London, 1950.
DOHNA, SOPHIE MATILDE GRÄFIN ZU. *Die ständischen Verhältnisse am Domkapitel von Trier vom 16. bis zum 18. Jahrhundert*. Trier, 1960.
DOLL, ANTON. "Entstehung und Entwicklung der Pfarreien der Stadt Speyer." In *900 Jahre Speyerer Dom*, edited by Ludwig Stamer, pp. 260–91. Speyer, 1961.
———. "Vögte und Vogtei im Hochstift Speyer im Hochmittelalter." *ZGO* N.F. 78 (1969):245–73.

———. "Zur Frühgeschichte der Stadt Speyer: Eine topographische Untersuchung zum Prozess der Stadtwerdung Speyers vom 10. bis 13. Jahrhundert." *MHVP* 52 (1954):133–200.

DOMARUS, MAX. "Der Reichsadel in den geistlichen Fürstentümern." In *Deutscher Adel 1555–1740: Büdinger Vorträge 1964*, edited by Hellmuth Rössler, pp. 147–71. Darmstadt, 1965.

DOMINICUS, ALEXANDER. *Baldewin von Lützelburg, Erzbischof und Kurfürst von Trier.* Trier, 1862.

DROEGE, GEORG. "Die finanziellen Grundlagen des Territorialstaates in West- und Ostdeutschland an der Wende vom Mittelalter zur Neuzeit." *Vierteljahrschrift für Sozial- und Wirtschaftsgeschichte* 53 (1966):145–61.

———. *Verfassung und Wirtschaft in Kurköln unter Dietrich von Moers (1414–1463).* Bonn, 1957.

DROLLINGER, KUNO. *Kleine Städte Südwestdeutschlands: Studien zur Sozial- und Wirtschaftsgeschichte der Städte im rechtsrheinischen Teil des Hochstifts Speyer bis zur Mitte des 17. Jahrhunderts.* VBW B, vol. 48. Stuttgart, 1968.

DUBY, GEORGES. *Rural Economy and Country Life in the Medieval West.* Translated by Cynthia Postan. London, 1968.

EDWARDS, KATHLEEN. *The English Secular Cathedrals in the Middle Ages.* 2d ed. Manchester and New York, 1967.

EHEBERG, [?]. "Die Münzerhausgenossen von Speyer." *ZGO* 32 (1880):444–80.

ENGEL, WILHELM. "Die Stadt Würzburg und die Kurie." *ZRG Kanon.* 37 (1951):303–59.

EPSTEIN, KLAUS. *The Genesis of German Conservatism.* Princeton, 1966.

EUBEL, KONRAD. "Zur Geschichte des Minoritenklosters zu Speier." *ZGO N.F.* 6 (1891):675–98.

EYER, FRITZ. *Das Territorium der Herren von Lichtenberg 1202–1480.* Strasbourg, 1938.

FABRICIUS, W. "Taxa generalis cleri Trevirensis." *Trierisches Archiv* 8 (1905): 1–52.

FATH, ADAM. "Bistum Speyer, 1939–1950." *AMKG* 3 (1951):385–90.

FEHR, HANS. "Das Waffenrecht der Bauern im Mittelalter." *ZRG Germ.* 35 (1914):111–211, and 38 (1917):1–114.

FEINE, HANS ERICH. *Die Besetzung der Reichsbistümer vom Westfälischen Frieden bis zur Säkularisation 1648–1803.* Kirchenrechtliche Abhandlungen, vols. 97–98. Stuttgart, 1921.

———. *Kirchliche Rechtsgeschichte: Die katholische Kirche.* 4th ed., rev. Cologne and Graz, 1964.

———. "Vom Fortleben des römischen Rechts in der Kirche." *ZRG Kanon.* 42 (1956):1–24.

FISHER, HERBERT A. L. *The Medieval Empire.* 2 vols. London and New York, 1898.

FLETCHER, J. M. "Wealth and Poverty in the Medieval German Universities."

In *Europe in the Late Middle Ages,* edited by John R. Hale, John R. L. Highfield, and Beryl Smalley, pp. 410–37. Evanston, Ill., 1965.

FOLZ, ROBERT. "Les assemblées d'états dans les principautés allemandes (fin XIIIe–début XVIe siècle)." *APAE* 36 (1965):163–91.

FOREVILLE, RAYMONDE. "Représentation et taxation du clergé au IVe Concile du Latran (1215)." In *XIIe Congrès international des sciences historiques,* pp. 55–74. Études, vol. 31. Vienna, 1965.

FOURNIER, EDOUARD. *L'Origine du vicaire général et des autres membres de la curie diocésaine.* Paris, 1940.

FOURNIER, PAUL. *Les officialités au Moyen Age: Étude sur l'organisation, la compétence et la procédure des tribunaux ecclésiastiques ordinaires en France, de 1180 à 1328.* Paris, 1880.

FRANZ, GÜNTHER. *Der deutsche Bauernkrieg.* 8th ed. Darmstadt, 1969.

FRIEDBERG, EMIL. *Lehrbuch des katholischen und evangelischen Kirchenrechts.* 2d ed., rev. Leipzig, 1884.

GANSHOF, FRANCOIS L. *Étude sur les ministeriales en Flandre et en Lotharingie.* Brussels, 1926.

GANZER, KLAUS. "Zur Beschränkung der Bischofswahl auf die Domkapitel in Theorie und Praxis des 12. und 13. Jahrhunderts." *ZRG Kanon.* 57 (1971): 22–82 and 58 (1972):166–97.

GÄRTNER, [?]. "Das Geschlecht der Ritter von Zeiskam." *MHVP* 5 (1875): 125–36.

Gerettete Wahrheit in einer diplomatischen Geschichte der Abtey Schwarzach am Rheine. 2 vols. Bruchsal, 1780.

GERHARD, DIETRICH. "Assemblies of Estates and the Corporate Order." In *Liber memorialis Georges de Lagarde,* pp. 283–308. Études, vol. 38. Paris and Louvain, 1970.

GERLICH, ALOIS. *Habsburg-Luxemburg-Wittelsbach im Kampf um die deutsche Königskrone: Studien zur Vorgeschichte des Königtums Ruprecht von der Pfalz.* Wiesbaden, 1960.

GESCHER, FRANZ. "Synodales: Studien zur kirchlichen Gerichtsverfassung und zum deutschen Ständewesen des Mittelalters." *ZRG Kanon.* 29 (1940):358–446.

GESELBRACHT, FRANKLIN. *Das Verfahren bei den deutschen Bischofswahlen in der zweiten Hälfte des 12. Jahrhunderts.* Leipzig dissertation. Weida, 1905.

GLADISS, DIETRICH VON. *Beiträge zur Geschichte der staufischen Reichsministerialität.* Historische Studien, vol. 249. Berlin, 1934.

GLASSCHRÖDER, FRANZ XAVER. "Das Archidiakonat in der Diözese Speier während des Mittelalters." *Archivalische Zeitschrift* N.F. 10 (1902):114–54.

———, ed. "Die Pfründen librae collationis des Speyerer Bischofs im Mittelalter." *FDA* N.F. 21 (1920):155–68.

———. "Zur Frühgeschichte des alten Speierer Domkapitels." *ZGO* N.F. 46 (1933):481–97.

GNANN, A. "Beiträge zur Verfassungsgeschichte des Domkapitels von Speyer." *FDA* N.F. 7 (1906):167–206.

GOLDSCHMIDT, HANS. *Zentralbehörden und Beamtentum im Kurfürstentum Mainz vom 16. bis zum 18. Jahrhundert.* Basel, 1908.

GOTTLOB, THEODOR. *Das abendländische Chorepiskopat.* Bonn, 1928.

————. *Der kirchliche Amtseid der Bischöfe.* Kanonistische Studien und Texte, vol. 9. Bonn, 1936.

GRASS, NIKOLAUS. "Alm und Landstände in Tirol." *APAE* 32 (1964):137–89.

————. "Aus der Geschichte der Landstände Tirols." In *Album Helen Maud Cam,* 2:297–324. Études, vol. 24. Louvain and Paris, 1961.

————. "Zur Kontinuität im bäuerlichen Rechte der Alpenländer." *ZRG Germ.* 66 (1948):516–24.

GRUNDMANN, HERBERT, ed. *Gebhardts Handbuch der deutschen Geschichte.* Vol. 1. 9th ed. Stuttgart, 1970.

GUERCHBERG, SÉRAPHINE. "The Controversy over the Alleged Sowers of the Black Death in the Contemporary Treatises on Plague." In *Change in Medieval Society,* edited by Sylvia Thrupp, pp. 208–24. New York, 1964.

GUGUMUS, JOHANN EMIL. "Die Speyerer Bischöfe im Investiturstreit: Forschungen zu Problemen über das Verhältnis von Kirche und Staat im ausgehenden 11. Jahrhundert." *AMKG* 3 (1951):77–144, and 4 (1952):45–78.

HÄBERLE, DANIEL. "Die Wüstungen der Rheinpfalz auf Grundlage der Besiedlungsgeschichte." *MHVP* 39–42 (1919–22):1–246.

HACKER, WERNER. *Auswanderungen aus dem früheren Hochstift Speyer nach Südosteuropa and Übersee im XVIII. Jahrhundert.* Kaiserslautern, 1969.

HAFFNER, FRANZ. "Die Bischöfe von Speyer bis zum Jahre 913 (918)." *ZGO* N.F. 74 (1965):297–359.

————. *Die kirchlichen Reformbemühungen des Speyerer Bischofs Matthias von Rammung in vortridentinischer Zeit.* (1464–1478). Speyer, 1961.

HAGEN, JULIUS. *Urkundliche Geschichte des Landauer Gebietes.* Landau, 1937.

HAIDER, SIEGFRIED. *Die Wahlversprechungen der römisch-deutschen Könige bis zum Ende des 12. Jahrhunderts.* Vienna, 1968.

HARSIN, PAUL. "Gouvernés et gouvernants dans la principauté de Liège du XIVe au XVIIIe siècle." *APAE* 33 (1951):79–86.

HARSTER, WILHELM. "Die letzten Veränderungen der reichsstädtischen Verfassung Speiers." *ZGO* N.F. 5 (1890):443–73.

————. "Die Veränderungen des Zunftregiments in Speier bis zum Ausgang des Mittelalters." *ZGO* N.F. 3 (1888):447–500.

————. "Die Verfassungskämpfe in Speier während des Mittelalters: I. Der Kampf der Zünfte und Patrizier." *ZGO* 38 (1885):210–320.

————. "Versuch einer Speierer Münzgeschichte." *MHVP* 10 (1882):1–166.

HARTUNG, FRITZ. *Deutsche Verfassungsgeschichte vom 15. Jahrhundert bis zur Gegenwart.* 8th ed. Stuttgart, 1950.

————. "Herrschaftsverträge und ständischer Dualismus in deutschen Territorien." *Schweizer Beiträge zur Allgemeinen Geschichte* 10 (1952):163–77.

HASELIER, GÜNTHER. *Geschichte des Dorfes und der Gemeinde Weiher am Bruhrain.* Weiher a. Rh., 1962.

HAUCK, ALBERT. *Friedrich Barbarossa als Kirchenpolitiker.* Leipzig, 1898.

————. *Kirchengeschichte Deutschlands*. Vol. 5, pt. 1. 2d ed. Leipzig, 1911.

HAUSRATH, HANS. *Forstgeschichte der rechtsrheinischen Theile des ehemaligen Bistums Speyer*. Berlin, 1898.

HELBIG, HERBERT. "Ständische Einungsversuche in den mitteldeutschen Territorien am Ausgang des Mittelalters." In *Album Helen Maud Cam*, 2:185–209. Études, vol. 24. Louvain and Paris, 1961.

HENNIG, ERNST. *Die päpstlichen Zehnten aus Deutschland im Zeitalter des avignonesischen Papsttums und während des grossen Schismas*. Halle, 1909.

HERZOG, ULRICH. *Untersuchungen zur Geschichte des Domkapitels zu Münster und seines Besitzes im Mittelalter*. Göttingen, 1961.

HEXTER, J. H. *Reappraisals in History*. New York, 1963.

HILDENBRAND, FRIEDRICH J. *Schloss Marientraut*. Speyer, 1922.

HINSCHIUS, PAUL. *Das Kirchenrecht der Katholiken und Protestanten in Deutschland*. 7 vols. Berlin, 1869–97.

HINTZE, OTTO. "Weltgeschichtliche Bedingungen der Repräsentativverfassung." *Historische Zeitschrift* 143 (1931):1–47.

HOFMEISTER, PHILIPP. *Bischof und Domkapitel nach altem und nach neuem Recht*. Abbey of Neresheim, 1931.

HOLBORN, HAJO. *A History of Modern Germany: 1648–1840*. New York, 1964.

HOLTZMANN, ROBERT. *Geschichte der sächsischen Kaiserzeit*. 4th ed. Munich, 1961.

HOYER, ERNST. "Gratian und der Blutbann der geistlichen Fuersten des mittelalterlichen deutschen Reiches." *Studia Gratiana* 4 (1956–57):131–83.

HUFFSCHMID, MAXIMILIAN. "Hochhausen am Neckar und die heilige Notburga." *ZGO* N.F. 1 (1886):385–401.

IMHOF, OTTO. *Die Ministerialität in den Stiftern Strassburg, Speier und Worms*. Freiburg i. B., 1912.

JACOB, ERWIN. *Untersuchungen über Herkunft und Aufstieg des Reichsministerialengeschlechts Bolanden*. Giessen, 1936.

JEDIN, HUBERT; LATOURETTE, KENNETH SCOTT; and MARTIN, JOCHEN, eds. *Atlas zur Kirchengeschichte*. Freiburg i. B., 1970.

KAISER, KARLWERNER. *Das Kloster St. German vor Speyer*. Speyer, 1955.

KÄMPF, HELLMUT, ed. *Herrschaft und Staat im Mittelalter*. Wege der Forschung, vol. 2. Darmstadt, 1965.

KANTOROWICZ, ERNST. "Inalienability: A Note on Canonical Practice and the English Coronation Oath in the Thirteenth Century." *Speculum* 29 (1954): 488–502.

KARST, THEODOR. "Pfälzische Klöster im Zeitalter der Reformation: Studien zu den Formen und Problemen der Säkularisation durch Kurpfalz." *MHVP* 62 (1964):36–58.

KAUL, THEODOR. "Der Klerus des Domstiftes von Speyer im Jahre 1542." *AMKG* 7 (1955):112–58.

————. "Das Verhältnis der Grafen von Leiningen zum Reich und ihr Versuch einer Territorialbildung im Speyergau im 13. Jahrhundert." *MHVP* 68 (1970):222–91.

KEINEMANN, FRIEDRICH. *Das Domkapitel zu Münster im 18. Jahrhundert.* Geschichtliche Arbeiten zur westfälischen Landesforschung, vol. 11. Münster, 1967.

KELLER, FRANZ. "Die Verschuldung des Hochstifts Konstanz im 14. und 15. Jahrhundert: Eine finanzgeschichtliche Studie nach archivalischen Quellen bearbeitet." *FDA* N.F. 3 (1902): 1–104.

KEMP, ERIC W. *Counsel and Consent: Aspects of the Government of the Church as Exemplified in the History of the English Provincial Synods.* London, 1961.

KIENER, FRITZ. "Zur Vorgeschichte des Bauernkrieges am Oberrhein." *ZGO* N.F. 19 (1904): 479–507.

KIMMELMANN, ALOIS. *Waibstadt: Geschichte einer verpfändeten, ehemals freien Reichsstadt.* Karlsruhe, 1936.

KIRCHHOFF, KARL-HEINZ. "Die landständischen Schatzungen des Stifts Münster im 16. Jahrhundert." *Westfälische Forschungen* 14 (1961): 117–33.

KISCH, GUIDO. *The Jews in Medieval Germany: A Study of Their Legal and Social Status.* Chicago, 1949.

KISKY, WILHELM. *Die Domkapitel der geistlichen Kurfürsten.* Weimar, 1906.

KLEIN, HERBERT. "Die Bauernschaft auf den Salzburger Landtagen." *Mitteilungen der Gesellschaft für Salzburger Landeskunde* 88–89 (1948–49): 51–78.

KLEINHEYER, GERD. *Die kaiserlichen Wahlkapitulationen: Geschichte, Wesen und Funktion.* Karlsruhe, 1968.

KLEWITZ, HANS-WALTER. "Königtum, Hofkapelle und Domkapitel im 10. und 11. Jahrhundert." *Archiv für Urkundenforschung* 16 (1939): 102–56.

———. *Reformpapsttum und Kardinalkolleg.* Darmstadt, 1957.

KLIMM, FRANZ. *Burg und Dorf Graben einst und jetzt.* Bruchsal, 1920.

———. *Der Kaiserdom zu Speyer.* 10th ed. Speyer, 1963.

KLINGELHÖFER, ERICH. *Die Reichsgesetze von 1220, 1231/32 und 1235.* Quellen und Studien zur Verfassungsgeschichte des deutschen Reiches im Mittelalter und Neuzeit, vol. 8, pt. 2. Weimar, 1955.

KLOE, KARL. *Die Wahlkapitulationen der Bischöfe zu Speyer (1272–1802).* Speyer, 1928.

KLUNZINGER, KARL. *Urkundliche Geschichte der vormaligen Cisterzienser-Abtei Maulbronn.* Stuttgart, 1854.

KNETSCH, GUSTAV. *Die landständische Verfassung und reichsritterschaftliche Bewegung im Kurstaate Trier, vornehmlich im XVI. Jahrhundert.* Historische Studien, vol. 75. Berlin, 1909.

KOLB, A. GUSTAV. *Die Kraichgauer Ritterschaft unter der Regierung des Kurfürsten Phillip von der Pfalz.* Freiburg i. B. dissertation. Stuttgart, 1909.

KORANYI, KAROL. "Zum Ursprung des Anteils der Städte an die ständischen Versammlungen und Parlamenten im Mittelalter." In *Album Helen Maud Cam,* 1:37–53. Études, vol. 23. Louvain and Paris, 1960.

KORZ, KARL HEINRICH. *Das Schultheissen- und Kämmerergericht von Speyer in den Jahren 1294–1689.* 1962 Mainz dissertation. Dusseldorf, n.d.

KRABBO, HERMAN. *Die Besetzung der deutschen Bistümer unter der Regierung*

Kaiser Friedrichs II. (*1212–1250*). Pt. 1. Historische Studien, vol. 25. Berlin, 1901.

KREBS, R. "Die Politik des Grafen Emich VIII. zu Leiningen und die Zerstörung des Klosters Limburg im Jahre 1504." *MHVP* 23 (1899):1–24.

KRIEG, JULIUS. *Die Landkapitel im Bistum Würzburg von der zweiten Hälfte des 14. bis zur zweiten Hälfte des 16. Jahrhunderts.* Kirchenrechtliche Abhandlungen, vol. 99. Stuttgart, 1923.

KRIEG VON HOCHFELDEN, GEORG H. *Geschichte der Grafen von Eberstein in Schwaben.* Karlsruhe, 1836.

KRIEGER, FRIEDRICH. *Die Burg Hornberg am Neckar.* Heilbronn, 1869.

KUTTNER, STEPHAN. "Cardinalis: The History of a Canonical Concept." *Traditio* 3 (1945):129–214.

LAGARDE, GEORGES DE. "Les Théories représentatives des XIVe–XVe siècle et l'église." In *Xe Congrès international des sciences historiques,* pp. 63–75. Études, vol. 18. Paris and Louvain, 1958.

LAGER, [?]. "Raban von Helmstadt und Ulrich von Manderscheid—ihr Kampf um das Erzbistum Trier." *Historisches Jahrbuch* 15 (1894):721–70.

LANDWEHR, GÖTZ. "Die Bedeutung der Reichs- und Territorialpfandschaften für den Aufbau des kurpfälzischen Territoriums." *MHVP* 66 (1968):155–96.

———. *Die Verpfändung der deutschen Reichsstädte im Mittelalter.* Forschungen zur deutschen Rechtsgeschichte, vol. 5. Graz, 1967.

LANGMUIR, GAVIN. "Counsel and Capetian Assemblies." In *Xe Congrès international des sciences historiques,* pp. 19–34. Études, vol. 18. Paris and Louvain, 1958.

LAUFNER, RICHARD. "Die Landstände von Kurtrier im 17. und 18. Jahrhundert." *Rheinische Vierteljahrsblätter* 32 (1968):290–317.

LEHMANN, JOHANN GEORG. *Urkundliche Geschichte der Burgen und Bergschlösser in den ehemaligen Gauen und Herrschaften der bayerischen Pfalz.* 5 vols. Kaiserslautern, 1857–65.

———. *Urkundliche Geschichte der ehemaligen freien Reichsstadt und jetzigen Bundesfestung Landau in der Pfalz.* Neustadt a. d. Haardt, 1851.

———. *Urkundliche Geschichte des gräflichen Hauses Leiningen-Hartenburg und Leiningen-Westerburg.* (Vol. 3 of his *Urkundliche Geschichte der Burgen und Bergschlösser.*) Kaiserslautern, 1860–61.

LEJEUNE, JEAN. "Les notions de 'patria' et d' 'episcopatus' dans le diocèse et le pays de Liège du XIe au XIVe siècle." *APAE* 8 (1955):1–53.

Lexikon für Theologie und Kirche. 2d ed., rev. 11 vols. Freiburg i. B., 1957–67.

LITZENBURGER, LUDWIG. "Die Besetzung des Speyerer Bischofstuhles im Jahre 1303: Sigibodo II., Herr von Lichtenberg 1302–1314." *AMKG* 11 (1959):310–13.

———. "Die Päpste und die Speyerer Bistumsbesetzung während der ersten Hälfte des avignonesischen Exils." In *Speculum historiale: Geschichte im Spiegel von Geschichtsschreibung und Geschichtsdeutung,* edited by Clemens Bauer, Laetitia Boehm, and Max Müller, pp. 599–606. Freiburg i. B. and Munich, 1965.

————. "Papst Pius II. providiert 1464 die Speyerer Kirche mit Matthias von Rammung." In *900 Jahre Speyerer Dom,* edited by Ludwig Stamer, pp. 292–302. Speyer, 1961.

LORD, ROBERT H. "The Parliaments of the Middle Ages and the Early Modern Period." *Catholic Historical Review* 16 (1930): 125–44.

LOSSEN, RICHARD. *Staat und Kirche in der Pfalz im Ausgang des Mittelalters.* Vorreformationsgeschichtliche Forschungen, vol. 3. Münster, 1907.

LOUSSE, ÉMILE. "Assemblées représentatives et taxation." In *XIIe Congrès international des sciences historiques,* pp. 19–32. Études, vol. 31. Vienna, 1965.

————. "Elenchus bio-bibliographicus Prof. É. Lousse." *APAE* 37 (1964):205–62.

————. *L'État corporatif au Moyen Âge et à l'époque moderne: Notes pour le cours d'histoire du droit à l'usage des étudiants en droit et en histoire.* Louvain, 1938.

————. "Gouvernés et gouvernants en Europe occidentale durant le bas Moyen Âge et les temps modernes: Rapport général." *APAE* 35 (1966):7–48.

————. *La Société d'ancien régime: Organisation et représentation corporatives.* Études, vol. 6. Louvain, 1943.

LÜBECK, KONRAD. *Die Fuldaer Äbte und Fürstäbte des Mittelalters.* Fulda, 1952.

LUCAS, HENRY S. "The Great European Famine of 1315, 1316 and 1317." *Speculum* 5 (1930):343–77.

LÜCKE, JUSTUS. *Die landständische Verfassung im Hochstift Hildesheim 1643–1802.* Quellen und Darstellungen zur Geschichte Niedersachsens, vol. 73. Hildesheim, 1968.

LYON, BRYCE. *From Fief to Indenture: The Transition from Feudal to Non-Feudal Contract in Western Europe.* Cambridge, Mass., 1957.

————. "Medieval Constitutionalism: A Balance of Power." In *Album Helen Maud Cam,* 2:155–83. Études, vol. 24. Louvain and Paris, 1961.

MAITLAND, FREDERICK W. *The Constitutional History of England.* Edited by Herbert A. L. Fisher. Cambridge, 1961.

MARONGIU, ANTONIO. *Medieval Parliaments: A Comparative Study.* Translated by Stuart J. Woolf. Études, vol. 32. London, 1968.

MAURER, HANS-MARTIN. "Die Entstehung der mittelalterlichen Adelsburg in Südwestdeutschland." *ZGO N.F.* 78 (1969):295–332.

MAZETTI, LUDWIG. "Die verfassungsrechtliche Stellung des Bistums und der Stadt Speier zur Zeit des Bischofs Beringer von Entringen." *MHVP* 48 (1927):3–98.

"Mediaeval Representation in Theory and Practice: Essays by American Members of the International Commission for the History of Representative and Parliamentary Institutions." In *Speculum* 29 (1954):347–476.

MEIER, RUDOLF. *Die Domkapitel zu Goslar und Halberstadt in ihrer persönlichen Zusammensetzung im Mittelalter.* Veröffentlichungen des Max-Planck Instituts für Geschichte, vol. 5. Studien zur Germania Sacra, vol. 1. Göttingen, 1967.

MERKEL, REINHARD. "Studien zur Territorialgeschichte der badischen Markgrafschaft in der Zeit vom Interregnum bis zum Tode Markgraf Bernhards I.

(1250–1431) unter besonderer Berücksichtigung des Verhältnisses der badischen Markgrafen zu den Bischöfen von Strassburg und Speyer." Freiburg i. B. dissertation, 1953.

METZ, WOLFGANG. *Staufische Güterverzeichnisse: Untersuchungen zur Verfassungs- und Wirtschaftsgeschichte des 12. und 13. Jahrhunderts.* Berlin, 1964.

————. "Die Urkunde König Sigiberts III. für das Bistum Speyer." *AMKG* 22 (1970):9–19.

MEUTHEN, ERICH. *Das Trierer Schisma von 1430 auf dem Basler Konzil: Zur Lebensgeschichte des Nikolaus von Kues.* Münster, 1964.

MEYER, AUGUST. *Geschichte der Stadt Lauterburg.* Weissenburg i. E., 1898.

MICHEL, FRITZ. *Forst und Jagd im alten Erzstift Trier.* Trier, 1958.

MILLER, EDWARD. *The Origins of Parliament.* Historical Association Pamphlets, no. 44. London, 1960.

MITTEIS, HEINRICH. *Der Staat des hohen Mittelalters.* 4th rev. ed. Weimar, 1953.

MOLLAT, GUILLAUME. *La Collation des bénéfices ecclésiastiques sous les papes d'Avignon (1303–1378).* Paris, 1921.

MONE, FRANZ J. "Die Besatzung zu Landau vom 13. bis 15. Jahrhundert." *ZGO* 3 (1852):299–309.

————. "Finanzwesen vom 13. bis 16. Jahrhundert in der Schweiz, Baden, Elsass und Bayern." *ZGO* 8 (1857): 257–306.

————. "Philipp II. Bischof zu Speier." *Badisches Archiv* 1 (1826):116–56.

————. "Stadtordnungen, von Heidelberg und Landau." *ZGO* 4 (1853):385–405.

————. "Ueber das Forstwesen vom 14. bis 17. Jahrhundert im Breisgau, der Markgrafschaft Baden, im Bistum Speier und Rheinhessen." *ZGO* 2 (1851): 14–33.

————. "Ueber das Geldwesen vom 12. bis 17. Jahrhundert." *ZGO* 3 (1852): 309–22.

————. "Ueber das Steuerwesen vom 14.–18. Jahrhundert in Baden, Hessen und Bayern." *ZGO* 6 (1855):1–37.

————. "Ueber die Bauerngüter vom 15. bis 18. Jahrhundert in Baden und der Schweiz." *ZGO* 5 (1854): 257–90.

————. "Ueber Zinsfuss und Ablösung im Mittelalter am Oberrhein." *ZGO* 1 (1850):26–36.

————. "Verbreitung des landsässigen Adels am Oberrhein vom 13. bis 17. Jahrhundert in Baden, Elsass, Bayern und Hessen." *ZGO* 8 (1857):385–406.

————. "Zur Geschichte der Volkswirtschaft." *ZGO* 10 (1859):257–316.

————. "Zur Geschichte des Bergbaues von Nussloch bis Durlach von 1439 bis 1532." *ZGO* 1 (1850):43–48.

————. "Zur Geschichte von Bruchsal vom 13. bis 15. Jahrhundert." *ZGO* 7 (1856):281–301.

MOSER, JOHANN JACOB. *Von den Teutschen Reichs-Ständen, deren Reichs-Ritterschafft, auch denen übrigen unmittelbaren Reichs-Glidern. . . .* Frankfurt, 1767.

MUNZ, PETER. *Frederick Barbarossa: A Study in Medieval Politics.* Ithaca and London, 1969.

MYERS, ALEC R. *Parliaments and Estates in Europe to 1789.* London, 1975.

NOPP, HIERONYMOUS. *Geschichte der Stadt und ehemaligen Reichsfestung Philippsburg.* Speyer, 1881.

O'DAY, ROSEMARY, and HEAL, FELICITY, eds. *Continuity and Change: Personnel and Administration of the Church in England 1500–1642.* Leicester, 1976.

OER, RUDOLPHINE FREIIN VON. "Estates and Diets in Ecclesiastical Principalities of the Holy Roman Empire (18th Century)." In *Liber memorialis Georges de Lagarde,* pp. 259–81. Études, vol. 38. Paris and Louvain, 1970.

———. "Landständische Verfassungen in den geistlichen Fürstentümern Nordwestdeutschlands." In *Ständische Vertretungen in Europa im 17. und 18. Jahrhundert,* edited by Dietrich Gerhard, pp. 94–119. Études, vol. 37. Göttingen, 1969.

OHLBERGER, JOSEPH. *Geschichte des Paderborner Domkapitels im Mittelalter.* Hildesheim, 1911.

OSWALD, JOSEF. *Das alte Passauer Domkapitel: Seine Entwicklung bis zum dreizehnten Jahrhundert und sein Wahlkapitulationswesen.* Munich, 1933.

OTTO, EBERHARD F. *Adel und Freiheit im deutschen Staat des Mittelalters: Studien über nobiles und Ministerialen.* Neue deutsche Forschungen, vol. 2. Berlin, 1937.

PENNINGTON, KENNETH J., JR. "A Study of Johannes Teutonicus' Theories of Church Government and of the Relationship between Church and State, with an Edition of His Apparatus to Compilatio Tertia." 2 vols. Ph.D. dissertation, Cornell University, 1972.

PÖSCHL, ARNOLD. *Bischofsgut und mensa episcopalis: Ein Beitrag zur Geschichte des kirchlichen Vermögensrechtes.* 3 vols. Bonn, 1908–12.

POST, GAINES. *Studies in Medieval Legal Thought: Public Law and the State, 1100–1322.* Princeton, 1964.

POSTAN, MICHAEL, ed. *The Cambridge Economic History of Europe,* vol. 1, *The Agrarian Life of the Middle Ages.* 2d ed. Cambridge, 1966.

POSTAN, MICHAEL; RICH, E. E.; and MILLER, EDWARD, eds. *The Cambridge Economic History of Europe,* vol. 3, *Economic Organization and Policies in the Middle Ages.* Cambridge, 1965.

PUFENDORF, SAMUEL VON (Severinus de Monzambano). *De statu imperii Germanici.* Geneva, 1667.

RAAB, HERIBERT. *Clemens Wenzeslaus von Sachsen und seine Zeit.* Vol. 1. Freiburg i. B., Basel, and Vienna, 1962.

RAPP, FRANCIS. *Réformes et Réformation à Strasbourg: Église et société dans le diocèse de Strasbourg (1450–1525).* Paris, 1974.

REINHARD, RUDOLF. "August, Graf von Stirum, Bischof von Speier, und die Zentralbehörden im Bistum Speier." *MHVP* 34–35 (1915):161–206.

REMLING, FRANZ XAVER. *Geschichte der Bischöfe zu Speyer.* 2 vols. Mainz, 1852–54.

————. *Urkundliche Geschichte der ehemaligen Abteien und Klöster im jetzigen Rheinbayern.* 2 vols. Neustadt a. d. Haardt, 1836.

RENGER, REINHARD. *Landesherr und Landstände im Hochstift Osnabrück in der Mitte des 18. Jahrhunderts.* Veröffentlichungen des Max-Planck Instituts für Geschichte, vol. 19. Göttinger, 1968.

RIEDER, KARL. "Die kirchengeschichtliche Literatur Badens im Jahre 1906 und 1907." *FDA* N.F. 9 (1908):323–73.

RIEDNER, OTTO. "Das Speierer Offizialatsgericht im 13. Jahrhundert."*MHVP* 29–30 (1907):1–107.

RIETSCHEL, SIEGFRIED. *Das Burggrafenamt und die hohe Gerichtsbarkeit in den deutschen Bischofsstädten während des früheren Mittelalters.* Leipzig, 1905.

ROEGELE, OTTO. *Bruchsal wie es war.* Karlsruhe, 1955.

ROSENKRANZ, ALBERT. *Der Bundschuh.* 2 vols. Heidelberg, 1927.

RUSSELL, JOSIAH COX. *Medieval Regions and Their Cities.* Bloomington, 1972.

SABEAN, DAVID W. *Landbesitz und Gesellschaft am Vorabend des Bauernkriegs: Eine Studie der sozialen Verhältnisse im südlichen Oberschwaben in den Jahren vor 1525.* Quellen und Forschungen zur Agrargeschichte, vol. 26. Stuttgart, 1972.

SANTIFALLER, LEO. *Zur Geschichte des ottonisch-salischen Reichskirchensystems.* 2d ed. Vienna, 1964.

SCHÄFER, ALFONS. "Das Schicksal des Weissenburgischen Besitzes im Uf- und Pfinzgau." *ZGO* N.F. 72 (1963):65–93.

————. "Staufische Reichslandpolitik und hochadelige Herrschaftsbildung im Uf- und Pfinzgau und im Nordwestschwarzwald vom 11.–13. Jahrhundert." *ZGO* N.F. 78 (1969): 179–244.

————. "Waren die Grafen von Eberstein die Gründer der Stadt Neuenburg a. d. Enz oder der ehemaligen Stadt Neuburg am Rhein?" *ZGO* N.F. 73 (1964):81–96.

SCHAUBE, KOLMAR. "Die Entstehung des Speierer Stadtrates." *ZGO* N.F. 1 (1886):445–61.

SCHNEIDER, PHILIP. *Die bischöflichen Domkapitel: Ihre Entwicklung und rechtliche Stellung im Organismus der Kirche.* 2d ed. Mainz, 1892.

SCHÖTTKE, GUSTAV. *Die Stände des Hochstifts Osnabrück unter dem ersten evangelischen Bischof Ernst August von Braunschweig-Lüneburg (1662–1698).* Münster dissertation. Osnabrück, 1908.

SCHREIBMÜLLER, HERMANN. *Die Landvogtei im Speiergau.* Kaiserslautern, 1905.

————. "Der Lutramsforst in seiner ursprünglichen Bedeutung." In *Von Geschichte und Volkstum der Pfalz,* edited by Kurt Baumann, pp. 39–42. Speyer, 1959.

————. *Pfälzer Reichsministerialen.* Kaiserslautern, 1910.

————. "Reichsburglehen in dem Gebiete der Landvogtei im Speyergau (bis 1349)." In *Von Geschichte und Volkstum der Pfalz,* edited by Kurt Baumann, pp. 75–94. Speyer, 1959.

SCHUBERT, ERNST. *Die Landstände des Hochstifts Würzburg.* Würzburg, 1967.

SCHUEGRAF, AUGUST. *Die Bistumsvereinigungen in der deutschen Kirche während des 14. und 15. Jahrhunderts.* Erlangen, 1935.

SCHULTE, ALOYS. *Der Adel und die deutsche Kirche im Mittelalter.* Kirchenrechtliche Abhandlungen, vols. 63–64. Stuttgart, 1910.

SCHÜTZE, CHRISTIAN. "Ziele und Mittel der pfälzischen Territorialpolitik im 14. Jahrhundert." *Pfälzer Heimat* 9 (1958):1–5.

SCHWICKERATH, WILHELM. *Die Finanzwirtschaft der deutschen Bistümer.* Beiträge zur kirchlichen Verwaltungswissenschaft, vol. 3. Breslau, 1942.

SEILER, ALOIS. "Die Speyerer Diözesangrenzen rechts des Rheins im Rahmen der Frühgeschichte des Bistums." In *900 Jahre Speyerer Dom,* edited by Ludwig Stamer, pp. 243–59. Speyer, 1961.

———. *Studien zu den Anfängen der Pfarrei- und Landdekanatsorganisation in den rechtsrheinischen Archidiakonaten des Bistums Speyer.* VBW B, vol. 10. Stuttgart, 1959.

SEMMLER, JOSEF. "Sinsheim, ein Reformkloster Siegburger Observanz im alten Bistum Speyer." *AMKG* 8 (1956): 339–47.

SMITH, CHARLES E. *Innocent III: Church Defender.* Baton Rouge, 1951.

SPANGENBERG, HANS. "Beiträge zur älteren Verfassungs- und Verwaltungsgeschichte des Fürstentums Osnabrück." *Mittheilungen des Vereins für Geschichte und Landeskunde von Osnabrück* 25 (1900):1–137.

———. *Vom Lehnstaat zum Ständestaat.* Munich and Berlin, 1912.

SPUFFORD, PETER. "Assemblies of Estates, Taxation and Control of Coinage in Medieval Europe." In *XIIe Congrès international des sciences historiques,* pp. 113–30. Études, vol. 31. Vienna, 1965.

STAMER, LUDWIG. *Kirchengeschichte der Pfalz.* 4 vols. Speyer, 1949–64.

STAUBER, A. "Kloster und Dorf Lambrecht." *MHVP* 9 (1880):49–227.

STENGEL, EDMUND E. *Abhandlungen und Untersuchungen zur mittelalterlichen Geschichte.* Cologne and Graz, 1960.

STEPHENSON, CARL. "Taxation and Representation in the Middle Ages." In *Anniversary Essays in Medieval History by Students of Charles Homer Haskins,* pp. 291–312. Boston and New York, 1929.

STIEFENHÖFER, HERMINE. *Philipp von Flersheim, Bischof von Speyer (1529–1552) und gefürsteter Propst von Weissenburg (1546–1552).* Speyer, 1941.

STOCKER, CARL W. *Der grossherzogliche badische Amtsbezirk Bruchsal.* Bruchsal, 1883.

TIERNEY, BRIAN. *Foundations of the Conciliar Theory: The Contribution of the Medieval Canonists from Gratian to the Great Schism.* Cambridge, 1955.

———. *Medieval Poor Law: A Sketch of Canonical Theory and its Application in England.* Berkeley and Los Angeles, 1959.

TROE, HEINRICH. *Münze, Zoll und Markt und ihre finanzielle Bedeutung für das Reich vom Ausgang der Staufer bis zum Regierungsantritt Karls IV.: Ein Beitrag zur Geschichte des Reichsfinanzwesens in der Zeit von 1250 bis 1350.* Vierteljahrschrift für Sozial- und Wirtschaftsgeschichte, Beiheft 32. Stuttgart and Berlin, 1937.

TUCHLE, HERMANN. "The Peace of Augsburg: New Order or Lull in the Fighting." In *Government in Reformation Europe, 1520–1560*, edited by Henry J. Cohn, pp. 145–65. London and New York, 1971.

———. "Das Zisterzienserkloster Maulbronn." *AMKG* 1 (1949):276–81.

VANN, JAMES A., and ROWAN, STEVEN W., eds. *The Old Reich: Essays on German Political Institutions 1495–1806*. Études, vol. 48. Brussels, 1974.

VEIT, ANDREAS. "Geschichte und Recht der Stiftsmässigkeit auf die ehemals adeligen Domstifte von Mainz, Würzburg und Bamberg." *Historisches Jahrbuch* 33 (1912):323–58.

VERRIEST, LEO. *Noblesse, chevalerie, lignages*. Brussels, 1959.

VOGT, WERNER. *Untersuchungen zur Geschichte der Stadt Kreuznach*. Mainz, 1955.

WALEY, DANIEL. *The Papal State in the Thirteenth Century*. London, 1961.

WATANABE, MORIMICHI. "The Episcopal Election of 1430 in Trier and Nicholas of Cusa." *Church History* 39 (1970):299–316.

WATT, JOHN A. "The Theory of Papal Monarchy in the Thirteenth Century." *Traditio* 20 (1964):179–317.

WEBER, FRIEDRICH J. *Die Domschule von Speyer im Mittelalter*. Freiburg i. B., 1954.

WEBER, MAX. *The Theory of Social and Economic Organization*. Edited by Talcott Parsons and translated by A. M. Henderson. New York and London, 1947.

WEISS, C. "Das Rechnungswesen der freien Reichstadt Speier im Mittelalter." *MHVP* 5 (1875):3–27.

WERLE, HANS. "Die Aufgaben und die Bedeutung der Pfalzgrafschaft bei Rhein in der Staufischen Hausmachtpolitik." *MHVP* 57 (1959):137–54.

———. "Die Landgrafschaft im Speyergau." *MHVP* 59 (1961):71–75.

———. "Die salisch-staufische Obervogtei über die Reichsabtei Weissenburg." *AMKG* 8 (1956):333–38.

———. "Staufische Hausmachtpolitik am Rhein im 12. Jahrhundert." *ZGO* N.F. 71 (1962):241–370.

———. "Studien zur Wormser und Speyerer Hochstiftsvogtei im 12. Jahrhundert." *Blätter für pfälzische Kirchengeschichte und religiöse Volkskunde* 21 (1954):80–89.

WERMINGHOFF, ALBERT. *Die deutschen Reichskriegssteuergesetze von 1422 bis 1427 und die deutsche Kirche*. Weimar, 1916.

———. "Ständische Probleme in der Geschichte der deutschen Kirche des Mittelalters." *ZRG Kanon.* 1 (1911):33–67.

———. *Verfassungsgeschichte der deutschen Kirche im Mittelalter*. 2d ed. Grundriss der Geschichtswissenschaft, vol. 2, pt. 6. Leipzig and Berlin, 1913.

WETTERER, ANTON. "Zur Geschichte des Speierer Generalvikariats im 18. Jahrhundert." *MHVP* 49 (1928–29):93–179.

WILD, KARL. *Staat und Wirtschaft in den Bistümern Würzburg und Bamberg*. Heidelberg, 1906.

WINKELMANN, EDUARD. *Jahrbücher der deutschen Geschichte: Philipp von Schwaben und Otto IV. von Braunschweig*. 2 vols. Leipzig, 1873–78.

WIRTZ, HEINRICH. "Donum, investitura, conductus ecclesiae: Ein Beitrag zur Geschichte des kirchlichen Stellenbesetzungsrechtes auf Grund rheinischer Urkunden vornehmlich des 12. Jahrhunderts." *ZRG Kanon.* 4 (1914): 116–50.

WITTE, BARTHOLD. *Herrschaft und Land im Rheingau.* Meisenheim, 1959.

WOLFRAM, GEORG. *Friedrich I. und das Wormser Concordat.* Strasbourg dissertation. Marburg, 1883.

YUNCK, JOHN A. "Economic Conservatism, Papal Finance, and the Medieval Satires on Rome." In *Change in Medieval Society,* edited by Sylvia Thrupp, pp. 72–85. New York, 1964.

ZIEGLER, PHILIP. *The Black Death.* New York, 1969.

Index